For Carl Schorske —
With deepest gratitude and
highest admiration

Walter Frisch
October 1999

THE EARLY WORKS OF ARNOLD SCHOENBERG, 1893–1908

Walter Frisch

THE EARLY WORKS *of* ARNOLD SCHOENBERG 1893–1908

UNIVERSITY OF CALIFORNIA PRESS BERKELEY LOS ANGELES LONDON

University of California Press
Berkeley and Los Angeles, California

University of California Press, Ltd.
London, England

First Paperback Printing 1997

Library of Congress Cataloging-in-
Publication Data

Frisch, Walter.
The early works of Arnold Schoenberg,
1893-1908 / Walter Frisch.
p. cm.
Includes bibliographical references and
indexes.
ISBN 0-520-21218-5 (alk. paper)
1. Schoenberg, Arnold, 1874-1951—
Criticism and interpretation.
I. Title.
ML410.S283F75 1993
780'.92—dc20 92-43829
CIP

Printed in the United States of America
9 8 7 6 5 4 3 2 1

The paper used in this publication meets
the minimum requirements of American
National Standard for Information
Sciences—Permanence of Paper for Printed
Library Materials, ANSI Z39.48-1984. ♾

For Anne

I'm very glad you received an offer to write a book about me. . . . That you wish to write only on the music is in accordance with my wishes. In my opinion: my biography as such is highly uninteresting and I consider the publication of any details embarrassing. A few place names, dates of composition, there's really nothing more to say. . . . It would be interesting to outline my development through the music.

SCHOENBERG
postcard to Berg, 8 December 1920, about a book project never completed

CONTENTS

List of Longer Musical Examples xi
Preface and Acknowledgments xiii
A Note on Abbreviations xix

PART I: SCHOENBERG AND THE BRAHMS TRADITION, 1893–1897

1. The "Brahms Fog": A Context for Early Schoenberg 3
2. The Instrumental Works 20
3. The Songs 48

PART II: EXPANDED TONALITY, EXPANDED FORMS, 1899–1903

4. The Dehmel Settings of 1899 79
5. *Verklärte Nacht*, op. 4 (1899) 109
6. *Gurrelieder* (1900–1901) 140
7. *Pelleas und Melisande*, op. 5 (1902–1903) 158

PART III: "THE DIRECTION MUCH MORE MY OWN," 1904–1908

8. The First String Quartet, op. 7 (1904–1905) 181
9. The First Chamber Symphony, op. 9 (1906) 220
10. The Second Chamber Symphony, op. 38, and the Second String Quartet, op. 10 (1906–1908) 248

Appendix of Longer Musical Examples 273
Bibliography of Works Cited 311
Index of Schoenberg's Compositions and Writings 321
General Index 323

LIST OF LONGER MUSICAL EXAMPLES

A. Piano Piece in C♯ Minor (1894), mm. 1–23 274
B. Scherzo for Piano in F♯ Minor (ca. 1894), mm. 1–44 275
C. Scherzo for String Quartet in F Major (1897), mm. 80–128 277
D. *Schilflied* (1893), mm. 1–13 279
E. *Ecloge* (1895), mm. 1–51 280
F. *Mädchenlied* (1897), mm. 1–13 283
G. *Waldesnacht* (1897), mm. 1–24 284
H. *Mädchenfrühling* (1897), complete 286
I. *Nicht doch!* (1897), mm. 1–12 289
J. *Nicht doch!* (1897), mm. 73–84 290
K. *Mannesbangen* (1899), complete 291
L. *Warnung* (1899), mm. 1–15 294
M. *Im Reich der Liebe* (1899), mm. 1–8 295
N. "So tanzen die Engel," from *Gurrelieder* (1900–1), piano-vocal score, mm. 443–88 296
O. "Du sendest mir einen Liebesblick," from *Gurrelieder*, mm. 653–67 299
P. "Du sendest mir einen Liebesblick," mm. 676–97 300
Q. First String Quartet, op. 7 (1904–5), mm. 1–35 302
R. Second Chamber Symphony, op. 38 (1906–8), I, two-piano arrangement, mm. 1–28 305
S. Second String Quartet, op. 10 (1907–8), I, mm. 1–55 307
T. Second String Quartet, op. 10, II, mm. 1–18 310

PREFACE AND ACKNOWLEDGMENTS

In an afterword to a reprint of Egon Wellesz's book *Arnold Schönberg* (1921), Carl Dahlhaus muses that since that first monograph, the literature on the composer "has grown to such enormous dimensions that it almost seems that those who read criticism about the music outnumber those who listen to the music itself" (Wellesz 1985, 153). Although the Schoenberg bibliography is indeed vast, the works of the earlier years, up to the so-called atonal compositions of 1908–9, have received relatively little attention. For several reasons, the time is ripe for a fresh investigation.

Aside from general surveys of Schoenberg's work, there are, to my knowledge, only five full-length studies that have focused in detail on this repertory: Friedheim 1963, Bailey 1979, Thieme 1979, Ballan 1986, and Hattesen 1990 (see Bibliography for complete citations). Each of these works originated as a master's or doctoral dissertation, and three of them remain unpublished; each has something of both the value and the limitations of the dissertation format.

In this book I have drawn readily and (I hope) appreciatively on some of these earlier studies, as well as on other important literature, stretching from Alban Berg's early analyses to the present day. (Although Berg never completed the book project mentioned in the epigraph to the present study, his own *Führer* to several Schoenberg works, as well as his other writings, are invaluable.) Of special value are the scores and critical reports that have appeared as part of Schoenberg's *Sämtliche Werke*. Most of the volumes pertinent to the music treated in this book have been edited over the past decade or so by Christian M. Schmidt—and edited for the most part in exemplary fashion. Schmidt's work, together with the generous policy adopted in the *Sämtliche Werke* of printing transcriptions of sketches, alternate or preliminary versions, and many fragments, has opened up a gold mine for the critic-historian.

Apart from the commentary in the critical reports, which is normally brief, and essentially documentary rather than analytical or interpretive, these sources have yet to be explored. The present book should be taken in part as a first step in that direction. During my research I had occasion to examine, and draw my own conclusions from, most of the primary manuscript sources to which I refer. I have also not hesitated, when it seemed appropriate, to modify or recast my ideas in light of the *Sämtliche Werke*, volumes of which continued to appear as I worked.

The bulk of this book consists of close, detailed musical analysis of selected works. The commentary attempts to take into account relevant aspects of the individual *Entstehungsgeschichte* and of the context of a composition among Schoenberg's other early works (and occasionally those of other composers). There are probably several hundred complete compositions or substantial fragments from Schoenberg's early years. To examine them all would swell this book (and test the reader's endurance) well beyond reasonable proportions. I have concentrated on those compositions that I believe are most important and interesting, and through which a development in Schoenberg's musical language can be traced.

I also believe it is important not to let any search for "development" override the aesthetic or technical qualities of individual pieces. Too often in musicological writing, compositions become primarily stages or steps in some broader evolution, either within a composer's work or within an entire historical style. (With his strong historicist orientation, Schoenberg himself was somewhat guilty of this attitude, although he did, of course, often analyze works, including his own, in loving detail.)

Theoretical writing often falls prey to a different, and in my view equally inadequate, practice: individual compositions are pillaged or dismembered for particular examples of harmony, rhythm, motive, and so forth. A book about the early Schoenberg could indeed be organized that way (or could be written solely about harmonic practice), but here again, I feel the qualities—both strengths and weaknesses—of the individual works would get lost in such a topical reshuffling. These qualities also tend to disappear in analyses such as those of Allen Forte (1972, 1978), which have a more specifically theoretical orientation.

The challenge, ultimately, is to find a balance between doing justice to the theoretical, technical, and aesthetic dimensions of the work and placing it persuasively in its compositional and historical context. My own solution—an attempt to provide detailed analyses in chronological or developmental order—is to some extent based on a fictional construct, but it is one that musical criticism is obliged, I think, to adopt.

A respected music theorist once told me I was brave (read "foolhardy") to be working on a repertory as complicated as the early Schoenberg, when Wagnerian chromatic practice is still so poorly understood. This remark reflects an unfortunate mind-set. We shall probably have to wait many years before comprehensive or systematic theories of Wagnerian and post-Wagnerian music emerge. And then, precisely because of the diversity and complexity of the music itself, any such theories would be so vast as to collapse under their own weight.

I make no claim to have invented or employed a theory in this sense for the early Schoenberg. The closest thing to a fully formed theoretical viewpoint that appears in this book is that of Schoenberg himself, upon whose writings I draw frequently, especially the *Theory of Harmony* (whose English title is a misrepresentation of *Harmonielehre*, a book that Schoenberg insisted embodied no "theory"). However illuminating and stimulating, Schoenberg's theoretical writings should not—and by their nature cannot—be applied like a template or key to his own compositions. Although Schoenberg the theorist and Schoenberg the composer were united in the same body, they were not always necessarily allied in spirit. This has long been recognized in the case of the twelve-tone works, which often violate the "theory," and it is true of the tonal works as well.

This book is fundamentally about Schoenberg the composer: about the compositional decisions he made and the compositional strategies he adopted or abandoned both in individual works and across or between works. The analyses represent my attempts to get inside the mind of Schoenberg—not systematically to retrieve his creative process, which would be impossible, but to evaluate and assess the results of that process. When Schoenberg the theorist can help, he is brought in, but only as an advisor, not as commander. Inevitably, this and other methods used in this study will seem ad hoc to more orthodox theorists still waiting for the key to unlock the chromatic music of 1850–1910. For this I make no apology; I wish only to make my own position clear.

The basic "story" told in this book is not a revisionist one. The three-stage picture of Schoenberg's early development, from a Brahms-oriented period (1893–97), to one in which Wagnerian expanded tonality becomes allied to Brahmsian techniques (1899–1903), to a more wholly individual synthesis (1904–8), has been adumbrated before, not least by the composer himself. The interest of the book will lie not in the periodization (three-stage, early-middle-late divisions seem to be universal in music-historical writing), but in the analyses of the compositional techniques Schoenberg employs within each of the three periods. If there is one overarching concept, it is that through the first movement of the Second Chamber Symphony and up to the beginning of the Second Quartet—thus until about the spring of 1907—Schoenberg is a profoundly tonal composer, one who manipulates theme, harmony, phrase design, and large-scale form to create coherent yet varied tonal structures.

This will certainly not be the last book written on Schoenberg's early tonal period. If it serves primarily as a stimulus for historical musicologists to tell a newer story, or for theorists to continue the search for a more systematic (but still, it is hoped, humane) approach to this repertory, it will have served its purpose.

A word is appropriate here about the musical examples transcribed from original sources. All transcriptions in this book are, except where specifically noted, my own and may differ in some details from those in the *Sämtliche Werke*. Since this book is a critical-historical study, and not a scholarly edition, my goal has been practical, rather than purely diplomatic and rigorous. Orchestral or chamber works (from both manuscript and printed sources) have been reduced to one or two staves and have sometimes been excerpted; occasionally, an ellipsis has been made in portions of a larger continuous sketch or draft. Details such as stem directions or accidentals have been adapted for these purposes. Where a significant ambiguity as to meaning may arise, my own editorial suggestions, such as clefs, time and key signatures, and accidentals, are placed in square brackets. In order to keep the examples free from unnecessary clutter, however, such markings have been used sparingly.

Portions of chapter 1 of this book have appeared in different form in *Brahms and His World* (Frisch 1990a); portions of chapters 3, 4, and 8 in the *Journal of the Arnold Schoenberg Institute* (Frisch 1986, 1988b); and other portions of chapter 8 in the *Journal of the American Musicological Society* (Frisch 1988a). I am grateful to Princeton University Press, the Arnold Schoenberg Institute, and the American Musicological Society, respectively, for permission to adapt this material.

The planning, researching, and writing of this book extended over many years and several grant periods and leaves; the work took place in various locations, with the support of numerous institutions and individuals. Rather than trying to formulate my gratitude too discursively, I offer my sincerest thanks in a more compact form to:

- The Schoenberg family, especially Lawrence, for generously authorizing access to many primary sources.
- Belmont Music Publishers, Pacific Palisades, California, for permission to use Schoenberg's music in musical examples within the text of the book and in the appendix.
- The staff of the Arnold Schoenberg Institute in Los Angeles, including its director (until the end of 1991), Leonard Stein, its associate director, Heidi Lesemann, and three successive archivists, the late Clara Steuermann, Jerry McBride, and Wayne Shoaf.

- The staff at the Library of Congress, especially Elizabeth Auman.
- The staff of the Austrian National Library, especially (during 1986) Rosemary Hilmar.
- J. Rigbie Turner of the Pierpont Morgan Library.
- The Music Division of the New York Public Library for the Performing Arts at Lincoln Center.
- A number of components of my home institution, Columbia University, including the Council for Research in the Humanities (for summer funds), the Arts and Sciences (for junior faculty leave), and the Music Department (for leave and sabbatical time).
- The National Endowment for the Humanities for a fellowship during 1985–86, during which much of the preliminary research was accomplished.
- The Alexander von Humboldt-Stiftung in Bonn for a grant, which brought me to the Musikwissenschaftliches Seminar of the University of Freiburg during 1990–91; and to Hermann Danuser, who served as welcoming *Gastgeber.*
- Reinhold Brinkmann, Ethan Haimo, Martha M. Hyde, Oliver Neighbour, and Richard Swift for insightful readings of all or part of the manuscript and for other advice generously offered.
- Don Giller, for preparation of the handsome musical examples.
- Karen Painter, for careful and perceptive research assistance in the preparation of the final manuscript.
- Michael Rogan, for the helpful transcriptions of passages from the autograph of *Verklärte Nacht*, prepared in conjunction with an M.A. essay at Columbia University in 1986.
- Ruth Spevack, for help in preparing the index.
- The staff at the University of California Press, including Pamela MacFarland Holway, Doris Kretschmer, Jane-Ellen Long, and Fran Mitchell, all of whom helped guide this book through the treacherous seas of production.
- My family, Anne, Nicholas, and Simon, the most wonderful, nourishing alternative to scholarly work imaginable.

A NOTE ON ABBREVIATIONS

Frequent reference is made in this book to Schoenberg's collected works, the *Sämtliche Werke* (Mainz and Vienna: Schott and Universal, 1966–). This publication is divided into two "series" (*Reihen*), A for scores, B for critical reports. Volume numbers are coordinated between the two series: thus, for example, volume 20 represents string quartets in both. The edition is separated by genre into *Abteilungen*, or divisions, indicated by Roman numerals.

In order to avoid cumbersome citations of the *Sämtliche Werke*, I have throughout this book employed the abbreviation *SW*, which is followed first by a letter indicating the series, A or B, then the volume number, then a colon and the page number. An indication of the *Abteilung* is not necessary, since the volumes are numbered consecutively throughout the edition.

Thus *SW* A4: 25–35, indicates the score series, volume 4, pages 25–35. If the volume itself has two parts, this is indicated by a Roman numeral: *SW* B11/II: 35–37, thus indicates part II of the critical report for the chamber symphonies, vol. 11. In the case of the two volumes of Lieder, the editors of the *Sämtliche Werke* have issued a two-part critical report that serves for both volumes in the A series, numbered 1 and 2. This report is thus cited as *SW* B1/2/I or *SW* B1/2/II.

PART I

Schoenberg and the Brahms Tradition, 1893–1897

CHAPTER ONE

The "Brahms Fog": A Context for Early Schoenberg

In a letter written in April 1894 to his friend Adalbert Lindner, the twenty-one-year-old Max Reger (1873–1916) staunchly defended Brahms against obstreperous journalistic opponents. Reger conceded that Brahms's music might at first be difficult to grasp, but noted:

> Brahms is nonetheless now so advanced that all truly insightful, good musicians, unless they want to make fools of themselves, must acknowledge him as the greatest of living composers. . . . Even if Lessman takes such pains to disperse Brahms and the Brahms fog [*Brahmsnebel*] (to use Tappert's term), the Brahms fog will remain. And I much prefer it to the white heat [*Gluthitze*] of Wagner and Strauss.
>
> REGER 1928, 39–40

Reger refers here to Otto Lessmann, editor of the *Allgemeine Musik-Zeitung* in Berlin from 1881 to 1907, and to Wilhelm Tappert, a prominent Wagnerian critic. I have not been able to locate where Tappert coined the term *Brahmsnebel*,[1] but it is not hard to see (or guess) what he—and Reger quoting him—may have meant by it. When paired with Reger's description of the "white heat" of Wagner and Strauss, Lessmann's phrase makes for an attractive characterization of the notorious dialectic that dominated Austro-German music in the later nineteenth century. Instead of the more common military metaphor— Brahmsians doing battle

1. Until 1888 Tappert was a regular contributor to two music journals, the Leipzig *Musikalisches Wochenblatt* and the Berlin *Allgemeine Musik-Zeitung*. The term *Brahmsnebel* does not appear in any of his writings for these journals that I have been able to discover. Nor does it appear in his several books on Wagner.

with Wagnerians—one composer and his followers are seen shrouded in a cold, dense mist, the other group radiating intense warmth and light.

Most scholars (and performers) have been attracted more readily to the brighter glow, to the phenomenon of Wagnerism and post-Wagnerism in Europe at the end of the nineteenth century. There has been less appreciation of the extent to which the "Brahms fog" penetrated to the heart of Austro-German music during the same period. "Brahms is everywhere," Walter Niemann remarked in 1912 near the end of an article in which he had briefly surveyed no fewer than fifty European composers whose piano music he said bore the unmistakable traces of the master's influence (Niemann 1912, 45). Hugo Leichtentritt observed similarly that "from about 1880 all chamber music in Germany is in some way indebted to Brahms" (Leichtentritt 1963, 449). The comments of Niemann and Leichtentritt could be applied equally to the vast quantities of Lieder issued by German and Austrian publishing houses in the same years.[2]

Perhaps as never before in the nineteenth century did young composers in German-speaking lands adhere so closely—and so proudly—to a single model when working in these genres. Reger could actually boast to Lindner in 1893 that "the other day a personal friend of Brahms's mistook the theme from the finale of my second violin sonata [op. 3] for a theme from one of Brahms's recent works. Even Riemann [Reger's teacher] told me that I really know Brahms through and through" (Reger 1928, 33).[3] Other testimony to Reger's *Brahms-Begeisterung* comes from the music critic Leopold Schmidt:

> What brought us together was our joint enthusiasm [*Schwärmerei*] for Brahms. At that time this feeling was stronger in Reger than even his undenied love for Bach. He saw in Brahms a protector, a figure who could fight against the "program music" that he [Reger] so hated, against everything that had no form, no limits. At that time there was no trace of the easygoing manner one could observe in the later Reger. Especially over a glass of wine, he could become absorbed in long, serious conversations.

2. Although there has been some investigation of individual *Nachfolger* of Brahms (mostly in routine life-and-works accounts, such as Deggeller-Engelke 1949, Holl 1928, and Kohleick 1943), nowhere do we get a genuinely critical or comparative account of Brahms's reception among composers of the period: of how his music affected that of his followers. Comprehensive bibliographies of *Brahms-Forschung*, arranged topically, may be found in Fellinger 1983, 192–96, and id., 1984, 203–6.

3. The main theme of Reger's finale echoes a number of Brahms themes; in particular, its rhythmic profile recalls the theme from the finale of Brahms's Cello Sonata No. 2 in F Major, op. 99, which could certainly count as one of Brahms's "recent" works (published in 1887). These two themes are shown together by Wirth 1974, 100 (who does not, however, note Reger's letter). More generalized Brahmsian "symptoms" of Reger's theme include the harmonic motion to chords a third away from the tonic, the dip down to B at the end of m. 1, and the complementary move up to F♯ at the beginning of the second phrase. The strongly Brahmsian features of Reger's first published works were remarked by Smolian 1894, 518–19, 597.

And his eyes would always shine brighter as soon as the discussion came around to "our Johannes."

SCHMIDT 1922, 160

Arnold Schoenberg would also in later years acknowledge his early admiration for and emulation of Brahms, not (as far as we know) over a glass of wine, but in essays, textbooks, and the classroom.[4] His earliest compositions also bear proud witness to this phenomenon. In the years through 1897, Schoenberg's works fall squarely into the three Brahmsian genres mentioned above: piano music, Lieder, and chamber music. From the point of view of style and technique, too, these works are very much enveloped in a Brahmsian fog. Evaluating and analyzing *Jugendwerke* like these compositions—the task of chapters 2 and 3 of the present study—gives rise to certain methodological problems. When a young composer turns to a powerful model, his works often become interesting more for what they reveal of his response to and assimilation of the model than for their own inherent aesthetic qualities. Study of such works may tend more toward reception history than to musical analysis. In the best music criticism, of course, the two endeavors should not be separated: a composition cannot easily be understood in isolation from its context, from its influences. In the commentary that forms the bulk of the next two chapters, I shall try to strike a balance between the two approaches—between an appreciation of the ways in which Schoenberg's earliest music is indebted to Brahms and an assessment of its more intrinsic qualities and merits.

In this regard it is worth letting the composer himself speak. The later Schoenberg would probably have been impatient with much of the Brahmsian imitation evident in his own early works and in those of other composers enveloped in the "Brahms fog." He had little respect for the imitation of a "style" in this sense, as he noted in an essay of 1934: "To listen to certain learned musicians, one would think that all composers did not bring about the representation of their *vision*, but aimed solely at establishing a style—so that musicologists should have something to do." Schoenberg felt that a work's "personal characteristics"—the style manifest in it—are merely "symptoms" laid over the essential "idea": "To overlook the fact that such personal characteristics follow from the true characteristic idea and are merely the symptoms—to believe, when someone imitates the symptoms, the style, that this is an artistic achievement—that is a mistake with dire consequences!" (Schoenberg 1975, 177–78).

4. Schoenberg's 1947 essay "Brahms the Progessive" (Schoenberg 1975, 398–441) is only the most famous of his numerous appreciations of Brahms. See my own discussion of Schoenberg's *Brahms-Kenntnis* in Frisch 1984, 1–18. A comprehensive account is Musgrave 1980.

This formulation—style versus idea—was central to Schoenberg's thought throughout much of his life, and, of course, it furnished the title for his collected essays, *Style and Idea*, in 1950.[5] It also furnished the ostensible justification for much of his music, in which he often resolutely refused to follow any "style." But a young composer—perhaps especially a self-taught one like Schoenberg, whose only textbooks were scores, whose principal teachers were the great masters—will almost always forge his own style out of that of an important predecessor or contemporary.[6]

Something like the style/idea distinction can be a valuable heuristic tool in understanding the early works of Schoenberg and his contemporaries. There are composers and works that seem clearly more caught up in trying to "sound" like Brahms on a superficial level (the "style"); and there are those that try to plumb Brahmsian depths by employing more subtle technical and expressive devices (the "ideas"). As a preliminary to examining Schoenberg's early works, it will be useful to assess a small control group of Brahmsian pieces composed by two of his most talented contemporaries, Zemlinsky and Reger, from these perspectives. Although the sample cannot claim to be objectively "representative" (whatever that may mean in the aesthetic realm), it may nevertheless serve to shed light on the Brahmsian context from which Schoenberg emerged.

Zemlinsky

Alexander von Zemlinsky (1872–1942), who in the period 1895–97 or 1896–97 became Schoenberg's only teacher in composition (we can be sure of neither the

5. Schoenberg fought hard to retain this title, about which the original publishers at Philosophical Library were not enthusiastic (see McGeary 1986, 184–88). The concept of a musical "idea," which Schoenberg reformulated many times, was to find its most complete exposition in a large manuscript, which remained unfinished, entitled "Der musikalische Gedanke und die Logik, Technik und Kunst seiner Darstellung." A scholarly edition of this work, the so-called *Gedanke* manuscript, will appear as Schoenberg 1994. For a survey of its contents, see Goehr 1977. On the various possible meanings of "idea" in Schoenberg's writings, see Cross 1980.

6. It is possible that Schoenberg's strong reaction against "style" as both a creative tool and critical yardstick was owing to his proximity in Vienna to the music historian Guido Adler (with whom he actually shared students, including Webern and Wellesz). Adler's highly influential methodological studies (see, for example, Adler 1911) form part of a much broader phenomenon of style consciousness among both practitioners and critics of the arts at the end of the nineteenth century. In German-speaking areas, especially, the visual arts and architecture were dominated by the notion of *Stilkunst* and of art having its own "will to style" (*Stilwollen*). In art history these concepts were given their strongest formulation by the Viennese curator and writer Alois Riegl, whose ideas are discussed by Schapiro (1953, 301–2) and Alpers (1987, 140–47); Riegl had a powerful influence on his compatriot and contemporary Adler. There is no evidence of animosity on Schoenberg's part toward Adler's method. (On the relationship and surviving correspondence between Schoenberg and Adler, see Reilly 1982, 99–100.) The composer may nevertheless later have felt that the contemporary obsession with "style" was excessive and misdirected.

exact dates nor the content of the instruction), was one of the most promising young musicians in Vienna in the the last decade of the century. After an auspicious study period at the Conservatory under such Brahms cronies as Anton Door and Robert Fuchs, he served as a conductor in several Viennese theaters and opera houses (including a stint under Gustav Mahler at the Hofoper in 1907) and was widely admired as pianist and accompanist. In 1911 he moved to Prague as opera director of the German theater.[7]

In his early Viennese period, Zemlinsky was fully, and willingly, enveloped in the "Brahms fog." In his brief memoir of Brahms, he reports: "I remember how even among my colleagues it was considered particularly praiseworthy to compose in as 'Brahmsian' a manner as possible. We were soon notorious in Vienna as the dangerous 'Brahmins'" (Zemlinsky 1922, 70). Zemlinsky recalls that he had first been introduced to the master in 1895.[8] In the following year, Brahms took enough interest in a string quintet by Zemlinsky to invite the younger composer around to his apartment to discuss it (a devastating experience, described vividly in Zemlinsky's memoir). Shortly thereafter, at a competition of the Wiener Tonkünstlerverein, Zemlinsky's Clarinet Trio in D Minor won the third prize, for which Brahms himself had put up the money. This time, Brahms thought highly enough of the composition to recommend it to his own publisher, Fritz Simrock, in a letter that also praised Zemlinsky as "a human being and a talent" (Brahms 1908–22, 4: 212). Simrock issued the Clarinet Trio as Zemlinsky's op. 3 in 1897.

The period of Zemlinsky's personal contact with Brahms and of his most ardently Brahmsian works coincided directly with the beginning of his own relationship with, and instruction of, Schoenberg. These compositions thus merit careful consideration by anyone interested in Schoenberg's early development.[9] It is striking that the compositions of the more accomplished and highly trained Zemlinsky, although *echt*-Brahms in "style," actually show less real understanding of Brahms than the best works by the more intuitive, largely self-taught Schoenberg. We can see this phenomenon better by examining a small sampling—one song and one movement of a string quartet—from Zemlinsky's Brahms period.

Zemlinsky was proud enough of the song *Heilige Nacht* to place it at the head of his first collection of Lieder, op. 2, published in 1897 (see ex. 1.1). The anonymous poem, a hymn of praise to night, which covers everything in a cloak of

7. For further biographical information on Zemlinsky, see Weber 1977.

8. The occasion was the premiere of Zemlinsky's Orchestral Suite at a concert of the Gesellschaft der Musikfreunde on 18 March. Brahms led his own Academic Festival Overture in the same program. The event is described in Kalbeck 1904–14, 4: 400–401.

9. A recent comprehensive study of Zemlinsky's early chamber works is contained in Loll 1990.

EXAMPLE 1.1 Alexander von Zemlinsky, *Heilige Nacht*, op. 2, no. 1.

tranquility ("even sorrow is sweet"), is of a type that attracted Brahms strongly.[10] The characteristics of Zemlinsky's song that derive from Brahms are (to this listener) so palpable that they can be itemized:

- the broad, descending triadic melody, mm. 1–4. Cf. Brahms's *Sehnsucht*, op. 49, no. 3, where the slow ascending arpeggios of the opening are inverted in the faster middle section. There are also ascending arpeggios at the opening of *Wie Melodien zieht es mir*, op. 105, no. 1, and *Maienkätzchen*, op. 107, no. 4.
- the strong, stepwise bass line, especially in mm. 1–6. Cf. *Dein blaues Auge*, op. 59, no. 8.
- the arpeggiated figuration in the right hand of the accompaniment, which is shaped as a diminution of the vocal rhythm and motives, mm. 1–8. Cf. *Mein wundes Herz*, op. 59, no. 7. (On this technique of "harmonic congruence," see Cone 1990.)
- the dip toward the subdominant at the very beginning, mm. 1–2. Cf. *An ein Veilchen*, op. 49, no. 2, where, however, the tonic root remains in the bass underneath the subdominant triad. (See also the discussion of sub- and pre-dominant chords in Brahms's intermezzi below.)
- the sudden move by third, from a G to an E♭ harmony in $^6_4$ position, mm. 6–7. Cf. "Wie bist du, meine Königin," op. 32, no. 9, and *Die Mainacht*, op. 43, no. 2, where the shift is from E♭ (via E♭ minor) to B major. In many instances, Brahms approaches the new key area through its own $^6_4$ harmony, as in "Von waldbekränzter Höhe," op. 57, no. 1, m. 20.
- the extension or augmentation of "während der heiligen Nacht" to create an irregular three-measure phrase, mm. 24–26. Cf. the augmentation of the phrase "tonreichen Schall" in *An die Nachtigall*, op. 46, no. 4, mm. 5–7.[11]
- the strong plagal cadence at the end of the song, mm. 29–30. Cf. the final cadence of *Die Mainacht*.

10. At least twelve of Brahms's works are set to such texts, including (in alphabetical order) *Der Abend*, op. 64, no. 2; *Abenddämmerung*, op. 49, no. 5; *Abendregen*, op. 70, no. 4; *An den Mond*, op. 71, no. 2; *Dämmrung senkte sich von oben*, op. 59, no. 1; *Gestillte Sehnsucht*, op. 91, no. 1; *In stiller Nacht*, WoO 33, no. 42; *Die Mainacht*, op. 43, no. 2; *Mondenschein*, op. 85, no. 2; *Mondnacht*, WoO 21; *O schöne Nacht!* op. 92, no. 1; and *Sommerabend*, op. 85, no. 1.

11. This and other examples of such phrase extension in Brahms's songs were pointed out admiringly by Schoenberg in "Brahms the Progressive" (Schoenberg 1975, 418–22).

Despite the distinguished, documentable pedigree of its technical devices, Zemlinsky's *Heilige Nacht* comes across as a pallid imitation of the master. First, the phrase structure is uncomfortably square. The rather rigid succession of two-measure units in the opening section, through m. 8, is scarcely concealed by the small modifications, such as in m. 6, where Zemlinsky repeats the words "dein Kuß" in order to extend the phrase another half measure. There is little here of the subtle asymmetry fundamental to Brahms's language. Nor would Brahms himself have undermined what is supposed to be a magical moment, the shift to the E♭$^6_4$ chord in m. 7, with an almost verbatim repetition of the opening theme. In Brahms, harmonic expansions of this kind are almost always accompanied by, or coordinated with, a farther reaching melodic or thematic development.[12]

Despite its apparent resemblance to Brahms, the harmonic syntax of *Heilige Nacht* also betrays awkwardness. Instead of an inflection toward the subdominant such as we might find in a Brahms song, the IV chord in m. 2 appears in root position; it is too emphatic, bringing the harmonic motion to a virtual standstill. Zemlinsky's actual cadence to F in mm. 8–9, though perhaps intended as a fulfillment of the opening harmonic gesture, is also unconvincing. The tonic has barely been reestablished in m. 7 when it is transformed into an augmented chord that is made to function as a dominant. The augmented sonority with an added seventh sounds especially bizarre in the prevailingly consonant context.

If I seem to be too hard on what is in many outward respects an attractive song, it is to point up that Zemlinsky is good at appropriating superficial stylistic traits from Brahms without really absorbing his fundamental compositional principles. This aspect of Zemlinsky's musical personality was recognized by Theodor Adorno, who in his penetrating essay of 1959 suggests that Zemlinsky was a genuine eclectic, "someone who borrows all possible elements, especially stylistic ones, and combines them without any individual tone" (Adorno 1978, 351). Adorno tries to strip the term *eclectic* of its pejorative connotations, arguing that Zemlinsky was in fact something of a genius in his "truly seismographic capacity to respond to all the temptations with which he allowed himself to be inundated" (354). I would argue that this "seismographic" receptivity actually prevented Zemlinsky from absorbing the essence of Brahms. He registered the aftershocks, so to speak, but failed to locate the epicenter of the tremor.

The same tendency can be seen in the first movement of Zemlinsky's String Quartet in A Major, which was published by Simrock as op. 4 in 1898. In the

12. See, e.g, the perceptive analysis of such techniques in the song *Feldeinsamkeit* in Schmidt 1983, 146–54.

first group (ex. 1.2), the notated meter 6/8 is continually subverted so as to yield a virtual encyclopedia—*grab bag* might be a more appropriate term—of Brahmsian metrical devices. At the very beginning, in mm. 1–2, the 6/8 measure unfolds as if in 3/4. In the next measure, the two lower parts move in 6/8, the second violin in 3/4, and the first violin somewhere in between. At the climax of the first group in mm. 9–12, Zemlinsky presents (although he does not notate) a dizzying alternation of 3/8 and 3/4 according to the pattern: 3/8–3/4–3/8–3/4–3/8–3/4–3/4. After the fermata, the metrical roller coaster gets under way once again.

In his commentary on this movement, Rudolf Stephan has suggested that "rhythmic complications of this kind point to the model of Brahms, who, however, does not employ them in this (almost) systematic fashion" (Stephan 1976, 128). The parenthetical "almost" betrays an appropriate diffidence, for I would maintain that there is little that is truly systematic in Zemlinsky's procedures. Indeed, it is Brahms who is more "systematic," if also more restrained, as can be shown by a brief comparative glance at the first movement of his Third Quartet in B♭, op. 67 (ex. 1.3). Brahms also continually reinterprets the notated 6/8 meter. But where his imitator dives headlong into complexity and conflict, Brahms unfolds a gradual and subtle process. In mm. 1–2 he places accent marks on the normally weak third and sixth beats. In m. 3 these accents are intensified by forzando markings. Only in m. 8 does Brahms introduce an actual hemiola, which serves an important structural function: it marks the first arrival on the dominant and the beginning of the B section of an ABA′ first group. The following transition flows unproblematically in the notated 6/8, but the conflict between duple and triple articulation of the measure surfaces again in the second group, which is in 2/4 (ex. 1.3b). As in the first group, the shift of meter is carefully coordinated with the thematic and formal procedures: the arrival of 2/4 coincides with a new theme and with the confirmation of the key area of the dominant.

To return for a moment to Zemlinsky's A-Major Quartet: Brahmsian symptoms are also evident in the ostentatious invertible counterpoint in mm. 5–6 and 7–8, and especially in the way in which the cadential neighbor-note motive of m. 4 (ex. 1.2) is taken up again in the transition to the second group (ex. 1.4). Here the motive, which sounds in 3/4 meter, is repeated and given in diminution, thus creating an implied 3/2 meter across mm. 27–28. The motive then retreats to the background in the viola and becomes the accompaniment to a new thematic figure, presented in dialogue between the violins.

Brahms is the direct inspiration for this whole procedure. Indeed, Zemlinsky must have had the first movement of the Second Symphony in his ears: his neighbor-note figure bears a distinct resemblance to Brahms's basic motive, D–C♯–D, which is subjected to similarly intensive processes of metrical augmentation and diminution. At the approach to the second group, Brahms treats both

EXAMPLE 1.2 Zemlinsky, String Quartet No. 1 in A Major, op. 4, I.

EXAMPLE 1.3 Johannes Brahms, String Quartet No. 3 in B♭ Major, op. 67, I.

EXAMPLE 1.4 Zemlinsky, String Quartet No. 1 in A Major, op. 4, I.

the neighbor-note figure and its triadic companion in diminution and then moves the latter into the background to become the accompaniment for the new theme. At precisely the analogous moment in the sonata form, Zemlinsky adopts this same technique using the neighbor-note motive.

The conclusion to be drawn from these analyses may seem self-evident: no one could compose Brahms as well as Brahms himself. But I am suggesting that a superbly equipped composer like Zemlinsky can actually manage to sound very like Brahms—as he put it, "to compose in as 'Brahmsian' a manner as possible"—without showing a deeper grasp of what "Brahmsianness" really is or could be.

Reger

Like Zemlinsky, the young Reger wrote his share (more than his share) of pieces that imitate many of the master's "symptoms."[13] But there is also one brief, and for Reger rather restrained, work that does something more (and less). It is a short piano piece written after Brahms's death on 3 April 1897 and intended specifically as a memorial tribute. Reger published it in 1899 as op. 26, no. 5, with

13. On the Reger-Brahms relationship, see especially Wirth 1974.

EXAMPLE 1.5 Max Reger, *Resignation*, op. 26, no. 5.

the title *Resignation* and the subtitle *3 April 1897—J. Brahms †*.[14] As a *tombeau* specifically intended to evoke the departed master, *Resignation* can hardly be taken as representative of Reger's work, or of that of other composers in the "Brahms fog" of the decades around 1900. Yet it shows perhaps better than any other individual work the different ways in which Brahms could be "received" compositionally.

We may distinguish four levels or degrees of Brahms reception in *Resignation.* Arranged in order from the most obvious or blatant to the most subtle, these might be called quotation, emulation, allusion, and absorption. The piece concludes with a direct, clear *quotation* of the theme from the Andante of Brahms's Fourth Symphony (ex. 1.5a). The reference could not be more patent; Reger even derails the tonic of *Resignation*, which up to this point has been A major, in order to bring the final quotation into its original key, E major, thus ending *Resignation* in the dominant!

14. *Resignation* has a kind of companion piece, entitled *Rhapsodie* and subtitled *Den Manen Brahms* (To the Memory of Brahms), which is a large, turbulent work modeled closely on Brahms's Rhapsodies, op. 79. It was published in 1899 as Reger's op. 24, no. 6. Both pieces are discussed briefly by Lindner 1938, 165, who notes their "strongly Brahmsian stamp." Both are printed in Reger 1957, where the editor, Helmut Wirth, attributes them to the summer of 1898, even though the autographs bear no dates. I suspect that at least *Resignation* may have been written a year earlier, perhaps just after Reger heard about Brahms's death.

EXAMPLE 1.5 *continued*

b.

The body of the piece that precedes this coda shows a considerable degree of *emulation*, by which I mean a general stylistic imitation of what Schoenberg would call the "symptoms." Such broader features of Brahms's piano style were aptly described by Niemann in 1912 as "motion by thirds and sixths, their orchestral doublings, the preference for wide spacings and for a sonorous, dark, low register, [and] a self-willed rhythmic language, with a tendency toward syncopated and triplet figures of all kinds" (Niemann 1912, 39). Reger's *Resignation* clearly strives for this more superficial kind of emulation, as can be seen in ex.

1.5b, which presents the opening portion of the piece. (The overall ABA′ form of *Resignation* is also typical of Brahms's late piano works.)

But Reger also goes beyond emulation to *allude* more specifically to at least three late Brahms intermezzi that share the two keys of *Resignation*: op. 116, nos. 4 and 6, both in E major; and op. 118, no. 2, in A major (see exx. 1.6a–d). Reger's deep bass octaves recall 1.6b; the distinctly polyphonic texture, with active middle voices, is a feature of both 1.6a and c. Reger also adopts the opening gesture characteristic of all three intermezzi: *Resignation* begins on an upbeat with a root-position tonic chord, which moves on the subsequent downbeat to a pre-dominant sonority, ii^6. Brahms uses similar harmonies on the downbeat: in ex. 1.6a, vi^6; in ex. 1.6b, first a passing chord on A, then ii; and in ex. 1.6c, a IV^6_4 chord. Although the actual configuration of the chord differs in each case, the basic gesture of an initial move from the tonic to some type of pre-dominant is the same.

In Reger, as in exx. 1.6a and b, the precise configuration of the pre-dominant chord is obscured by appoggiaturas and (as in 1.6a) by the holding of notes over the bar line. These rhythmic and/or melodic devices serve in each case to create harmonic ambiguity: we do not know whether to interpret the first chord as a tonic or as V of IV. In ex. 1.6b, Brahms also generates considerable metrical ambiguity. Our ear tends to hear the strong root-position chord as a downbeat, and the subsequent phrasing suggests a broad $\frac{3}{2}$ meter that contradicts the notated $\frac{3}{4}$. A bit later in op. 118, no. 2 (ex. 1.6d), Brahms introduces a similar kind of ambiguity: the notated third beat begins to take on the character of a downbeat. (We cannot speak here, however, of a real metrical *displacement*, since the hairpins support the downbeat, which is in any case fully restored by m. 20.)

At the approach to the dominant in *Resignation*, mm. 6–9, Reger draws upon precisely these kinds of metrical ambiguity or conflict. As we listen—at least for the first time—mm. 5–6 suggest a $\frac{3}{2}$ hemiola superimposed over the notated $\frac{3}{4}$, an effect very characteristic of Brahms. But the downbeat of m. 7 does not, as we might expect, restore the notated meter unequivocally. Instead, the implied $\frac{3}{2}$ measure is, as it were, stretched to accommodate the cadential approach to E through the circle of fifths, C♯–F♯–B–E (as shown in ex. 1.5b). Reger now accelerates the harmonic rhythm, so that while the C♯ lasts a half note, or a full beat in $\frac{3}{2}$, the F♯ and B are only a quarter note each. The cadential goal, E, thus arrives on the notated last beat of m. 7. The two subsequent measures confirm E with the Phrygian cadence made from F and C, a gesture that foreshadows the actual quotation from Brahms's Fourth Symphony and also owes something to the similar harmonies in op. 118, no. 2 (ex. 1.6d). This Phrygian passage extends the metrical ambiguity long enough to bring the phrase to a close on the notated second beat of m. 9, thus allowing the varied restatement of the opening to begin in its proper position, on beat 3. The tonic now reappears with another Brahms-

EXAMPLE 1.6 Brahms Intermezzi.

a. Intermezzo in E Major, op. 116, no. 4

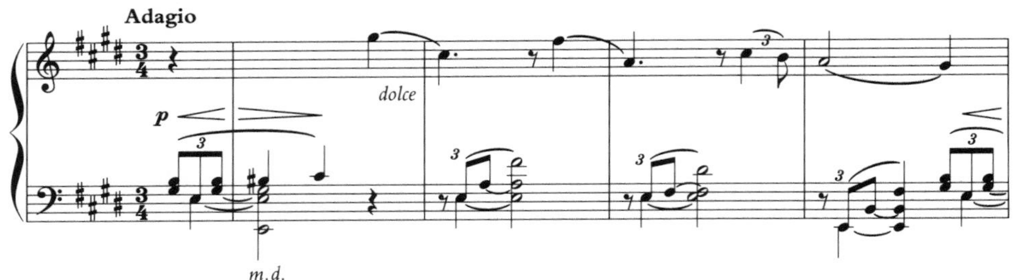

b. Intermezzo in E Major, op. 116, no. 6

c. Intermezzo in A Major, op. 118, no. 2

d. Intermezzo in A Major, op. 118, no. 2

ian gesture: the A enters a half-beat too "early," sounding deep in the bass underneath the prevailing dominant harmony.[15]

The elegant procedures involving meter, harmony, and phrase structure that I have analyzed in mm. 6–9 of Reger's *Resignation* fall into the last, most subtle category, *absorption*. Reger is making no apparent quotation of, or allusion to, any specific passage in Brahms; rather he has fully internalized some of Brahms's most characteristic compositional techniques. This is the kind of "influence" that Charles Rosen has characterized as the most profound, and also the least easily detected: no precise model can be found, and the search for one becomes essentially an endeavor of "pure musical analysis" (Rosen 1980, 100).

Resignation obviously appeared too late to have served as any kind of model for Schoenberg's early Brahms assimilation. A further investigation of possible "influence" in this traditional sense would have to examine the works of Reger that appeared before 1897, thus his opp. 1–16 (1893–96). (Unlike in the case of Zemlinsky's music, where we can assume that Schoenberg would have been familiar with works composed or published in the mid 1890s, we cannot be sure just what early Reger works Schoenberg might have known.) My point in examining *Resignation* has not been to claim that Reger served as model for Schoenberg, but rather to suggest how Brahms may really have served as model for them both. Even at its most "symptomatic," a work like *Resignation* can show deeper points of contact with the compositional essence of Brahms, as in mm. 6–9. It is this kind of absorption, rather than the more superficial imitation evident in some of the Zemlinsky works, toward which the young Schoenberg strove; this will be the essential subject of the next two chapters.

15. Although I have found no specific instance of this procedure in Brahms's piano music, the overlapping of dominant and tonic at moments of return occurs in a variety of ways in the orchestral and chamber music. See Frisch 1984, 138–39, for a discussion of this procedure in the Andante of Brahms's Third Symphony.

CHAPTER TWO

The Instrumental Works

A substantial number of compositions, both instrumental and vocal, survive complete from Schoenberg's Brahmsian period; there are also many fragments and torsos. Because some of the works and most of the fragments were not dated by the composer and are not firmly datable by either internal musical or external biographical means, it is impossible to construct anything like a definitive chronology. But a survey of the surviving juvenilia suggests that it was through his assimilation of Brahms that Schoenberg really began to grow as a composer.[1]

This process started at least as early as 1893, with the first datable Lieder, was well under way with the Piano Pieces of 1894, and culminated in 1897 with two Lieder based on poems by Paul Heyse (to be examined in chapter 3) and the D-Major String Quartet. The principal instrumental compositions of Schoenberg's early period through 1897, not including the smaller fragments, are listed in table 1.[2] In this chapter we trace an ever more sophisticated assimilation of Brahmsian principles across three of the main works, the Piano Pieces of 1894 (and a fragmentary scherzo probably composed at the same time), the Serenade of 1896, and the D-Major Quartet and F-Major Scherzo for Quartet of 1897.

1. Biographical information on Schoenberg's early years is scarce. Aside from such standard secondary sources as Stuckenschmidt 1978 and valuable but brief memoirs like Zemlinsky 1934 and Bach 1924, Schoenberg's 1949 essay/lecture "My Evolution" (in Schoenberg 1975, 79–92) is the best known and most often cited account of his youth. See also the autobiographical remarks in Schoenberg's 1949 "Notes on the Four String Quartets" (in Rauchhaupt 1971, 35–36).

2. The most extensive inventory of compositions and fragments from this period is given in Maegaard 1972, 1: 26–28 and 147–66. In compiling his catalogue from materials in the United States (mainly in the Schoenberg *Nachlaß* in Los Angeles), Maegaard did not have access to the Nachod collection (originally from Schoenberg's brother-in-law Hans Nachod), which is now at North Texas State University and is catalogued in Kimmey 1979. More recently, a small portion of the Nachod collection that had been retained by the last private owners has come into the possession of the Arnold Schoenberg Institute.

TABLE 1 Schoenberg's Principal Completed Instrumental Works through 1897

Date	*Work*	*Maegaard 1972, 1*	*Publication*
1894	Three Piano Pieces	p. 26	*SW* A4: 73–83
Ca. 1895	Presto, string quartet, C major	p. 151	*SW* A20: 143:64
Dedicated, 14 February 1896	Six Piano Pieces, four hands	p. 26	*SW* A5: 81–92
Fall 1896	Serenade for Small Orchestra (only 1st mvt. complete)	p. 26	facs. Thieme 1979, 98–102
March 1897	Gavotte and Musette for String Orchestra	p. 27	facs. Thieme 1979, 108–10
Fall 1897	Scherzo, string quartet, F major	p. 7	*SW* A20: 167–76; Schoenberg 1984
Fall 1897	String Quartet, D major	pp. 27–28	*SW* A20: 179–215; Schoenberg 1966

The Three Piano Pieces and Scherzo of 1894

As I have suggested elsewhere, a symphony theme cited by Schoenberg as having been written by him in about 1892 already shows a familiarity with Brahms's Tragic Overture specifically, and with Brahms's procedures of thematic evolution more generally (Frisch 1984, 159). Schoenberg's Three Piano Pieces of 1894 (printed complete in *SW* A4: 73–83), the first substantial instrumental compositions that survive, show that the twenty-year-old composer had continued to study Brahms intensively—in this case, the short piano works published recently in Brahms's collections opp. 116, 117, 118, and 119 (1892–93).

What is striking in the first of Schoenberg's 1894 pieces, an Andantino in C♯ minor, is the concentration with which he pursues one particular technical element of Brahms, here metrical displacement, to the virtual exclusion of others. Although the piece is notated in $\frac{2}{4}$, it unfolds from the very beginning as if in $\frac{6}{8}$ (Appendix ex. A). Both hands fully support the $\frac{6}{8}$ until mm. 9–10, where Schoenberg disrupts the pattern. The C♯ chord in m. 9 is not followed, as we would expect, by an eighth note upbeat. Instead, the next phrase begins an eighth note "early" on the notated downbeat of m. 10. Although notated and perceived downbeats coincide here, the $\frac{2}{4}$ meter is not unequivocally restored, since the rhythmic pattern of the melody and accompaniment continues to suggest $\frac{6}{8}$.

The last two sixteenth notes of m. 10 hover uneasily in a kind of metrical void: they sound neither like the last beat of a $\frac{2}{4}$ measure (since the preceding rhythmic figure has come to be heard solely in $\frac{6}{8}$) nor the fourth beat of a $\frac{6}{8}$ pattern (since the notes are given no bass support, as we might expect on the strong fourth beat, and as has been the case earlier, for example, on the notated downbeat of m. 2). The last beat of m. 10 thus conforms to what David Lewin has called a "transformational beat," one that serves to mediate between two different metrical frameworks (Lewin 1982, 25). The $\frac{6}{8}$ pattern begins again on the downbeat of m. 11. Unlike in m. 10, the last eighth note of this measure *does* now fit into the established $\frac{6}{8}$ pattern; as in mm. 2–3 it is tied to the succeeding downbeat.

Schoenberg's complex metrical procedures derive directly from Brahms, who often shifts the entire framework by a beat so that notated and perceived meters are out of phrase for long stretches.[3] But in his almost single-minded concentration on the metrical dimension of the music, Schoenberg tends to leave the others underdeveloped. The harmonic language of the Andantino remains very conventional, as does the basic phrase structure. Despite the metrical blip in mm. 9–11, the whole first section of the piece, up to the double bar, comprises four phrases in $\frac{6}{8}$ arranged according to a traditional pattern resembling what Schoenberg in his *Fundamentals of Musical Composition* would call a "sentence" (Schoenberg 1967, 20–24). A sentence generally consists of a two-measure idea, its restatement (often on the dominant), and a four-measure continuation and close; the whole is thus in the proportion 1:1:2.

In Schoenberg's Andantino, mm. 1–3 constitute the first statement, beginning and closing on the tonic; mm. 4–6 are the "complementary repetition," beginning on the tonic and moving to III;[4] mm. 7–12, comprising twice as many measures as each of the preceding parts, are the developmental continuation and

3. See my discussions of metrical procedures in Brahms's Piano Quintet, op. 34, and Third Symphony, op. 90, in Frisch 1984, 87–95 and 133–39. Schoenberg would surely, for example, have studied the way Brahms displaces the notated $\frac{4}{4}$ meter by a quarter note at the close of the exposition of the first movement of the piano quintet, and then at m. 96 returns to the original framework with a "transformational beat." Another example of large-scale metrical displacement is to be found in the exposition of the first movement of Brahms's Second Symphony, mm. 136–52.

4. In Schoenberg's formulation (1967, 21–24) the second phrase is called the "dominant form," normally beginning on V (his *locus classicus* is the opening of Beethoven's Piano Sonata in F Minor, op. 2, no. 1). He also acknowledges other possible harmonic schemas, including beginning the second phrase on the tonic and concluding it in a contrasting key.

EXAMPLE 2.1 Schoenberg, Piano Piece in C♯ Minor (1894).

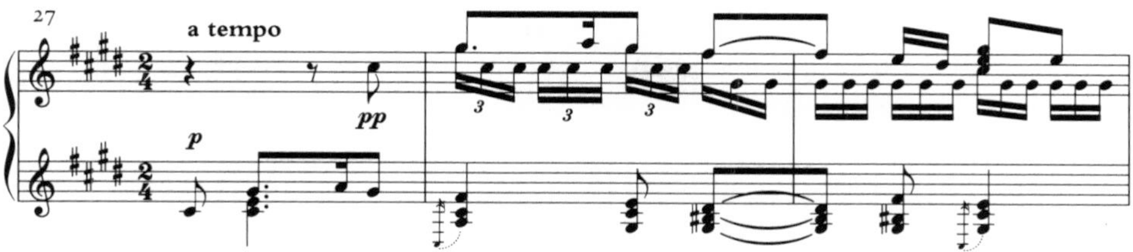

conclusion (ending on VI). Schoenberg observes in *Fundamentals of Musical Composition* that the "development" in the last portion of a sentence usually consists of reducing the thematic material to its smallest components, a process he calls "liquidation" (1967, 58). Liquidation is lacking in the piano piece, however: the basic three-measure unit (in notated measures) remains essentially intact and is given two full presentations in mm. 7–12.[5] What is "developed" is clearly the metrical aspect: the "early" arrival in m. 10 and the mysterious "extra" beat at the end of the same measure constitute the most dramatic changes in the basic unit.

Like many of Brahms's short pieces, and like Reger's *Resignation*, the Andantino has a ternary form; in this instance the middle section (mm. 13–26) serves as a kind of development of the opening material. As in mm. 7–12, the development is primarily metrical in nature. Indeed, it is the same C♯-major triad (cf. mm. 9 and 14) that seems to trigger the change of pattern. Schoenberg interprets this chord on the downbeat of m. 14 as the proper first beat of a $\frac{2}{4}$ measure, and the notated $\frac{2}{4}$ meter seems to govern the right hand through m. 16, while the left-hand arpeggios continue in the $\frac{6}{8}$ pattern. The downbeat of m. 17 is, like the last beat of m. 10, an ambiguous "extra" or transformational beat given no chordal or accompanimental support; it leads us back to the original $\frac{6}{8}$ pattern (which is, however, immediately disrupted in the same way).

Schoenberg varies the return of the opening section in m. 27 (ex. 2.1): the main theme now appears in canon between the two hands, decorated with an inner part moving in triplets. The canon here serves not purely as a contrapuntal variation of the material, but as further *metrical* manipulation, which now obscures both the notated and perceived frameworks.

Schoenberg's Andantino, then, can be said to adopt certain outward "symp-

5. The sixteenth-note ornamentation of the neighbor-note figure in the right hand of m. 11, where the original is transferred to the left hand (C–D♮–C), would be considered a "variant," not a real development (Schoenberg 1967, 9).

toms" of Brahms's style, evident in the arpeggiated bass and in the piano texture in general, and one more specific technical aspect, that of metrical development. But the piece may be said to founder precisely because the areas of motivic development, harmony, and phrase structure are not treated at the same level as, and are not adequately coordinated with, the metrical procedures (as happens, for example, in the first movement of Brahms's B♭ Quartet, examined briefly in chapter 1).

In these respects the third of the piano pieces, a Presto in A minor, is more ambitious and, it might be said, more successful. In his brief memoir of Schoenberg's youth, David Josef Bach makes the intriguing remark that "with its remarkable rhythm" this piece "already contains the seed of the later Schoenberg" (Bach 1924, 318). Unfortunately, Bach specifies neither what aspect of its rhythm is remarkable nor what prefigures the later Schoenberg. But he is right to imply that the piece is the most advanced of the three.

The progressiveness is not apparent in the phrase structure, which, as in the Andantino, is in itself quite square. The opening eight measures (ex. 2.2a) form what Schoenberg calls a "period" (Schoenberg 1967, 25–31), comprising a four-measure phrase and its varied restatement, or what we can call an antecedent and a consequent. (A period generally has two phrases of equal length, unlike a sentence.) In the Presto, both antecedent and consequent end on the dominant; the antecedent begins on the tonic, the consequent on a diminished seventh. The progressive aspect consists of the way this traditional design is filled out with chromatic harmony, specifically with what Schoenberg would later call "vagrant" chords (Schoenberg 1978, 134, 257–67); these are harmonies, such as diminished or half-diminished ones, that are ambiguous and can be led in different directions. Although the tonic is clearly implied by the bass in the first half of m. 1, it is nevertheless obscured by the right-hand arpeggiation of the diminished triad, F–G♯–B, and by the chromatic descent in both hands in m. 2. The second half of the antecedent (m. 3) begins on a remote V^7/II, and moves through II and iv^6 before settling on the dominant at the end of m. 4. The identity of the tonic is never in doubt, but the tonic is enriched by the annexation of other chromatic degrees, either as passing tones or (in the case of the A♯ in m. 3) actual chord tones. (In fact, all degrees of the chromatic scale are touched upon in mm. 1–4.)

Brahms is an obvious source for this kind of controlled, intense chromaticism, as, for example, in the Capriccio, op. 116, no. 3, where the tonic G minor is continually subverted until the end of the A section.[6] The Brahmsian pedigree of the Presto is even more evident in Schoenberg's striving to make the entire tex-

6. Thieme 1979, 81–82, has pointed to the importance of Brahms's Capriccio, op. 76, no. 1, as a model for the texture and figuration of the middle section of Schoenberg's Presto.

EXAMPLE 2.2 Schoenberg, Piano Piece in A Minor (1894).

EXAMPLE 2.2 *continued*

ture "thematic." The alto inner voice of the B section is derived from the main theme of the A section (ex. 2.2b). Later, the B theme moves into the bass and is presented simultaneously in diminution in the right hand (ex. 2.2c).[7]

The middle section lies in the key of the dominant; but Schoenberg avoids any strong cadential V–i motion at the return to the A. Instead, the return is made via the half-diminished ii⁷ chord, a vagrant harmony that is sustained for ten measures (mm. 63–72) by means of the energetic working of a descending motive A–F–E–D (ex. 2.2d).[8] The coda (mm. 92–101; ex. 2.2e) is built from the same harmony and motive; the motive is now compressed or diminuted even further and is subject to rhythmic displacement similar to that used in the Andantino in C♯ minor. (As Thieme [1979, 83] asserts, the coda may well contain the "remarkable" rhythm to which Bach was referring.) At m. 94 the $\frac{2}{4}$ meter appears to shift one eighth note to the right: the right-hand cluster B–D–E takes on the quality of a downbeat (this becomes especially apparent in mm. 95–96, when the bass note B reappears, now on the perceived downbeat). The final beat of m. 96

7. For the first procedure, see, for example, the first movement of Brahms's Second Symphony, where the arpeggio of the first theme forms (in diminution) the accompanying inner part to the second theme (as mentioned in the previous chapter). For the second, see Brahms's song *Mein wundes Herz*, op. 59, no. 7, where both voice and accompaniment are derived from the same material.

8. As Thieme has pointed out (1979, 82–83), this motive is a variation of the final theme of the middle section (A–G♯–E–C♯).

acts as the transformational beat, and the notated meter returns on the first beat of m. 97. The final cadence to the tonic in mm. 100–101 is made not via the dominant, but from a final appearance of the half-diminished (now in first inversion).

The intensity with which the ii^7 chord is manipulated, both motivically and harmonically, suggests something of the later early Schoenberg: in the next chapter we shall see him exploiting the same sonority throughout the song *Mädchenfrühling* (1897). Yet because the phrase structure tends to remain four-square (even the B section unfolds in rigid four-measure units) and because the melodic invention is less than inspired, our final impression is one of a rather static, undevelopmental form.

A more fluid and sophisticated approach to phrase structure is evident in an eighty-measure fragment in F♯ minor, labeled a scherzo by Schoenberg.[9] The fragment, which was probably drafted at about the same time as the three piano pieces, has a rondo-like form, with a main theme and two contrasting themes. The eight-measure main theme and its slightly varied repetition extend from m. 1 to m. 16 (see Appendix ex. B). Although the theme and its repetition comprise a regular number of measures (8 + 8), the harmony and meter are out of phase: each eight-measure unit begins with a measure of a dominant harmony, which resolves to the tonic in the second measure (mm. 2 and 10). The first measure is therefore in a strong metrical position, but a weak harmonic one. The conflict becomes apparent after m. 17. At first, this measure of dominant harmony would appear to be analogous to mm. 1 and 9, and thus to begin a new group like the first two. The harmony does in fact resolve to the tonic in m. 18, but the move is accompanied by a sudden diminuendo and a change in texture.

The first contrasting theme begins with this measure of tonic (not with the preceding dominant) and, like the main theme, consists of two parallel groups of eight measures. The first (mm. 18–25) moves from the tonic to its relative major, A, the second (mm. 25–32) back to the dominant. But these groups overlap, so that the final measure of the first (m. 25) is also the initial measure of the second. The ambiguity is heightened by the initial measure of each phrase (18 and 25), which remains in a sense athematic: the principal motive appears only in the *second* measure (19 and 26). The result is that m. 18 tends to sound like an introduction and m. 25 like a transition, even though these measures form an integral part of the overall phrase structure.

Thus, although they add up to an even number on the largest scale, the first thirty-two measures of the scherzo do not divide squarely into 8 + 4, as tends to

9. See Maegaard 1972, 1: 149. The piece, edited by Reinhold Brinkmann, is published in *SW* B4: 101–4.

happen in the Three Pieces of 1894. Rather, the "extra" measure, m. 17, and the compensating overlapping measure, m. 25, make the internal division asymmetrical:

MAIN THEME

Unit 1: mm. 1–8

Unit 2: mm. 9–16

"Extra" measure: m. 17

FIRST CONTRASTING THEME

Unit 1: mm. 18–25

(Overlapping measure: m. 25)

Unit 2: mm. 25–32[10]

Within the contrasting theme, the motivic working seems more fluid than in the other pieces of 1894. In the first phrase (mm. 18–21), as we have seen, the basic motive appears in the second measure (accompanied by figuration derived from m. 2 of the main theme) and then is rhythmically augmented and transformed across the third and fourth (20–21). In the second phrase the motive appears in the first two measures (22–23), but is absent from the cadential motion of the second two (24–25). The two phrases are thus not simply parallel, as is often the case in the piano pieces of 1894.

Serenade for Small Orchestra (1896)

In 1895 Schoenberg joined the small amateur orchestra Polyhymnia as cellist. It may well have been for this group that he began to compose what appears to be his first large-scale instrumental work, the Serenade in D Major. Schoenberg completed only the first movement; a scherzo, slow movement, and finale survive as fragments. The first movement is dated 1 September 1896 on the first page and 3 September on the last. The scherzo was begun on 30 November. The slow movement and finale bear no date.[11]

10. By repetition Schoenberg extends the cadence past m. 32; the first theme reappears in m. 38.

11. The slow movement fragment (microfilm no. U265–67 at the Schoenberg Institute), which bears no date, has not previously been identified as belonging to the Serenade. Maegaard 1972, 1: 26, includes only the other three movements in his entry for the Serenade; the slow movement is described on p. 152 as a separate work. Thieme 1979, 94, also identifies only three movements. Although it is not dated, the Andante clearly belongs to the Serenade. It has the same instrumentation as the other movements. It also has similar handwriting and is copied on the same kind of 28-stave paper as the scherzo movement (the other two movements are on 24-stave paper).

The orchestral serenade was a popular medium within the Austro-German-Bohemian sphere in the last decades of the nineteenth century. Schoenberg would surely have been acquainted not only with the two early serenades of Brahms (opp. 11 and 16), but also with more recent ones by Robert Volkmann, Antonín Dvořák, Josef Suk, and Robert Fuchs. A well-worn score of Fuchs's Serenade for Strings in D Major, op. 9 (published 1874), filled with performance indications in an unidentified hand, survives in the archives of the Schoenberg Institute. This may well have been a score used by Polyhymnia and may also have provided inspiration for Schoenberg's own work in the same key. For his first movement, however, he found a more compelling structural-technical model in Brahms, and in particular in the first movement of Brahms's Second Symphony, also in the key of D major.

The overall design of Schoenberg's movement owes little directly to Brahms; it takes the form of a small-scale and somewhat oddly proportioned sonata, with a very brief exposition (mm. 1–12), consisting of a single long phrase moving from tonic to dominant; a substantial modulatory development (13–44); a conventional recapitulation (45–58); and a lengthy coda (58–77).[12] But the actual thematic ideas and their treatment are strikingly close to Brahms's first movement. Both movements begin with a theme (marked *a* in ex. 2.3a) in the low strings (violas in Schoenberg, cellos in Brahms) consisting of a neighbor-note figure that surrounds the tonic; the theme falls to the dominant note A. Unlike Brahms, however, Schoenberg accompanies this theme from the outset with a repeated rhythmic figure in the woodwinds (marked *b*). After two bars (one in Brahms), a new triadic idea (*c*) enters above motives *a* and *b*. This theme is treated imitatively by the violins while being accompanied continuously by the other two ideas. At the climax of the short exposition, the violin theme takes on the *rhythm* of motive *b*.

What is especially distinctive here is Schoenberg's creation of a texture in which—as in Brahms—each part is given a motivic or thematic function. The effort is more successful than in the A-minor Presto for piano. Also impressive is Schoenberg's handling of the retransition and arrival of the recapitulation. This is always a crucial moment in Brahms's sonata forms, one for which he developed many elegant and ingenious procedures that Schoenberg must have studied carefully. By m. 33, in the development section, Schoenberg has modulated to G♭ major, which is then reinterpreted enharmonically as F♯, or V of B minor. Schoenberg cadences in this key at m. 34 (ex. 2.3b), where the actual retransition can be said to begin. The B in the bass becomes part of a seven-measure preparation of the dominant A, which is circumscribed by its diatonic upper neighbor,

12. See Thieme 1979, 97, for a formal diagram of the movement, as well as an analysis.

EXAMPLE 2.3 Schoenberg, Serenade for Small Orchestra (1896), I.

EXAMPLE 2.3 *continued*

c.

B, and its chromatic lower neighbor, G♯. In mm. 39–40 the G♯ supports a diminished-seventh chord, which resolves onto a tonic $^6_4$ harmony in m. 41. In m. 43 this becomes a dominant seventh, leading to the entrance of the recapitulation at m. 45.

The motivic-thematic process complements this harmonic one. For the ten measures preceding the retransition, Schoenberg has avoided developing motive *c*, which now reemerges at the arrival on B minor, accompanied by motive *b* in the cellos and basses. At the climax of the crescendo, in m. 40, the theme is dissolved or "liquidated" in diminution—much as Brahms treats his own analogous triadic theme at various points in the first movement of his Second Symphony (cf. mm. 59ff.). Throughout this passage, *c* has been presented by the strings (first violins and violas), while the horns reiterate only the dotted upbeat figure as a kind of ostinato on octave F♯s. In mm. 39–40 the F♯ drops to F♮, which forms part of the diminished-seventh harmony over G♯. In the next measure, at precisely the moment when the strings liquidate motive *c* and sustain a high A (mm. 40–41), the horn resolves the F♮ back up to F♯ and takes over the theme. Schoenberg shifts the dotted figure from the second beat, where it has appeared in mm. 34–39, to the last beat, where it becomes the proper upbeat to *c*. The theme is thus taken up by the horns, while diminution continues in the strings. The actual recapitulation begins at m. 45, where *c* moves to the cellos and bassoons. This whole process recalls some of Brahms's smoothest and most elegant retransitions, where the main theme appears to evolve gradually out of its various components.[13]

The other portion of this movement that deserves commentary is the conclu-

13. See, for example, the retransition and entrance of the recapitulation in the Andante of Brahms's Third Symphony, discussed in Frisch 1984, 137–40.

sion of the coda, where the tonic is reached not via the dominant, but directly from an augmented sixth chord (a German sixth, spelled B♭, D, F, A♭), which resolves over a D pedal (ex. 2.3c). Hardly unusual in itself, the harmonic device in this context represents a conscious intensification of, and complement to, the harmonic process of the retransition. There, we recall, the D$^6_4$ chord was approached from a diminished-seventh chord built on G♯ (mm. 39–41, ex. 2.3b). The German sixth of m. 70ff. differs from that diminished seventh by only one note; and its B♭ comes to sound like a chromatic intensification of the diatonic sixth degree, B♮. The final cadence recalls the earlier process of resolving the dissonant harmony by neighbor motion.

Although the harmonic vocabulary is relatively simple, the association between the two passages, retransition and coda, shows Schoenberg already thinking of harmonic function in terms of large-scale structure. The retransition and coda occupy analogous, or perhaps complementary, places within the sonata form: the retransition represents the moment of greatest harmonic tension, the coda the moment of least tension. To point up the relationship, Schoenberg employs dissonant harmonies that resolve by means of neighbor motion.

In the ways just analyzed, the first movement of the Serenade in D Major is a great step forward from the piano works of 1894. The work is a more effective, persuasive composition largely because Schoenberg has begun to internalize, to make his own, some of Brahms's more important techniques. In terms of the spectrum proposed in chapter 1, we might say that Schoenberg's emulation and allusion are now giving way to absorption. As we listen to the first movement of the serenade, we are less aware of the model than of the skill and naturalness with which Schoenberg manipulates the principles taken over from it.

The D-Major String Quartet and F-Major Scherzo (1897)

Many of the formal, thematic, and harmonic techniques that are beginning to bud in the Serenade in D Major come to fruition in the first large-scale instrumental work that Schoenberg was actually to complete (or allow to survive complete), the D-Major String Quartet. We can be certain that the quartet was revised extensively with Zemlinsky's advice. According to Egon Wellesz—and the information was confirmed by the composer—Schoenberg wrote the work in Vienna in the summer of 1897, then showed it to Zemlinsky upon the latter's return from a holiday. The first and last movements were considerably rewritten, and a new movement was composed in place of the original second one. Apparently at the time he showed Zemlinsky the quartet, Schoenberg had only just begun a third movement (it is not clear whether the fourth was complete); here too another movement was substituted for the planned one.[14] At the instigation of Zemlinsky, the quartet was given a private performance at an evening of the Wiener Tonkünstlerverein on 17 March 1898. The public premiere was given by the Fitzner Quartet at the Bösendorfersaal of the Gesellschaft der Musikfreunde on 20 December of the same year.[15]

For the D-Major Quartet, there exist an autograph and a set of parts (at the Library of Congress), neither of which shows signs of the extensive revisions or substitutions mentioned by Wellesz and Schoenberg. The original second movement survives, however, as a Scherzo in F Major, for which the manuscript is dated 27 July 1897 at the beginning and 7 August 1897 at the end.[16]

Taken together, the D-Major Quartet and the F-Major Scherzo constitute the most successful instrumental works of Schoenberg's Brahmsian period, and as such they bear more extended analysis. The first movement of the quartet was Schoenberg's most expansive sonata form to date. The exposition, which is especially rich in thematic material, has the following shape:

Theme 1a, mm. 1–12
Theme 1b, mm. 13–16
Theme 1a′, mm. 17–28
Transition, mm. 29–38
Theme 2a, mm. 39–46

14. This information about the genesis of the quartet is gleaned from Wellesz 1925, 12–13, supplemented by information that Schoenberg provided Wellesz after the appearance of the latter's book in German in 1921. In the book Wellesz reports that the third movement remained unchanged, but Schoenberg wrote to him that "auch hier kam ein ganz anderer Satz an Stelle des geplanten." Schoenberg's remarks to Wellesz were passed on by Wellesz in 1965 to Oliver Neighbour, who reports them in the preface to Schoenberg 1966. (They also appear in *SW* B20: XII.) It should be noted that the English translation of Wellesz's biography, first published in 1925, already contained some corrections that Schoenberg had furnished to the author (and that the author had passed on to the translator), although not the information about the third movement of the D-Major Quartet. These other corrections are reported by Carl Dahlhaus in his afterword to a reprint of the German edition of the Wellesz biography (1985, 158–59). I am grateful to Neighbour for providing me with a photocopy of Wellesz's letter to him and for suggestions regarding the genesis of the D-Major Quartet.

15. See Maegaard 1972, 1: 27–28; Hilmar 1974, 163. See also Zemlinsky 1934, 34.

16. Published as Schoenberg 1984 and in *SW* A20. For further information on this scherzo, see also Maegaard 1983. Oliver Neighbour has suggested (personal communication) that a brief sketch contained near the bottom of the scherzo manuscript might have been intended originally as the theme for the third movement. This sketch is reproduced in *SW* B20: 222; another, much longer version of it is found at the bottom of a leaf containing a fragmentary Heyse setting, *Vorfrühling*, in the Nachod Collection in Texas (reproduced in Kimmey 1979, 222, item 97; mentioned in *SW* B1/2/I: 45). Although Neighbour's notion is potentially attractive, it seems unsupported by the theme itself, which is in $\frac{2}{4}$ meter and the key of E♭ major. It bears a resemblance to neither the eventual third movement nor the Intermezzo that replaced the Scherzo. This E♭ theme seems to demand a relatively rapid tempo (none is actually indicated by Schoenberg) and would thus be unsuitable for a slow movement, which is what we would expect to follow a scherzo.

Theme 2a′, mm. 47–54
Theme 2b, mm. 55–64
Theme 2b′, mm. 65–78
Theme 2c, mm. 79–86
Codetta, mm. 87–96

This exposition shares with the Serenade in D Major a preoccupation—not to say obsession—with motivic and thematic development. Unlike in the earlier work, however, Schoenberg does not set out three different motivic ideas more or less simultaneously. Instead, the opening theme is presented in unison and octaves by all four instruments, as if Schoenberg wishes to begin as transparently as possible. Example 2.4a shows the first two themes, 1a and 1b, of the tripartite first group. Already in its third measure, theme 1a begins to be "developed": mm. 3–4 form a free but recognizable retrograde of mm. 1–2.

The first twelve measures function as a period, in which mm. 1–4 are an antecedent and mm. 5–12 an expanded consequent that derives quite clearly from what has preceded it. The rhythm of four slurred eighth notes in m. 5 (labeled *y*) is developed from the last two beats of m. 3. The rhythmic profile of m. 6 derives from the figure spread across the bar line between mm. 1–2 and 2–3 (*x*), where the dotted quarter note receives an accent. The consequent phrase explores the implications of that accent by shifting the figure so that it begins on the downbeats of mm. 6 and 8.

In the brief B section of the first group (mm. 13–16), *y* is further modified (hence *y*′): a rest appears in place of the first note. The pitch content retains the neighbor-note motion of the consequent form (as in mm. 5, 7, and 9), but now shifts it one eighth note to the right, so that in m. 13, B–C♯–B and G–A–B do not begin on strong beats.

In the first group, Schoenberg saturates the texture with the rhythm and pitch content of *y*. In the consequent phrase, the bass presents an inversion (D–C♯–D–C♯) of the motive played by the first violin in the preceding measure (C♯–D–C♯–D). Related motives appear in the other parts throughout mm. 7–9. Although many of these ideas may appear to represent simple melodic embellishments, in this context they function as genuine, if obvious, motivic developments. As in the Serenade in D Major, Schoenberg is attempting to make all parts of the texture thematically significant.

This developmental process continues past the first group, as is shown in ex. 2.4b, which is the climax of the transition and the beginning of theme 2a. Here motive *y* forms the beginning of a two-measure idea, of which the second measure is almost a rhythmic retrograde of the first. In the diminuendo and ritar-

EXAMPLE 2.4 Schoenberg, String Quartet in D Major (1897), I.

a.

dando of mm. 37–38, the motive is liquidated to a single neighbor-note figure, F♯–G–F♯. (It might be said that in these two measures the neighbor-note figure shifts from the rhythm of *y* to the rhythm of *x*.) Motive *y* is then immediately regenerated in the inner parts of 2a, while the tail of the liquidated motive, G–F♯ (m. 38), generates the opening of the cello figure that accompanies the new theme.

If the first group is especially impressive for its motivic concentration, the very broad second group of the first movement is striking for large-scale harmonic control. In this movement (unlike in the D-Major Serenade), Schoenberg avoids the dominant as a second key area, instead orienting the second group around B

EXAMPLE 2.4 *continued*

b.

minor and major. The potential importance of the sixth or submediant degree is made apparent at the very opening of the movement: the pitch B is accented in m. 1; a B-minor triad is prominently outlined in mm. 2–3; and the consequent phrase begins in m. 5 with a sustained B in the first violin. At the end of 1a, Schoenberg begins to realize the harmonic implications of these initially melodic details: theme 1a ends with a half-cadence on F♯, V of B minor, and theme 1b begins in B minor, before returning to the dominant of D.

The second group of the exposition returns to, and remains in, the key of the submediant. What is most remarkable—and bears some scrutiny here—is how Schoenberg manages to sustain harmonic tension across the very broad, fifty-six-measure expanse of the second group. Theme 2a begins over a dominant pedal (F♯, m. 39), which (as suggested above) arises when the tail of the F♯–G–F♯ motive of m. 38 is transformed and transferred to the bass. Throughout 2a and its counterstatement 2a′, this F♯ never resolves definitively to B in root position. (The B-major triad on the downbeat of m. 41 is a transitory phenomenon.) The first cadence is to F♯ itself via its own dominant, C♯ (m. 46). Theme 2a′ moves in m. 54 to D♯ major, which functions here as V/vi in B: Schoenberg appears to be moving to the submediant's own submediant. But this move is thwarted. Theme 2b begins unstably as this D♯ resolves deceptively *downward* to D♮, which supports a German sixth chord in a distinctive third inversion. When this process is repeated sequentially up a minor third in m. 59, we are brought back to F♯, the dominant of B, alternating with its own German sixth (a G^7 chord).

All this chromatic activity and sequential motion makes 2b more of a transitional than a "thematic" section. Theme 2b′ now serves to stabilize and, as it were, thematicize this material. Like 2a, however, this theme begins over a dominant pedal and touches down only fleetingly on the tonic B. At its climax this theme moves to V/V, C♯, and theme 2c begins *subito pianissimo* over yet another F♯ pedal. At the counterstatement of the four-measure theme (mm. 83–86) the pedal is transferred into the first violin and the cello begins tentatively, on the weak beats 2 and 4, to introduce the tonic; but the prominent F♯s (also in the viola) still tend to dominate. B is confirmed—now as a radiant major—only at the downbeat of m. 87, the start of the brief codetta that reintroduces theme 1a.

The various harmonic diversions and the constant return to an F♯ pedal enable Schoenberg skillfully to avoid confirming the submediant. He also carries even further the kind of structural use of harmony evident in the D-Major Serenade. There, we recall, the diminished-seventh and the German sixth sonorities appeared in analogous places in the sonata form, and the latter sonority was made to seem an intensification of the former. In the quartet movement, the German sixth is first introduced in third inversion in mm. 55 and 57 in theme 2b (ex. 2.5). The chord returns in the same inversion (but at a different pitch level, with a B♭ root) at the end of the development section, at mm. 157–58 and 160–61 (ex. 2.5b). Our ears cannot, I think, fail to make the association with the earlier occurrence. Now, however, the German sixth reshapes itself into the more conventional inversion, with the B♭ in the bass. This pitch resolves downward to A (in the viola) as the recapitulation begins in m. 167. The beginning of the recapitulation is in its way as elegant as that of the serenade: the actual entrance of the main theme is obscured or disguised in a Brahmsian fashion (ex. 2.5b). When 1a enters in m. 167, its first two measures (167–68) are repeated an octave higher (168–69), thus creating an "extra" pair of measures and leaving us unsure which pair constitutes the "real" moment of recapitulation.

As a whole, then, the first movement of the D-Major Quartet shows an impressive grasp of principles associated most closely, or most immediately, with the music of Brahms. By comparison, the possible influence of Dvořák on this work seems insignificant. To be sure, as Reinhard Gerlach has noted, the outer movements of the quartet have a strongly Slavic flavor (Gerlach 1972, 124). He points especially to Dvořák's F-Major Quartet, op. 96 (1894), which opens with a pentatonic-style theme not unlike Schoenberg's. But the resemblance is only superficial, for in the D-Major Quartet the emphasis on the sixth degree is not merely a local effect: as we have seen, Schoenberg goes on to build important structural features of the movement from the submediant degree. In its diatonic

EXAMPLE 2.5 Schoenberg, String Quartet in D Major (1897), I.

form as B♮, it forms the key area for the second group; in its chromatic form as B♭, it shapes the retransition. In the coda of the movement, Schoenberg replaces the B♭ by its lower fifth counterpart, the Neapolitan E♭, which is sustained for four measures (mm. 263–66) before resolving to the tonic.

Moreover, Schoenberg need not have looked to Dvořák for a pentatonic melody; one still more similar to his own, and in the same key as his quartet, can be found in Brahms's op. 71, no. 1, the song *Es liebt sich so lieblich im Lenze!* (1877). Brahms's vocal melody (ex. 2.6) is in fact shaped very much like Schoenberg's

EXAMPLE 2.6 Brahms, *Es liebt sich so lieblich im Lenze!* op. 71, no. 1.

theme, forming a broad triadic arch with the F♯ at its apogee. It is also characteristic of Brahms—and of the kind of technique adapted by Schoenberg—that the principal motive of the accompaniment is a retrograde diminution (B–A–F♯–D) of the first four notes of the vocal line. Schoenberg responded strongly to this contrapuntal, "congruent" aspect of Brahms (see Cone 1990), a dimension that (as Gerlach admits) is lacking in Dvořák.

What keeps the first movement of the D-Major Quartet rather earthbound, however, despite its motivic and harmonic elegance, is the four-square nature of its phrase structure and rhythmic-metrical language. Virtually every theme or section unfolds in four- or eight-measure units. The original second movement of the quartet, the F-Major Scherzo, shows greater flexibility in this regard, and (on a smaller scale) is equally accomplished in its motivic, formal, and harmonic aspects.

The main theme of the scherzo, presented by the viola (ex. 2.7), is one of the most economical and concentrated—and in these respects, prophetic—in all of early Schoenberg. The five-measure antecedent consists of malleable two-note motivic units (marked by brackets in the example) that take on various rhythmic and metrical shapes. In the first measure the unit begins on the downbeat with a quarter note. The initial note is then reduced to an eighth and placed in a weak metrical position as the upbeat to m. 2; this pattern is twice repeated within (and across) mm. 2–3. Schoenberg's manuscript fails to provide a slur from the upbeat in m. 3 to the downbeat of m. 4, but our ears can still trace the two further modifications of the two-note unit leading up to the cadence on F on the last beat of m. 4.

The treatment of the unit in mm. 2–3 implies (in the viola part only) a hemiola—a broad measure of $\frac{3}{2}$ superimposed on the two notated $\frac{3}{4}$ measures. The

EXAMPLE 2.7 Schoenberg, Scherzo in F Major for String Quartet (1897).

effect is distinctive here because the hemiola extends across the two *interior* measures of a four-measure phrase. Even in Brahms, the ostensible model for the device, a hemiola will usually begin on a strong bar (as in m. 25 of the third movement of the B♭ String Quartet, op. 67).

In the consequent phrase (mm. 6–9), Schoenberg expands the basic motivic unit to three notes, which now remain comfortably within the bar line as the music takes on a more lyrical regularity. The cadence on iii, or A minor, leads to a new thematic idea in the first violin (m. 10). This new idea, an ascending fourth, is presented initially as a two-note unit, a free but conspicuous augmentation of the opening rhythmic shape. This motive is now answered by a phrase in which the two-note ascending fourth, in rhythmic diminution, becomes the first component of a figure that rises to A, then sinks back through G to the starting point, D.

Two aspects of this process are of particular interest. First, as in theme 1a of the first movement of the D-Major Quartet, Schoenberg shows a predilection for palindromic or retrogradable themes (D–G–A–G–D). Of greater significance is the way the five-note thematic figure of mm. 12–13 synthesizes the two rhythmic elements of the first theme: the two-note unit is now joined with, and completed by, a three-note one. That the A–G–D component is a three-note unit, despite the slur that covers all five notes in mm. 12–13, is confirmed by the independent appearance of the motive in mm. 20–21.

The motivic-rhythmic process traced here across the first part of the scherzo equals in fluidity that of the first movements of the serenade and quartet. The same might be said of the elegant recapitulation within the scherzo proper (Appendix ex. C). The recapitulation enters over a dominant pedal, but it is the dominant of D, not F. The retransition has been governed by an intense E pedal, which pushes toward a resolution on A. When the A arrives in the bass in m. 88, after a dramatic one-beat *Generalpause*, it supports neither an A-major chord (the expected resolution) nor a first-inversion chord on the true tonic, F (which might have provided a clever way to introduce the tonic), but a D-major $^6_4$. This is the least stable possible resolution of the E: one dominant pedal has moved to another.

In its turn, the A also proves deceptive. Instead of resolving to D, it moves up to B♭, whence begins a threefold sequence descending from B♭ (m. 92), through A (m. 94), G (m. 96), and at last to the tonic F (m. 98). The tonic is not confirmed, however, but initiates another statement of the sequence in which the established pattern is disrupted: instead of the half-step that would give the expected D♮ on the downbeat of m. 99, the bass moves a whole step to D♭, which opens an attractive harmonic detour into the key of G♭, the Neapolitan of the tonic. The true dominant pedal arrives only at m. 107, the tonic at m. 113 with a full unison-and-octave statement of the original scherzo theme.

The entire recapitulation, then, shows a control of form, harmony, and voice-leading so impressive that we can only wonder why Zemlinsky advised Schoenberg to replace the scherzo. Perhaps the suggestion had more to do with *Stimmung* than with compositional technique: Zemlinsky may have felt that a relatively bumptious scherzo was no longer appropriate in chamber music at the fin de siècle. In his own works of this period, Zemlinsky tended either to substitute for the scherzo a more gentle allegretto in the manner of Brahms (the String Quartet, op. 4) or to eliminate the scherzo altogether (the Clarinet Trio, op. 3, which has only one inner movement, a slow one). In the D-Major Quartet, Schoenberg decided on the former route: the second movement became a lilting Intermezzo in F♯ minor, marked Andantino grazioso (a very Brahmsian designation).

The F-Major Scherzo and the Intermezzo that replaced it have in common the use of the viola as the principal melodic voice, a feature that seems to derive most directly from the third movement of Brahms's B♭-Major String Quartet, op. 67 (ex. 2.8). The motivic language of Brahms's Agitato seems also to have been in Schoenberg's ear as he worked on the scherzo. The first six measures of the Brahms are based on a three-note dotted rhythm that is very similar in content and in spirit to Schoenberg's. But Schoenberg goes beyond mere emulation or allusion; he forges from this material a thematic-metrical process so fluid that it might even be said to surpass the model. (He also adopts the figure from

EXAMPLE 2.8 Brahms, String Quartet No. 3 in B♭ Major, op. 67, III.

EXAMPLE 2.9 Schoenberg, String Quartet in D Major (1897), III.

Brahms's first and second violins in mm. 7–8 as one of the principal accompanimental motives, which appears in the second violin, in mm. 1, 3, etc.) By comparison, the newer intermezzo seems tame. Schoenberg takes over the *Klangfarbe* of the Brahms (muted strings) with some elegance, but he loses the motivic-rhythmic élan.

In suggesting that the scherzo be replaced, Zemlinsky may have felt that it was too close in general style and specific motivic content to Brahms's op. 67. If so, he failed to see (or hear) past the symptoms, to see how flexibly and creatively Schoenberg had reinterpreted Brahms's compositional techniques. To be sure, the new Intermezzo gave Schoenberg's quartet a more symmetrical, and unusual, tonal plan: across the four movements, the keys rise by major third, D–F♯–B♭–D. But the original scherzo would have fitted nicely into the quartet as a whole, since it bears a close thematic relationship to the third movement, a theme and variations. Like the scherzo theme, the variation theme (ex. 2.9) unfolds at first in distinct two-note groups; indeed, the two themes begin almost identically, with a falling second that is then expanded outward (to a fourth in the scherzo, to a third in the Andante). These relationships suggest that at least the theme of the original third movement was retained when that movement was replaced by the present one.

In his brief reminiscences of Schoenberg, Zemlinsky remarks that although much of the D-Major Quartet was derivative from Brahms, "a middle movement already strikes an individual tone" (Zemlinsky 1934, 34). Recent commentators have assumed that by "middle," Zemlinsky meant the new second movement, the Intermezzo, whose composition he apparently encouraged (Gerlach 1972, 125; Thieme 1979, 113). But I suspect he intended the third, which in many respects is the most innovative and impressive of the five movements that survive.

The gnomic eight-measure theme (ex. 2.9) is, to my knowledge, unique in the variation literature in that the first half is played unaccompanied and the second half consists of two lines in counterpoint. (The texture and procedure are very different from baroque variations on a ground, and bear only a distant relationship to the finale of Beethoven's *Eroica*, where the "theme" is at first a single line, which is then joined by a counterpoint in the first variation.) There are two basic rhythmic motives, which are developed to some extent independently of intervallic concerns: the two-note figure of m. 1 (*x*) and the more extended four-note figure of m. 2 (*y*), which can also be heard as a combination of two two-note motives. Rhythm *y*, which serves to conclude both the antecedent and consequent of the first half of the theme, initiates the second half (mm. 5–6).

The two phrases of the first half are well balanced intervallically: the descending third of the antecedent (B♭–G♭, m. 1) is answered by the ascending thirds in the consequent (B♭–D♭ and C♭–E♭, m. 3). In the antecedent of the second half of the theme (mm. 4–6), the interval content of the viola theme is subtly related to the end of the preceding consequent in the cello. If the viola's rising sixth, F–D♮, is understood as the inversion of a descending third, the *Hauptstimme* of mm. 4–5 can be heard as the transformation of a pair of descending thirds (F–D♮, E♭–C)—a complement to the pair of rising thirds in mm. 3–4.

Because of the sparse texture of the theme, the slightest chromatic detail seems to take on special significance. The emphasis on G♮ (m. 2) and the Neapolitan C♭ (m. 4) has consequences both for the second half of the theme and the subsequent variations. The D♮–D♭ shift in mm. 5–6 recalls the C♮–C♭ shift in the preceding consequent. And the cadence to VI, or G♭, in m. 6, which brings with it a melodic C♭, serves to integrate the latter pitch into the larger harmonic design.

One other aspect of the theme deserves particular mention: the emphasis on imitation in the antecedent of the second half, where the cello follows the viola in a rhythmic canon at the distance of a quarter note. The principle of imitation will prove important in the following variations, as will the particular relationship between the parts at this point in the theme.

The autograph score of this movement contains seven variations (five in minor, two in major) and a coda. Schoenberg indicated two of the variations for deletion, those between the present 3 and 4 (in minor), and 4 and 5 (in major).[17] Throughout the variations, Schoenberg makes good, as it were, on the polyphonic-contrapuntal implications of the theme. The idea of canonic imitation proposed in the antecedent of the second half is taken up and developed in different ways—and at different moments—in each variation. In variation 1, the two-note groups of the theme (the first violin) are imitated two beats later by the two-note groups in the cello. A similar but modified relationship exists in the varied repetition of the first part of variation 2 (mm. 21ff.), where the violin begins the two-note group on the upbeat, the cello on the downbeat. In the second half of the variation, all three upper instruments engage in imitation (mm. 25–26). In the first two measures of variation 3, the first violin and cello are in free rhythmic imitation; in the second half, Schoenberg intensifies the imitation at the place analogous to the preceding variation: all four instruments now participate. In variation 4, the violin and cello are again in rhythmic imitation, now at the close distance of a sixteenth note. In variation 5, the second violin and viola are in imitation.

Another significant feature of the variations is the way Schoenberg treats the rhythmic motive *y* at the beginning of the second half. From variation 1 on, the originally subordinate imitative voice begins to take on a motivic life of its own (let's call it *z*). In variation 1 (m. 13), *y* appears in the second violin; it is imitated, less strictly than before, in the viola and cello (*z*), where the first note is now shortened from a quarter to an eighth and the pitch contour is altered (ex. 2.10a). In the analogous spot in variation 2 (ex. 2.10b), *y* is varied with continuous eighth notes, and treated imitatively by the second violin, first violin, and viola (mm. 25–26). Motive *z* has now completely shed its imitative role: in the viola and cello, it remains in the rhythmic form it assumed in the preceding variation (with the opening leaps inverted). Similarly, in variation 3 (ex. 2.10c), a further diminution of motive *y* is treated imitatively independent of motive *z*, which appears in the first and second violins (m. 33).

Motive *z* is absent in variation 4 and in the two rejected variations, but receives its apotheosis, so to speak, in the final variation, variation 5 (ex. 2.10d). Here it changes position within the variation structure, appearing at the very opening (m. 63) instead of at the beginning of the second half. It thus stands in place of the expected two-note motive, *x*. Furthermore, *z* now generates its own imita-

17. The two rejected variations appear in both Schoenberg 1966 and *SW* B20: 276–78. In the former, they are placed in the score in their original positions and are marked, respectively, A and B. In the latter, the rejected variations, printed only in the critical report, are called IV and VI. To avoid possible confusion with Roman numerals indicating harmonic function, I here adopt the A and B labels for the two variations, as well as the measure numbering of Schoenberg 1966.

EXAMPLE 2.10 Schoenberg, String Quartet in D Major (1897), III.

a. Variation 1

b. Variation 2

c. Variation 3

tion, between second violin and viola. At the opening of the second half of the theme—the customary position for *z*—Schoenberg retains only a small hint of the motive in the syncopated rhythm that begins in the viola (m. 70) and moves into the second violin (ex. 2.10e).

The evolution undergone by *z* helps to give the entire variation structure a coherent shape. (Perhaps this is one reason Schoenberg deleted two of the variations, A and B, that bore no trace of *z* and thus did not contribute to the overall

EXAMPLE 2.10 *continued*

d. Variation 5

e. Variation 5

shape.) So too does Schoenberg's treatment of harmony. The initial harmonic structure of the theme is adhered to closely in variations 1 to 3. In each, as in the theme, the antecedent of the first half moves to V, the consequent back to i; the antecedent of the second half begins in the tonic major and moves to VI; the consequent returns to the tonic. This design is changed significantly for the first time in variation 4, where the second half begins directly in G♭, or VI, then moves to C♭. Between mm. 49 and 50—in the middle of the antecedent phrase—Schoenberg literally wrenches the harmony up an augmented second (enharmonically a minor third) to D major (m. 50), whence the preceding pattern is repeated, leading from D major to G major. The harmonic shift serves to set in relief the altered scale degrees III and VI (D♮ and G♮), which were already highlighted by the chromatic inflections in the theme. A diminished-seventh chord built on E♮ leads the consequent back to a cadence in B♭ minor.

The annexation, or integration, of these altered scale degrees is carried still further in the two major variations, B and 5. Instead of returning to I, the first half of variation B moves to III, or D major, the key approached so forcibly in the preceding variation (4). The choice of key is significant in another respect: D, lying a major third above the tonic, serves as the symmetrical counterpart to the

G♭ that served as the analogous tonal goal in variations 1–3. (This same symmetrical array of keys is reflected in the tonal plan of the quartet as a whole, D–F♯–B♭–D.)

The slow variation 5 is the first in which Schoenberg actually expands the original phrase structure: each half of the theme now lasts eight measures instead of four. In this way Schoenberg creates the temporal space, as it were, in which to synthesize important features of preceding variations. (We have already noted the "apotheosis" of motive *z*.) As in variation B, the second of the rejected variations, the harmony moves first to V, then to III, but now the pattern changes. In the second half, Schoenberg returns to the tonic relatively soon (mm. 72–73), but then, after a notated *Luftpause*, shifts abruptly to G♭ major, where the music remains delicately suspended for two and a half measures. In m. 76 the bass (high up in the cello) moves to F♭, thus forming a German sixth chord in third inversion precisely like those encountered at important structural moments in the first movement of the quartet. On the downbeat of m. 77, the bass (enharmonically an E♮) resolves upward a half-step to F♮ and the tonic $^6_4$ chord.

With this elegant passage, Schoenberg has reintegrated into the *major* mode the G♭ that served as an important secondary harmony of the *minor* variations—thus making explicit its role as symmetrical counterpart to the D major of the first half of the variation. Moreover, he creates a clear reference to the role played by the ♭VI in the first movement, as upper neighbor to the dominant and as the root of a German sixth chord appearing in third inversion.

The final variation is a remarkable testimony to the young Schoenberg's powers of synthesis and long-range planning. And the variation movement as a whole stands as his finest achievement within the Brahms chamber music tradition. The D-Major Quartet is, in fact, Schoenberg's last work that falls directly within that tradition. Between the composition of the quartet in the summer and fall of 1897 and the composition of the sextet *Verklärte Nacht* almost exactly two years later, he was not to complete another piece of instrumental music. Any link between the two works seems to have been forged not in the realm of instrumental music, but in that of Lieder.

CHAPTER THREE

The Songs

By far the largest proportion of Schoenberg's early works consists of Lieder. There survive autographs for thirty-two complete songs (and more fragments) that were written before the end of 1900 but did not appear among Schoenberg's first published collections, opp. 1, 2, and 3 in 1903–4.[1] Since fewer than a third of the manuscripts were actually dated by Schoenberg (only after 1897 did he begin to provide dates with some consistency), the problem of establishing a firm chronology is even harder than in the instrumental works. First attempts along these lines were made by Walter Bailey (1979) and Ulrich Thieme (1979, 127–43), who (independently of each other) separated the early songs, principally on the basis of style, into three main periods: a largely autodidactic phase up to about 1894; a distinctly Brahmsian phase up to about 1897; and a more chromatic, Wagnerian phase from 1897 to 1899. The development thus charted is plausible and agrees essentially with that outlined by Schoenberg himself in his writings.

A more precise chronology, based principally on paper types and handwriting in the song manuscripts, has been proposed more recently (1989) by Christian M. Schmidt in the critical report for *SW* B1/2/I: 42–52. The results are persuasive and are basically consistent with the stylistic development suggested by Bailey and Thieme, as well as with the picture of the early Schoenberg that has been drawn thus far in part I of the present study. In the absence of precise datings from Schoenberg himself or from other biographical sources, Schmidt's work should be accepted as the most accurate available; it forms the basis of the list of early songs through 1897 given in table 2.

1. The early songs, which are scattered among several collections and institutions, were first inventoried by Stein 1977 and Bailey 1979, whose work has now been superseded by, and incorporated into, the comprehensive critical report prepared by Christian M. Schmidt for *SW* B1/2. Seven of the early songs were published as Schoenberg 1987. All have now appeared in *SW* A1 and A2.

TABLE 2 Schoenberg's Completed Songs through 1897

Date	Song (Poet)	Publication in SW *A2*
1893	*In hellen Träumen* (Alfred Gold)	1–3
	Schilflied (Nikolaus Lenau)	4–7
Before 1895	*Einst hat vor deines Vaters Haus* (Ludwig Pfau)	8–10
	Das zerbrochene Krüglein (Martin Greif)	11–12
	Daß gestern eine Wespe (unknown)	13–15
	Juble, schöne junge Rose (unknown)	16–17
	Warum bist du aufgewacht (Pfau)	18–19
	Im Fliederbusch ein Vöglein saß (Robert Reinick)	30–33
	Daß schon die Maienzeit vorüber (Ada Christen)	34–36
	Könnt' ich zu dir, mein Licht (Pfau)	37–40
	Mein Schatz ist wie ein Schneck (Pfau)	41–42
	Gott grüß dich, Marie! (Pfau)	43–44
	Der Pflanze, die dort über dem Abgrund schwebt (Pfau)	45–46
	Einsam bin ich und alleine (Pfau)	47–49
	Nur das thut mir so bitterweh' (Oskar von Redwitz)	50–52
	Du kehrst mir den Rücken (Pfau)	55–56
	Ich grüne wie die Weide grünt (Wilhelm Wackernagel)	57–59
	Mein Herz, das ist ein tiefer Schacht (unknown)	60–62
Before September 1895	*Zweifler* (Pfau)	53–54
	Vergißmeinnicht (Pfau)	20–25
1895	*Ecloge* (Jaroslav Vrchlický)	67–78
Before March 1896	*Mädchenlied* (Emanuel Geibel)	63–64
	Sehnsucht (Joseph Christian von Zedlitz)	65–66
Before 1897	*Lied der Schnitterin* (Pfau)	26–29
1897	*Waldesnacht* (Paul Heyse)	81–85
	Mädchenlied (Heyse)	79–80
	Mädchenfrühling (Richard Dehmel)	86–88
	Nicht doch! (Dehmel)	89–95

Based on a fresh assessment of these works, and in light of the more precise chronology now available, I would refine and reshape somewhat the version of Schoenberg's development given by Bailey and Thieme. We can discern a four-stage development, which forms the basis for the analytical commentary in this chapter and can be summarized as follows:

1. Most of the songs that appear to antedate 1894 are rather pallid imitations of Brahms and Schumann, with one exception, *Schilflied* ("Drüben geht die Sonne scheiden") of 1893, which shows a highly original, if still tentative, compositional voice.
2. With *Ecloge* of 1895, which went through three different versions (more than any other surviving early song), Schoenberg breaks free of the the more obvious Brahmsian imitation and refines certain harmonic-formal techniques explored in *Schilflied.*
3. With the two Heyse settings *Mädchenlied* and *Waldesnacht*, which were almost certainly composed in 1897, Schoenberg seems to return more self-consciously to Brahms, but now achieves a genuine internalization or absorption fully on a level with that of the contemporaneous D-Major Quartet.
4. Schoenberg moves definitively away from the Brahms idiom—but not from its fundamental compositional principles—in the two Dehmel settings from the fall of 1897, *Mädchenfrühling* and *Nicht doch!* Here he reaches toward the newer, more individual kind of musical expression that was to culminate in his works of 1899.

One aspect of Schoenberg's activity as a song composer that appears quite early on (although it is by no means unique to him) is a tendency toward concentrated involvement with specific poets for short periods. Moreover, the quality of the poetry seems directly related to the musical results. Thus, in the earliest period, up to about 1895, there are eleven relatively uninspired complete (and other fragmentary) settings of poems by Ludwig Pfau, a minor figure from the sentimental, *volkstümlich* romantic tradition. With the two Heyse settings and then the Dehmel settings of 1897, the higher quality of the poetry seems to stimulate a higher level of musical composition.

Schilflied

Schilflied, which Schoenberg's childhood friend David Josef Bach has testified was composed in 1893 (Bach 1924, 317), brought Schoenberg his first semi-official recognition: it was awarded a composition prize by the amateur Viennese orchestra Polyhymnia, the group Schoenberg was to join as cellist in 1895.[2] In another song datable to 1893, *In hellen Träumen*, Schoenberg worked with a rather mawkish text by his schoolmate Alfred Gold. In *Schilflied*, he turned to a more venerable poem, one of a set of five *Schilflieder* published in 1832 by the romantic author Nikolaus Lenau. (Although *Schilflied* thus refers as a title to the set of poems, and not the individual text, which begins "Drüben geht die Sonne scheiden," I shall for ease of reference continue to call Schoenberg's song *Schilflied* in the present chapter.) This group of poems became extremely popular with composers of the nineteenth century. A scan of Ernst Challier's *Grosser Lieder Katalog* reveals that by the time Schoenberg wrote his song, in 1893, at least fifty-seven settings of this particular text, "Drüben geht die Sonne scheiden," had appeared in print (Challier 1885). Conceivably the choice of text was dictated by the Polyhymnia prize competition.

The poem (printed here as it appears in Schoenberg's manuscript) is in many respects a characteristic creation of German romanticism, in which nature becomes a metaphor for, or projection of, the feelings of a solitary protagonist:

Drüben geht die Sonne scheiden,
Und der müde Tag entschlief.
Niederhangen hier die Weiden
In den Teich, so still, so tief.

Und ich muß mein Liebstes meiden:
Quill, o Träne, quill hervor!
Traurig säuseln hier die Weiden,
Und im Winde bebt das Rohr.

In mein stilles, tiefes Leiden
Strahlst du, Ferne! hell und mild
Wie durch Binsen hier und Weiden,
Strahlt des Abendsternes Bild.

2. As has been realized by Schmidt, the entry for *Schilflied* in Maegaard 1972, 1: 156, is in error in stating that the manuscript is part of group of Lieder (at the Morgan Library) enclosed in a wrapper headed "4 Lieder korrigiert 16." This information led Bailey (1979, 53–54) to suggest that the surviving manuscript of *Schilflied* may represent a later revision. The wrapper actually belongs to drafts of four songs from the *Hanging Gardens* cycle, op. 15, also at the Morgan (nos. 3, 4, 5, and 8; see Maegaard, 1: 62, and *SW* B1/2/I: 24 and 50–51). (Schmidt seems to accept that the wrapper reads "korrigiert" and thereby acknowledges a potential problem with the *Hanging Gardens* songs, for which a 1916 revision is unlikely. To my eye, the scribble is by no means definitively readable as "korrigiert.") In short, there is no physical evidence to contradict Bach's suggestion that *Schilflied* is a song of 1893.

Over there the sun goes down, and the weary day closed its eyes. Here the willows droop in the still, deep pond.

And I must stay away from my beloved: flow, my tears, flow forth! Here the willows are rustling in sadness, and the reed trembles in the wind.

Into my still, deep suffering you shine, O distant one! Bright and gentle, as through rushes here and willows, shines the image of the evening star.

Schoenberg shapes Lenau's three stanzas into a rounded four-part song, in which the central stanza is divided musically into two parts: the overall form is thus A (m. 1), B (m. 19), C (m. 27), A′ (m. 35). The song represents perhaps the earliest surviving example in Schoenberg's works of the kind of motivic-rhythmic concentration that was to become a hallmark of his compositional technique and that we have noted in the D-Major Quartet and F-Major Scherzo.

The prelude (Appendix ex. D) is dominated by an almost obsessive repetition of a two-note, short-long figure, which is traded between the two hands. When the voice enters in m. 5, the motive continues in the accompaniment, but its articulation is now modified. The left hand plays as before, but in the right, slurs now join the longer note to the succeeding shorter note. The motivic forms in the voice at the end of the stanza, in mm. 11–13, are clearly heard as further modifications of the original two-note figure.

The economy of the motivic language may well have been inspired by Schoenberg's early encounters with Brahms's music, but there is in fact little else of a recognizable Brahms style in *Schilflied*. In the harmonic language, especially, Schoenberg seems engaged in an empirical or intuitive exploration of the kind of chromatic chords he was later to label "vagrant." Extensive use of vagrant harmonies is, of course, a major aspect of the style of Liszt, Wagner, and Wolf, a repertory that Schoenberg claimed to have discovered only in 1898–99 (as reflected in works discussed in succeeding chapters). *Schilflied* in no way invalidates that claim, for in it the augmented, diminished, and half-diminished chords are employed in a manner very different from that of Wagner or Wolf. These harmonies do not arise primarily from the kind of stepwise chromatic voice-leading that might be called Tristanesque. Instead, they occur to extend, delay, or obscure basic diatonic progressions. Hence my characterization of Schoenberg's harmonic language here as "empirical" and intuitive; it is as if he is discovering the properties of vagrant chords on his own.

The prelude essentially sustains or prolongs a dominant, E-major harmony. However, as I have indicated with the brackets underneath mm. 1–4 in Appendix ex. D, the bass line actually arpeggiates not the dominant triad, but a more ambiguous half-diminished seventh chord, E–G–B♭–D–E. The first vocal phrase carries the ambiguity a step further: it ends in m. 8, not with the expected dom-

EXAMPLE 3.1 Tonal structure of *Schilflied.*

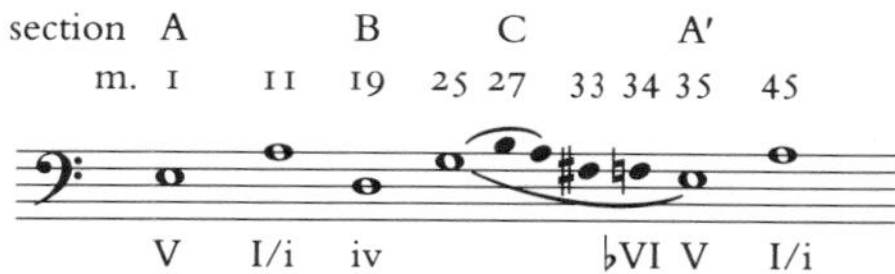

inant triad, but with an augmented chord spelled E–G♯–C. The C can be understood as an upper neighbor to the implied B of the dominant triad; but the C conspicuously fails to resolve and is instead carried over in the harmonies of the first measure of the next phrase. The conclusion of the A section is also colored by the augmented triad, which evolves by chromatic motion into two other vagrant harmonies under the repeated E of the voice in mm. 12–13.

In this first section of the song, then, Schoenberg uses the vagrant harmonies to deemphasize the tonic-dominant axis and thereby capture something of the general *Müdigkeit* or lassitude conveyed by the poem. In the impassioned B and C sections, the vagrant harmonies surge more forcefully and continuously. The initial key area of the B section, D minor, is immediately overridden by a succession of seventh chords: minor, half-diminished, and diminished. Particularly striking here is the tritone motion in the bass of mm. 22–24, supporting the juxtaposition of a C-minor seventh chord and a second-inversion augmented triad with a B♭ root and F♯ bass. Only in m. 25 is a stable G-minor triad reached. The more tranquil C section is oriented around F major; just before the fermata of m. 34, the F appears in the bass to establish itself as the root of a German sixth chord in A minor and usher in the reprise.

If we step above, or behind, the many harmonic regions touched on in *Schilflied*, what emerges is a coherent, if idiosyncratic, large-scale structure, which is sketched in ex. 3.1. The song proceeds essentially by fifth through the arrival on G minor in m. 25. The status of G minor as the long-range goal of this "progression" helps to explain why it is given such emphasis in mm. 25–26—more emphasis, indeed, than is given to the tonic in the A section. At the end of the C section, this G can be heard to descend stepwise to F, or the sixth degree in A minor, which in turn drops to E to begin the A′ section.

Because of the tension sustained in this way across large spans, the song can even be heard as having some of the tonal dynamic characteristic of a sonata form: the A section functions as a kind of exposition, centered around tonic and dominant; the B section is a far-ranging "development," reaching a remote G minor; C is a "retransition," moving to a sonority that becomes recognizable as the sixth degree, upper neighbor to the dominant; A′ functions as a "recapitulation." I use these terms not to imply that Schoenberg was attempting a song in sonata form, but to suggest that the song manifests ambitious "instrumental" impulses that might be said to strain against the traditions of the song medium.

Ecloge

Some of these same impulses can be detected in another remarkable song, *Ecloge*, which, although not dated by the composer, was probably composed in 1895. The poet, not named on any of the three manuscripts for the song, has recently been identified (*SW* A2: 67) as the Czech Jaroslav Vrchlický (a pseudonym for Emil Frida). Schoenberg appears to have taken this text from a German translation of some of Vrchlický's lyrics that appeared in 1895.[3] The poem is not an eclogue in the strictly classical sense of a pastoral dialogue, but is rather an attractive romantic lyric associating spring, described in stanzas 1 and 2, with love, described in parallel terms in stanzas 3 and 4:

Duftreich ist die Erde und die Luft krystallen,
Und das Moos erzittert unter deinem Fuß,
Aus dem Schilfrohr hör'ich's wie von Pfeifen schallen,
Und vom Hagedorn fällt heller Blütengruß.
Und das Aug' von Freude naß,
Fragst du: Ja, was soll all das?
"Was?"
Ruft der Vogel und die Blume spricht:
"Anders kommen doch des Lenzes holde Wunder nicht!"

Hell dein Blick, dein Atem süß vom Duft der Erlen,
Und es bebt dein Busen, wie ich dich umfang';
Wie aus hartem Felsen springen Quellenperlen,
Bricht aus meinem Herzen glühender Lieder Drang.
Und das Aug von Freude naß,
Fragst du: Ja, was soll all das?
"Was?"
Ruft der Vogel und die Blume spricht:
"Anders kommen doch der Liebe holde Wunder nicht!"

3. See *Gedichte von Jaroslav Vrchlický*, translated by Friedrich Adler (Leipzig: Reclam, n.d.). Since Adler's preface is dated December 1894, we can assume the volume appeared in 1895. This book was only one of several collections of Vrchlický's poems published in German, beginning in 1886. The poem "Duftreich ist die Erde," no. 5 in a volume of ten eclogues originally published in Czech in 1880, appeared in several of the German collections; but only the Adler translation of 1895 matches the one used by Schoenberg (with minor differences of spelling and punctuation). Thus we can safely assume (with Schmidt, *SW* B1/2/I: 11) that this volume served as Schoenberg's source. The date of 1895 also fits in plausibly with the stylistic-compositional development traced in this chapter. The text of the poem as printed here is taken from the Adler volume. In the Adler volume the generic title "Ekloge" is given with a *k*, whereas in the only one of Schoenberg's manuscripts to bear the title at all (at the Schoenberg Institute), it appears with a *c*. In *SW*, Schmidt follows Adler's spelling; here I have followed Schoenberg's, hence *Ecloge*.

The earth is rich with scents, the air crystalline, and the moss trembles under your foot. From the reed I hear a sound like that of pipes, and from the hawthorn descends the bright greeting of blossoms. What does all this mean? you ask, your eyes wet with joy. "What?" calls the bird, and the flower responds: "The sweet miracle of spring comes in no other way."

Your gaze is bright, your breath sweet with the scent of alder, and your breast throbs as I embrace you. As pearls of water spring forth from hard stones, thus does a rush of radiant songs burst from my heart. What does all this mean? you ask, your eyes wet with joy. "What?" calls the bird, and the flower responds: "The sweet miracle of love comes in no other way."

Following the poem, Schoenberg's setting is strophic on the largest scale: it is based on an almost exact repetition of a musical unit of 49 measures. The way in which the musical strophe is shaped—and, among the three manuscripts, reshaped—bears certain resemblances to *Schilflied.* The overall form of the strophe can be considered A (mm. 1–15), A′ (16–23), B (24–30), A″ (31–49) (see Appendix ex. E).

As in *Schilflied,* Schoenberg attempts in this song continually to sidestep the tonic, A♭, which is reached in only m. 4 as the last component of a sequence moving V$^{6}_{5}$/ii–ii–V$^{6}_{5}$–I (as shown in the Appendix). Because A♭ arrives in this way, with no special emphasis or preparation, we may not even recognize it as the tonic. Nor is it confirmed in what follows. The vocal part in the A section breaks off in m. 12 in midstream, as it were, on a ii$^{6}_{5}$ chord. In the two-bar transition between sections, mm. 14–15, Schoenberg again treats the tonic simply as part of an ongoing sequence, ii^{7}–V–I–IV, leading to the return of A′.

The broad, dissonant leaps make the vocal part of *Ecloge* considerably more advanced than that of *Schilflied.* The piano part also has a more independent, continuous motivic process, which unfolds in the tenor range, underneath the cascading eighth notes. As in the other song, the basic motive is a very concise one, here the four-note A♮–E♭–D♭–C figure of m. 1. Measure 2 presents a rhythmic variant of this motive and serves to mark off a basic two-bar unit, which is then repeated sequentially. At the respective conclusions of the four-bar groups in mm. 4 and 8, the motive is further transformed into a three-note figure, quarter–dotted quarter–eighth. This in turn becomes the sole motive form to appear in mm. 9–12, where Schoenberg builds to the conclusion of the A section.

The virtually equal status of piano and voice in *Ecloge* is confirmed by the exchange at the start of the A″ section. In mm. 31–34, the voice takes over the thematic skeleton of the right-hand eighth-note figuration of mm. 1–4, and the right hand of the piano plays the disjunct theme formerly sung by the voice. The exchange ends in m. 35 as Schoenberg introduces new vocal material and a new kind of texture for the line beginning with "Anders kommen." It is here that we find the first real signs of technical unsureness in the song. The passage seems clumsy, unmotivated, perhaps because we have not had enough of a real "return" to justify a new departure, which is then followed by a sudden push toward the apparent climax of the song on the big $^6_4$ chord and high A♭ of "Wunder" in m. 42.

My own dissatisfaction with the passage beginning at m. 35 was apparently shared by Schoenberg, who altered it in each of the three autographs for *Ecloge*. Although none of the three manuscripts bears a date, their order of completion can be surmised on the basis of the passage in question. The earliest version is a fragment (in the Nachod collection at North Texas State University; reproduced in Kimmey 1979, 204–6), which breaks off after the first musical strophe (and in which Schoenberg has inadvertently substituted "der Liebe," from stanza 2, for "des Lenzes" from stanza 1). The version of the song at the Pierpont Morgan Library (as reproduced in Appendix ex. E), close in handwriting style to the Texas copy, is almost certainly the second in order: it is a complete draft of the song, but shows signs of intended revision in mm. 24–25 and 35–37, which have wavy lines drawn across them. The copy at the Schoenberg Institute is the third manuscript. A fair copy with breathing marks written in, it was apparently intended for performance.[4]

Originally, the Schoenberg Institute copy (the third) corresponded almost exactly to the Morgan one (the second), but Schoenberg began to revise extensively at precisely one of the spots marked with a wavy line in the Morgan copy, at "Anders kommen" in mm. 35ff. Although the crossouts and pasteovers in the Institute copy do not in fact yield a complete, coherent draft of the song, we can reconstruct at least the state in which he left the "Anders kommen" passage before apparently abandoning work on the song. The three versions of this passage are superimposed in ex. 3.2.

In Schoenberg's first attempt, ex. 3.2a, the parallel-fauxbourdon texture at "Anders" involves even the bass, which is high in its register and plays in eighth notes. The vocal line and the top part of the piano here are initially a fourth higher than in the version of 3.2b. In 3.2b, Schoenberg brings the first "Wunder nicht" (mm. 7–8) down a minor third, to F–E♮, probably so as to avoid usurping the climactic A♭ to be reached on the later "Wunder" of m. 12. Text repetition is also handled differently in 3.2a and b. In 3.2a, Schoenberg repeats the line of text intact in mm. 9–13; in 3.2b, he adds still more text, in effect delaying the arrival on the final "nicht."

The most far-reaching changes, however, come in the third version, 3.2c. Two aspects are particularly striking: the different figuration at "Anders" and the new

4. That this third draft of *Ecloge* forms part of a gathering with *Waldesnacht*, which was almost certainly composed in 1897, has led Schmidt to suggest that Schoenberg may have attempted this revision in 1897, thus two years after the first draft (*SW* B1/2/I: 45).

EXAMPLE 3.2 Comparison of versions of *Ecloge.*

EXAMPLE 3.2 *continued*

a. *continued*

10
Lie - be hol - de Wun - der nicht An - ders kom - men doch der Lie - be hol-de

b. *continued*

10 (40)
Len - zes hol - de Wun - der nicht An - ders kom - men doch des Len - zes hol-de
f

c. *continued*

Len - zes Wun - der nicht,
des

a. continued
Wun - der nicht
ritardando
b. continued
15 (45)
Wun - der, des Len - zes Wun - der nicht.
f rit.
dim.
pp
c. continued
10
Len - zes hol - de Wun - der nicht.
rit.

harmonization from "Blume" onward. As to the first: Schoenberg must have realized that the parallel chordal style is too anomalous, especially in a recapitulatory section. He thus abandons it and reintroduces the basic slurred eighth-note figuration of the A section. At the same time he reshapes the harmonic progression so as to avoid arriving on the tonic at "spricht" in m. 4. He understood that this tonic made for too much closure in versions a and b and that it tends to undercut the arrival on the tonic $^6_4$ at "Wunder." Moreover, by this point we have heard this particular progression, V^6_5/ii–ii–V^6_5–I, twice before, at the beginning of the A and A′ sections.

Schoenberg thus reharmonizes the F♭–E♭ in the voice at "Blume spricht." As shown in ex. 3.2c, he displaces the V^6_5 to m. 4 ("spricht"), preceding it at "Blume" with a neighbor-chord spelled as a G♭-minor seventh (the chord has no functional label in A♭). The resolution of the dominant now falls on "Anders," in m. 5, a bar later than in the earlier versions. Rather than closing off harmonic motion, as happened in versions 3.2a and b, the tonic now forms the beginning point of a strong rising bass line that pushes forward more quickly to the secondary dominant on "nicht" and then to the tonic $^6_4$.

In 3.2c, Schoenberg has shifted the weight and placement of the climax. In the earlier versions the $^6_4$ chord had been reached more circuitously, and its power had then been vitiated somewhat too quickly by the immediate melodic cadence to A♭ (m. 13). In 3.2b, the extension by word repetition does not change this fundamental situation, since the voice hovers on A♭ for the last four measures. But in 3.2c, the voice descends more slowly—and appropriately—to the final A♭, which now coincides with the actual arrival of the root in the bass.

I have dwelled on the successive revisions of this small passage from *Ecloge* because they have a significance broader than their immediate context. They show Schoenberg grappling with fundamental compositional issues of thematic, formal, and harmonic balance. More than in *Schilflied*, he seems to be questioning the proper shape and status of a "recapitulation" or return: how to prepare it harmonically, how long it needs to be to accomplish its formal purpose, how it should transform earlier material, and so forth.

In these ways, both *Schilflied* and *Ecloge* open up a number of promising paths that Schoenberg might have been expected to follow immediately in 1895. In fact, it is not clear just what direction his song composition took over the next one or two years. This was the period of his private study with Zemlinsky, who may have encouraged Schoenberg to return to and master the Brahmsian model, to "get it right," so to speak (something that, as I suggested in chapter 1, Zemlinsky himself failed to do in *Heilige Nacht*). In any case, this period culminates in Schoenberg's most profoundly Brahmsian songs, *Mädchenlied* and *Waldesnacht* (1897). Here we find the kind of assimilation and absorption missing from earlier efforts, especially apparent in the phrase structure, motivic development, and harmonic expansion. Each of the two songs seems to draw consciously on a different *Stimmung* typical of Brahms—the first light and folk-like, the second slow and broadly lyrical. In both, Schoenberg turns to Paul Heyse, whose poems Brahms himself had set on several occasions, and who is a substantial cut above Ludwig Pfau.

Mädchenlied

Schoenberg sets the poem "Mädchenlied" as a modified strophic song in which two poetic stanzas are grouped into one musical strophe:

Sang ein Bettlerpärlein
Am Schenkentor,
Zwei geliebte Lippen
An meinem Ohr:

Schenkin, süße Schenkin,
Kredenz dem Paar,
Ihrem Dürsten biete
Die Labung dar!

Und ich bot sie willig,
Doch der böse Mann,
Biß mir wund die Lippen,
Und lachte dann:

Ritzt der Gast dem Becher
Ein Zeichen ein,
Heißt's er ist zu eigen
Nur ihm allein.

A pair of beggars sang at the tavern door; two seductive lips at my ear said:

Barmaid, sweet barmaid, serve this pair. For their thirst offer refreshment.

And I offered it gladly, yet the wicked man bit and hurt my lips and laughed:

If a guest carves his sign on a cup, they say it belongs to him alone.

The song (first strophe in Appendix ex. F) is a direct counterpart to the first movement of the D-Major Quartet from the same year, not only in key and mood but also in the triadic/pentatonic build of the opening melody, which likewise emphasizes the sixth degree, B, and a B-minor harmony. Brahms, of course, is the ultimate model. Indeed, Schoenberg seems to have had a specific Brahms song in his ear: *Ständchen*, op. 106, no. 1, whose first phrase concludes with the same $\hat{6}$–$\hat{3}$–$\hat{5}$ melodic figure, harmonized by vi–I.

It is in the more subtle relationships between voice and piano and in the fluid phrase structure that Schoenberg's song reveals a more genuine Brahmsian inheritance. In the first two phrases, mm. 1–5, the accompaniment repeats a brief three-note motive, *x*, the neighbor-note figure heard first as F♯–E♯–F♯. In the second half of the first strophe, mm. 6–7, *x* migrates from the piano into the voice, at "süße" and "kredenz dem."

This motivic transference forms part of a still more sophisticated exchange of material between voice and piano. As the voice reaches the half-cadence on the dominant in m. 5, the piano begins a restatement of what was originally the vocal theme, now in the dominant. From the second half of m. 6 this restatement begins to deviate slightly from the original (an exact transposition would bring an E in the right hand on beat 3 of m. 6), but the contour and rhythms are fully recognizable through m. 7.

This piano statement actually overlaps with the conclusion of the first vocal phrase in m. 5 and the beginning of the next one in m. 6. There is thus an asynchronous relationship between voice and accompaniment here, perhaps intended by Schoenberg as a kind of musical corollary of the drunken beggars outside the tavern. The voice and accompaniment could be said to get back into phase in m. 8, for the final phrase of the strophe.

The flexible relationship between piano and voice in *Mädchenlied* makes the analogous techniques in *Ecloge*—the piano's motivic development and the interchange of material at the recapitulation—look rudimentary. More significantly, the comparison suggests that it was in emulating Brahms's music that Schoenberg found the ways to expand on techniques already present in his own earlier songs.

Waldesnacht

If *Mädchenlied* pays homage to Brahms's sophisticated *Volkston*, Schoenberg's *Waldesnacht* draws impressively on the rich fund of broad, slow songs like *Feldeinsamkeit*. Where Heyse's "Mädchenlied" poem is concise and epigrammatic, his "Waldesnacht" is expansive, almost hymnic:

> Waldesnacht, du wunderkühle,
> Die ich tausend Male grüß',
> Nach dem lauten Weltgewühle
> O wie ist dein Rauschen süß!
> Träumerisch die müden Glieder
> Berg' ich weich ins Moos,
> Und mir ist, als würd' ich wieder
> All der irren Qualen los.

Fernes Flötenlied, vertöne,
Das ein weites Sehnen rührt
Die Gedanken in die schöne,
Ach, mißgönnte Ferne führt!
Laß die Waldesnacht mich wiegen,
Stillen jede Pein,
Und ein seliges Genügen
Saug' ich mit den Düften ein.

In den heimlich engen Kreisen
Wird dir wohl, du wildes Herz,
Und ein Friede schwebt mit leisen
Flügelschlägen niederwärts.
Singet, holde Vögellieder,
Mich in Schlummer sacht!
Irre Qualen, löst euch wieder;
Wildes Herz, nun gute Nacht!

Forest night, wondrous cool, I greet you a thousandfold; after the noisy turmoil of the world, oh, how sweet is your rustling! Dreamily I bury my weary limbs in the soft moss, and it is as if I were freed from all my confused torments.

Sound, distant flute song, which stirs a vast longing and leads my thoughts to the lovely distance, oh so begrudged! Let the forest night lull me and silence my pain, and I breathe a blissful contentedness with its fragrance.

In your secretive, close confines you will recover, restless heart. And peace floats downward on gently beating wings. Sing me to gentle slumber, tender bird songs! Begone, delirious torments; good night, then, restless heart!

Schoenberg's setting of the poem is modified strophic; the changes come principally in the vocal part of lines 5–6 of each stanza, analogous to mm. 14–17. (Appendix ex. G gives only the first musical strophe in full.) For this song, Schoenberg had a direct model in Brahms's own setting of the Heyse's "Waldesnacht" as a song for mixed chorus, op. 62 (ex. 3.3). A comparison of the opening phrase in the two settings will show how Schoenberg responds to Brahms's predilection for asymmetry. The first two lines of the poem, which have eight regular metrical stresses, would fall naturally into a phrase of four full measures, divided 2+2. Where in one of his earlier songs Schoenberg would almost certainly have followed the four-square approach, here he emulates Brahms in extending the first phrase to five measures, or eighteen quarter beats. But he follows the spirit rather than the letter of Brahms's practice: Brahms augments the note values on "kühle" and "die"; Schoenberg creates a beautiful ascending melisma

EXAMPLE 3.3 Brahms, *Waldesnacht*, op. 62, no. 3.

on the first syllable of "wunder." By means of word repetition, Brahms extends his second phrase still further, to six full measures, or twenty-four quarter beats. Schoenberg moves in the opposite direction, compressing lines 3–4 into four measures plus an upbeat, or seventeen quarter beats.

Schoenberg's integration of chromatic detail within a diatonic context places this song well beyond his other Brahmsian efforts and can, indeed, stand beside Brahms's own practice in chromatic passages like mm. 6–10 of the choral song *Waldesnacht*. We might note especially Schoenberg's elegant treatment of the flatted sixth degree, G♮. This is the first non-diatonic note heard in the song; it appears in the bass of m. 5 to color the word "kühle." The same pitch, enhar-

EXAMPLE 3.4 Schoenberg, *Waldesnacht,* strophe 3, mm. 58–61 (vocal part only).

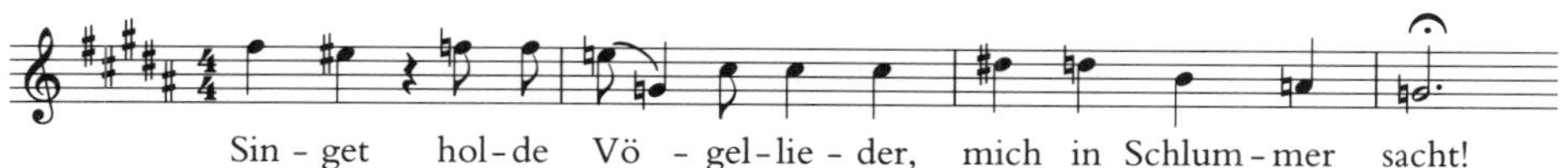
Sin - get hol-de Vö - gel-lie - der, mich in Schlum - mer sacht!

monically respelled as F𝄪, reappears on the corresponding rhyme "wühle," in m. 9, as part of a strong stepwise bass progression. At the cadence in mm. 11–12, the G♮ appears in the voice and piano as an appoggiatura to the dominant.

The G♮ becomes the basis for chromatic effects that reach still farther in mm. 14–17, where it forms part of a German sixth chord in the tonic minor, spelled G–B–D–E♯ (mm. 14 and 16; the chord has the G in the bass in m. 16). This harmony does not resolve to the dominant; it bypasses F♯ in the bass and steps down to a ii^7 chord at the fermata. The G♮ is never actually resolved as such; it is rather "neutralized," as Schoenberg would say, by the return of the diatonic sixth degree G♯ in m. 19.

Two other aspects of the song merit comment here. The first is the subtle evolution of the piano texture across the strophe. The staggered arpeggiation of mm. 3–12 gives way in m. 13 to full chords alternating between the hands. After the fermata of m. 17, this texture evolves into the parallel chordal style in which the piano doubles the voice. We have encountered this texture before, in the "Anders kommen" section of *Ecloge.* There it seemed merely awkward, and Schoenberg eventually abandoned it (see ex. 3.2c above). In *Waldesnacht,* however, the parallel chordal style has been carefully prepared and makes for a wonderfully effective climax to the musical strophe.

The second aspect of the song that is noteworthy is the transformation of the vocal part in the third strophe, at mm. 58–61 (ex. 3.4; cf. mm. 14–17 of Appendix ex. G). Here the voice in essence takes over the top line of the piano part (with the addition of a downward sixth leap at "Vogel"). The enharmonic and chromatic steps carry this phrase well beyond the Brahmsian idiom of the rest of the song. Indeed, this kind of line—as well as its harmonic underpinning, including a whole-tone chord on the last beat of m. 14/58—would be at home in a Schoenberg work of 1899, or perhaps in *Gurrelieder.*[5]

5. This vocal line actually represents a revision written by Schoenberg over the original line, which was as in strophe 1. In *SW* A2: 85, Schmidt opts for the original version and banishes the chromatic revision to the critical report (*SW* B1/2/I: 294). This seems to me an unfortunate editorial decision. Schoenberg 1987 gives mm. 58–61, as in my ex. 3.4.

This passage shows quite vividly that *Waldesnacht* marks the farthest Schoenberg could go within the Brahms "style." Together with the variation movement of the D-Major String Quartet (examined in the previous chapter), the song can be said to represent the culmination of his period of Brahms study; it is his graduation piece, so to speak, or the work pointing the way out of the "Brahms fog." That path was to be opened still more forcefully in the fall of 1897 with Schoenberg's turn away from the kind of poetry represented by Heyse to the newer kind of verse embodied in the works of Richard Dehmel.

The Dehmel Settings of 1897

In one of the early manifestos of German modernism, a polemical essay of 1885 called "Die neue Lyrik," the literary critic Karl Bleibtreu called for a reaction against the folk-like tradition in German poetry as represented by Heyse. He bemoaned the fact that "the Volkslied, coming by a detour through Goethe, is taken by most critical papists as the only valid norm of the so-called 'genuine [*echte*] lyric.'" He added, with obvious sarcasm, "Ah, the 'genuine lyric' is indeed so easy: a little mood, a little rhyme, and the masterwork is ready." Bleibtreu demanded a new kind of poetry that would exhibit not only greater naturalism (the first catchword among the early modernists) but also greater subjectivity: "In the first place, *subjectivity* must be released, in order to break the stiffness of the conventional patterns" (in Ruprecht 1962, 51–53).

The new subjectivity or individualism in poetry, strongly influenced by Nietzsche in the late 1880s and 1890s, was to take many forms in expression and technique. But it was nowhere embodied more strikingly than in the verse of Richard Dehmel (1863–1925), whose first collection of poetry appeared in 1891.[6] By the late 1890s, Dehmel was perhaps the most famous poet in Germany (or with Stefan George, one of the two most famous). The public and press were at once attracted and scandalized by Dehmel's eclectic blend of what the critic Julius Hart in 1896 characterized as "archaism, symbolism and allegory, everyday-realistic naturalism, with elements of sexuality, immorality and Satanism, and the Nietzschean superman" (in Ruprecht and Bänsch 1970, 15).

This poetry apparently held no attraction for the older generation of composers; Brahms dismissed it as "not well suited for musical treatment" (in Birke 1958, 280). But the younger musicians, including Richard Strauss, Zemlinsky,

6. The principal collections of Dehmel's poems published in the 1890s include *Erlösungen: Eine Seelenwandlung in Gedichten und Sprüchen* (Stuttgart: Göschen, 1891); *Aber die Liebe: Ein Ehemanns- und Menschenbuch* (Munich: Albert, 1893); *Lebensblätter: Gedichte und Anderes* (Berlin: Verlag der Genossenschaft PAN, 1895); *Weib und Welt: Gedichte* (Berlin: Schuster & Loeffler, 1896); and *Erlösungen: Gedichte und Sprüche*, 2d ed., rev. (Berlin: Schuster & Loeffler, 1898).

Reger, Schoenberg, and (slightly later) Anton Webern, were strongly drawn to it.[7] Dehmel was the first major contemporary poet to whom Schoenberg devoted sustained creative attention. And it was a conversion that was to have far-reaching implications for his musical style.

In a well-known letter to Dehmel of 1912, Schoenberg himself acknowledged the poet's profound impact, noting that

> your poems have had a decisive influence on my development as a composer. They were what first made me try to find a new tone in the lyrical mood. Or rather, I found it even without looking, simply by reflecting in music what your poems stirred up in me. People who know my music can bear witness to the fact that my first attempts to compose settings for your poems contain more of what has subsequently developed in my work than there is in many a much later composition.
>
> SCHOENBERG 1964, 35

In another letter, written a year later, Schoenberg reiterated Dehmel's influence on the younger generation: "Far more than any musical model, it was you who determined the platform of our musical experiments" (Birke 1958, 285).[8] These are strong sentiments, but they constitute no great exaggeration when we consider the enormous role played by Dehmel in Schoenberg's early works: between 1897 and 1906 he was to sketch or complete at least eighteen works based on Dehmel's poetry. Among these are some of his most important early compositions.

The two earliest Dehmel songs, completed in September 1897, were *Mädchenfrühling* and *Nicht doch!* After a hiatus, Schoenberg returned to Dehmel in the spring of 1899 (as we shall see in the next two chapters). A single Dehmel collection, *Weib und Welt* (1896), was to provide the source for all of Schoenberg's Dehmel works of 1899. For the two settings of 1897, Schoenberg turned to an earlier volume, *Aber die Liebe* (1893). It seems significant that Schoenberg selected Dehmel poems that, although tinged with erotic subjectivity, nevertheless show their allegiance to the folk-like tradition represented by the Heyse texts for *Mädchenlied* and *Waldesnacht*. There is, however, enough difference in the poetry to

7. See Sichardt 1990. After Schoenberg, Strauss composed the most Dehmel works. His ten songs, composed between 1895 and 1902, comprise *Stiller Gang*, op. 31, no. 4; *Mein Auge*, op. 37, no. 4; *Leises Lied, Der Arbeitsmann, Befreit*, and *Lied an meinen Sohn*, op. 39, nos. 1, 3, 4, and 5; *Wiegenlied* and *Am Ufer*, op. 41, nos. 1 and 3; *Notturno*, op. 44, no. 1; and *Waldseligkeit* and *Wiegenliedchen*, op. 49, nos. 1 and 3. None of these texts overlaps with the ones set by Schoenberg. On the personal and professional relationship between Strauss and Dehmel, see Schuh 1982, 437–45.

8. For more extensive citation of these letters and discussion of their aesthetic implications for Schoenberg's style, see Frisch 1986, 138–42.

have liberated Schoenberg from the more obvious kind of Brahmsian symptoms and to have encouraged him to reach for something more individual, more "subjective."

Mädchenfrühling

In Dehmel's poem, the arrival of spring is developed as a metaphor for the emergence of feelings of love and sexuality in the young maiden. The work derives its tension from setting the process of nature—that of April buds becoming May blossoms—against the unnatural recalcitrance of the boy, who seems not to share the vernal urges. In the first stanza the boy's failure to react is conveyed by the blunt, intentionally wooden rhyme of the one- and two-syllable lines, "und / *sein* Mund." In the last line of the poem the maiden's frustration is captured by the repeated "fühlt":

Dehmel	*Schoenberg*
Aprilwind;	Aprilwind;
alle Knospen sind	alle Knospen sind
schon aufgesprossen,	schon aufgegangen,
es sprießt der Grund,	es sprießt das Grün,
und	und
sein Mund	*sein* Mund
bleibt so verschlossen?	bleibt so verschlossen [?]
Maisonnenregen;	Maisonnenregen;
alle Blumen langen,	alle Blumen langen,
stille aufgegangen,	stille aufgegangen,
dem Licht entgegen,	[line omitted]
dem lieben Licht.	dem lieben Licht.
Fühlt, fühlt er's nicht?	Fühlt, fühlt er es nicht [?]

> April wind; all the buds have burst forth [Schoenberg: opened], the ground [Schoenberg: green] is sprouting and *his* mouth remains closed?
>
> May sunshowers; all the flowers yearn, having quietly risen, toward the light, to the lovely light. Doesn't, doesn't, he feel it?

To the right of Dehmel's poem I give the text as it appears in both of Schoenberg's autographs.[9] Two of the variants, the substitution of "aufgegangen" for

9. Schoenberg's setting has been discussed in three studies: Bailey 1979, 82–85; Thieme 1979, 157–59; and Dümling 1981, 149–54. Bailey and Dümling erroneously print as Dehmel's "original" the rather different, revised version of the poem that Dehmel prepared for his ten-volume *Gesammelte Werke* (Berlin: Fischer, 1906–9), where it appears in the collection *Erlösungen*. This situation is un-

"aufgesprossen" in line 3, and "das Grün" for "der Grund" in line 4, upset the original rhyme scheme of stanza 1 ("-sprossen" / "-schlossen" and "Grund" / "Mund"). The first substitution repeats (actually anticipates) the participle in line 10 of the poem. Thus it seems clear that these are inadvertent errors made in copying the text. The other principal alteration, however, the omission of Dehmel's line 11, may have been a more conscious structural decision, as I suggest below.

The music of *Mädchenfrühling* (Appendix ex. H) shows clearly that what gripped Schoenberg was less the textual detail than the sonorous potential of the opening word/image, "Aprilwind" (and also of the initial word of stanza 2, "Maisonnenregen"). The image of "Aprilwind" gave rise to the swirling arpeggiated accompaniment figure and the half-diminished harmony that dominate the song—sweep through it, one might say. The C♯–E–G–B harmony functions ostensibly as ii^7 in B minor, and thus a pre- or subdominant chord.[10] But since a firm tonic is avoided for the entire first stanza—B minor is touched on only in mm. 17–18, where it serves as a passing harmony between A minor and C major—the half-diminished seventh remains tantalizingly ambiguous or vagrant. The whole first stanza seems suspended above this and the related subdominant sonority, E minor, to which the dominant, F♯, always resolves deceptively (mm. 7–8, 9–10, 23–24). Even the final cadence of the song, to B major (mm. 45–48), is made not via the dominant, but directly from the same half-diminished seventh, presented successively in root position, first inversion, and second inversion.

The first stanza is, indeed, a remarkable study in harmonic *Flüchtigkeit* and understatement. Schoenberg avoids establishing not only the tonic, but also the conventional secondary key, the relative major. The D^6_4 harmony with the strong A pedal in mm. 13–14 would seem to indicate a move toward III, but no cadence is forthcoming. The expected A-major chord (V of III) appears instead as A mi-

fortunately typical of the Schoenberg literature, which often fails to take account of the complex publication history of Dehmel's poetry. As in the case of "Mädchenfrühling," Dehmel often transferred and revised poems between collections, both in the original individual volumes and in the two later editions of his collected works.

Schoenberg's personal library, preserved at the Arnold Schoenberg Institute, contains only the ten-volume *Gesammelte Werke* (and the individual volume *Schöne wilde Welt* [Berlin: Fischer, 1913]), which obviously did not serve as the source for his settings of 1897–1905 (see Steuermann 1979, 215). At the Schoenberg Institute there is also a single undated leaf in Schoenberg's hand, headed "Gedichte von Richard Dehmel," onto which the composer copied six poems from various sources: "Bitte," "Liebe," "Gieb mir," "Geheimnis," "Klage," and "Mannesbangen." Only the last of these was set to music.

10. In Schoenberg's *Theory of Harmony* (Schoenberg 1978), this chord (not named as a "half-diminished") is illustrated on pp. 231–33 (ex. 164 f, g, i, k, and ex. 165) as deriving from the minor subdominant. Schoenberg later examines its more radical possibilities as a "vagrant" chord (the "Tristan" chord) on pp. 255–56 (ex. 189). These compositional possibilites are exploited by Schoenberg in a Dehmel setting, *Mannesbangen*, to be discussed in chapter 4.

nor (mm. 15–16), and moves through a passing B minor, to the Neapolitan C major (m. 19). The structural function of the A minor has been to introduce the crucial Neapolitan pitch C♮. The Neapolitan is the strongest sub- or pre-dominant sonority employed to this point; but it fails, like the others, to lead directly to a dominant; instead, in m. 21, it moves to its own dominant, G. Only in the piano interlude is the dominant at last reached. In m. 22, the Neapolitan C♮ is replaced by the diatonic II, C♯, which now leads to a definitive half-cadence on F♯ in m. 25.

The fleeting harmonies of the first stanza give way to more stable ones in the second stanza. The dominant of the interlude resolves to a broad B major. A pedal point on B is sustained for ten measures and leads purposefully to a half-cadence on F♯ at "dem lieben Licht" (mm. 37–38). The "Aprilwind" half-diminished chord reappears in the following measure, now functioning clearly—as it did not earlier—as subdominant, resolving to V on the downbeat of m. 44. In the postlude the original evanescent harmonic language returns, as the dominant dissolves back into the "Aprilwind" chord.

The remarkable harmonic planning and control in *Mädchenfrühling* are complemented by—actually, inextricably linked to—Schoenberg's sophisticated treatment of meter and rhythm, and by the large-scale design of the vocal line. After the strong downbeat orientation of the accompaniment in the first five measures, the syncopations of the left hand in mm. 6–10 come into conflict with the right-hand figuration. This rhythmic displacement is a corollary to the harmonic avoidance of a firm cadence, discussed above. The end of the second vocal phrase is marked not by a clear downbeat, but by further ambiguity, a Brahmsian hemiola that creates one large measure of $\frac{3}{4}$ out of mm. 10–11. Schoenberg then further attenuates the subdominant chord on the downbeat of m. 12 by tying the E over the bar line; the subsequent D-major and A-minor chords in the left hand of mm.13–16 are also tied. The hemiola returns for the piano interlude in mm. 23–24, leading at last to rhythmic-metrical stability with the arrival of B major at "Maisonnenregen."

The very active accompaniment of *Mädchenfrühling* is a foil to the laconic, understated vocal part, whose unfolding provides one of the finest and most fluent examples of developing variation among the early works of Schoenberg. The initial B–E motive materializes out of the accompaniment figure simply by picking two chord tones from the half-diminished chord. This "Aprilwind" motive then becomes the source for almost all subsequent vocal material, at least in the first strophe. The next two phrases both fill in and expand the range of the initial motive: "Alle Knospen" extends the range upward to F♯, "es sprießt" downward to A.

The developing variation also involves a progressively greater emphasis on the upper F♯ in the vocal line. The first phrase goes up to E, the second up to F♯ on the weak beats of mm. 7 and 9. The F♯ receives more prominence in phrase 4, with the quarter note on "und"; the pitch still, however, falls on a weak beat. With the first syllable of "Maisonnenregen," F♯ appears for the first time on a downbeat; the phrase as a whole traces a broad arpeggio down to the same note an octave lower. The phrase "dem lieben Licht" climbs up to, cadences on, and sustains the F♯, which is thereby given the greatest emphasis so far. And yet the process is not over, for as the piano returns to the opening material, the vocal line (m. 41) reaches briefly, wistfully still one half-step beyond, to the highest note in the song, the G♮ that represents the top of the "Aprilwind" figuration. One could scarcely imagine a more elegant, effective conclusion.

Finally, a word about the formal structure of *Mädchenfrühling* and a speculation on why Schoenberg omitted line 11 of Dehmel's poem. Schoenberg understood that the two stanzas of the poem, although roughly parallel, could not sustain a strophic or modified strophic setting: the musical form needed to reflect the process of growth or evolution described in the text. And yet the final line—where the maiden laments the boy's unresponsiveness—undercuts the optimism of the second stanza. To capture this design Schoenberg creates an abbreviated ternary or ABA′ form. Since the A′ is brief (mm. 40–48, or only 40–43, not counting the piano postlude), Schoenberg may well have felt it was necessary to truncate the poetry of the B section ("Maisonnenregen") somewhat in order to achieve a rounded musical form that would not be grossly imbalanced. He thus dropped one of the two clauses involving "Licht," a tactic that destroys the rhyme "regen / entgegen," but not the actual syntactical sense of the stanza.

The musical transition back to A′ is fashioned most subtly. At m. 37, underneath the rising half-cadence of "dem lieben Licht," the piano begins to return to the opening "Aprilwind" figuration. The actual return, however, comes two measures later on the last beat of m. 39, as the G♯ at the top of the arpeggio is replaced by the familiar G♮. This return is achieved with a sophistication worthy of, and perhaps inspired by, Brahms, who often ushers in the reprise gradually in his ternary songs, so that we cannot point to a specific moment where it begins.[11] Also Brahmsian is the way Schoenberg momentarily obscures the bar line at the beginning of the piano postlude. The "Aprilwind" figuration appears first in the *left* hand, instead of the expected right hand, on the last beat of m. 43; then the right hand begins an overlapping statement on the subsequent downbeat—a metrical position it has not occupied before. This statement is truncated to allow the right hand to begin its next statement in the "proper" place, on the last beat

11. See, for example, the song *Die Kränze*, op. 46, no. 1, mm. 47–50, discussed in Frisch 1984, 100–101.

of m. 44. As in many passages of Brahms, the metrical ambiguity across the bar line between mm. 43–44 is momentary, but telling, adding interest or "development" to a recapitulation.

Perhaps the most remarkable aspect of these Brahmsian techniques is how well they are integrated into the newer, more individual musical idiom of *Mädchenfrühling*. Gone are the Brahmsian "symptoms" still evident in *Mädchenlied* and *Waldesnacht*; but the fundamental principles of Brahms's harmony, phrase structure, and thematic variation, remain—and are indeed used with still greater elegance.

Nicht doch!

The sense of evanescence, even incompleteness, imparted by the truncated form and ambiguous harmonic close of *Mädchenfrühling* suggests that the song was not meant to stand alone. I believe it was conceived as part of a complementary pair with the other Dehmel setting of 1897, *Nicht doch!* This also survives in two manuscripts, a rough draft (incomplete) and a fair copy. The draft, which breaks off at the measure corresponding with m. 32 of the fair copy, forms part of the same bifolium as the dated draft of *Mädchenfrühling*. In addition to their association on music paper, the songs are linked by certain poetic and musical features. Schoenberg encountered the two poems on successive pages of Dehmel's *Aber die Liebe*. Although Dehmel himself does not specifically pair the two poems, they can be read—as Schoenberg apparently did—as a kind of before-and-after of the maiden's encounter with the young man. In the first poem he is unresponsive, but in the second he at last reacts, sweeping the maiden off her feet with a skillful seduction:

> Mädel, laß das Stricken—geh,
> thu den Strumpf bei Seite heute;
> das ist was für alte Leute,
> für die jungen blüht der Klee!
> Laß, mein Kind;
> komm, mein Schätzchen!
> siehst du nicht, der Abendwind
> schäkert mit den Weidenkätzchen.
>
> Mädel liebes, sieh doch nicht
> immer so bei Seite heute;
> das ist was für alte Leute,
> junge sehn sich ins Gesicht!
> Komm, mein Kind,
> sieh doch, Schätzchen:
> über uns der Abendwind
> schäkert mit den Weidenkätzchen . . .

Siehst du, Mädel, war's nicht nett
so an meiner Seite heute?
Das ist was für junge Leute,
alte gehn allein zu Bett!—
Was denn, Kind?
weinen, Schätzchen?
Nicht doch—sieh, der Abendwind
schäkert mit den Weidenkätzchen . . .

Maiden, leave off your mending—go; put the stocking aside today; that kind of thing is for old people; for the young, the clover is blooming! Leave it, my child; come, my treasure! Don't you see the evening breeze flirting with the willow catkin?

Dear maiden, don't still avert your gaze today; that kind of thing is for old people; the young look each other in the face! Come, my child; look here, treasure: above us the evening breeze is flirting with the willow catkin . . .

Do you see, maiden, wasn't it nice to be by my side today? That kind of thing is for young people; old folks go to bed alone!—Well now, child? Are you crying, treasure? Come now—look, the evening breeze is flirting with the willow catkin . . .

Schoenberg created several significant musical connections between the two songs (see Appendix ex. I for the opening of *Nicht doch!*). Despite somewhat different tempo/mood markings (the fair copy of *Mädchenfrühling* is marked "rasch, etwas flüchtig, durchwegs leise," *Nicht doch!* simply "leicht"), both songs seem to demand a similar pace. Such at least is suggested by their strikingly similar metrical-rhythmic profiles. Both have an almost continuous flow of sixteenth notes, and although *Mädchenfrühling* is notated in $\frac{3}{8}$ and *Nicht doch!* in $\frac{6}{8}$, a listener without a score might well hear both songs in the same meter (probably $\frac{3}{8}$), at least initially.

The upward flourish that occupies the first three beats of *Nicht doch!* is separated distinctly from the second half of the measure by a vertical wedge, a *subito piano*, and a change in figuration. It thus tends to be heard as a single measure of $\frac{3}{8}$. Indeed, in m. 6 Schoenberg treats this figure in precisely that manner, as an "extra" half-measure. The effect of m. 1 is then repeated in m. 9. In both songs the notated meter is overridden at the ends of phrases by an almost identical hemiola of $\frac{3}{4}$ in the accompaniment.

The songs display a similar piano figuration, especially at the opening. Although rising arpeggios or scales are, of course, common accompanimental devices in nineteenth-century Lieder, Schoenberg treats them in a special way here. If the two songs are played in succession, the opening of *Nicht doch!* seems to recall, and then suddenly abandon, the figuration of *Mädchenfrühling*. The upward-moving figure, whose contour recalls the "Aprilwind" of the first song,

EXAMPLE 3.5 *Nicht doch!* mm. 25–30 (piano part only).

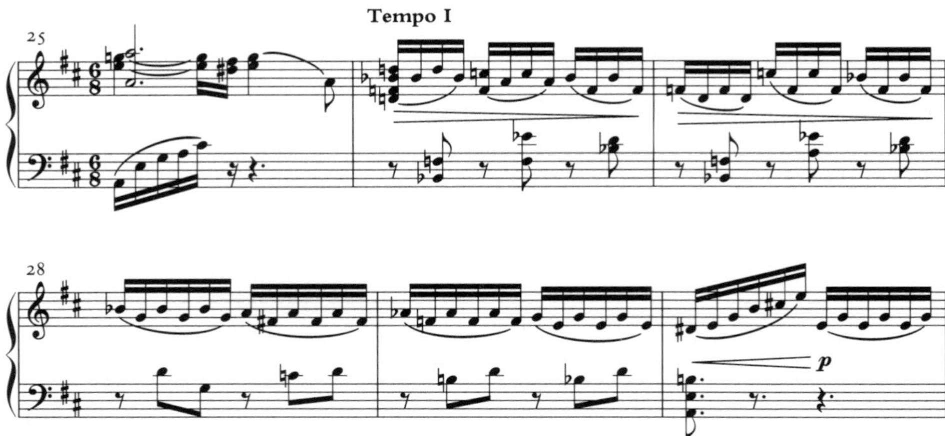

gives way rather abruptly to a very different figuration oscillating between two notes a third apart. It is as if the upward-moving sixteenth-note figure has come to represent the kind of innocent, vernal love depicted in *Mädchenfrühling*, which gives way to the coarser, simpler sentiments of *Nicht doch!*

Mädchenfrühling and *Nicht doch!* also share certain tonal features, including a key signature of two sharps (also shared by the D-Major Quartet and *Mädchenlied* of the same year). *Mädchenfrühling* is in B minor-major, *Nicht doch!* in D major. Although in the abstract this relationship could hardly be taken as evidence of harmonic planning, Schoenberg's treatment of D in the first song is suggestive. The D major sought but not reached in mm. 13–14 of *Mädchenfrühling* (as discussed above) becomes the tonic of *Nicht doch!*—a relationship that becomes apparent only if the songs are performed together.

Although *Nicht doch!* is not as harmonically elegant as its companion song, one particular procedure points clearly to Schoenberg's growing control of large-scale tonal structure, control of a kind already discussed in the case of the contemporaneous D-Major String Quartet. The piano interlude that appears between strophes 1 and 2 (mm. 25–30; see ex. 3.5), and 2 and 3 (mm. 54–59), makes a sudden detour from the dominant seventh of D to the key of B♭, then after three measures comes around again, via G minor, to the dominant ninth that opens the strophe.

During the first two strophes this harmonic diversion to the flatted sixth, the upper neighbor of the dominant, remains a detail confined to the interludes. But in the third strophe, Schoenberg picks up and expands the idea. Here the second quatrain ("Was denn, Kind?") begins not in the tonic, as in strophes 1 and 2, but in iii (Appendix ex. J). B♭ major arrives with dominant preparation on the downbeat of m. 75 to accompany the appearance of the title words, "Nicht doch!" The harmony now works its way definitively back to the song's dominant by circumscribing the A in the bass: B♭–A–G♮–G♯–A, arriving on the tonic $^6_4$ in m. 77. The whole harmonic process is reiterated as the first two lines of the second quatrain are repeated (mm. 79–83, as happened in previous strophes), except that the relation of the vocal part and accompaniment is adjusted so that the arrival of the tonic now coincides with the words "Nicht doch!" As in the D-Major Quartet, then, Schoenberg has effectively integrated the flatted sixth degree and the tonic.

The two Dehmel songs of 1897 make a telling complement or sequel to the pair of Heyse settings. If the latter pair represent a saturation point of Schoenberg's Brahms absorption, the former two, especially *Mädchenfrühling*, represent something of a new beginning. Had Schoenberg's encounter with the poetry of Dehmel been limited to these two works, we might not be inclined to see the poetry itself as initiating this new direction. But after a relatively fallow year in 1898, Schoenberg returned to Dehmel in 1899. The works of that year mark the real milestone in his early compositional development. This fact suggests that Dehmel's verse played a crucial role, one that must be examined further in the next two chapters.

PART II

Expanded Tonality, Expanded Forms, 1899–1903

CHAPTER FOUR

The Dehmel Settings of 1899

Schoenberg and Weib und Welt

If, indeed, as the stylistic and paleographic evidence suggests, all the compositions discussed in part I of this study were completed by the end of 1897, then 1898 appears to have been a relatively fallow year in Schoenberg's early creative life. The only works that we can attribute to it with relative certainty are the two songs, op. 1, and the aborted symphonic poem *Frühlings Tod.*[1] The songs of op. 1 are strikingly different both from what preceded them in 1897 and from what followed them in 1899. Schoenberg turns away from both the folk-like poetry of Heyse and the modified folk style of the two Dehmel poems toward two longer, more discursive texts—examples of what has been called *Begriffspoesie*—by another contemporary, Karl von Levetzow (1871–1945).[2] The expansive, cantata-like musical settings, with their extravagant piano parts, contain many splendid moments, but they were ultimately an expressive dead end for Schoenberg. He was to find his own path, his own voice, in his rediscovery of Dehmel's verse, specifically the collection *Weib und Welt.* Schoenberg's involvement with this volume in 1899 was so intense that I believe it can be said that his remarkable development that year, culminating in the sextet *Verklärte Nacht,* grew directly out of his search for a musical language appropriate to the poetry of *Weib und Welt.*

1. Although the autographs for the op. 1 bear no date, there is a partial preliminary draft of no. 1, *Dank,* at the Schoenberg Institute, dated 30 July 1898 (see *SW* B1/2/II: 143). The particell for the symphonic poem is dated ten days earlier than the song sketch, 20 July 1898 (see Maegaard 1972, 1: 28). This work will be discussed briefly at the beginning of the next chapter.

2. The texts were taken from Levetzow's collection *Höhenlieder: Gedichte und Aphorismen* (Vienna: Carl Konegen, 1898), where (like the Dehmel poems set in 1897) they appear on consecutive pages. Here, however, *Dank* (Schoenberg's no. 1) comes after *Abschied* (Schoenberg's no. 2).

TABLE 3 Schoenberg's Works or Fragments of 1899 Based on the Original 1896 Edition of *Weib und Welt* by Richard Dehmel

Work	*Page in* Weib und Welt	*Date of composition, 1899*	*Publication in SW*
Mannesbangen	56	Spring	A2: 99–101
Warnung (first version), op. 3/3	79	7 May	B1/2/II: 18–22
Gethsemane	114–18	11 May	B3: 253–58
Erwartung, op. 2/1	80–81	9 August	A1: 23–25
Aus schwerer Stunde	96–97	August	B1/2/II: 148
Im Reich der Liebe	82	Fall	B1/2/II: 149–51
Jesus bettelt, op. 2/2	57	Fall	A1: 26–28
Erhebung, op. 2/3	126	16 November	A1: 29–30
Verklärte Nacht, op. 4	61–63	September–1 December	—

There survive fragments, drafts, or completed manuscripts for eight compositions of 1899 based on the poems from *Weib und Welt* (table 3). The only other works firmly attributable to this year are the songs *Die Beiden* (Hofmannsthal), composed on 4 April, and *Mailied* (Goethe), composed on 8–9 May. On the same type of paper as these two songs, and probably composed about the same time (although undated), is a setting of Dehmel's *Mannesbangen*. The earliest dated Dehmel song manuscript of 1899, the first version of *Warnung* (op. 3, no. 3), was written on 7 May, a day before *Mailied*. The apparent chronology, then, suggests that Schoenberg's preoccupation with *Weib und Welt* began in the spring of 1899 and very soon displaced all other poetic interests, even in such high-quality verse as that of Hofmannsthal and Goethe.[3]

Weib und Welt, which appeared in the fall of 1896, marked an analogous milestone in Dehmel's poetic development. In a letter to a friend in October of that year the poet himself noted that in this volume, "I believe I have finally found

3. In light of the fluid publication history of Dehmel's poems—especially the fact that poems were transferred and reprinted among different collections—it may seem risky to assume that Schoenberg drew all his 1899 and 1905–6 poems directly from *Weib und Welt*. But the high incidence of compositions based on poems that appear in that volume (wherever else they may also have appeared) points strongly to the composer's acquaintance with it. Moreover, it is clear that he had access to *Weib und Welt* at least in 1906: the sketch for *Besuch* bears the annotation "Dehmel 112," a reference to the precise page on which this poem appears in *Weib und Welt*.

the *proper* simplicity, the balance between form and content, which is distinguished from the 'classical' style only in that it gives expression to my own time and eternity" (Dehmel 1923, 256). *Weib und Welt* had a great impact on younger poets, inspiring the twenty-one-year-old Rainer Maria Rilke to write an unabashed fan letter: "Since I have come to know *Weib und Welt*, my admiration for you has grown enormously. A book of poetry like this comes along only once in a century."[4]

The appearance of *Weib und Welt* also brought the greatest public notoriety of any of Dehmel's works. In June 1897 the poet was called into a Berlin courtroom to defend himself against charges of blasphemy and immorality. On 23 June he responded with a remarkable "open letter," which bears partial quotation here for the light it sheds on the poetry to which Schoenberg was to be drawn so strongly:

> First, I must disagree that to an unprejudiced mind the overall content of the book can appear immoral [*unsittlich*]—whether blasphemous or lewd [*gotteslästerlich, unzüchtig*]. To be sure, the book shows how a human being, contrary to his holiest principles, abandons himself to a sensual passion, and is thereby driven by the most painful emotional turmoil, finally to a disgraceful death. Clearly it cannot be the artist's task to disguise or conceal the seductive charms that lie naturally within every passion. But I believe that anyone who helps the human soul open its eyes to its bestial urges serves true morality better than many a moralistic accuser.
>
> DEHMEL 1963, 126

Dehmel's open letter reveals something of the inner "turmoil" he was himself experiencing at the time. *Weib und Welt* is a largely autobiographical work, inspired by the poet's infatuation with Ida Auerbach, whom he met in the fall of 1895. Their affair was to lead to the breakup of his marriage to Paula Oppenheimer, and to his eventual marriage to Auerbach in 1901.[5]

It may have been the publicity surrounding the court proceedings of the summer of 1897 that first brought Dehmel to Schoenberg's attention: as we saw in chapter 3, his earliest Dehmel settings date from the fall of 1897. Even though he might have come to know *Weib und Welt* at this time, Schoenberg initially turned to earlier, less steamy verses of Dehmel's. Only in 1899 was he inclined to take

4. Cited in Dehmel 1963, 195. For more information on the creation of and reaction to *Weib und Welt*, see Bab 1926, 194–203.

5. On Ida Auerbach, or "Frau Isi," see Bab 1926, 175–93.

on musically the full-blown eroticism of *Weib und Welt*. Schoenberg's biographer H. H. Stuckenschmidt has noted plausibly that this compositional activity coincided with his courtship of Mathilde Zemlinsky, whom he was to marry in 1901 (Stuckenschmidt 1978, 40).[6]

Only four of Schoenberg's Dehmel song efforts of 1899 were actually to be completed and published by him: as op. 2, nos. 1 (*Erwartung*), 2 (*Jesus bettelt*), and 3 (*Erhebung*); and op. 3, no. 3 (*Warnung*). These collections appeared, respectively, in October 1903 and April 1904.[7] At least one of the songs, *Warnung* (to be discussed below), was extensively revised, probably shortly before publication. *Erwartung* and *Erhebung* are virtually identical in their 1903 publication to the dated drafts of 1899.

Given Schoenberg's Dehmel infatuation and the generally high quality of his settings, it is noteworthy that he did not choose to make his op. 2 an all-Dehmel set, indeed an all–*Weib und Welt* one, with *Warnung* as the fourth song (or as one of the four). The publication of *Warnung* was delayed until op. 3, and a weaker if attractive song, *Waldsonne*, set to a text by Johannes Schlaf, was inserted to round out op. 2. These actions suggest that by the fall of 1903 Schoenberg was still not satisfied with *Warnung*, and that he needed to find a last-minute substitute.

Whatever the precise details and dates of their *Entstehungsgeschichte*—here as elsewhere it is not possible to establish a watertight chronology—the Dehmel settings of 1899 merit close attention because it is through them that Schoenberg moves definitively beyond the Brahms style to explore and gain mastery over a more progressive chromatic language and more ambitious musical forms. There is no question that this language owes much to Wagner, and probably something to Wolf and Richard Strauss, all composers for whom Schoenberg developed an

6. The turn to Dehmel's more intensely erotic poems, as well as to a more chromatic musical style, may also have been spurred in part by Zemlinsky's Dehmel settings of 1898, especially *Entbietung*, op. 7, no. 2, which is in the same key and shows certain other similarities to Schoenberg's *Mannesbangen*. For further discussion, see Frisch 1986, 172–73.

7. These dates of publication are taken from a postcard in Alban Berg's *Nachlaß* at the Österreichische Nationalbibliothek in Vienna. To my knowledge, they have never been discussed before. When preparing a book on Schoenberg (which he never completed), Berg wrote to Verlag Dreililien to get exact publication dates for the early works. The firm responded with a card (dated 14 February 1921) that noted:

op. 1 erschienen im Okt. 1903
op. 2 " " " "
op. 3 " " April 1904
op. 4 " " Mai 1905
op. 7 " " Febr. 1907
op. 6 " " Jan. 1907

These dates, for which the firm must have checked its own files, should probably be taken as definitive.

appreciation in the last few years of the century. As with some of the Brahmsian works examined in part I, we now find many Wagnerian "symptoms," such as surging model-and-sequence constructions. One particularly bald example is the lengthy instrumental introduction to *Gethsemane*, a fragment for baritone and orchestra, which is modeled directly on the Prelude to *Tristan*. As the piece unfolds, the sequences become progressively shorter and the climax is reached (on the "Tristan" chord, of course) approximately three-fourths of the way through (m. 25).

The interest and importance of the works of 1899 lie in the way Schoenberg assimilates some of these Wagnerian techniques to the Brahmsian ones he had already absorbed. Schoenberg himself pointed to this kind of synthesis in *Verklärte Nacht* (Schoenberg 1975, 80), which was completed toward the end of 1899; but the other Dehmel works form an indispensable part of this process. Based on the style and technique of the surviving music and on the chronology suggested by the paper types, we can trace, in brief, the following development in Schoenberg's *Dehmeljahr*.

He turned first, in the spring of 1899, to two of the most explosive poems in *Weib und Welt*, "Mannesbangen" and "Warnung." In the first of these settings, the chromatic harmony and the motivic language—the Wagnerian and Brahmsian spheres, so to speak—are poorly coordinated. *Warnung* is in these respects more successful, but still awkward; Schoenberg himself was dissatisfied enough to undertake a major revision in 1903–4. The draft of *Warnung* was followed by *Gethsemane*, set to a very different kind of poem, a long monologue spoken by Jesus on the eve of his arrest. Here, too, Schoenberg came to a dead end, breaking off the piece after 88 measures.

With the song *Erwartung*, composed on 9 August, Schoenberg managed to strike the right balance between chromatic expansion and formal control; the song embodies perfectly on a small scale those processes to be expanded in *Verklärte Nacht*, begun in September. The last two completed Dehmel settings of 1899, *Jesus bettelt* ("Schenk mir deinen goldenen Kamm") and *Erhebung*, may be seen to divide between them the dual, Wagner-Brahms musical inheritance of the Dehmel year. The former shows a great mastery of chromatic harmony and thematic transformation, the latter of motivic development, polyphonic density, and flexible phrase structure. Something of what is achieved in these last two songs is adumbrated in the fragment *Im Reich der Liebe*, also composed in the fall.[8]

8. After the intense involvement with Dehmel's poetry in 1899, Schoenberg returned to it during two later periods, in 1905–6, and again in 1914–15. At neither time did the verse seem to strike the same spark. With the exception of the song *Alles*, op. 6, no. 2 (September 1905), to be discussed briefly in chapter 8 below, all these other Dehmel works remained fragments (see Frisch 1986, 170–71, and Bailey 1984, 79–118).

Mannesbangen

In "Mannesbangen," as in many poems of *Weib und Welt*, the speaker is a man addressing a woman, and there is a great emphasis on physical, specifically sensual, detail—the eyes, hands, hair, head, and loins. Also like many poems in the collection, "Mannesbangen" has a symmetrical structure. The central seven lines of physical description are framed by the opening and closing couplets, which articulate the poem's basic conceit of fear:

Du mußt nicht meinen,
ich hätte Furcht vor dir.
Nur wenn du mit deinen
scheuen Augen Glück begehrst
und mir mit solchen
zuckenden Händen
wie mit Dolchen
durch die Haare fährst,
und mein Kopf liegt an deinen Lenden:
dann, du Sündrin,
beb' ich vor dir—

You must not think I am afraid of you. Only when you with your shy eyes desire happiness and with such quivering hands like daggers run through my hair, and my head lies upon your loins: then, you sinful woman, I tremble before you—

Two autographs survive for Schoenberg's setting of *Mannesbangen*, one a fragment extending only ten measures, the other a slightly altered revision complete except for one measure, m. 6 (Appendix ex. K). There are many aspects that place the song light years beyond the Dehmel settings of 1897: the extraordinarily busy piano accompaniment; the angular vocal part, with large dissonant leaps; and the profusion of vagrant harmonies, especially the augmented triad, the diminished seventh, the half-diminished seventh, and the French sixth. In a clear attempt to capture the framing aspect of the poem, Schoenberg fashions an ABA′ form in which the outer sections (mm. 1–6 and 21–25, the latter in fact the piano postlude) are diatonic and the central one (mm. 7–20) is dominated by the vagrant harmonies.

Ulrich Thieme has suggested that the B section of the song is in fact oriented around a diatonic sonority, the subdominant B minor, which is touched upon three times in passing (mm. 11, 12, and 15) and then approached with more em-

EXAMPLE 4.1 *Mannesbangen*, cadential articulation points.

phasis in m. 17.[9] Although Thieme's analysis is persuasive, it does not account sufficiently for the way C♯, the supertonic of that B minor and the dominant of the song as a whole, governs the harmonic and melodic aspects of the middle section. Indeed, up until the climax of the song in mm. 17–18, every cadence, half-cadence, or principal point of articulation occurs on a sonority based on C♯, as shown in example 4.1. Only the first occurrence, the broad half-cadence on the song's dominant in m. 5, is diatonic. The central section begins by retaining the C♯ root of m. 5 but transforming the harmony to a vagrant half-diminished seventh (m. 7), which is sustained by means of bass arpeggiation for four measures. (In m. 9 Schoenberg momentarily transforms the chord to a full-diminished; the chord note B is replaced by A♯.)

This is literally the same chord that dominated much of *Mädchenfrühling*, but the different treatment it receives shows how far Schoenberg's harmonic language has traveled. In the earlier song the half-diminished was treated exclusively as a pre-dominant (at the end, a dominant substitute) of B minor. In *Mannesbangen*, Schoenberg more extensively exploits the chord's vagrant possibilities along the lines of the tongue-in-cheek description he provides in *Theory of Harmony*, where vagrant chords are characterized as "homeless phenomena, unbelievably adaptable and unbelievably lacking in independence: spies, who ferret out weaknesses and use them to cause confusion; turncoats, to whom abandonment of their individuality is an end in itself; agitators in every respect, but above all: most amusing fellows" (Schoenberg 1978, 258). Although the chords cause considerable fluidity and ambiguity in the middle section, Schoenberg demonstrates an impressive concern for overall coherence by organizing the articulation points with a large-scale bass arpeggiation of the C♯ triad, as shown in ex. 4.1. In this way, C♯, rather than B, becomes the real functional tonal center for the middle section.

The large role played by C♯ in supporting vagrant harmonies in the B section of the song has the effect of weakening its power as an actual dominant of F♯

9. See Thieme 1979, 167–68. The song is also discussed briefly in Bailey 1979, 103–4.

EXAMPLE 4.2 *Mannesbangen*, cadences omitting dominant.

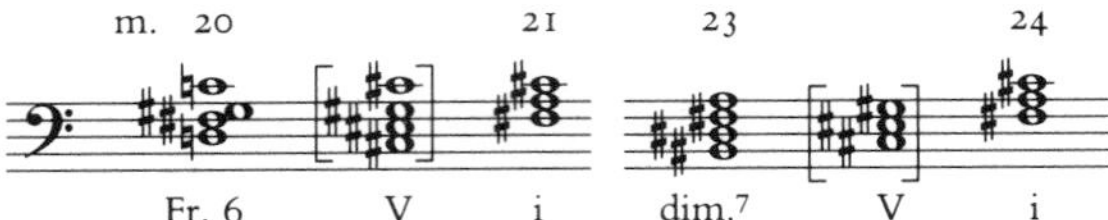

minor. Schoenberg realized that the final cadences to the tonic could not be effectively made via its own dominant. Thus F♯ is approached first from the French sixth (mm. 20–21) built on D (with a notated B♯ instead of C♮), then from a diminished seventh on B♯ (mm. 23–24). As shown in ex. 4.2, both are elliptical progressions, omitting the expected dominant seventh.[10] These kind of ellipses become more common in the music of Schoenberg (and of other composers) as a result of the weakened cadential power of the traditional dominant. *Jesus bettelt*, op. 2, no. 2, a song in the same key as *Mannesbangen*, ends with an elliptical cadence (mm. 42–43) much like that in mm. 23–24 of *Mannesbangen*: the tonic is approached directly from V^6_5 of V.[11]

Despite the large-scale control manifested by Schoenberg's organization of the vagrant harmonies around C♯, *Mannesbangen* remains an awkward song in several respects. Its motivic language seems stiff, even clumsy, by comparison with the elegant use of developing variation in *Mädchenfrühling*. The basic motive of the song is the stepwise third, which is heard ascending in m. 1 (F♯–G♯–A), and ascending and descending across mm. 2–3 (B–C♯–D♮–C♯–B♯). Unlike the "Aprilwind" motive in the earlier song, however, this one seems not to undergo significant expansion or transformation. Despite the general atmosphere of *Leidenschaft*, it remains earthbound, appearing only in slight variants of the original forms of mm. 1–3 (mm. 7 and 10–11: E–F♯–G♮–F♯–E♮; mm. 8 and 11. D–C♯–B; m. 12, A–G♮–F♯–[G]; mm. 14–15, B–C♯–D–C♯–B). To be sure, the rising third assumes different rhythmic shapes and metrical positions: in m. 1 it appears in quarter notes, beginning on beat 2; in m. 7 it is quarter-note triplets, beginning on the downbeat; in m. 10, it is eighth notes, beginning (as an upbeat) on beat

10. Thieme's harmonic reduction/analysis of the first cadence, in mm. 20–21, is confusing (Thieme 1979, 168). He misrepresents the French sixth by showing an F♯ bass and then describing the sonority as "a dominant seventh of the dominant, in second inversion [although his example demonstrates third inversion], with a lowered fifth."

11. In *Jesus bettelt*, the penultimate chord is a second-inversion G♯ seventh; in *Mannesbangen* the chord has an A, not G♯. Thieme, who notes the resemblance between the cadences, erroneously calls the endings "the same" (Thieme 1979, 168). In his transcription of *Mannesbangen* (p. 166) the A of the right-hand chord in m. 23 drops to G♯ on the last eighth note. This represents a misreading of the autograph, where the final chord in m. 23 retains the A.

3½. Yet these alterations do not really give motivic life to the song; they fail to generate process or development.[12]

Only at the climax of the song does the motive undergo more significant modification. Here the descending form is extended across two full measures in a dramatic sequence (F♯–E–D, mm. 17–18, and E♭–D–C♮, mm. 19–20). The expansion coincides with the principal phrase—the "punch line"—of the poem, beginning with "dann" (the preceding seven lines are part of a subordinate "wenn" clause). The moment is indeed effective, and yet it has not really been "earned" by preceding motivic development.

The other principal flaw of *Mannesbangen* is the great discrepancy between diatonic and chromatic harmony. As mentioned above, Schoenberg attempts to reflect the structure of the poem by "framing" the central chromatic portion of the song with diatonic segments. But the contrast between the stodgily diatonic A section and wildly chromatic B section is too extreme, too unmediated. Indeed, the fact that m. 6 remained incomplete—with only a solitary E-minor triad in the right hand—suggests that Schoenberg himself found the gap difficult to bridge. He could not decide how to move persuasively from the broad, conventional half-cadence on the dominant C♯ in m. 5 to the vagrant half-diminished seventh chord of m. 7. The two chords share the same root but occupy two different universes.

Warnung

In Dehmel's "Warnung," the imploring, submissive persona of "Mannesbangen" has become a jealous figure who poisons his dog and threatens his beloved with a similar fate if she is not careful:

> Mein Hund, du, hat dich bloß beknurrt
> und ich hab ihn vergiftet;
> und ich hasse jeden Menschen,
> der Zwietracht stiftet.
>
> Zwei blutrote Nelken
> schick ich dir, mein Blut du,
> an der einen eine Knospe;
> den dreien sei gut, du,
> bis ich komme.

12. According to the criteria Schoenberg himself adopts in *Fundamentals of Musical Composition* (Schoenberg 1967, 8), these changes in the motive would constitute "variants" rather than genuine "developing variations." With the latter "there is something which can be compared to development, to growth. But changes of subordinate meaning, which have no special consequences, have only the local effect of an embellishment. Such changes are better termed *variants*."

Ich komme heute Nacht noch;
sei allein, sei allein, du!
Gestern, als ich ankam,
starrtest du mit Jemand
ins Abendrot hinein—Du:
denk an meinen Hund!

My dog, you, merely snarled at you, and I have poisoned him; and I hate everyone who sows discord.

I send you, my blood you, two bloodred carnations, on one of which is a bud; be good to the three, you, until I come.

I'm still coming tonight; be alone, you! Yesterday when I arrived, you were staring deep into the dusk with someone—you: think of my dog!

Given the musical style of *Mannesbangen*, one might expect Schoenberg to give the still more violent "Warnung" an analogously more florid setting. In fact, however, with his May 1899 setting of this poem, Schoenberg reins in some of the earlier pianistic and harmonic extravagance to create a tauter, more intense song. Above all, he seems to be striving for a new kind of relationship—new in his own work—between piano and voice. In *Warnung*, the piano bears almost the full weight of musical continuity, while the vocal part is broken up or dissolved into relatively small declamatory fragments that sometimes unfold independently of the phrase structure of the accompaniment. Perhaps to offset the fluidity of the voice, the piano part is decidedly square in terms of rhythm, meter, and phrase structure. In the A section of the song—the song as a whole has a ternary structure—the piano has essentially two thematic ideas, *x* and *y* (Appendix ex. L; complete 1899 version in *SW* B1/2/II: 18–22), which appear in alternation: *x* twice (1–4), *y* (5–6), *x* twice (8–11), *y* expanded (12–16). The second *x*–*y* pair is transposed up a fourth. The vocal part in mm. 1–3 overrides, or floats free of, the 2 + 2 structure of the piano: the conjunction "und," which actually begins the second vocal phrase, appears on the last note of *x* in m. 4.

A particularly significant aspect of *Warnung* is the role played by thematic transformation in shaping the B section of the song. Indeed, we have here one of the earliest examples in Schoenberg's works of a theme being reshaped (rather than pulled apart or developed) to yield an entirely different affect.[13] The piano's five-note figure *x* from m. 1 is reworked in m. 17 such that it retains its original contour and identity, although its intervals are adjusted (see ex. 4.3). The lower neighbor now appears on the third beat (F in m. 17) rather than the second (A♮ in m. 1); the interval of the third (D♭–B♭) now becomes a whole-step appoggia-

13. For more detailed discussion of the distinction between thematic transformation and thematic development, see Frisch 1984, ch. 2, and Friedheim 1963, 13–14.

EXAMPLE 4.3 *Warnung*, thematic transformation (piano part only).

tura (A♭–G♭). The upward arpeggio (F minor in m. 2) is inverted, becoming a downward arpeggio (G♭ in m. 18).

Schoenberg elegantly shifts harmonic weight in the transformation. In mm. 1–2 the progression is iv–i–v; the most emphasis falls in the second half of the first measure, with the tonic triad. In the transformation in mm. 17–18, the harmonic progression is now adjusted to move toward the key area of G♭ (VI); the metrical weight thus coincides with the G♭ triad on the downbeat of m. 18. (In the 1899 version this G♭ chord is in $^6_4$ position, with D♭ in the bass; in the revised version published in op. 3, Schoenberg places an octave G♭ deep in the bass to reinforce the key.) The kind of thematic transformation evident in *Warnung* is, of course, nothing new in the nineteenth century, but it does show Schoenberg fastening, perhaps for the first time, on a way to achieve greater continuity and coherence in his musical language: this kind of coherence was lacking in the frenetic motivic world of *Mannesbangen*.

Despite the more flexible relationship between voice and piano and the role played by transformation, the 1899 draft of *Warnung* remains awkward. The vocal line of the A section swings clumsily between very small intervals (seconds at "Mein Hund, du" and "ich hab ihn vergiftet") and large octave leaps (at "hasse," "Menschen," and "Zwietracht"). The chords falling every half-measure in the left hand in the A section make for metrical heavy-handedness. The return to A′ in m. 38 is also disappointingly literal, coming from the pen of a composer preoccupied with fashioning subtle returns in some of his earlier songs (as in an earlier Dehmel setting, *Mädchenfrühling,* examined in chapter 3). In the 1899 *Warnung*, Schoenberg opts for an exact return of *x* and *y* from mm. 1–6 in the piano (mm. 38–43).

Schoenberg clearly felt the need for a substantial postlude to take up or dissipate the intense energy of the song. But the long-winded postlude he wrote in 1899 surely makes for one of the least persuasive endings among the early songs. Transposed but literal statements of *y* (mm. 42–46; cf. mm. 11–15) and *x* (mm. 47–50; cf. mm. 1–4) give way to a repeated cadential figure moving to the tonic major (mm. 53–56). This figure, which bears no meaningful relation to *x* or *y*, seems peculiarly unmotivated or arbitrary in a song that has been so taut in its motivic economy (if also square in phrase structure).

All the features that I have characterized as weak were altered when Schoenberg came to revise *Warnung* in 1903–4. Strictly speaking, those revisions lie outside the scope of this chapter, for they obviously form no part of Schoenberg's development in 1899. (A chronologically oriented discussion of them would belong somewhere between chapters 6 and 7 of the present study.) But for the convenience of the reader, and because the revisions have, to my knowledge, never been taken into account in the general Schoenberg literature,[14] I shall summarize them here. (I include no musical examples from the op. 3 revision; readers should refer to the available published score.)

- When Schoenberg came to revise *Warnung*, he altered both the stiff phrase structure and rhythms of the piano and the melodic shape of the vocal line. In the op. 3 version, the second part of the A section (mm. 7–13) is now compressed and varied: it begins like the 1899 version, with a sequential repetition of *x*, but then deviates from the second half of m. 8. As Schoenberg must have realized, the repetition of *y* material in mm. 12–16 of the original version is unnecessary from the musico-poetic point of view: it serves only to complete the formal plan, *x y x y*, and leaves six awkward measures of silence in the vocal part. Underneath a revised vocal part (mm. 9–13), Schoenberg omits *y* altogether and introduces octaves and sequential imitation based on *x*.
- Another weakness of the 1899 version, the strong metrical stress on each half-measure, is removed in op. 3. In the *x* material, mm. 1–4 and 7–8, Schoenberg replaces the regular dotted quarter notes in the left hand with brief figures or chords that begin off the beat. This greater rhythmic nervousness captures much more effectively the spirit of the text and also provides better contrast with the stressed beats in the *y* material of mm. 5–6 and 9–13.
- In the op. 3 version Schoenberg also gives the vocal line greater continuity and coherence. He eliminates some of the short-breathed quality—without sacrificing any declamatory force—by filling some of

14. For example, the analyses of *Warnung* in Stuckenschmidt 1978, 38–40, and Friedheim 1963, 91–94, are based on the version published in op. 3, which is tacitly assumed to be identical to the draft of 1899 and thus is discussed as if it were a composition of that year. Most of the musical features discussed by these two authors are in fact a result of the later revisions.

the large temporal gaps and rests with sustained notes ("du" and "und"). He also brings closer together lines 2 and 3 of the poem, thus bringing forcefully forward the phrase "ich hasse" and eliminating the long vocal pause in mm. 5–7 of the 1899 version. Schoenberg also moderates the intervallic extremes of the 1899 song, in the process giving the text greater definition. The first "du" is now given greater emphasis by the descent of a fourth, to C, from which the vocal line rises logically upward to the high B♭ of m. 3. The continuation, in the new mm. 4–10, is also made more coherent and less hysterical by the elimination of the octave leaps and by the dramatic rise from the sustained low D♭ of "und" in m. 4 to the high E♭ (the highest note in the song) on "hasse."

- A small but striking difference between the A section in the two versions of *Warnung* involves the harmony of the *y* component. In the 1899 version, the inner voice of the piano in mm. 5–7 plays a thirty-second figure with D♭–B♭. The chord thus formed on the second half of mm. 6 and 7 is a conventional dominant seventh of A♭ (the key of the following *x* material). In the revision, the B♭ becomes a B♭♭ throughout these measures (mm. 5–6), a change that transforms the chords into vagrant whole-tone harmonies. In the second half of m. 5, the chord becomes F–G♮–B♭♭–D♭; in the last half of m. 6, the harmony is now a dominant seventh with a lowered fifth (a French sixth type of chord), E♭–G♮–B♭♭–D♭.[15] What was a conventional progression in the 1899 version thus becomes much more "vagrant" in 1903–4. This change is wholly characteristic of the more advanced tonal language of the op. 3 version and places it logically in the context of the First Quartet, op. 7, to be examined in chapter 8 (see also mm. 43–45 of the revised song for more whole-tone formations).
- Two other important aspects of the 1899 *Warnung* that were altered in 1903–4 involve the extent of the return in A′ and the piano postlude. Schoenberg radically modified the entire A′ section, first by avoiding a literal return in the piano. The second two measures of *x* (mm. 37–38), instead of repeating the first two (cf. 3–4), are now transposed up a tone. Moreover, from m. 39 the accompaniment continues as if recapitulating mm. 9ff., the *x* passage reworked with sequence and imitation.

15. Schoenberg demonstrates this way of altering a dominant seventh in his *Theory of Harmony* (Schoenberg 1978, 355, ex. 287). However, he does not specifically mention the chord's whole-tone properties in this context. Rather, he sees the whole-tone scale as arising from a dominant seventh with a *raised* fifth (and thus an augmented triad) (Schoenberg 1978, 391).

- Schoenberg also alters the voice part. At the return in the 1899 song, he seems determined to compress the three lines of text (lines 12–14) into three measures (mm. 38–40), where at the opening the same musical space had been filled by only one line of the poem. The vocal part of mm. 38–41 is declaimed with very small note values. As Schoenberg came to realize, the compression is too great, especially at the fast tempo of the song. In the revision Schoenberg allows lines 12–14 of the poem to unfold over six measures, but compensates somewhat for the expansion by marking the return "Sehr rasch." He also introduces a hemiola on "jemand" in m. 38 and extends the final "Du" and the admonition "Denk an meinen Hund" over a much broader expanse of five measures (mm. 41–45), as compared with the three of the 1899 version.
- In the revised *Warnung* Schoenberg completely recasts the postlude. He builds to a large, triple *forte* climax at m. 48, then winds down. Only the G♭–F appoggiaturas ($\flat\hat{6}$–$\hat{5}$) from the original mm. 56–58 remain. The obtrusive cadences to B♭ major are eliminated, and the final chord remains hauntingly ambiguous in its mode: it is presented only as a bare fifth, B♭–F, with no defining third.

Erwartung, op. 2, no. 1

The more flexible vocal style and the more motivically coherent accompanimental foundation toward which Schoenberg is apparently striving in the May 1899 version of *Warnung* are fully achieved in *Erwartung*. With its mastery of large-scale ternary form, the control and coordination of melodic and harmonic processes, and the balanced relationship between voice and piano, *Erwartung* is the gem among the *Dehmellieder* of 1899. Schoenberg himself must have felt thus, when several years later he placed it at the head of his op. 2. With *Erwartung,* Schoenberg turned from frenetic texts to a more understated poem:

Aus dem meergrünen Teiche
neben der roten Villa
unter der toten Eiche
scheint der Mond.

Wo ihr dunkles Abbild
durch das Wasser greift,
steht ein Mann und streift
einen Ring von seiner Hand.

Drei Opale blinken;
durch die bleichen Steine
schwimmen rot und grüne
Funken und versinken.

Und er küßt sie, und
seine Augen leuchten
wie der meergrüne Grund:
ein Fenster thut sich auf.

Aus der roten Villa
neben der toten Eiche
winkt ihm eine bleiche
Frauenhand.

Out of the sea green pond, near the red villa, under the dead oak, shines the moon.

Where her dark image reaches through the water, a man stands and draws a ring from his hand.

Three opals glimmer; red and green sparks swim through the pale stones and sink away.

And he kisses them, and his eyes glow like the sea green depths: a window opens.

Out of the red villa, near the dead oak, the pale hand of a woman beckons to him.

Dehmel's "Erwartung" is about sexual anticipation, not about unbridled fulfillment. The speaker is an impersonal narrator, not an impatient or threatening lover; emotions are controlled, as he or she describes, not the love encounter itself, but the expectation of it. "Erwartung" is also one of the most visually evocative poems in *Weib und Welt*, constituting a perfect example of the technique at which Dehmel hints in a diary entry of 1894: "Nowadays we aim to make poetic technique more sensuous by incorporating painterly and musical effects, just as painting and music attempt to learn new means of expression from the sister arts" (Dehmel 1926, 21). Dehmel claims that there are limitations to this kind of technical interchange but suggests, for example, that the poet might "associate a color word with a particularly strong upwelling of a certain emotional state" or might intensify his verse "through the use of sound symbols."

In "Erwartung," color words become more than simply adjectives describing the setting: Dehmel achieves "painterly effects" by treating them in a fashion that is almost abstract, stylized. Each line of the first stanza either states or implies a different color. The pond is "sea green," the villa "red," the oak "dead"—hence black or dark brown—and the moonlight pale white. These colors are then repeated and transformed. In stanza 3 the opals are "pale," the sparks "red and green." In stanza 4 the *Grund*, apparently referring to the immobile bottom of both the pond and the stones, is again "sea green." The final stanza acts as a return or (in musical terms) a recapitulation. "Red" and "dead" reappear, and the "pale," with its color value of white, is now transferred to the woman's hand.

By introducing the paired juxtapositions in stanza 1, red–green and black–white, Dehmel may consciously have sought to exploit color complementarity.[16] Indeed, he seems to endow the colors with strong psychological associations much like those Wassily Kandinsky was to outline in *Concerning the Spiritual in Art* of 1911. Kandinsky calls the elements of each such pair "antithetical." Green is passive, "the most restful colour that exists"; its opposite, red, is warm and intense. Black represents a "totally dead silence," white "a silence . . . pregnant with possibilities" (Kandinsky 1977, 36–41).

In Dehmel's poem, the shining moon, the blinking stones, and the waving hand of the woman—the physical images most closely linked to the lovers' anticipation—are pale or white, and thus appropriately "pregnant with possibilities." The villa, presumably the actual scene of the lovemaking to come, is red. The images implying less motion, the dead oak and the tranquil pond, are black and green.[17] "Erwartung," then, is truly a study in poetic color, a fine example of what one Dehmel scholar has called a *Farbenspiel* (Fritz 1969, 71). The coloristic and painterly qualities of "Erwartung" also suggest an affinity with one of the leading contemporary movements in the visual arts, Jugendstil.[18]

The poem has a symmetrical structure that might also be considered painterly. The two outer stanzas, which are similar in content, frame the poem even more strongly than the beginning and closing couplets in *Mannesbangen*. There is an elegant inner symmetry as well. The two principal unidirectional actions of the poem, the man pulling the ring from his hand, and the window going up, are presented in the second and fourth stanzas. At the still center of the poem are the most circular or static actions: the opals glimmer, the sparks swim (although they also sink).

Schoenberg was, to the best of my knowledge, the only major composer of the time to set "Erwartung" to music.[19] His musical imagination was clearly kindled by the possibilities of realizing the "painterly" aspects of the poem, especially the *Farbenspiel*. At the very opening (ex. 4.4a), the words "meergrünen" and "roten" are accompanied by a distinctive five-note harmony built from the tonic note E♭

16. Red and green are considered psychologically complementary colors, as are black and white. See the useful discussion in Osborne 1970, 258.

17. Even if the oak is taken to be brown instead of black, similar associations prevail: Kandinsky calls brown "unemotional, disinclined for movement" (1977, 40).

18. On Dehmel's personal contacts and/or collaborations with Jugendstil artists, see Fritz 1969, 39–43. The best general treatments of Jugendstil in the visual arts can be found in Schmutzler 1962, in Hamann and Hermand 1973, and in the essays collected in Hermand 1971. For further discussion of the affinities or connections between Schoenberg's music and Jugendstil, see Frisch 1990b.

19. I have found no evidence to support Ernst Hilmar's claim that Zemlinsky also set the poem (Hilmar 1976, 57–58). Zemlinsky published no setting, and no such manuscript exists in his *Nachlaß* at the Library of Congress. Challier's song catalog does, however, report that a setting of Dehmel's "Erwartung" by a W. Jordan appeared sometime between July 1904 and July 1906 (Challier 1906, 1951), thus shortly after Schoenberg's.

EXAMPLE 4.4 *Erwartung*, op. 2, no. 1.

a.

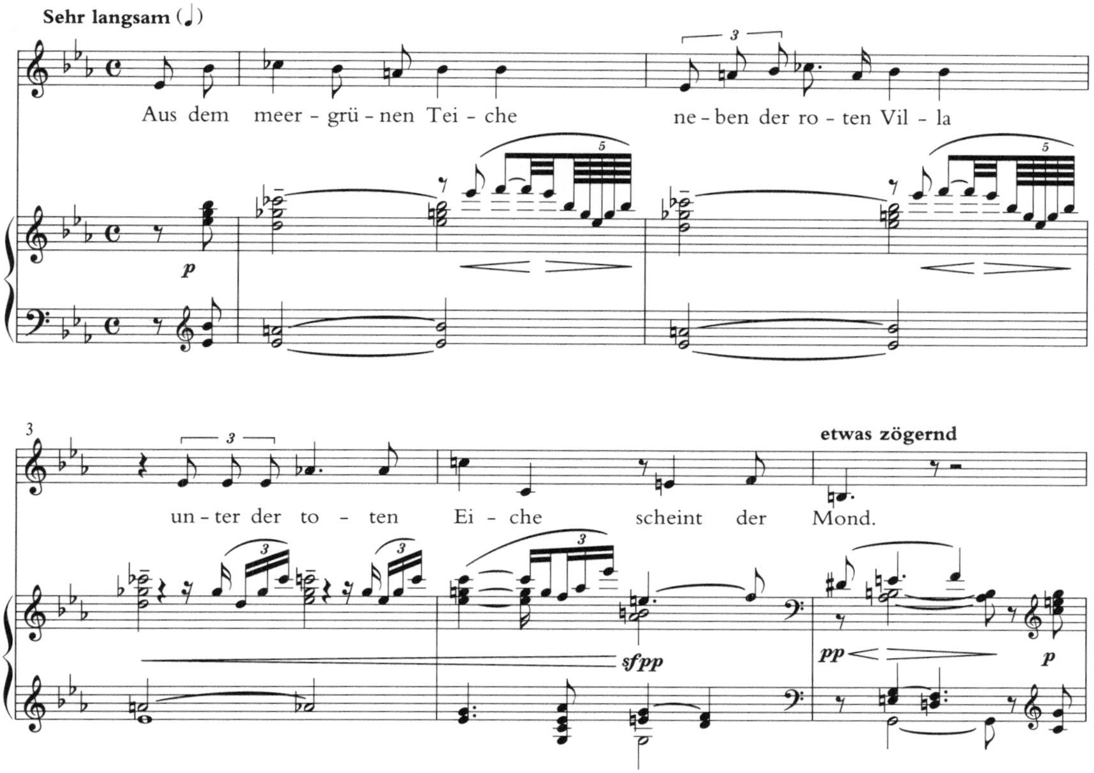

Sehr langsam (♩)
Aus dem meer - grü - nen Tei - che
ne - ben der ro - ten Vil - la
p
3
un - ter der to - ten Ei - che
scheint der Mond.
etwas zögernd
sfpp
pp
p

b.

20
zurückhaltend
wie der meer - grü - ne Grund:
f
zart
p
dim.

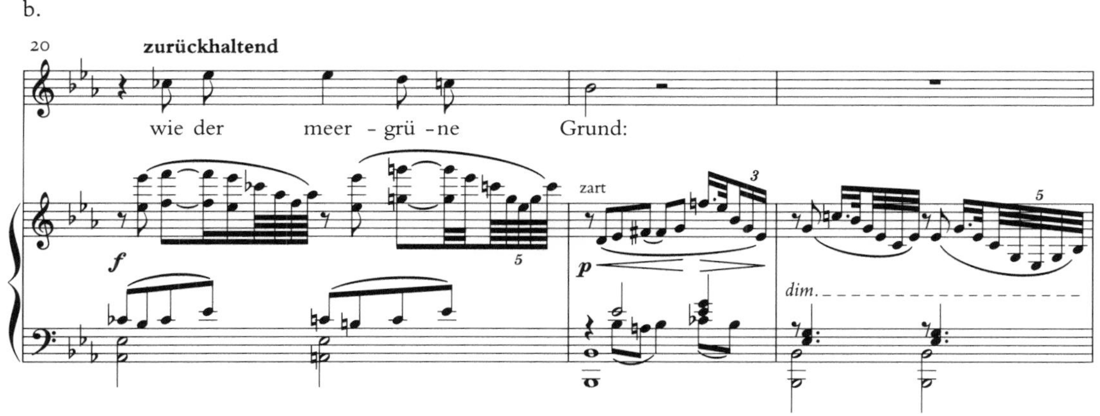

EXAMPLE 4.5 *Erwartung*, transformations of color chord.

and four neighbor notes. Schoenberg proceeds to make this "coloristic" chord structural, much as Dehmel does with the color words in the poem. In a manner reminiscent of, but more sophisticated than, *Mädchenfrühling* of two years earlier, this single *Klang*, or harmonic configuration, comes to dominate the song.

Edward T. Cone has shown how the color chord is successively transformed in the song.[20] In ex. 4.5 I elaborate on aspects of his sensitive but brief analysis. *W* represents the chord as it appears in mm. 1–3. Respelling and inverting the chord, placing D in the bass, give *X*, a dominant thirteenth sonority with the seventh omitted and the ninth flatted.[21] It is in this form transposed down a fifth, *Y*, that the chord appears on the third and fourth beats of m. 4, at "scheint der Mond." In context, the E♮ actually functions as an appogiatura to F♮, whereby the transformed chord (*Y*′) assumes more clearly the shape of a dominant seventh, with flatted ninth. It is this chord that pervades the entire middle section of the song (stanza 3) and then returns, transposed to the real dominant, B♭, for the piano postlude.

At the opening of the second stanza, the entire initial progression is repeated, transposed down a minor third, in the key of C major. This level of transposition assures maximum intersection between the pitches of the original (*W*) and transposed color chord (*Z*). A comparison of chords *W* and *Z* in my example will reveal three pitches in common (C♭/B♮, G♭/F♯, and E♭). Only one of the ten other possible transpositions, up a minor third, yields as many common pitches.

In that it resolves to the tonic twice in mm. 1–2, the color chord in its initial, neighbor-note form (*W*) may be considered a kind of enhanced or substitute dominant. And, as I have just argued (following Cone), it is transformed into just such a chord at m. 4 (*Y* and *Y*′) and in the middle section of the song. But

20. See Cone 1974, 28–29. Other published analyses of *Erwartung* include Just 1980; Brinkmann 1984, 27–28; and Friedheim 1963, 98–103.

21. Friedheim (1963, 98) suggests that the five-note chord should be interpreted not as an appoggiatura chord, but as an "altered supertonic ninth without the root." I find this analysis misrepresents the way the chord is actually presented and transformed. At first the chord clearly functions as an appoggiatura to the tonic triad; only later is it reinterpreted as a kind of ninth chord (though not on the second degree and not with an absent root).

Y is the dominant of C major, not of E♭; and the larger form of *Erwartung* derives its tension precisely from the way Schoenberg sets up but avoids the arrival of the real dominant, a process we shall now explore.

With "Erwartung," Schoenberg finally settled on a Dehmel poem perfectly suited to a rounded musical structure, to which some of the earlier settings could be fitted only with difficulty. The broad five-part form might be analyzed as:

A	A′	B	C	transition	A″
m. 1	m. 6	m. 12	m. 18	m. 23	m. 26

After the delicate, flickering stasis of mm. 1–2, the harmony begins to move toward the dominant via the subdominant sonorities of mm. 3–4 (the voice at "unter der toten Eiche" outlines a sudominant triad). But on the last two beats of m. 4 (at the *sfpp*), Schoenberg abruptly substitutes a dominant on G (chords *Y* and *Y′*), and the vocal part cadences on B♮, a half-step above the expected B♭.

This G dominant continues to replace B♭ until the splendid climax of the song (ex. 4.4b), at the end of the C section, where the subdominant reappears and now leads firmly, by means of half-step motion in the bass, toward the dominant. On the downbeat of m. 21, B♭ is articulated in strong, stark octaves by the piano and the voice. (It seems likely that in setting the word "Grund" to these lone B♭s, Schoenberg was creating a kind of musical pun, but also reading his text with great sensitivity.) The B♭ then supports a cadential $\substack{6\\4}$ harmony; but no dominant chord is forthcoming. Instead, on the downbeat of m. 23 the original color chord reappears in a low register.

The moment is indeed "magical," as Cone has said, though I would not agree that the chord "is accorded the status of a true dominant" (Cone 1974, 29). There can, I think, be only one "true" dominant; and Schoenberg's compositional strategy, as I have been describing it, is precisely to *avoid* articulating the dominant harmony. He continues to do so throughout the transition and the recapitulation (A″). Only in the piano postlude is the entire dominant chord presented; and, as if to make up for its previous absence, it is repeated again and again. The dominant functions here as the final transformation of the color chord, which now appears in its *Y′* form, transposed to the dominant.

The elegant harmonic process of *Erwartung* supports an equally elegant vocal part, one that is metrically much more flexible than in *Mannesbangen*, where the stresses tended to fall on the downbeat with some regularity, or in the original *Warnung*, where the freer declamation generated a vocal line that bordered on incoherence. In the A section of *Erwartung* (ex. 4.4a), each phrase lies slightly differently in relation to bar line. Phrase 1 begins with an upbeat figure ("Aus dem"), which is then in varied form ("Neben der") squeezed into the downbeat of phrase 2. This rhythmic-metrical migration continues in phrase 3, where the equivalent "upbeat" ("unter der") now falls on the notated second beat of the measure, while the notated downbeat remains empty. This progressive metrical shift of the prepositions ("Aus," "neben," "unter") serves to bring the musical climax of mm. 1–4, the C♮ of "Eiche," onto the notated downbeat of m. 4. The subsequent verb phrase and the real grammatical goal of the first stanza, "scheint der Mond," also assumes a normal or expected position vis-à-vis the bar line, across mm. 4–5.[22]

The large-scale control evident in the harmonic and melodic aspects of *Erwartung*—specifically the treatment of the color chord, the withholding of the dominant, and the declamatory and metrical fluidity of the vocal part—is not to be found in Schoenberg's earlier works. He instinctively realized that the rather frantic style of *Mannesbangen* or the surging, Tristanesque harmonic language of *Gethsemane* would not be appropriate here. "Erwartung" is a poem not of passionate intensity or of Wagnerian-Schopenhauerian *Sehnsucht*, but of heightened anticipation.

The magisterial breadth and pacing of *Erwartung* give it a quality that might be justly called symphonic. Indeed, it is probably no coincidence that the composition of the song in August 1899 was followed shortly by work on what was to become Schoenberg's first instrumental piece truly to deserve that label, *Verklärte Nacht*. There are even certain similarities between the two poems, "Erwartung" and "Verklärte Nacht." Both have as their subject a nocturnal encounter between a pair of lovers. Both are framed by stanzas in which a narrator describes the scene (in "Verklärte Nacht," however, the characters also speak), a feature that inspired Schoenberg to create in both works a broad recapitulatory closing section. I suspect that the achievement represented on a smaller scale by *Erwartung* may have encouraged Schoenberg to undertake the ambitious sextet.

Im Reich der Liebe

Erwartung may be said to represent the still center, and also the musico-poetic high point, of Schoenberg's *Dehmellieder*. In what appear to be the last three settings of 1899, Schoenberg moves to consolidate more consciously, or at least more obviously, Brahmsian and Wagnerian compositional principles. Both together inform the fragment *Im Reich der Liebe*, in which Schoenberg set only the first of three stanzas (a full setting was probably to have a ternary form):

22. For a brilliant and extended analysis of the metrical implications of vocal lines in certain later works of Schoenberg, see Lewin 1982.

O Du, dein Haar, wie stralt dein Haar,
das ist wie schwarze Diamanten!
O—weil wir uns als Herrscherpaar
der ewigen Seligkeit erkannten,
Du!

Oh, you, your hair, how your hair shines, it's like black diamonds! Oh—because we knew ourselves rulers of eternal bliss, you!

In musical style and mood, the setting resembles *Mannesbangen* (see Appendix ex. M for the first eight measures). But where in the earlier song the succession of vagrant harmonies seemed out of control, here such chords—initially a half-diminished seventh (m. 3), a German sixth in third inversion (m. 4), and an augmented triad, notated in second inversion (m. 5)—are connected and supported by a strong bass line that descends by step (E–D–C♯–B–A♯–A♮–G♯).

In m. 6 of *Im Reich der Liebe*, Schoenberg interrupts the stepwise motion to prepare a cadence in the relative major, G: the bass now moves by fifth A–D–G. But the cadence is subtly sidestepped by both the harmonic resolution and the phrase structure; the next phrase actually begins *before* the harmonic arrival. In the measure of dominant preparation (m. 6), Schoenberg begins a new rising stepwise line in the right hand of the piano; the voice enters on the second beat, moving in parallel thirds and sixths. In the following measure, at the cadence to G minor, the rising line is transferred to the bass, where it is then repeated sequentially through m. 9. The sophistication here is threefold. First, Schoenberg overlaps the beginning of the new phrase in m. 6 with the harmonic cadence, which is not completed until m. 7. Second, the cadence is blurred by the motivic imitation or interchange between the right and left hands across the juncture of mm. 6–7. And third, the actual cadence is made to G minor rather than the expected major. In these ways, Schoenberg achieves continuity between the phrases.

Together with its Wagnerian (or post-Wagnerian) harmonic language, this passage provides a fine example of a technique characteristic of Brahms, which Schenker called the *Knüpftechnik*, or linkage technique: a motive introduced at the very end of a phrase is taken over to initiate the next one (see Frisch 1984, 15–16). Schoenberg's linkage is even more elegant than many in Brahms, since the harmony and phrase structure are made to be out of phase with one another; the new phrase begins in m. 6, but the cadence is completed only in m. 7.

Jesus bettelt ("Schenk mir deinen goldenen Kamm"), op. 2, no. 2

The song *Jesus bettelt* pulls together various technical and expressive threads of the earlier completed Dehmel settings of 1899. It develops further the chromatic style of *Mannesbangen*; it resembles *Warnung* in the declamatory flexibility of the vocal line and in the use of thematic transformation to shape the central section of the song; and it has something of the broad pacing, the control of the large scale, evident in *Erwartung*. A highly sensual appeal by Jesus to Mary Magdalene (and only slightly more chaste than the approaches of Wilde's Salome to Jokanaan), the poem is surely one of the texts of *Weib und Welt* viewed as bordering on blasphemy and obscenity:

> Schenk mir deinen goldnen Kamm;
> jeder Morgen soll dich mahnen,
> daß du mir die Haare küßtest.
> Schenk mir deinen seidnen Schwamm;
> jeden Abend will ich ahnen,
> wem du dich im Bade rüstest—
> o Maria!
>
> Schenk mir Alles, was du hast,
> meine Seele ist nicht eitel,
> stolz empfang'ich deinen Segen.
> Schenk mir deine schwerste Last;
> willst du nicht auf meinen Scheitel
> auch dein Herz, dein Herz noch legen—
> Magdalena?
>
> Give me your golden comb; each morning should remind you that you kissed my hair. Give me your silken sponge; each evening I will envision you preparing for your bath, O Mary!
>
> Give me everything that you have; my soul is not vain, proudly I receive your blessing. Give me your heaviest burden; will you not also lay your heart upon my head, Magdalene?

The formal structure of Schoenberg's song is more ambitious than that of any of the earlier settings. Rather than fashioning a modified strophic or ternary form, Schoenberg treats the second stanza (mm. 19–38) as a kind of development or expansion of the first. The first stanza consists essentially of a six-measure statement and its sequential repetition up a half-step, followed by a climactic setting of Jesus' direct address, "o Maria." The music for "o Maria" returns in the second stanza for the analogous "Magdalena," but what precedes it constitutes essentially a development of motives from the first stanza.

The opening two-and-a-half-measure theme in the piano furnishes the basic material for the song. This theme has two components (labeled *x* and *y* in ex. 4.6a), which are developed separately in the second stanza. The basic principle resembles that of *Warnung*, but now the two thematic ideas are handled with

EXAMPLE 4.6 *Jesus bettelt* ("Schenk mir"), op. 2, no. 2.

greater fluidity. The theme remains relatively intact during the first fourteen measures. (Motive *x* is used for the transition between the statements of the sequence.) At m. 14, *y* is for the first time isolated and treated sequentially, in diminution, as Schoenberg builds to a climax at "o Maria." The second stanza is dominated at first by sequential repetition of *y* (mm. 19–23), which then gives way to sequential diminution of *x*. The diminution of *x* is first introduced in m. 23, then retreats and reappears to dominate all of mm. 26–33 (ex. 4.6b).

The modification of *x* in the accompaniment at the "wieder langsamer" of m. 26 manifests the same impulse toward thematic transformation seen in the B section of *Warnung*. The contrast in mood is, to be sure, not as marked as that between the angry opening of *Warnung* and the "carnation" transformation. But in *Jesus bettelt*, the *Stimmung* has definitely changed at m. 26, from "ausdrucksvoll" to "sehr innig." And this change is accompanied or reflected by the new treatment of *x*.

Also more successful is Schoenberg's treatment of harmony. Two aspects are especially worthy of discussion. The first is the way Schoenberg underpins the chromatic voice-leading with strong fifth-oriented bass progressions. At the very opening (see ex. 4.6a), the bass steps down from F♯ to D, supporting a move from the tonic F♯ minor, to a half-diminished seventh, which resolves by appoggiatura to a regular diminished seventh (D–F–A♭–B). The bass now begins to move by fifth, D–G–C–F–B♭, a progression that gives coherence to the succession of vagrant chords and appoggiaturas. The end point of the progression, the whole-note B♭ in m. 4, is initially treated as the root of a minor-seventh chord. But by the second half of the measure, it has become an enharmonic substitute for A♯: the chord formed on the last eighth note (B♭, D♭, G♭) is a first-inversion triad that is enharmonically the tonic major. This is why the A^7 chord on the downbeat of m. 5 sounds somewhat shocking; the A♮ in the bass is in essence a cross-relation with, rather than a half-step resolution of, the preceding B♭.[23]

Strong root progression in the bass emerges again in mm. 14–19. Here the effect is even more striking than at the opening of the song because of a very basic cadential I–II–V–I succession, in which, however, the diatonic *Stufen* are harmonized with vagrant chords (see ex. 4.7a). This passage shows how skillfully Schoenberg can extend or delay arrival on the tonic. The first cadence in the song, at "küßtest" in m. 6, is made to the tonic major. At the parallel spot in m. 14 ("rüstest") Schoenberg wants to avoid closure to the tonic so as to lead into the climactic "o Maria." The tonic note, F♯, appears in the bass under "rüstest," but it is harmonized with the half-diminished "Tristan" chord (supporting the dim-

23. For a somewhat different harmonic reading of this passage, see Smith 1986, 127. On the first cadence to F♯ in m. 6, see also Cone 1974, 25.

EXAMPLE 4.7 *Jesus bettelt*, vagrant harmonies with diatonic roots (piano part only).

a.

b.

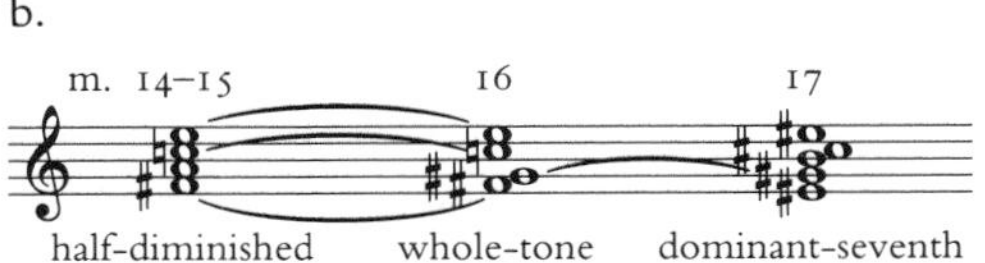

inution of motive *y*), which is sustained for two measures. This chord then gives way to another vagrant harmony, a whole-tone chord with a G♯ (the diatonic II) in the bass. The sonority is like that of a French sixth, but the chord does not function that way (a true French sixth in F♯ would be D♮–F♯–G♯–B♯, resolving to the dominant). Five of the six notes of the whole-tone scale are present in m. 16 (only A♯/B♭ is missing), making this one of the earliest uses of the whole-tone complex in Schoenberg. (One measure of *Waldesnacht*, examined in chapter 3, also used a whole-tone harmony.) In m. 17, the G♯ in the bass resolves to C♯ and the whole-tone chord to the dominant seventh; this in turn resolves to the tonic major in m. 19.

The succession of chords in these measures shows Schoenberg attempting to connect vagrant harmonies by means of smooth voice-leading. As is suggested in ex. 4.7b, the first two of the three harmonies—the "Tristan" half-diminished and the whole-tone chord—differ from each other only by one half-step. Further half-step voice-leading produces the third chord, the dominant seventh. (The C♮ of the second chord might be heard to "split" into the C♯ and B♮ of the third.) With the strong I–II–V bass progression, Schoenberg is able to give the chromatic voice-leading much greater coherence than in *Mannesbangen*.

Toward the end of the song, Schoenberg reworks the "o Maria" passage at the

EXAMPLE 4.8 *Jesus bettelt,* mm. 34–38 (piano part only).

parallel place in the stanza (ex. 4.8), where he manages to delay the tonic still longer. At mm. 34–36 (cf. mm. 14–17), a I–II–V supports, as before, the "Tristan" chord, the whole-tone chord, and the dominant seventh. But the dominant now resolves deceptively to a IV^6 chord (which in turn moves on in the second half of the measure to a vi). This is an especially lovely moment, largely because up to this point in the song there has been no emphasis on the subdominant. Its appearance here at the conclusion fulfills, or at least begins to fulfill, the same tension-releasing function as in many classical and romantic codas. But instead of descending to C♯, the bass drops only to D♮; the upper voices remain in place, thus forming another vagrant harmony, an augmented triad (with the G♯ of the appoggiatura providing a fifth note of the whole-tone scale). Although this augmented chord seems to be left hanging, it in fact differs by only one note from the succeeding tonic major triad that begins the postlude in m. 39. Thus even across the fermata and the change of register, Schoenberg is careful—as he is throughout this song—to create smooth voice-leading connections.

The final cadence of *Jesus bettelt,* as suggested above, resembles that of *Mannesbangen* and is motivated by similar harmonic procedures. In both cases the dominant is elided and the tonic is approached directly from what is normally a predominant chord, the French sixth in the earlier song, V/V in *Jesus bettelt.* The rationale for this procedure in both songs is that the dominant has in some sense exhausted its cadential powers; in *Jesus bettelt,* the dominant has featured strongly in the big climax at mm. 17–18 and the more restrained one at 35–36.

In *Jesus bettelt,* then, Schoenberg has tightened the harmonic and motivic procedures of the earlier Dehmel settings. This is accomplished above all through a more moderate and transparent accompaniment, a more focused motivic language, and a strong emphasis on stepwise connection between vagrant chords, which are here often underpinned with basic diatonic progressions.

Erhebung, op. 2, no. 3

The song *Erhebung* appears to be Schoenberg's final Dehmel setting of 1899. (Its composition may well have taken place contemporaneously with the copying of the score of *Verklärte Nacht.*) The poem is the briefest of the texts selected by Schoenberg in 1899:

> Gieb mir deine Hand,
> nur den Finger, dann
> seh ich diesen ganzen Erdkreis
> als mein Eigen an!
>
> Oh, wie blüht mein Land!
> sieh dir's doch nur an,
> daß es mit uns über die Wolken
> in die Sonne kann!

> Give me your hand, only your finger; then will I see the whole circle of this earth as my own!
>
> Oh how my land is blossoming, look at it now, so that it can rise with us over the clouds toward the sun!

Rather than floating on top of an accompaniment that provides continuity, as in *Warnung* and *Erwartung*, the voice part of *Erhebung* is a full participant in the polyphonic texture. The voice is often doubled, or at least shadowed closely, by one line of the piano part. This kind of texture, also apparent in *Jesus bettelt*, contributes in *Erhebung* to a still more extreme motivic-thematic concentration and development. This concentration is apparent not only on the largest scale—the setting is a compact modified strophic one, A (mm. 1–11) A′(12–24)—but on the most detailed level. The melodic line at the very opening (see reduction in ex. 4.9) seems almost a programmatic announcement of the large role to be played by developing variation: the melodic line of m. 2 is clearly heard as a transposed retrograde of the m. 1: the descending triad of A, followed by the leading tone G♯, becomes in m. 2 the leading tone E♯, followed by an ascending triad of F♯ minor.

Each of the two strophes of *Erhebung* is comprised essentially of a phrase and its varied or developed repetition. In the first strophe, mm. 5–9 constitute a modification and expansion of mm. 1–4, fashioned more subtly than anything we have seen up to this point. Schoenberg adjusts the metrical alignment of the melody and bass in ways that directly anticipate parts of *Gurrelieder*, in particular Tove's song "Du sendest mir einen Liebesblick," to be examined in chapter 6.

EXAMPLE 4.9 *Erhebung*, op. 2, no. 3, mm. 1–9 (piano and vocal parts reduced).

The A in the bass on the last half of m. 4 represents both the end point of the first phrase (which consists of eight half notes) and the beginning of the second (consisting of ten). Although it is slurred with the previous G♯, this A also begins a bass pattern whose contour closely resembles the pattern of the first phrase in mm. 1–4: it rises from A to C (cf. D in m. 2), descends back through A to F♯ (cf. beat 1 of m. 3, beat 3 of m. 6), then rises again to A (cf. beat 3 of mm. 4 and 7). Measures 8–9 constitute the extension. Over this bass pattern, the vocal part also presents a variation of its original melody. Although it begins with the tied quarter note on the last beat of m. 4, and thus on the same beat as the bass A, the second vocal phrase proceeds to orient itself to the bar line like the first one (cf. mm. 2 and 6). Thus in the second phrase, bass and vocal line are essentially one half-measure out of phase through the end of m. 7; or, rather, they are each varied in a way that places the original components in a different metrical-rhythmic relationship. These sophisticated variation procedures also involve the harmony. The original I–I^6–ii^6–I pattern of mm. 1–2 is circular, reflexive; its varied repetition is more chromatic, less regular. The second phrase is oriented more toward the submediant, F♯, where it will cadence in m. 9. As in *Jesus bettelt*, the bass line now supports a series of vagrant rather than diatonic harmonies.

Where mm. 5–9 expanded the original thematic material, the first phrase of the second strophe, mm. 12–14, now compresses it into three measures, in prepara-

EXAMPLE 4.10 *Erhebung*, mm. 15–21 (piano and vocal parts reduced).

tion for a final, still greater expansion, mm. 15–21 (ex. 4.10). This expanded last phrase shows Schoenberg's powers of motivic-thematic development at their height in the 1899 Dehmel songs. By analogy to the preceding statements of the basic phrase, the high C♯ on the last beat of m. 16 would be followed by an E on the downbeat of m. 17 (cf. mm. 3, 7, 14). But Schoenberg withholds that E, rising up to it dramatically through B–C♯–D♯; the E is reached on the downbeat of m. 18 ("uns"). Again by analogy to earlier places (mm. 3, 7, 14), the E would descend immediately (as an appoggiatura) to D♯. But Schoenberg delays that resolution as well: the E of m. 18 instead pushes upward to the A of "Sonne" in m. 20, the melodic high point of the song. This A descends to the orginal E, which then resolves to the expected D♯ on the downbeat of m. 21. In mm. 17–21, then, Schoenberg has essentially expanded a one-measure gesture to five measures.

Even more than in the earlier Dehmel songs of 1899, Schoenberg avoids strong dominant resolutions in *Erhebung*. In *Mannesbangen* and *Jesus bettelt* the dominant (C♯ in both cases) is often present but does not resolve to the tonic; in *Erwartung*, as we have seen, the dominant (B♭) is withheld for much of the song, but features in the approach to the return and in the coda. In *Erhebung*, Schoenberg seems to avoid any straightforward dominant whatsoever: pure E major is nowhere to be found. It is implied by the rising melodic line at "daß es mit uns" in mm. 17–18, and suggested by the big $^6_4$ sonority on the downbeat of m. 17. But the vocal E of "uns" is harmonized deceptively, with a C♯-minor triad. In both the piano transition between strophes (mm. 9–11) and the postlude (mm. 21–22), the tonic is approached directly (as in *Jesus bettelt*) from a form of V/V that has an F♯ in the bass. The final tonic is reached via a still more vagrant whole-tone chord, D♯–F♮–A♮–C♯, which makes for a tritone leap in the bass, D♯–A.

In *Mannesbangen* and *Jesus bettelt*, the cadences to the tonic might be said to be relatively tentative and unconvincing. *Erhebung* is most impressive for the way in which the "false" dominants of mm. 11, 21, and 23 lead strongly, persuasively to the tonic. This effect is in part a function of, or corollary to, the thematic-motivic processes, which impart considerable continuity and thrust to the musical discourse.

In this sense, *Erhebung* represents the culmination of Schoenberg's Dehmel songs of 1899. Although traditional harmonic syntax has been loosened, it is compensated for by a dynamic motivic language and fluid phrase structure, which carry along and give meaning to the vagrant chords and the unusual harmonic resolutions. Even if we might prefer *Erwartung* as the most perfect song of Schoenberg's *Dehmeljahr*, *Erhebung* nevertheless embodies more than any other song the techniques that were to be developed in *Gurrelieder* and other later works.

CHAPTER FIVE

Verklärte Nacht, op. 4 (1899)

The string sextet *Verklärte Nacht* was both the culmination of Schoenberg's *Dehmeljahr* and his first instrumental masterpiece. At once chamber music and program music (a novel combination acknowledged as such by contemporary critics), it hovers generically and chronologically between the Brahms tradition represented by the D-Major Quartet of 1897 and the Liszt-Strauss tradition that was to be explored further by Schoenberg in the symphonic poem *Pelleas und Melisande* (1902–3).

The sextet was preceded by three attempts at program music, each of which remained a fragment. One is a brief thirteen-measure draft (in short score) for a symphonic poem entitled *Hans im Glück*, which appears to date from 1898 (see Maegaard 1972, 1: 152; Bailey 1984, 44–45). A more substantial fragment, begun in the summer of 1898, is the symphonic poem *Frühlings Tod*, based on a poem by Nikolaus Lenau (the poet of *Schilflied*). A short score of the piece extends 255 measures, a full score 135. Because *Frühlings Tod* has been discussed in detail twice (Thieme 1979, 183–215, and Bailey 1984, 45–51), it will not be treated here. Suffice it to say that it shows Schoenberg beginning to grapple with chromatic harmony and Wagnerian sequential construction on a scale broader than he had attempted before. The third fragment, which is closest in style and medium to *Verklärte Nacht*, is a string sextet entitled *Toter Winkel*, a 34-measure fragment in B minor, based on a poem by Gustav Falke. The manuscript of *Toter Winkel* is undated, but it probably was written in 1898 or early 1899.[1]

In each of these cases, it may have been the poetic source that failed to sustain

1. The work is discussed in detail by Thieme (1979, 173–83) and Bailey (1984, 38–44), both of whom include a complete facsimile of the score.

the initial creative spark ignited in Schoenberg. As in his Lieder, so in his program music, the encounter with Richard Dehmel's work was to be decisive. Indeed, as I have suggested in the preceding chapter, it was probably the composer's successful engagement with the poetry of Dehmel in the songs of the spring and summer of 1899 that inspired him to attempt—and complete—the sextet that became op. 4.

The exact date of composition of *Verklärte Nacht* in relation to the songs of 1899 cannot be precisely determined. The handful of sketches are undated; the autograph manuscript, which shows considerable revision and recomposition (to be treated below), is dated 1 December 1899. Egon Wellesz, an authoritative source, whose information was in many cases provided (or corrected) by Schoenberg himself,[2] reports that the sextet was composed in September (Wellesz 1925, 14). Schoenberg himself says that the sextet was composed in three weeks, but gives no specific dates (Schoenberg 1975, 55).[3] Zemlinsky tried to have the work performed at the Wiener Tonkünstlerverein, which had given the D-Major Quartet in the preceding season (1898–99), but the sextet was rejected (Zemlinsky 1934, 34). It was given its premiere by the Rosé Quartet (augmented by two players) in March 1902; the score was published, after many delays, by Verlag Dreililien in May 1905.[4]

From all this evidence, it seems logical to assume that the sextet was conceived and written during a relatively short span in September 1899, then was revised intermittently over the course of the fall, so that the complete score was finished on 1 December. Another tantalizing possibility is that the major revisions reflected in the manuscript were undertaken just over two years later in preparation for the first performance (no manuscript parts survive for this performance), or even later still, as Schoenberg was preparing the score for publication. The most likely scenario, however, is that the essential inspiration and creative work, as well as the most intensive revisions, took place in the late summer and fall of 1899, when the composer was strongly in the thrall of Dehmel's poetry.

It was suggested in the previous chapter that the Dehmel poem "Verklärte Nacht" is similar in several respects to "Erwartung" and is less sexually explosive than some of the other poems from *Weib und Welt* selected by Schoenberg in 1899. Like "Erwartung," "Verklärte Nacht" has a clear, almost rigidly symmetrical

2. See chapter 2, n. 14, above.

3. Willi Reich (Reich 1971, 7) misquotes Zemlinsky as saying, "In the summer of 1899 (during a holiday together in Payerbach) Schoenberg composed a sextet." In fact, Zemlinsky does not specify a date, implying only that the sextet was composed "soon after" the first performances of the D-Major Quartet (Zemlinsky 1934, 34).

4. On the date of publication, see chapter 4, n. 7.

structure, in which the first, third, and fifth stanzas are spoken by an implied narrator, the second and fourth by one of the two protagonists:

Zwei Menschen gehn durch kahlen, kalten Hain;
der Mond läuft mit, sie schaun hinein.
Der Mond läuft über hohe Eichen,
kein Wölkchen trübt das Himmelslicht,
in das die schwarzen Zacken reichen.
Die Stimme eines Weibes spricht:

Ich trag ein Kind, und nit von dir,
ich geh in Sünde neben dir.
Ich hab mich schwer an mir vergangen;
ich glaubte nicht mehr an ein Glück
und hatte doch ein schwer Verlangen
nach Lebensfrucht, nach Mutterglück
und Pflicht—da hab ich mich erfrecht,
da ließ ich schauernd mein Geschlecht
von einem fremden Mann umfangen
und hab mich noch dafür gesegnet.
Nun hat das Leben sich gerächt,
nun bin ich dir, o dir begegnet.

Sie geht mit ungelenkem Schritt,
sie schaut empor, der Mond läuft mit;
ihr dunkler Blick ertrinkt in Licht.
Die Stimme eines Mannes spricht:

Das Kind, das du empfangen hast,
sei deiner Seele keine Last,
o sieh, wie klar das Weltall schimmert!
Es ist ein Glanz um Alles her,
du treibst mit mir auf kaltem Meer,
doch eine eigne Wärme flimmert
von dir in mich, von mir in dich;
dir wird das fremde Kind verklären,
du wirst es mir, von mir gebären,
du hast den Glanz in mich gebracht,
du hast mich selbst zum Kind gemacht.

Er faßt sie um die starken Hüften,
ihr Atem mischt sich in den Lüften,
zwei Menschen gehn durch hohe, helle Nacht.[5]

5. The text is reproduced here as it appears in Dehmel's *Weib und Welt* (Berlin, 1896), 61–63. There are certain small variants between this version and that printed at the head of the score of Schoenberg's *Verklärte Nacht*.

Two people walk through the bare, cold woods; the moon runs along, they gaze at it. The moon runs over tall oaks, no little cloud dulls the heavenly light, into which the black points reach. A woman's voice speaks:

I bear a child, and not by you. I walk in sin alongside you. I have gone seriously astray. I believed no longer in good fortune, yet still had a great longing for a full life, for a mother's happiness and duty; then I became reckless; horror-stricken, I let myself be taken by a stranger and even blessed myself for it. Now life has taken its revenge: now have I met you, oh, you.

She walks with clumsy gait. She gazes upward; the moon runs along. Her somber glance drowns in the light. A man's voice speaks:

The child that you conceived, let it be no burden to your soul; oh, look, how clear the universe glitters! There is a radiance about everything; you drift along with me on a cold sea, yet a special warmth glimmers from you in me, from me in you. It will transfigure the strange child, you will bear it me, from me; you have brought the radiance into me, you have made me a child myself.

He holds her around her strong hips. Their breath mingles in the air. Two people walk through the high, clear night.

The poem was apparently conceived the day after Dehmel's first amorous encounter with Ida Auerbach in November 1895, and, except for the pregnancy, directly reflects that experience. In a letter of 30 November, he reminded her of "the moonlight" and asked, "Did you also feel it, this radiance [*Glanz*, as in the poem] coming through the clouds while I led you through the streets? You, me. Everything glowed [*glänzte*]" (Dehmel 1923, 224–25). Dehmel was proud of the structure of "Verklärte Nacht" and claimed to have found in it "the form for the new ballad, which owes nothing to the old-fashioned masquerade; it is a form that permits the entire life of a soul and human fate to be depicted in a thousand variations" (Dehmel 1923, 225). In fact, Dehmel was to go on to make "Verklärte Nacht" the model for (and the first poem in) an entire collection of poems with the same basic 36-line structure, *Zwei Menschen: Ein Roman in Romanzen* (1903).

Form in Verklärte Nacht

Cast in a single movement, and lasting just under half an hour, *Verklärte Nacht* is the most extensive, ambitious instrumental structure completed by Schoenberg up to this point. Its formal disposition has prompted divergent analytical perspectives. Webern, probably the earliest commentator, described *Verklärte Nacht* as simply "frei phantasierend" (Webern 1912, 23). Schoenberg's own discussion, written for record liner notes in 1950, seems to take a similar tack in that he does not explicitly treat the larger form, but rather associates certain specific musical themes with portions of the poem.[6] In 1921, Wellesz proposed a more intimate relationship between the overall structure of the sextet and the Dehmel poem:

> The structure of *Verklärte Nacht*, in accordance with the poem, is made up of five sections, in which the first, third, and fifth are of more epic nature and so portray the deep feelings of the people wandering about in the cold moonlit night. The second contains the passionate plaint of the woman, the fourth the sustained answer of the man, which shows much depth and warmth of understanding.
>
> WELLESZ 1925, 67

In more schematic terms, what Wellesz proposes as the larger musical form of *Verklärte Nacht* is something corresponding to the five poetic stanzas as ABA′CA″. A, A′, and A″ represent the more "epic" or narrative segments; B and C, the direct speeches of the protagonists. Wellesz's plan is persuasive, although the actual unfolding of the sextet is, of course, considerably more complex than the rondo-like scheme implied by the letter designations. As Carl Dahlhaus has suggested, "the rondo ground-plan, which gives the work formal support, is as it were covered with a web of thematic and motivic relationships, a web which becomes tighter and thicker as the work proceeds" (Dahlhaus 1987, 97). In other words, the different segments of *Verklärte Nacht* are closely related by motivic variation, and toward the end of the work earlier themes are recalled.[7]

The Wellesz-Dahlhaus analytical stance toward *Verklärte Nacht* is, I believe, the most reasonable one to assume, since it grants to the sextet a form that is musically coherent and yet at the same time reflective of the broader structure of the poem. Several commentators, however, including Wilhelm Pfannkuch and Richard Swift, have gone further in according to *Verklärte Nacht* a more purely musical shape, that of sonata form. In this respect, the sextet is seen implicitly as the successor of the forms of the D-Major Quartet and explicitly as the direct precursor of the large one-movement instrumental works Schoenberg composed in 1902–6, including *Pelleas und Melisande*, op. 5; the First Quartet, op. 7; and the First Chamber Symphony, op. 9.

In 1963, Pfannkuch suggested that *Verklärte Nacht* represents, if only "vorstufenhaft," Schoenberg's first attempt to blend sonata form with a larger structure resembling the standard four-movement format. According to Pfannkuch, the sextet consists of two principal themes (mm. 1–49); a transition (50–104); a sec-

6. Schoenberg's commentary appears in the booklet accompanying the Columbia recording *The Music of Arnold Schoenberg*, vol. 2. It is excerpted in Bailey 1984, 31–34.

7. On the relationships between the poem and motivic and formal procedures in *Verklärte Nacht*, see also Schmidt 1978, 181–84.

ondary theme (105–31); a "development" (132–80); a brief "reprise" (181–87); a transition, further reprise, and more transition (188–228); an inserted "adagio" movement (229–369); and a reprise/coda (370–418) (Pfannkuch 1963, 269–70). (The exact measure numbers, although not given in Pfannkuch's analysis, have been added here.)

In 1977, Swift argued that *Verklärte Nacht* consists of a pair of sonata forms, preceded by an introduction, linked by a transition, and followed by a coda (Swift 1977, 7). In this plan, the A, A′, and A″ segments of the Wellesz-Dahlhaus scheme constitute, respectively, the introduction, transition, and coda; the B and C portions become the two sonata forms. Swift's analysis remains highly problematic on the detailed level, essentially because it employs the traditional labels of sonata form without arguing effectively for their applicability. Rather than being passed over quickly, however, his analysis should be dealt with at some length because it raises issues of formal structure important to an understanding not only of Schoenberg's early music, but of much of the post-Wagnerian instrumental repertory.

There are three major problems with Swift's approach. First, as even he admits, Schoenberg's sextet is lacking in much of the tonal polarity that lies at the basis of sonata form even late into the nineteenth century. Not only is there "an astonishing absence of emphasis upon the dominant as a large-scale tonal area" (Swift 1977, 9), but there is no consistent dominant substitute. (As will be suggested below, the dominant does play a significant role in the latter part of the sextet, but not as a large-scale key area.) Second, as Klaus Kropfinger has observed, it seems misleading for Swift to relegate what is really the primary thematic material of the sextet—material that returns prominently in the first violin of the "second group" of Sonata II—to an "introduction," "transition," and "coda," terms that imply secondary status (Kropfinger 1984, 142). Third, the proportions of the various sections in Swift's "sonatas" are suspiciously unbalanced, and his partitioning tends to obscure other more plausible interior formal arrangements. For example, the "bridge" of his Sonata I lasts 42 measures, longer than either the first or second groups, and its supposed boundaries override or obscure a clear A (mm. 50–62) B (63–68) A′ (69–74) thematic-formal structure (involving what I call themes 3a and 3b; see below, ex. 5.1), which is followed by a new theme (4a) at m. 75. In Swift's analysis, theme 3a appears in the "first group," while the contrasting 3b (stepwise and chromatic) and the return of 3a are relegated to the bridge.

Swift acknowledges that the second sonata incorporates thematic material from the first, but his diagram does not adequately reflect the way or the places in which earlier themes are brought in. All of mm. 229–44 is lumped in the "first group," although an important articulation point is surely provided in m. 236 by the entrance of the theme from m. 29 (2a). The "bridge" of the second sonata is surprisingly brief—only five measures—by comparison with the earlier bridge. While the broad theme in F♯ major (7a), which is given substantial preparation, might be reasonably said to have the feel of a "second theme," the continuation from m. 266 is distinctly different and less stable.

At issue here is the necessity of invoking sonata form at all, when so many distortions are required to make it fit. A brief comparison may be appropriate between *Verklärte Nacht* and a roughly contemporary programmatic work, Strauss's *Don Juan* (1889). Though the medium and the mood differ, both works are in a single movement of about the same length. In both works the poetic source is printed at the front of the score and could be said to bear a similar relationship to the musical form.[8] Yet *Don Juan* is much more closely tied to principles of sonata form (see Hepokoski 1992, 192ff.). The first 148 measures form a clear "exposition." The bold E-major theme of m. 9 functions as a first theme, and the first group closes with a firm cadence on the tonic at m. 40 (rehearsal letter **B**). This is followed by a transition based on the first theme and some new material, leading up to the strong preparation of a contrasting key beginning at m. 71 (**D**). The preparation involves an extended V/V pedal (F♯), which at last resolves to the dominant, B, at m. 90, whence arrives a broad new lyrical melody. This archetypical "feminine" second theme is spun out at great length until the deceptive cadence onto E minor at m. 149, which can be heard to mark either the beginning of a "development" or a transition to a development that begins with the return of the first theme in C major at m. 169 (**H**).

In fact, Strauss provides no development as traditional in design as the preceding exposition. Instead, he moves to a stable G (minor, then major) and introduces three new themes (m. 199, **K**; m. 236, **L**; m. 299, **N**). The G then serves as dominant to the bold horn theme presented in C (actually, first *on* G as dominant) at m. 316. Only after this are earlier themes combined and fragmented in the manner of a classical-romantic development section. This section concludes with an extremely long dominant pedal (mm. 425–49, 459–75) that clearly suggests "retransition." The recapitulation, beginning at m. 476 (**W**), is truncated but unmistakable: it incorporates the first theme and the horn theme, both in the tonic.

Even allowing for Strauss's imaginative reworkings of the standard form from

8. Walter Bailey (1984, 28) has suggested that Schoenberg did not initially want to include the poem with the printed score. The evidence to which Bailey points is a letter of 2 August 1905 in which Schoenberg's publisher, Max Marschalk of Verlag Dreililien, urges him to furnish the program ("raus mit dem Programm"). This letter, however, refers, not to *Verklärte Nacht*, which had already been published in May (see chapter 4, n. 7, above), but to *Pelleas und Melisande*, a score the composer was trying to persuade Marschalk to accept for publication. The letter is part of the extensive correspondence from Marschalk in the Schoenberg Collection of the Library of Congress. What we *do* know about the poem and the sextet (gleaned from contemporary reviews) is that at the premiere of *Verklärte Nacht* in March 1902, the text was distributed only to critics, not to the general public.

the "development" on, *Don Juan* is much more clearly shaped by sonata principles than is *Verklärte Nacht.* (It is not surprising that Strauss presents a very traditional exposition before beginning to deviate from the formal model.) For one thing, the fashion in which Strauss lays out broad diatonic key areas and sustains them—at least in the background—for long periods is characteristic of sonata form, as are the prominent tonic-dominant relationships. The surface of Schoenberg's sextet is much more chromatic and—*pace* Swift—any diatonic background is less audible. Schoenberg also annexes (as will be seen) a greater number of key regions, and they tend to be more remote from the tonic than Strauss's keys (even than his G–C harmonic axis).

Another important difference involves the number of themes. Strauss's exposition is normative (even restrictive) in this regard: one main theme for the first "group," one for the second. Schoenberg's *Verklärte Nacht* is, as we shall see below, characterized by a relative profusion of themes, most of them very brief. There are no fewer than five theme groups in the first part, some comprising two or more distinct ideas. To pigeonhole some of these into a "first group," others into a "bridge," others into a "second group," is fundamentally to falsify the thematic and formal processes of the sextet.

There is no question, however, that *Verklärte Nacht* employs certain techniques and has certain sections that are reminiscent of sonata form (as Pfannkuch suggests). The presentation and unfolding of themes up to m. 132 fulfills an "expository" function. The broad theme in E major at m. 105 (5a) can be heard to resemble a "second theme" because it is preceded both by more agitated developmental (transitional) material characteristic of a "bridge" and by dominant preparation. Even though there is considerable motivic variation and development, the portion of the sextet up to m. 132 is clearly different in nature from what follows, up to m. 180. This latter part functions and sounds like a "development," because of an almost schematic use of modulation, sequence, thematic fragmentation, and contrapuntal combination. The segment from m. 370 on, in which various earlier themes are combined in the tonic major, clearly acts as a kind of reprise or "recapitulation." But to try to force *Verklärte Nacht* into a sonata form (or two) is to create a Procrustean bed (or twin beds) that the material simply will not fit.

Thematic Style and Structure

Verklärte Nacht can more accurately be said to be shaped by thematic processes and large-scale harmonic procedures lying largely outside the sonata tradition. The thematic material in *Verklärte Nacht* is unfolded by continuous transformation that is more malleable and subtle than anything we have seen in Schoenberg's earlier works. Example 5.1 presents the basic thematic ideas; the numbering bears

EXAMPLE 5.1 *Verklärte Nacht*, op. 4, principal themes.

no relation to sonata-form "groups," but attempts to reflect the way themes are clustered in the sextet, where sections tend to be separated off from one another by such articulative features as distinct ritardandos (as at m. 28, before 2a), fermatas (as at m. 49, before 3a), changes of meter (as at mm. 74–75, before 4a), or modulation and dominant preparation (mm. 100–4, before 5a). For ease of reference I shall refer to the section of the sextet that extends up to the arrival in D major in m. 229 as part I and to everything thereafter as part II. It is hoped this broad partitioning will be as uncontroversial as possible, so as to allow the thematic connections and processes to "speak for themselves." In ex. 5.1 the themes of each part of the sextet are aligned vertically to show relationships and derivations as clearly as possible. Relationships not easily or conveniently demonstrable in the example are suggested by "cf." and are explained more fully in the prose commentary that follows below. The example makes no attempt to show an entire thematic statement (or the harmonic context), but only the basic unit from which Schoenberg works.

It is one of the distinctive features of *Verklärte Nacht* that the basic thematic kernels tend to be very brief, usually only a measure long. A frequent pattern (as in themes 2a, 3a, and 5a) is a twofold presentation of the one-measure unit, which is then extended by means of sequence or variation. This practice represents a kind of compression and modification of the classical-romantic thematic structure that Schoenberg was to call a "sentence," in which a unit (usually of two measures) is first presented on the tonic, then on the dominant, and then "developed" and "liquidated" in a continuation (usually in four measures). The overall proportion is thus 1:1:2, or 2:2:4 (see Schoenberg 1967, 58–59). The themes of *Verklärte Nacht* differ significantly from this model in that the repetition is normally not on the dominant, but at the original pitch level; harmonic motion takes place in the continuation. The short thematic units of *Verklärte Nacht* serve to give part I of the piece a somewhat breathless, urgent quality unlike anything in Schoenberg's earlier instrumental work, but rather like the motivically intense Dehmel songs of 1899, especially *Warnung*.

Two other features are particularly characteristic of part I of the sextet: the themes tend to appear in pairs (indicated as "a" and "b" in the example), and the initial theme of each of the first three groups (1a, 2a, and 3a) is in the lower register, from which the range tends to rise during the unfolding of a section. Theme 1a is clearly intended to be somewhat "neutral" and introductory. It is characterized by the stepwise descent from the sixth to the first degree of the D-minor scale and by the dotted rhythms of the second and fourth beats. The dotted rhythm continues through mm. 9–10, then forms part of theme 1b, which can be heard as an elaboration of 1a; like 1a it has an upbeat, followed by a quarter note on the downbeat, then a dotted rhythm, then a longer note value. Theme 1b also prominently features the first and sixth degrees, now heard in disjunct form rather than connected by a stepwise scale. Theme 1c shares with 1a the upbeat moving down a half-step to a quarter note on the downbeat. As in both 1a and 1b, the second beat involves some kind of diminution—the dotted rhythm has now been fleshed out to four sixteenths—and the third beat has a longer note value.

Theme 2a, the woman's agitated first theme, is distinctly (and appropriately) different in mood from the theme 1 family, but the relationships are still strong. The theme returns to the low register of 1a, whose $\hat{6}$–$\hat{1}$ descent, B♭–D, is now presented as a disjunct leap. The span and the dissonance level are increased by the addition of the leading tone, C♯. The dotted rhythm is present on the second beat, as in the theme 1 complex, but now the first beat of the measure, as well as the preceding upbeat, are distinctly empty. (It might be said that the upbeat has been compressed *within* the measure.) The rhythmic changes, especially the gaping silence on the downbeat, and the incorporation of the leading tone within the theme mirror perfectly the change in mood that occurs at the "etwas bewegter," where the woman begins to pour out her sad story.

In the third measure of 2a, the D–C♯ appoggiatura of two quarter notes is placed up an octave and condensed into a dotted figure, from which the C♯ leaps upward to F. At m. 34, this figure takes on more independent thematic status, hence 2b, which is distinctive for being the first thematic unit to *begin* on a downbeat and to be two measures in length. (Although the thematic unit may seem at first to be four measures long [mm. 34–37], the repetition in fact begins in m. 36, where the second violin takes up the theme and the bass repeats the pattern of mm. 34–35.) Another distinctive feature of 2b that is to be echoed and/or transformed in later themes is the initial half-step followed by a leap. In this theme the leap is resolved by half-step, so that we are made aware of a pair of semitone motives, A–G♯ and D–C♯ (the latter already prominent in theme 2a).

Theme 3a, presented in B♭ minor and separated from the earlier ones by the dramatic climax and liquidation of mm. 41–49, marks the first real tonal departure from D minor. But it has intimate thematic links with the preceding sections. Like 2b it begins on a downbeat and has paired semitone motives, of which the second incorporates the tonic and leading tone (now B♭–A♮). As in 2a, the rhythmic activity in the first half of the measure, including the familiar dotted rhythm, gives way to a longer note value on the third beat. There is no question, however, that theme 3a marks a new larger segment of *Verklärte Nacht*. It initiates a group of themes, including 3, 4, and 5, that is distinctive for brief binary or ternary structures. The formal plan might be represented as follows:

3a, mm. 50–62
3b, mm. 63–68

3a′, mm. 69–74
4a, mm. 75–78
4b, mm. 79–82
4a′, mm. 83–86
4b′, mm. 87–90
Sequential development of 4a, mm. 91–99
Transition / introduction to 5a, mm. 100–104
5a, mm. 105–10
5b, mm. 111–14
5a′, mm. 115–20
5b′, mm. 121–23
Sequential development of 4a and 5b, mm. 124–32

What is perhaps most striking about this segment is the close relationship among the "b" themes. Theme 3b consists of descending semitones culminating in a turn figure; 4b keeps the semitone descent F–E–E♭, but precedes it with an upward leap and then registrally displaces the turn; 5b is virtually the same as 4b, with the necessary changes made for meter and key. As several commentators have pointed out (including Schoenberg himself, as will be seen below), there is also an intimate relationship between the first three notes of 2b, 4a, and 5a: a descending semitone followed by the leap of a diminished fifth or augmented fourth. (It might be said that 3a represents a further transformation: descending semitone followed by a minor third.) An important rhythmic distinction exists between the three themes, however. Theme 2b, as suggested, is significant for being the first theme to begin emphatically on a downbeat. In 4a, the downbeat (as in 2a) is noticeably empty. In 5a, Schoenberg has now restored the upbeat characteristic of the theme 1 family. In a sense, then, the thematic sequence 3a–4a–5a can be said to reverse the rhythmic process of 1a–2a, in which the upbeat was gradually suppressed.

The unfolding of the paired theme groups 3 and 4 seems so logical and persuasive that it is hard to imagine any other possible ordering. But the autograph manuscript of *Verklärte Nacht* (at the Library of Congress) reveals that Schoenberg originally set down the themes in a different arrangement:

3a (the present mm. 50–60)
3b (mm. 63–68)
4a (mm. 75–78)

4b (mm. 79–82)
4a′ (mm. 83–86)
4b′ (mm. 87–90)
3a′ (mm. 69–74)
Sequential development of 4a, mm. 91–99

In this ordering, 3a′ is separated off from 3a and 3b and inserted before the sequential development of 4a. It seems clear that Schoenberg conceived both 3a′ and the sequential development of 4a as passages that would together form a kind of continuous development or developmental transition leading up to theme 5a. But he reconsidered this scheme, perhaps deciding that despite the close thematic relationship between 3a and 4a, 3a′ would remain too isolated amidst all the material from the theme 4 group; or, to look at it the other way around, that 3a′ would interrupt the continuous flow of theme 4 material.[9]

By moving 3a′ back to just after 3b (and by adding the present mm. 60–62 between 3a and 3b), Schoenberg thus created a rounded ternary structure for the theme 3 group and a more plausible sequence from two presentations of the 4a–4b pair into a sequential development based on 4a. It could be said that the final arrangement "de-sonatifies" the passage. Where the original ordering tends to group developmental or transitional gestures together, the revision spreads them out so that each theme group has its own developmental segment and is more self-contained.

To return to the final version: given the constant and fluid evolution of thematic shapes and the relative lack of exact repetition up to this point in *Verklärte Nacht*, the presentation of 3b, 4b, and 5b—especially the identity between the latter two—has a powerful effect. It is almost as if the thematic discourse of the sextet is beginning to collapse, to double back on itself. And, indeed, the discourse does in a sense break down here with the collapse onto to the octave Ds at m. 132, followed by the awesome drop to the low unison E. This is the moment that marks the start of what is often called the "development."

Schoenberg introduces relatively few new themes in part II of *Verklärte Nacht*, largely because there is considerable recapitulation or reappearance of themes from part I. There is also less of an emphasis on paired or multiple theme groups. In general, the new themes of part II are broader and less chromatic than those of part I, although several of them still show a preoccupation with semitone movement. Themes 6 and 7a, both distinctly associated with the man, are closely

9. The reshuffling of material in this section of *Verklärte Nacht* is discussed briefly in Stephan 1974, 270.

related. Theme 6 is so limpidly diatonic that the chromatic passing note in the accompanying voice in m. 232 (B♭, shown in smaller notes in ex. 5.1) stands out in this context. The chromatic descending three-note figure in the second viola acts as counterpoint to the ascent of the third in the theme. A very similar sonority occurs in 7a, where the diatonic melodic ascent, A♯–B–C♯, is supported by an inner voice descending chromatically in contrary motion, D♯–D♮–C♯ (also shown in smaller notes). Theme 7a also clearly derives the quarter–half–quarter rhythm of its second and fourth measures from the rhythmic shape of the first measure of theme 6.

Theme 7a relates not only to its immediate predecessor, but also to the numerous themes in part I that juxtapose a dissonant leap (here A♯–E♯) with a semitone (E♯–F♯) (cf. 2b, 3a, 4a, 5a). The "new" themes that follow refer still more overtly to part I. Theme 8 returns to both the register and the rhythm of 3a. Theme 9b is clearly derived from the stepwise sixth descent of theme 1a, which is actually replicated at the same pitch level (B♭–D), despite the different key. Theme 10 directly recalls 2b (and the group of themes related to that one).

The theme in D♭, 11, the last new theme before the climax and return to theme 6, is closely related to theme 7a. In 7a a pair of descending fourths (A♯–E♯, D♯–A♯) is followed by a stepwise ascent through a third (A♯–B–C♯). In theme 11 there seems to be a complementary process: two *ascending* fourths are followed by a stepwise (now chromatic) *descent* (G♭–F–E♮).

Schoenberg's basic strategy in part II of the sextet appears to be to increase the associations with part I across themes 7a–10, then to pull back for one especially distinctive final theme (11). The "recapitulation" continues with the return of the first theme of part II, theme 6, which in turn ushers in the actual return of theme 1a, in combination with 7a and 10, at m. 370. While some of these compositional procedures can be seen clearly to relate to traditional instrumental forms, the actual thematic-formal structure of both parts of *Verklärte Nacht* is sui generis.

Tonal-Harmonic Relationships

Equally distinctive is the web of harmonic or tonal relationships from which the sextet is spun. Throughout, Schoenberg explores the possible intersections between what might be called diatonic/dominant and chromatic/half-step worlds. By *diatonic/dominant* I mean those relationships that revolve mainly around the tonic-dominant axis, especially V–I (or V–i). Although, as Swift notes, the dominant is absent as a "large-scale key area" in *Verklärte Nacht*, it is nonetheless present as a significant harmonic force, especially in the recapitulatory portions of part II (as will be seen below, in the next section). Other significant relationships are based primarily on half-step motion around certain important pitches or key areas—hence the designation *chromatic/half-step*.

It has been suggested above how half-steps are also important motivic elements in many of the individual themes. This phenomenon, and its relation to the larger tonal dimension of the sextet, was articulated by Schoenberg himself in a remarkable two-page analytical document entitled "Konstruktives in der Verklärten Nacht," which was written out, as the composer notes on the manuscript, "on a sleepless night" in Barcelona in 1932 (see plate 1).[10] This document, which offers a good starting point for a consideration of tonal aspects of the sextet, consists of ten numbered examples (and several other unnumbered ones), each of which demonstrates the larger-scale harmonic resonances of semitones within the themes:

I: Refers to theme 2b (m. 34). Shows how certain notes of the theme outline a C♯-minor triad, others a D-minor triad.

II: Refers to theme 4a (m. 75). Shows how certain notes outline E♭ major, others D major. To the lower right of II is another short example referring to theme 2a (m. 29), in which Schoenberg highlights the semitone pairs A–B♭ and D–C♯, and (with the bracket underneath) the whole-step G–F.

III: Refers to several places in the score, to mm. 34 (theme 2b), 225–28, 229, 320–322 (theme 11). Shows what Schoenberg also suggested on other occasions: how the large-scale tonal structure of *Verklärte Nacht* is shaped by symmetrical half-step relations around the tonic.[11] The D minor of the first part is juxtaposed with the E♭ minor at the end of the transition. The D major of the second part is approached first from above, from the E♭ minor, then later from below, from D♭ (enharmonically C♯) major.

IV: Refers to themes 3a (m. 50) and 2b (m. 34). Shows the intervals of "minor seconds" in these themes.

V: Shows the relationship, consisting of a descending semitone and an augmented fourth, between the first three notes of themes 5a (m. 105) and 4a (m. 74). (I have discussed this aspect of the themes above.)

VI: Refers to themes 7a (m. 255) and 9a (m. 279). The lower brackets show half-step motion. The upper ones show how, although theme 7a is in F♯ major, certain notes form a D♯-minor triad, enharmonically E♭. Theme 9 is indicated as being in D♭. Although Schoenberg does not

10. The "Konstruktives" manuscript has been reproduced and briefly discussed twice before, in Thieme 1979, 216–21; and Bailey, 1984, 31–32 and 36–37.

11. See the remarks reported by Dika Newlin in Newlin 1978, 214, and Newlin 1980, 229.

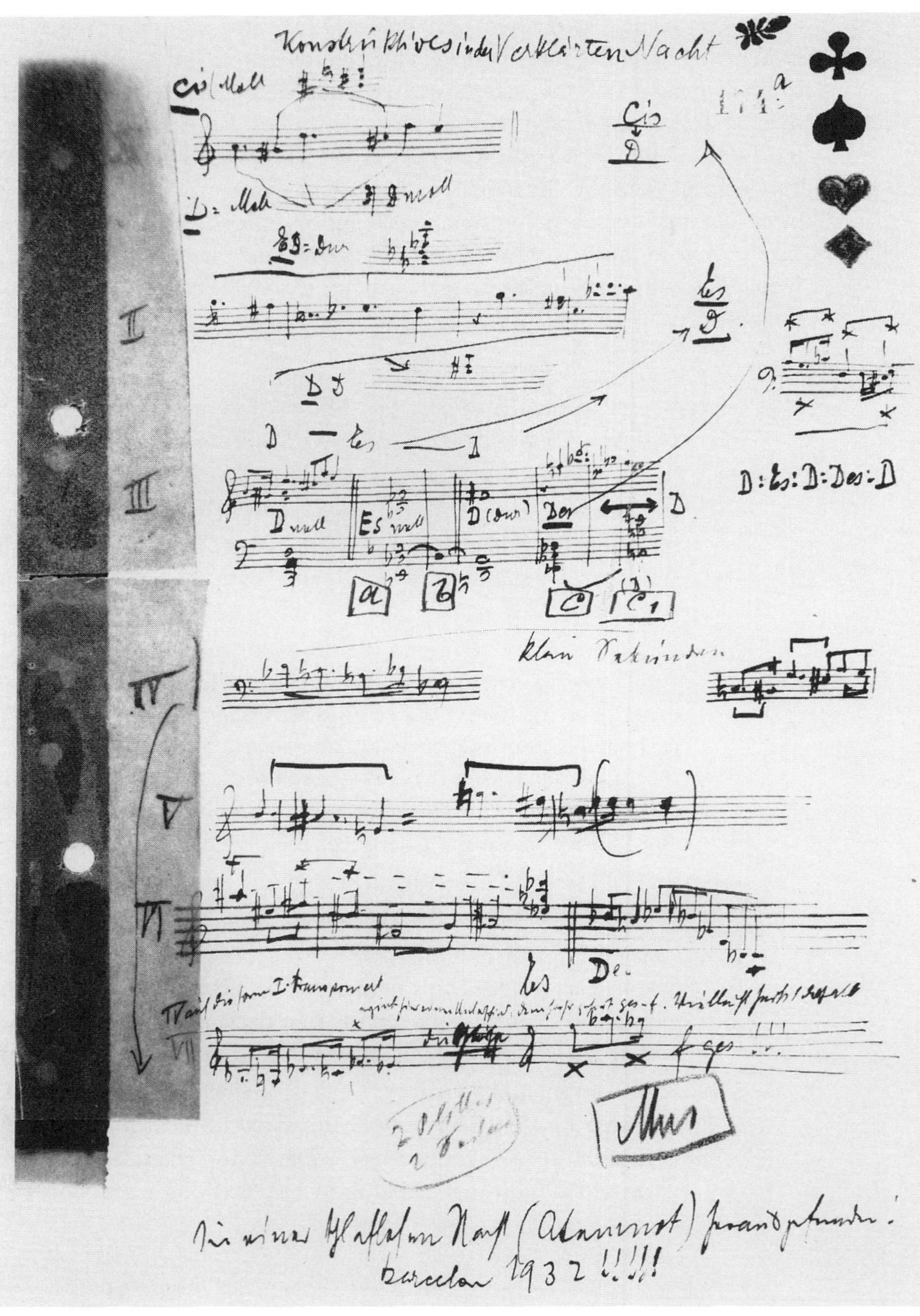
Konstruktives in der Verklärten Nacht
D : Es : D : Des : D
1932 !!!!!

PLATES 1A AND 1B "Konstruktives in der Verklärten Nacht," manuscript reproduced by permission of the Arnold Schoenberg Institute.

specify the relationship he is trying to demonstrate, it seems that he is again indicating how the D♯ and D♭ surround the tonic D from above and below. A similar relationship is shown in his example VIII.

VII: The larger handwritten text above at left reads: "IV auf die form I transponiert." (The remaining text in VII is not readily decipherable.) The music at the left is not found in *Verklärte Nacht* in this form. Its pitch content is close to the second violin in m. 156 (except for the first two notes, which should be A♭–G); but the rhythm resembles that of mm. 311 and 313. Schoenberg's comment seems to suggest that the paired semitones of IV (D♭–C♮, A♮–B♭, A–G♯, D–C♯) are here "transposed" into the contour of I—that of descending semitone pairs a perfect fourth apart.

Music at right refers to the first violin obbligato to theme 3a at m. 50.

VIII: Refers to theme 7a (m. 255) and to 6 (m. 230), which appears centered, below 7a. Schoenberg's remark "noch einmal VI" suggests that the example shows (as in VI) how the first two measures of 7a outline a D♯/E♭-minor triad, and how mm. 3–4 outline C♯/D♭ major. As in VI above, then, Schoenberg appears to be suggesting how the two implied triads circumscribe the tonic D major, which here is explicitly shown in theme 6.

IX: Refers (like VI above) to theme 9a (m. 279), which, although in the key of D♭, is shown to outline an E♭-minor triad and then (in the first viola) to descend to D♮.

X: Refers to the continuation of theme 7b at mm. 264–65 (at left), to the continuation of theme 3a at mm. 52–54 (at right), and to the further continuation of this theme at mm. 57–60 (below). The brackets and Xs isolate the scale figure descending from $\hat{5}$ to $\hat{1}$ in B♭ minor.

At the bottom of page 2 Schoenberg notes that "of all these motivic and structural connections, I was conscious only of those under III a-b-c-c1. Everything else was the diligent effort of my brain, working 'behind my back,' without seeking my approval."[12] In other words, Schoenberg claims to have intended only the symmetrical circumscription of the tonic a half-step above and below. (In the reports of Dika Newlin, however, Schoenberg is said to have claimed *not* to have been aware of this structural principle while composing. See Newlin 1978, 213–14; Newlin 1980, 229.)

Schoenberg frequently praised the power of his own subconscious in creating musical relationships (see, for example, Schoenberg 1975, 85–86). What should concern us here is less their documentable intentionality (or lack thereof) than their significance within the composition. Some of Schoenberg's observations in the "Konstruktives" analysis seem of minor importance for *Verklärte Nacht*—for instance, the demonstration in example VIII that certain notes of theme 7a outline E♭ minor, others C♯ major. It is hardly surprising that a theme in F♯ major will feature the diatonic pitches of the dominant and submediant triads. Other relationships seem merely coincidental, such as in IX, where pitches in the D♭ theme 9a are shown to highlight the supertonic triad, E♭ minor. But the basic

12. The German reads: "Von all diesen motivischen und konstruktiven Zusammenhängen war mir nur die unter III a-b-c-c1 bewußt. Alles andere sind Fleißaufgaben meines Hirns, die es 'hinter meinem Rücken' gemacht hat, ohne meine Zustimmung einzuholen." I am grateful to Anita Lügenbuhl for help with the transcription of Schoenberg's handwriting.

analytical premise of "Konstruktives"—that *Verklärte Nacht* is built on both the large and small scale around a few specific tonal relationships—is undoubtedly appropriate. The areas surrounding the tonic by semitone from below and above, C♯ and E♭, do indeed play an important role, as do other half-step relationships, which are often treated symmetrically. These are the kind of relationships, moreover, that become more prominent in later works by Schoenberg, including those to be examined in subsequent chapters (see also Lewin 1968).

Especially significant at the opening of the sextet are the symmetrical relationships pointed out by Schoenberg in the small example at the far right of II: those deriving from the half-step above the fifth degree, B♭, and the half-step below the tonic, C♯. Schoenberg's example refers specifically to theme 2a; but in fact the highlighting of these relationships begins on the first page of the work. The B♭ is the starting point of the stepwise descent in theme 1a; in m. 9 the pedal D yields for a moment to the C♯. Still greater prominence is accorded the B♭/A–C♯/D half-steps in theme 2a, as Schoenberg himself demonstrates. The A–B♭ motive begins to take on further *harmonic* significance in mm. 41ff. Here the bass of the dominant seventh resolves deceptively up by half-step to the B♭, which supports the famous chord that Schoenberg described as an inverted ninth (Schoenberg 1978, 346).[13] In fact, the bass line continues up by step well past the B♭ (reaching D♮ in m. 44). But in m. 45, it returns to the A, which after more lower-neighbor motion (F♯–G–A♭–A), again resolves upward to B♭ in mm. 48–49. The B♭ now supports an augmented chord less dissonant than the "ninth," and after the fermata it becomes the root of the new harmonic region, B♭ minor.

Across the first fifty measures of the sextet, then, Schoenberg has reversed the original roles of the B♭ and A. In themes 1a and 2a, B♭ clearly functions as as a dissonant upper neighbor. In the passage with the inverted ninth chord, both notes are effectively dissonant: the A is a dominant, the B♭ is the deceptive resolution. But at the fermata the augmented triad begins to take on some harmonic stability; and with the arrival of theme 3a, the B♭ triad becomes fully consonant.

The half-step manipulation is one part of a broader harmonic strategy at the opening of *Verklärte Nacht*. This strategy seems to have two goals: gradually to infiltrate a purely diatonic D-minor sound with chromatic tones and to unfold a large-scale cadential structure whose basic root motion is i–ii–V–i, as is suggested in ex. 5.2. Let us consider first the chromatic infiltration. As the opening section unfolds, the diatonicism is sustained, not only by the tonic triad, but by the subdominant-type chord, the half-diminished ii^7. This harmony is familiar from several of the songs examined in the previous chapter: the reader will also recall that it formed the central *Klang* around which *Mädchenfrühling* was shaped. It

13. A stimulating essay about the function and the context of the "inverted ninth" chord in *Verklärte Nacht* is Lewin 1987.

EXAMPLE 5.2 *Verklärte Nacht*, mm. 1–29, harmonic reduction.

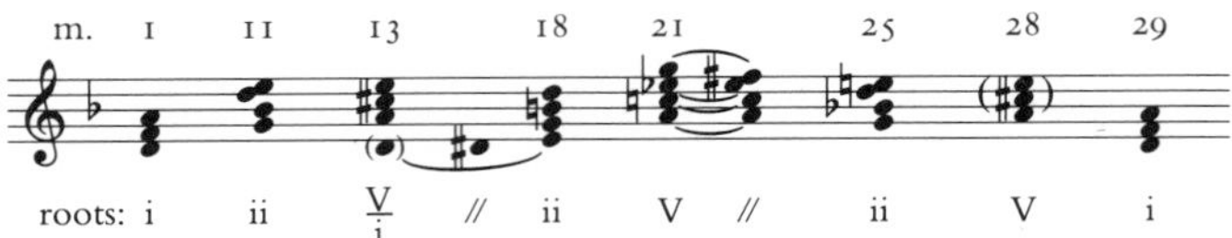

likewise forms the most important non-tonic sonority in the first section of *Verklärte Nacht*. The first significant intimation comes at the sustained, double-dotted quarter note in mm. 5–6, the longest melodic note value up to this point. Locally, the E and G of this chord are upper neighbors to the D–F of the tonic triad; but if we add an implied or inferred B♭ to the chord—the note is never far away on the opening page of *Verklärte Nacht*—we have E–G–B♭–D, or ii^7 in D minor.

In m. 9, Schoenberg introduces the first non-diatonic pitch. The leading tone C♯ appears in the bass, not as part of a dominant, but in an augmented triad spelled F–A–C♯. In mm. 11–12 the upper strings ascend to a higher register and Schoenberg intensifies the gesture of mm. 5–6: the tonic root now alternates with G, which supports the complete half-diminished harmony in first inversion (ii^6_5). With m. 13, the steady D pedal resumes, but now the descending stepwise opening theme is transposed to the dominant (what Swift has called the "dominant hexachord" [1977, 7]). Just as the ii^6_5 has taken on more definition, so now does the mysterious C♯ introduced in mm. 9–10. It is now in the uppermost voice and has annexed an additional note of the dominant triad, A; it is sustained for a half-note and given its own dominant note, the upbeat G♯, which provides a quasi-cadential melodic motion.

Schoenberg has distinctly upped the level of dissonance: as the dominant of the leading tone, this G♯ is the most remote pitch heard up to this point. Meter and rhythm also play a role in giving the C♯ of mm. 14 and 16 more prominence. Previous dissonant or non-tonic chords have appeared on the weaker second half of the measure (mm. 5–6, 9–10); the C♯ now falls on the downbeat.

From m. 17 on, the dissonance level is intensified still further. The bass at last moves definitively off the D, rising chromatically up to the E. This E supports a ii^7 chord with a raised fifth (B♮), which resolves up by fourth to a half-diminished on A. The progression is repeated in m. 19, then again in augmentation across mm. 20–21; in both instances the first chord is now the original half-diminished, E–G–B♭–D. As in the song *Jesus bettelt*, examined in the last chapter, Schoenberg provides strong, explicit root movement underneath vagrant harmonies. The A chord is thus made to seem like a consonance, or at any rate a chord of resolution, until the second half m. 21, where it resolves by appoggiatura to a full diminished seventh (A–C–E♭–G♭). This latter chord marks the first real articulation point in the piece. The sequence of mm. 22–23 is, like what has preceded it, based on vagrant chords, the diminished and half-diminished sevenths, and we end up in m. 24 on the familiar ii^6_5 of D minor (cf. m. 11), which is now sustained for four measures. The dominant to which it resolves in m. 28 is intentionally perfunctory; it consists only of unison and octave As.

From the viewpoint of root motion, the large cadential structure that extends over the first section of *Verklärte Nacht* is twice interrupted: i–ii–V // ii–V // ii–V–i (ex. 5.2). But, as I have suggested, this tonal scaffolding is by no means straightforward or conventional, since the diatonic roots, very much as in mm. 14–17 of the song *Jesus bettelt*, often support vagrant chords. The cadential framework is also unusual in that the pre-dominant ii chord gets considerably more weight than the dominant by virtue of its presence in mm. 11–12, 18–20, and 24–27. The dominant pitch A never supports or is supported by an actual dominant harmony: in mm. 13–17, a D pedal underlies the "dominant hexachord" in the melodic voices; in mm. 18–21 the chords above the bass A are half-diminished and diminished; and in m. 28 there is no harmonization of the A at all.

The dominant withheld in the first section becomes more apparent—indeed, insistent—in the theme 2 group, mm. 29–49. Here the half-diminished ii chord returns in mm. 34–38, where the ascending stepwise bass outlines the diminished fifth E–B♭. The chord leads via a still more intense diminished seventh (B–D–F–G♯, in m. 40) to a standard i^6_4–V^7 cadential progression. The resolution, however, is twice interrupted: first by the "inverted ninth" chord, second (m. 46) by a diminished-seventh chord built on F♯. With this last deceptive move, Schoenberg leaves the tonic region for the remainder of part I of *Verklärte Nacht*. At m. 181, theme 2a returns, now accompanied by the harmonic progession of mm. 41–44. Although labeled the first "recapitulation" by Swift, this passage cannot be heard as a tonal return to D minor. The harmony remains intentionally ambiguous and open-ended, leaving the way open for the definitive return to the tonic in part II.

The Tonal-Formal Structure and Revisions of Part II

One of the most intriguing aspects of the large-scale design of *Verklärte Nacht* is the way in which Schoenberg sets about establishing the tonic major in part II, a process that forms a complement or corollary to the thematic plan discussed above, whereby part II takes on an increasingly recapitulatory function. The half-step approaches to D major of which Schoenberg was so proud, as represented in example III of plate 1, tell only part of the story. The actual confirmation of D takes place through strong dominant preparation, of the kind hinted at, but then left unfulfilled, before m. 50. Both *Verklärte Nacht* as we know it and the revisions evident in the autograph suggest that Schoenberg was entirely confident neither about how much dominant was necessary to assure closure, nor just

EXAMPLE 5.3 *Verklärte Nacht*, key areas and dominant preparations in part II.

where the dominant should be applied. If there is any compositional weakness in the sextet, it lies in this area.

After the initial presentation of D major at m. 229, D is given dominant preparation (or at least persuasive cadential preparation) four different times in part II, as shown in the tonal overview in ex. 5.3. The first instance is at the approach to theme 11, where the tonic is actually withheld and the A^7 resolves to D♭ (ex. 5.4a). The second time occurs about twenty-two measures later, at the climax of theme 11, where we do get an actual resolution to D (ex. 5.4b). At the third passage, beginning at m. 365, a more languid dominant leads to a contrapuntal recapitulation in D major of themes 1a, 7a, and 2b/10, thus themes from both parts I and II (ex. 5.4c). The fourth passage of dominant preparation occurs at m. 391, where Schoenberg recapitulates the climax of m. 338 (ex. 5.4d, cf. b).

The autograph of *Verklärte Nacht* reveals that Schoenberg originally included yet a fifth passage of dominant preparation near the very end, comprising ten measures between what are now mm. 406 and 407 (ex. 5.5). Here the dominant gathers force during a big crescendo in the last five measures, then resolves to a *subito pianissimo* at m. 407. These ten measures are indicated for deletion in the autograph, and the present mm. 406 and 407 are linked together by the marks "VI-" and "-DE." Although Schoenberg rightly came to sense the redundancy of this passage, we might regret its omission especially because of the striking fashion in which the A^7 is approached; in mm. 5–6 of the deleted passage, it is approached directly from the D♭ chord. Schoenberg thus seems to allude to the same progression in mm. 319–20 of theme 11 (see ex. 5.4a).

Although he eliminated this redundancy, Schoenberg decided to let stand another that is much more striking and has greater formal ramifications: the triple *forte* climax of mm. 338–40 is replicated quite closely by the "Sehr gross" of mm. 391–93 (ex. 5.4b, d). At least one sensitive musician was disturbed by this "double" climax. In 1943, while preparing a performance of the string orchestra arrangement of *Verklärte Nacht*, the conductor Bruno Walter wrote to the composer to point out the repetition and to request a large cut, comprising the omission of my ex. 5.4b and the subsequent 46 measures leading up to ex. 5.4d. He

EXAMPLE 5.4 *Verklärte Nacht,* dominant preparations of D.

noted, "For me it will create a difficulty in performance that the soulful development that follows these measures [338–42] of definitive status ends up in the same measures."[14] Even if Schoenberg could not approve such a large cut, asks Walter, would he consider eliminating the developmental-sequential passage in mm. 378–89? "Don't you find," he wrote, "that all conflicts have already been

14. Letter in the Schoenberg Collection at the Library of Congress, dated 18 December 1943. The original reads: "Das die seelenvolle Entwicklung, die diesen Takten des *Definitiven* folgt, in die gleichen Takte muendet, wird mir . . . auch zum Auffuehrungsproblem."

EXAMPLE 5.4 *continued*

c.

EXAMPLE 5.5 *Verklärte Nacht*, passage of dominant preparation deleted from autograph (reduction).

resolved with the passage at m. 338, so that here [at m. 378] we have attained spiritual readiness for the coda [probably mm. 401ff.]?"[15]

No reply from Schoenberg survives, but to judge from a subsequent letter from Walter, and from responses made by Schoenberg to other similar requests, the composer absolutely refused to join what he had in 1918 called the "cutting conspiracy" (Schoenberg 1964, 54). At that time, when Zemlinsky had requested a similar large-scale cut in *Pelleas und Melisande* (to be discussed in chapter 7), Schoenberg replied:

> I am against removing tonsils although I know one can somehow manage to go on living even without arms, legs, nose, eyes, tongue, ears, etc. In my

15. The original German reads: "Finden Sie nicht, dass alle Konflikthafte bereits mit der Periode um 338 geloest ist, so dass wir hier bereits die seelische Bereitschaft für die Coda erreicht haben?"

> view that sort of bare survival isn't always important enough to warrant changing something in the programme of the Creator who, on the great rationing day, allotted us so and so many arms, legs, ears and other organs. And so I hold the view that a work doesn't have to live, i.e., be performed, at all costs either, not if it means losing parts of it that may even be ugly or faulty but which it was born with.
>
> SCHOENBERG 1964, 54

Schoenberg obviously felt the same in the case of his sextet. He may also have felt that the "double" climax is no redundancy: although the passages at mm. 338–40 and 391–93 are similar, each leads into very different material. The first culminates in theme 6, the second in the chromatic progression taken over from mm. 41–45. Thus, the first returns us only to the beginning of part II of the sextet; the second takes us back further, to a significant element of part I, an element that, moreover, served as a climactic conclusion to part I in mm. 181–84. The chromatic progressions at mm. 181–84 and 394–97 therefore occupy analogous positions near the endings of parts I and II respectively. And, of course, only at the latter occurrence does the G♯ diminished chord of the progression at last resolve properly: to a major $^{6}_{4}$ chord (m. 397), a dominant seventh (400), and the tonic (401).

It may be as hard for us as it was for Schoenberg to envision a reduction of 54 measures, or about 13 percent, in a work as seemingly compact as *Verklärte Nacht.* But Walter, a sensitive musician, was definitely on to something. What he isolated with his proposed cut was, in a sense, a symptom of Schoenberg's main compositional problem or task in part II of the sextet: the establishment of the tonic D major by means of its own dominant, and the concomitant fulfillment of the demands of the chromatic/half-step relationships.

The basic tonal structure of part II is outlined above in ex. 5.3. Initially, the large-scale key structure appears to point toward a symmetrical division of the D octave into major thirds: D–F♯–(B♭)–(D). But the final D major is delayed by a long and complex process, unfolding between mm. 270 and 401, and involving the keys of D and D♭ and their respective dominants. It is here that Schoenberg strives to reconcile the chromatic and diatonic worlds of *Verklärte Nacht.*

After the D major of theme 6, the first tonal region touched upon is F♯ major, which has already been adumbrated within theme 6 itself, at the cadence to F♯ minor or iii in m. 235. At m. 265, just before the change of key signature, the harmony comes momentarily to rest on III of F♯, or A♯ major. In this measure Schoenberg also prepares the enharmonic respelling: the upper five instruments play B♭s; the second cello, A♯. The music now turns briefly to E♭ minor (m. 266) and then, after the fermata of m. 269, to a prolonged dominant pedal of D♭ major. The D♭ resolution at m. 283 is only a momentary one, and Schoenberg

EXAMPLE 5.6 Derivation and function of the German sixth chord.

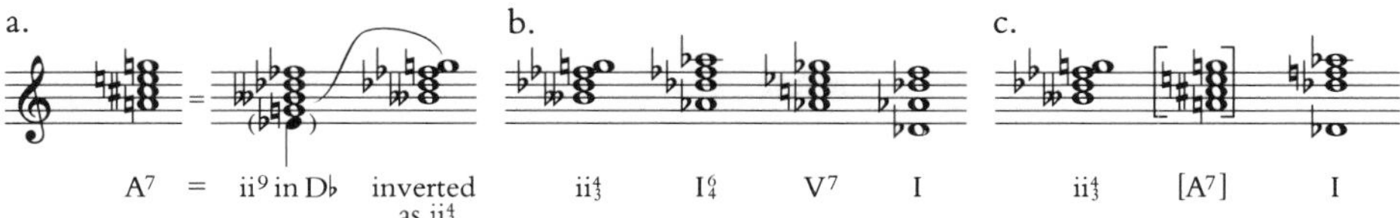

moves on toward F major at m. 291 (the harmony becomes more stable at m. 294). This F major leads on to the most developmental/sequential passage in part II, which culminates *fortissimo* on the A^7 harmony of mm. 316–19. It is this harmony that resolves directly to the D♭ theme, theme 11, of m. 320 (see above, ex. 5.4a).

This resolution represents the nexus of Schoenberg's chromatic and diatonic strategies in *Verklärte Nacht*, especially in part II: A^7, ostensibly the dominant of D, is redefined as the German sixth of D♭. In his *Theory of Harmony*, Schoenberg derives this chord as a ninth chord built on the second degree, with the root omitted, as shown in ex. 5.6a (cf. Schoenberg 1978, 248, ex. 184). The normal complete resolution is to a $^6_4$ chord, a dominant, and a tonic, as shown in ex. 5.6b. If the two intermediary chords are omitted (ex. 5.6c), the augmented sixth can resolve directly to the tonic.[16]

It is striking how the German sixth–tonic resolution not only introduces theme 11, but becomes an integral part of it. The half-cadence that ends the first phrase in m. 322 is made not to the dominant, but to the German sixth (see ex. 5.4a). This progression is repeated in m. 324 and three more times at the climax in mm. 332–36. The goal of what follows could be said to restore to A its rightful function as the dominant of D. The process begins in earnest at m. 337, where the chromatic progression containing the A^7 is at last pushed sequentially up a half-step (see ex. 5.4b), thus reaching B♭^{7}, which resolves in the proper manner of a German sixth, to a cadential $^6_4$ on A. To redefine A in its original role as the dominant of D, Schoenberg has, as it were, needed to meet the A^7 on its own terms—thus to precede it with its own German sixth on the last beat of m. 337. The entire D♭ episode, through the arrival on D, thus begins to fulfill what I have suggested was the main compositional demand of part II of the sextet: the integration of the chromatic/half-step and diatonic/dominant worlds, specifically, the approaches to the tonic by key area a half-step away (C♯/D♭–D) and by conventional dominant preparation.

16. When the chord is spelled as an A^7, as in *Verklärte Nacht*, there is obviously no actual augmented sixth (B♭♭–G). Nevertheless, I shall refer to the chord as a German or augmented sixth because functionally/enharmonically it is equivalent to one, as Schoenberg himself realized.

In fact, the rehabilitation of the dominant is not completed at the approach to D at mm. 337–42. The bass resolves down to A, but not to a dominant seventh; instead, the A passes swiftly to a sustained G, which supports a *subdominant* type of sonority (ii^6 on the downbeat of m. 339). The actual cadence to D in mm. 342–43 is made not via its own dominant, but from the subdominant. Only after the harmonic energy of the preceding D♭ segment has been defused, during the gentle, repeated plagal cadences in mm. 349–52, can the dominant of D begin to emerge in its proper role. The redefinition of the A^7, as it were, is the purpose of the sequential passage leading up to its appearance as the dominant of D, which occurs at last in mm. 365–70 (ex. 5.4c).

The autograph manuscript of *Verklärte Nacht* suggests that the harmonic elegance of part II was not easily achieved. While part I was written out with relatively few revisions (the most significant have been discussed above), Schoenberg apparently found it more difficult to balance the various demands of tonal resolution and thematic recapitulation in part II. Beside the removal of ten measures of dominant in the coda, discussed above (ex. 5.5), there are several other important revisions that relate specifically to the D♭ theme, theme 11.[17]

The first revision involves the approach to theme 11. The present mm. 310–19 represent an actual addition or interpolation; in the earlier layer represented in the autograph, theme 11 (m. 320) was approached directly from something like the present m. 309, as shown in ex. 5.7a.[18] The D♭ is reached not from its German sixth, A^7, but directly and much less strikingly from a diminished seventh on C♯ (cf. m. 1 of ex. 5.7a and m. 309 of the final version), which is followed by a D♭ major arpeggio. In adding the sustained A^7 of mm. 316–19, Schoenberg sought to introduce the harmony and harmonic relationship that is to become so prominent within theme 11 itself.

The most important changes come within theme 11 itself and in the "half-step" approach to D major. In the earlier version evident in the autograph, the second three-measure phrase of the theme is identical to the first; in the revision Schoenberg changes the G♭ half note of m. 6 to A♭–G♭ quarter notes (m. 324). In the early version, instead of making a single, decisive half-step shift upward (at m. 337), Schoenberg alternates between two versions of the chromatic progression a half-step apart (ex. 5.7b). It is striking that the F♯ of the melody (downbeat of

17. In addition to the autograph manuscript for *Verklärte Nacht*, there survive four loose pages of sketches (numbered 984–87 at the Schoenberg Institute), most of which concern revisions for part II and were probably made in conjunction with changes evident in the autograph.

18. In the autograph, all of the present mm. 309–44—incorporating the sequential passage just before the *fortissimo* A^7, theme 11 itself, and the first big resolution to D major—are contained on a large *Einlage* that was inserted by Schoenberg into the manuscript between the numbered pages 26 and 27. Of the music on the *Einlage*, only mm. 310–19 represent an actual *addition*; the rest served to replace passages crossed out by Schoenberg. Measures 310–19 are also sketched or drafted on p. 987 of the sketches.

EXAMPLE 5.7 *Verklärte Nacht*, passages from autograph (reductions).

second full measure in ex. 5.7b) is harmonized, not with a D^6_4 chord, as in the final version (m. 336, beat 3), but with an F♯-minor chord (thus with C♯ instead of D). The D-major sonority of the final version can be said to be more effectively integrated with the overall harmonic thrust of the passage toward D.

Schoenberg's revision makes this passage much more powerful, not only by eliminating the seesawing and by focusing the harmonic motion, but by adding powerful metrical expansion and contraction. In mm. 331–35, the notated 4/4 meter becomes stretched to an implied 3/2, as each phrase now takes in six quarter notes (see ex. 5.4b, where m. 334 and the first half of m. 335 function as a measure of 3/2). In mm. 335–36, Schoenberg compresses the meter once again to 4/4. (In order to bring the four-note melodic pattern back in conjunction with the bar line, he writes a single measure of 2/4 in m. 336. The measure is perceived, however, as part of a 4/4 bar beginning on the second half of m. 335.)[19]

The actual approach to and arrival on D major (cf. ex. 5.4b) are also handled very differently in the early version represented in the autograph, as shown in ex. 5.7c. The B♭ bass of the German sixth chord of m. 1 in the example (comparable to the last beat of m. 337) moves up to B♮ and a rather tepid half-diminished chord before resolving downward to A. Schoenberg then proceeds to circumscribe the dominant note A from above (B♮) and below (G♯). The passage is far less compact and compelling than its replacement in the final version of the sextet, in part because of thematic differences. In the final version, Schoenberg repeats theme 11 one final time over the bass A, in D major and triple *forte* (ex. 5.4b). The last note of the theme, D in m. 340, overlaps with the first note (also D) of theme 6. This wonderful thematic elision is absent from the early version shown in 5.7c, where Schoenberg abandons theme 11, instead anticipating in a fanfare-like manner the first two notes of theme 6, D and F♯, and then presenting the theme itself in a high register. This appearance of theme 6 serves to rob the subsequent, alto-register statement (shown at the end of ex. 5.7c, corresponding to m. 341) of its expressive and formal power.

The immediate aftermath and confirmation of the D-major arrival, corresponding to mm. 344–55, remained unchanged from the early to the final version, but the continuation from the present m. 356 was originally quite different. Especially significant or suggestive is that in the early version there is no hint of the elegant contrapuntal recapitulation of themes now at m. 370 (see ex. 5.4c). Instead, the developmental/sequential passage following m. 356 culminates in a return of theme 11 in the tonic, D major (ex. 5.7d). At this point, the autograph trails off to a single line, then after theme 11 breaks off altogether. Yet as far as

19. The revision of theme 11 (melodic line only) is drafted on p. 985 of the sketches. This seems to represent an intermediate stage between the early and final versions in the autograph. The sequential seesawing has been eliminated, but the metrical expansion and contraction are not yet evident.

it goes, the early draft clearly suggests that Schoenberg planned to "recapitulate" theme 11 in the tonic, something that does not occur in the final version of the sextet.

As he came to a halt here and rethought his compositional strategy, Schoenberg must have realized that theme 11, first heard in D♭, did not need to be recapitulated in the tonic. In the final version, it functions as a retransition, leading swiftly and directly into the climax and the return to D major at m. 343. A further appearance of theme 11 in D would have been redundant and would have robbed the earlier statement of its dynamic, climactic role. In revising, Schoenberg came to understand that it would, however, be appropriate to recapitulate—to bring into the tonic—the important themes of parts I and II; hence the multiple reprise at m. 370. As we know, Schoenberg did let stand one other passage that might be considered redundant: the reappearance at m. 391 of the climax from m. 338 that so troubled Bruno Walter (ex. 5.4b, d).

Thus it can be said that even in its final form, the sextet still reveals something of Schoenberg's struggle to achieve adequate formal, thematic, and harmonic closure. None of this takes away from the work's status as a masterpiece. In *Verklärte Nacht*, composed only two years after the D-Major Quartet, Schoenberg was working for the first time with a freer, extended instrumental form. To this endeavor, he brought (and to later such endeavors would continue to bring) all his basic instincts for assuring tonal and formal coherence, instincts that had only recently been put into the service of much more conservative, traditional forms.

CHAPTER SIX

Gurrelieder (1900–1901)

During the year following the completion of *Verklärte Nacht* in December 1899, Schoenberg was occupied principally with *Gurrelieder*, which evolved into his most ambitious composition to date. The broad outlines of the chronology of *Gurrelieder* were provided by Schoenberg to Berg when the latter was preparing his *Gurrelieder-Führer*, in which Schoenberg is cited directly (Berg 1913, 18). The genesis as described by Schoenberg can be summarized as follows:

March 1900: parts I, II, and "much of part III" composed

March 1901: part III completed

August 1901: orchestration begun

Mid 1902: orchestration continued

1903: orchestration continued up to ca. p. 105 of vocal score (near beginning of part III)

July 1910: orchestration completed up to final chorus

1911: final chorus completed

Although Schoenberg's chronology is probably in most respects accurate, it must be amended slightly in light of the piano-vocal drafts for the first nine songs (at the Arnold Schoenberg Institute), which bear dates in the composer's hand entered from March through 14 April 1900 and thus suggest that at least through mid April of that year, he was occupied almost exclusively with this portion of part I. The dates appear on songs 1, 3, 4, and 5 as follows (with the original keys):

1. Waldemar, "Nun dämpft die Dämmrung," E♭ (dated March 1900)

2. Tove, "O, wenn des Mondes Strahlen," E♭ (later transposed to G♭)
3. Waldemar, "Ross! Mein Ross!" E major (dated 7 April 1900)
4. Tove, "Sterne jubeln," B major (dated 14 April 1900)
5. Waldemar, "So tanzen die Engel," D major (dated 14 April 1900)
6. Tove, "Nun sag' ich dir zum erstenmal," D major
7. Waldemar, "Es ist Mitternachtszeit," D minor (–major)
8. Tove, "Du sendest mir einen Liebesblick," G major
9. Waldemar, "Du wunderliche Tove," E♭

Although Schoenberg stopped dating these manuscripts after song 5, we can reasonably assume that the first intensive compositional activity on *Gurrelieder* unfolded over the early spring of 1900. The portion composed at this time can be seen to draw together the major tendencies of the preceding *Dehmeljahr*: an interest in song, a desire to grapple with large-scale structures (as reflected in *Verklärte Nacht*), and intensive involvement with the work of a single poet. As before, Schoenberg's poetic enthusiasm was shared (and perhaps stimulated) by Zemlinsky, who also worked with Jacobsen texts at this time.[1]

It can be established with some certainty that Schoenberg did not first approach *Gurrelieder* as a lyric-dramatic whole; rather, he chose the first nine poems, which alternate between Waldemar and Tove, as the basis of a piano-accompanied song cycle. In his comprehensive dissertation on *Gurrelieder*, Simon Trezise has established, through consultation of the records of the Wiener Tonkünstlerverein, that a competition for piano-accompanied song cycles had been announced in late 1899 or early 1900, and that about forty entries were submitted (Trezise 1987, 20). Zemlinsky, who was apparently to be one of the judges, recalled later:

> Schoenberg, who wanted to win the prize, composed a few songs after poems by Jacobsen. I played them for him. . . . The songs were wonderful and truly original, but we both had the impression that precisely on that account they would have little chance of winning the prize. Schoenberg nevertheless went on to compose the whole large cycle of Jacobsen. But no longer for a single voice; he added large choruses, a melodrama, preludes, and interludes, and the whole was set for gigantic orchestra.
>
> ZEMLINSKY 1934, 35

1. There are three settings of Jacobsen in Zemlinsky's Lieder sets opp. 7 and 8, probably composed in 1900 (see Oncley 1977, 297–98). There is also a Jacobsen poem in Zemlinsky's op. 10 (probably composed in 1901).

In a remark reported by Dika Newlin, Schoenberg observed (in 1940) that he had begun the work as a cycle of nine songs for piano and voice but then "finished them half a week too late for the contest and this decided the fate of the work!" (Newlin 1980, 225). The excuse of the late completion date has a somewhat different implication from Zemlinsky's assertion that Schoenberg withheld the songs because they were unlikely to win. Nevertheless, it is clear from these various bits of verbal evidence, as well as from the manuscript materials, that Schoenberg did begin *Gurrelieder* as a cycle for soprano and tenor consisting of the first nine songs of the present work, without the transitions. It is not absolutely determinable from these sources just when Schoenberg's conception changed from that of a nine-song, piano-accompanied cycle to the massive cantata-like *Gurrelieder* that we know today. (In the drafts, the 16-stave paper, used by Schoenberg from the beginning, changes to a larger format only in "Die wilde Jagd," but as Trezise points out [1987, 26], parts of the draft of the Wood Dove's song are not executable at the keyboard.) In any case, that evolution must have occurred within a short span of time in the spring of 1900.

The poetic source, *Gurresange*, written by Jacobsen (in Danish) in 1868–69, had appeared posthumously in 1886. In 1897 the *Gurresange* were included in a collection of his poems published in a German translation (as *Gurrelieder*) by Robert Franz Arnold. These translations, further amended by Arnold, were taken over into a larger three-volume German edition, which appeared in 1898 (Glienke 1975, 22–23, 39). Trezise has established definitively that it was the original 1897 translation that served as the source for the Jacobsen settings of both Schoenberg and Zemlinsky (Trezise 1987, 57, 68, 85–86).

In the Danish original, the nineteen individual poems of *Gurrelieder* are arranged into nine divisions articulated by Roman numerals:

- I: Waldemar (one poem)
- II: Tove (one poem)
- III: Waldemar (one poem)
- IV: Tove (one poem)
- V: "Meeting," comprising five poems: Waldemar—Tove—Waldemar—Tove—Waldemar
- VI: Wood Dove (one poem)
- VII: Waldemar (one poem)
- VIII: "Die wilde Jagd" (The Wild Hunt), comprising seven poems: Waldemar—Peasant—Waldemar's Men—Waldemar—Klaus Narr—Waldemar—Waldemar's Men

IX: "Des Sommerwindes wilde Jagd" (The Wild Hunt of the Summer Wind) (one poem)

Although the Roman numerals were removed in the German translation used by Schoenberg, the divisions were retained by means of extra line spaces between the original groupings. This somewhat asymmetrical arrangement of the poems points up the diverse, highly heterodox nature of the *Gurrelieder*, which embraces a variety of literary styles and genres. Bernhard Glienke has suggested in his excellent study of the poetry that the cycle is

> a lyrical-dramatic-musical development of the traditional northern romance cycle toward a concentration characteristic of the *Singspiel*. It functions as a seamless transition between romanticism, Biedermeier, and symbolism. With its folk-song strophic forms [parts I and II], with *Edda* pastiche [part VI], with *Knittelvers*[2] and madrigal verse, it reaches far back into tradition. With its four Lieder in free rhythms [poems 3–5 of part V; poem 7 of part VIII] . . . it partakes in the development of modern poetry.
>
> GLIENKE 1975, 201–2

Jacobsen's divisions correspond essentially to scene-like articulations within the larger cycle. Glienke further groups these "scenes" into "acts." His act 1, which he calls "The Monologues," comprises Jacobsen's I–IV. Act 2, corresponding to the poet's V, is "The Dialogues." Act 3, called rather loosely "Hawk and Dove; King and Fool," comprises VI and VII. Act 4, "Die Nacht," comprises VIII; and act 5, "Morning," IX. Whatever the larger articulation that a reader can discern, it is clear that Jacobsen's cycle combines lyrical and dramatic or narrative elements in a distinctive fashion, one that Glienke aptly characterizes as filmic:

> Instead of stage scenes and acts, we might speak rather of different camera positions, so that, for example, Waldemar's ride to Gurre [IV] and the whole "Wild Hunt" [VIII] are presented more from the angle of characters in motion, [and] the introductory poems [I–III] and "Together" [V] from that of the fixed camera. The sudden scene changes are like film "cuts."
>
> GLIENKE 1975, 180

2. According to the *Oxford Companion to German Literature* (Garland 1976, 478), *Knittelvers* is a verse form first used in the fifteenth century and then revived in the late eighteenth. In it, four stresses occur with an irregular number of unstressed syllables, varying from four to eleven. The lines usually occur in rhyming pairs.

EXAMPLE 6.1 *Gurrelieder*, large-scale key structure of songs 1–9.

Schoenberg's *Gurrelieder* shows him to have been highly responsive to many of the kinds of techniques and devices outlined by Glienke. For the purposes of the present study, we shall concentrate only on "acts" 1 and 2—that is, the first nine songs. It is in the formal, thematic, and harmonic aspects of this portion of Schoenberg's *Gurrelieder* that we see most clearly a connection with, and growth from, the songs and instrumental music of 1899. The more overtly dramatic and extended sections, especially part III, are necessarily less coherent as closed formal and lyrical structures.

The Large-Scale Design of Songs 1–9

Although Schoenberg abandoned his original plan for a nine-song cycle, the first nine numbers made—and in the final form still make—a nicely rounded entity beginning and ending in the key of E♭. On one manuscript page of the original drafts (p. 2183) we can see what was clearly intended to be the ending of the cycle, a conclusion to Waldemar's song, "Du wunderliche Tove," with a substantial piano postlude in E♭ and a double bar. At this stage (March–April 1900), Tove's first song, "O wenn des Mondes Strahlen," was set in the key of E♭ (MS pp. 2172, 2177); it was later transposed to G♭. In the absence of the orchestral prelude, which had not yet been written, the original key of song 2 was thus intended to provide more time spent in the "tonic" E♭, before the tonal excursions of songs 3–8. When he later added the prelude, which hovers around the key of E♭ and leads directly into song 1 in that key, Schoenberg may have felt it was no longer necessary to keep song 2 in E♭, and, indeed, that a move away would be desirable.

Within the E♭ frame, one can discern a tonal grouping of songs 3 and 4 (E–B), and of 5–8 (D–G) (ex. 6.1) that shows Schoenberg's sensitive response to the arrangement of Jacobsen's verse as outlined by Glienke. The first two "monologues," both originally set in E♭, present individual portraits of the two lovers apart; each is contemplating the beginning of evening. The E♭ tonality of the original draft of song 2, then, is perhaps closer in spirit to the design of Jacobsen's cycle. But when transposed to G♭ in the final version of *Gurrelieder*, the song forms more of a tonal bridge or mediator between the E♭ tonal area of the orchestral prelude and song 1 and the E–B matrix of songs 3–4: G♭ is both ♭III of E♭ and (as F♯) dominant of B major.

In the third and fourth poems, the "action" begins with the increased anticipation of the meeting of Waldemar and Tove. Schoenberg shifts to a new tonal region, E major. Waldemar rides to Gurre, and in the last line of poem 3 actually sees Tove, who is probably watching from her window. Poem 4, set in B, the dominant of E, expresses Tove's jubilation at Waldemar's arrival. In the last four lines, Waldemar runs up the steps to her and falls into her arms.

In poems 5–9, or part V of Jacobsen's original, the two lovers participate in what Glienke calls the "dialogues" (or act 2). Like the first two songs of the cycle (in the original drafts), the first two of this section share a key, now D major. With Waldemar's announcement of midnight (song 7), the tonality shifts to D minor, but turns back to major for the central section (mm. 581–615) and the coda (646–52). For Tove's final song, the D resolves as dominant to G major. This move can be said to complement—actually to reverse—on another tonal plane, the move from E to its dominant B between songs 3 and 4.

Song 9, the final song of the original cycle, returns to the key, the mood, and even to some of the thematic-harmonic material of the first. As in song 1, there is considerable emphasis on the sixth degree, C, which is often sounded with the tonic harmony. Although it returns emphatically to the key of E♭, the final song also seeks to integrate within that key references to the key of the preceding song (and by implication, the preceding four songs). Thus the middle section of song 9 (mm. 758–84) is set in the key of G major (and a V^7 of G returns prominently at m. 797). (This move to G major is not present in the original piano-vocal draft of the song, where the segment beginning "Auf der Lippe" remains in the principal key of E♭.)

Large-scale tonal design is only one of the devices by which Schoenberg gives a collective shape to the first nine songs of *Gurrelieder.* Another is the strategic placement of two large and distinctive musical climaxes. The first comes near the conclusion of the "monologues," in song 3, at the words "Volmer hat Tove gesehen (mm. 330–32). This represents the first contact (albeit eye contact) between the two lovers; the preceding songs (and the preceding portion of song 3) have all been concerned with the anticipation of their union. Schoenberg marks the moment with a broadening of the tempo and a *fortissimo.* The second large climax comes at the end of song 8, at Tove's "So laß uns die goldene Schale leeren," specifically at the word "Kuß!" in m. 705. This moment represents a still more significant peak within the first nine songs: physical union. After this climax near the end of song 8, song 9 functions as a kind of epilogue.

Individual Aspects of Songs 1–9

The great variety of formal structures among the individual songs in *Gurrelieder* goes well beyond anything we have encountered in Schoenberg's earlier Lieder, and indeed beyond nineteenth-century song traditions. Trezise has rightly emphasized that despite the regularity of much of the poetry, Schoenberg's forms tend to be "progressive" rather than rounded or strophic:

> An overwhelming impression left by the work is of forward, goal-directed movement. This is achieved by the weakening or absence of closure in the songs; the use of interludes that make only a veiled distinction between postlude, transition, and introduction. The tendency of the music to be exposing new material, rather than preparing major structural recapitulations of earlier material, is also a contributing factor.
>
> TREZISE 1987, 188

Yet as in the best of Schoenberg's songs of the 1890s, and as in *Verklärte Nacht*, the urge to through-composition is tempered by an equally strong impulse toward recapitulatory structures. One of the most compelling aspects of *Gurrelieder*, at least for this listener, is the variety of ways in which Schoenberg handles returns or reprises within the separate songs, especially those in the "dialogue" section of part I.

Before turning to these songs, brief consideration should be given to the way Schoenberg manipulates form and harmony to delineate the individual characters, especially that of Tove, in the "monologue" section before their union. Waldemar's songs, 1 and 3, tend to be more complex; Tove's songs, 2 and 4, project the portrait of a far simpler personality. This image is reflected in the verse structure created by Jacobsen and his translator, Arnold. Poem 2, "O, wenn des Mondes Strahlen," cast entirely in rhymed couplets (six in all), may derive from the *Knittelvers* tradition to which Glienke refers, and which here seems to be regularized into something like iambic pentameter:

> O, wenn des Mondes Strahlen leise gleiten,
> Und Friede sich und Ruh durchs All verbreiten,
> Nicht Wasser dünkt mich dann des Meeres Raum,
> Und jener Wald scheint nicht Gebüsch und Baum.
> Das sind nicht Wolken, die den Himmel schmücken,
> Und Tal und Hügel nicht der Erde Rücken,
> Und Form und Farbenspiel, nur eitle Schäume,
> Und alles Abglanz nur der Gottesträume.[3]

3. The orthography and layout of this and the other poetic texts from *Gurrelieder* cited below are reproduced from Berg 1913.

Oh, when the moon's beams glide gently, and peace and silence spread themselves over everything, then the expanse of the sea does not seem like water to me, and that forest does not appear like thickets and trees. Those aren't clouds that decorate the sky, nor do hill and vale cover the earth, and the play of forms and colors is only empty fluff, and everything is merely the reflection of God's dream.

Schoenberg captures the uncomplicated faith of Tove, for whom each natural beauty is only a reflection of God, by returning to the tonic at the end of *each* line of poetry except line 6. Even though it ends on a different chord (A♭), the musical setting of line 6 is in fact a sequential repetition up a whole tone of line 5 and thus in spirit retains the simplicity of the overall formal-harmonic design. Line 7 concludes on an F♯-minor chord, enharmonically the tonic minor, and line 8 returns us directly to the tonic major. It is striking, too, how in each case the tonic at the end of the poetic line is approached, not from its dominant, but from either a diminished-seventh chord or a German sixth. Dominant resolutions would sound too "strong," too forceful (not to mention monotonous). The cadences created by Schoenberg tend to sound appropriately "weak."

Jacobsen maintains this vision of Tove in her next song, as does Schoenberg in turn. "Sterne jubeln" (no. 4) is an overenthusiastic litany of subject-verb pairs expressing joy, pride, and similar emotions:

Text	*Musical Structure*
Sterne jubeln, das Meer, es leuchtet,	strophe 1
Preßt an die Küste sein pochendes Herz,	
Blätter, sie murmeln, es zittert ihr Tauschmuck,	
Seewind umfängt mich in mutigem Scherz,	
Wetterhahn singt, und die Turmzinnen nicken,	strophe 2
Burschen stolzieren mit flammenden Blicken,	
Wogende Brust voll üppigen Lebens	
Fesseln die blühenden Dirnen vergebens,	
Rosen, sie müh'n sich, zu späh'n in die Ferne,	strophe 3
Fackeln, sie lodern und leuchten so gerne,	
Wald erschließt seinen Bann zur Stell',	
Horch, in der Stadt nun Hundegebell.	(strophic structure breaks off)
Und die steigenden Wogen der Treppe	
Tragen zum Hafen den fürstlichen Held,	
Bis er auf alleroberster Staffel	
Mir in die offenen Arme fällt.	

Stars rejoice, the sea is shining, it presses the shore to its beating heart. Leaves are murmuring, their dewy cover quivers, sea wind enwraps me in bold play, weathervane sings, and tops of towers nod, young boys strut with sparkling glances, in vain do the blossoming girls repress the heaving breast full of sensual life, roses try to peer out into the distance, torches blaze and shine happily, forest instantly reveals its magic, hear the barking of dogs in the city. And the rising waves of the staircase bear the princely hero to the harbor until, on the highest step, he falls into my open arms.

Until near the end of the song, the musical setting is organized into almost schematically clear two- and four-measure groups, which are placed into a modified strophic setting. The vocal melody swings along in a regular, unproblematically articulated triple meter. Even the harmonic rovings, among the most advanced in Schoenberg's work up to this time, take place with a bluntness that seems well suited to the character of Tove. As Berg points out (1913, 32), Schoenberg uses the same diminished-seventh chord to change gears abruptly from B to A♭ (m. 354) in the first strophe and then from B to A major in the second (m. 370).

The disruption of this regularity comes at m. 395 ("Horch, in der Stadt"), when Tove first becomes aware of the arrival of Waldemar. Until then, the first eight lines are set as two slightly varied musical strophes beginning in the tonic, B major. The third strophe begins in the mediant, E♭, and although further varied, shows strong similarities to the first two; but the strophic design is broken off after the third line as Tove hears the barking dogs that mark the arrival of Waldemar.

With the "dialogue" section of part I of *Gurrelieder*, Schoenberg attains new heights in the integration of form, theme, and harmony. Song 5, Waldemar's "So tanzen die Engel," is in this respect a miracle of recapitulatory subtlety. The poem comprises four four-line stanzas, each with an identical rhyme scheme (the stanzas are not actually separated by line spaces in the Arnold translation used by Schoenberg, although the structural divisions are readily apparent):

Text	*Musical Structure*
So tanzen die Engel vor Gottes Thron nicht,	A
Wie die Welt nun tanzt vor mir.	
So lieblich klingt ihrer Harfen Ton nicht,	
Wie Waldemars Seele Dir.	
Aber stolzer auch saß neben Gott nicht Christ	B
Nach dem harten Erlösungsstreite,	
Als Waldemar stolz nun und königlich ist	
An Tovelilles Seite.	
Nicht sehnlicher möchten die Seelen gewinnen	C
Den Weg zu der Seligen Bund,	
Als ich deinen Kuß, da ich Gurres Zinnen	
Sah leuchten vom Oeresund.	
Und ich tausch' auch nicht ihren Mauerwall	D
Und den Schatz, den treu sie bewahren,	
Für Himmelreichs Glanz und betaübenden Schall	A′
Und alle der Heiligen Scharen!	

> The angels do not dance before God's throne as the world now dances before me. Their harps do not sound as lovely as Waldemar's soul does to you. Even Christ, after the hard struggle of redemption, did not sit beside God more proudly than Waldemar now proudly and royally sits at Tove's side. The souls could not desire more passionately to win access to the holy band than I to your kiss, when I saw Gurre's battlements shining from the Danish straits. And I wouldn't exchange its walls and the treasure they firmly guard even for the glow of heaven and the stupefying noise and all the holy bands!

As it unfolds, Schoenberg's setting seems to be almost entirely through-composed (see letters to right of text above; the music of the song appears in Appendix ex. N). Then at the third line of the final quatrain (m. 490) Schoenberg returns quite unexpectedly, and quite splendidly, to the opening theme, which appears not in the tonic, D major, but in the key of the Neapolitan, E♭. The tonic arrives only in the piano postlude (m. 480), after the end of the vocal text (not shown in ex. N).

Although it may seem unprepared, the E♭ return on "Himmelreichs" in fact forms the climax of what has been a very gradual and subtle return of the opening material, extending well back into the C section. The recapitulatory process can be summarized in the following stages:

1. At m. 467 the tonic returns in first inversion and in minor. There is at this point no direct thematic reference to the "So tanzen" theme, although its A–D–A profile is suggested by the chromatic ascent and descent between A and D in the melody of mm. 467–69.
2. At mm. 471–72, the opening theme is adumbrated still more strongly by the setting of the words "ich deinen Kuß," which is also a recurrence of one of the principal leitmotives of *Gurrelieder.* The motive, which can be taken in a general sense to stand for the love between Waldemar and Tove (see Trezise 1987, 197–201), occurs first in song 2 at m. 223 (ex. 6.2a) and reappears frequently throughout the work. Here in Waldemar's song it also constitutes a decorated reprise of the opening theme. A juxtaposition of this passage with the opening of the song (ex. 6.2b, c) shows that the correspondence is quite close for four measures. The only significant melodic difference is the emphasis on E in m. 473, different from the F♯ in m. 446. The return here is a harmonic as well as thematic one, although like the thematic one, it is oblique: as in stage 1, the tonic chord appears in first inversion in mm. 472 and 474 and is approached not from its dominant but from V^7/V.

   Measures 475–76 recall another portion of the opening of the song:

EXAMPLE 6.2 *Gurrelieder*, "So tanzen die Engel," transformation of motive.

a.

b.

c.

the approach to V/vi in mm. 456–48. The original harmonic motion from G to F♯ is here condensed or compressed.

3. The third stage, beginning in m. 477, brings the tonic in root position and another quotation from earlier in *Gurrelieder:* the first two phrases from the coda to Waldemar's first song (m. 146, "Und jede Macht"). In its original context, this passage served to depart from, and then confirm, a tonic (E♭) that had already been firmly established. It is thus striking that in song 5, Schoenberg brings the material back in a context where the tonic has not yet been confirmed—where no clear return has yet occurred. Because we first heard it as a coda in song 1, we tend to hear a similar function here: that is, leading away from the tonic. The D major on the downbeat of m. 477 is soon reinterpreted as a D^7, inflecting toward the subdominant (a gesture typical of codas) and its own supertonic (m. 480).
4. At this point, the opening theme of the song returns at last, not in the tonic, but in the Neapolitan, E♭. The gesture seems to reach back harmonically to the similarly abrupt turn to the Neapolitan in m. 459 of this song. The final phrase (mm. 485–88), an augmentation of the phrase from stage 3 (m. 477) and song 1, brings the song back into the tonic realm—but not to the tonic chord. The diminished-seventh

EXAMPLE 6.3 *Gurrelieder*, "Nun sag ich dir zum erstenmal," tonal design.

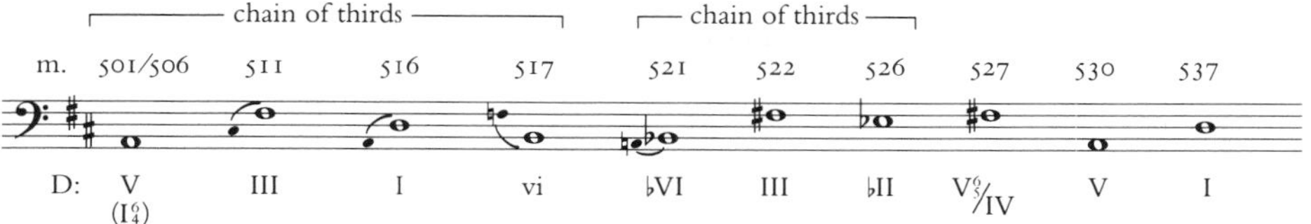

chord prolonged here (E♯–G♯–B–D) relates to both E♭ (D as leading tone) and D major (G♯ as leading tone to the dominant), thus to both the Neapolitan and the true tonic.

The ways in which harmonic, thematic, and formal returns are greatly expanded and kept out of phase in this song far surpass anything we have seen in Schoenberg's work to date, although there are clear points of contact with the kinds of practices examined in *Verklärte Nacht*. In "So tanzen" there is no single moment of return, but rather an intricate, multiphase reprise spread out over eighteen measures.

The withholding of the final tonic is intended to lead smoothly into Tove's song, no. 6 ("Nun sag' ich dir zum erstenmal"), in the same key, perhaps the most admired (or at least the most analyzed) individual number in *Gurrelieder* (see Webern 1912, 25–26; Wellesz 1925, 77–79; Gerlach 1985, 74–87). Several critics, including Schoenberg himself, have pointed to the main melody, with its broad leaps, as a harbinger of his later vocal style. In its harmonic practice, however, the song relates most directly to its immediate predecessor in the cycle and to *Verklärte Nacht*. We recall that in part II of the sextet the tonic D major forms the fulcrum or focal point for a wide range of tonal relationships: some third-based, as in the initial ascent from D to F♯ to B♭; some based on half-steps, as in the circumscription by D♭ and E♭; some diatonic, as in the strong emphasis on the dominant, A. Something similar, but in more compressed form, occurs in Tove's song (ex. 6.3).

The tonic D (unlike in the sextet or in "So tanzen die Engel") is not sounded in root position in the opening measures; rather, the harmony hovers around the dominant note A, which underpins the first "cadences" to D (in $^6_4$ position) in mm. 501 and 506. The first root-position triad is F♯ in m. 511. (Here I would disagree with Berg, who hears the F♯ functioning as a dominant within the region of B minor [Berg 1913, 38]. The F♯ is prepared by its own dominant, C♯, and does not have the feel of a half-cadence.) From here Schoenberg returns to D major in mm. 513–15, but only as a way station for further forays. B minor is touched upon in m. 517, and a strong cadence is made to B♭ in m. 521. We might expect, as in *Verklärte Nacht*, the B♭ to function as ♭VI, dropping down to the dominant A. In fact, however, it behaves enharmonically as A♯: in the following measure, m. 522, Schoenberg returns directly to F♯ major. He then flips just as rapidly back to the flat side with the strong plagal approach to E♭ major in mm. 524–26.

From the viewpont of local harmonic syntax, the song might appear a patchwork, but in fact the principal bass motion since the beginning can be heard as two interlocking chains of thirds connected by half-step.[4] The first chain is A–F♯–D–B; the second, B♭–F♯–E♭. The role of E♭ here recalls its role in *Verklärte Nacht*, where it forms one of the means of approach to the tonic D. In this song, however, the final approach to D is made tantalizingly more elusive. Measures 527–29 seem to hint at a move toward the subdominant, G: a first-inversion dominant of G appears on the downbeat. This alternates with an augmented dominant triad of B♭. In the second half of m. 529, this triad resolves to B♭, which now acts as flatted sixth and drops down to A (the dominant of D), an approach that recalls the first climax in part II of *Verklärte Nacht* (mm. 337–38).

Together, songs 5 and 6 of *Gurrelieder* show Schoenberg exploring further the kinds of harmonic and formal issues adumbrated in the sextet, especially the sustaining of harmonic tension and formal expectation over a large span and the attempt to integrate dominant-related with chromatic or third-based tonal processes.

A similar mastery is evident in song 8, Tove's last song ("Du sendest mir einen Liebesblick"). The poem is one of the least regular in structure of any in *Gurrelieder*, perhaps one of the freest that Schoenberg had set up to this point in his career. Here Tove has, as it were, fully left behind the naive versifying of her earlier "monologues":

Text	*Musical structure*
	Part I
Du sendest mir einen Liebesblick	A1, mm. 653-67
Und senkst das Auge,	
Doch der Blick preßt deine Hand in meine,	
Und der Druck erstirbt;	
Aber als liebeweckenden Kuß	
Legst du meinen Händedruck mir auf die Lippen.	
Und du kannst noch seufzen um des Todes willen,	A2, 668–74
Wenn ein Blick auflodern kann	

4. For another analysis of the song that stresses the role of third or mediant relationships, see Ballan 1986, 56–67.

Wie ein flammender Kuß?	
Die leuchtenden Sterne am Himmel droben	B, 675–79
Bleichen wohl, wenn's graut,	
Doch lodern sie neu jede Mitternachtszeit	
In ewiger Pracht.—	
So kurz ist der Tod,	transition, 680–82
Wie ruhiger Schlummer	
Von Dämm'rung zu Dämm'rung,	
Und wenn du erwachst:	A1′, 683–90
Bei dir auf dem Lager	
In neuer Schönheit	
Siehst du strahlen	
Die junge Braut.	
	Part II
So laß uns die goldene	A, 691–97
Schale leeren	
Ihm, dem mächtig verschönenden Tod:	
Denn wir gehn zu Grab	B, 698–705
Wie ein Lächeln, ersterbend	
Im seligen Kuß!	orchestra: A′, 705ff.

You send me a glance of love and lower your gaze. And the glance presses your hand in mine, and the pressure dies away. But as a love-awakening kiss, you press your hand to my lips, and can you still sigh in longing for death, when a glance can flare up like a flaming kiss? The shining stars in the heavens above turn pale when dawn comes, but blaze anew in full glory each midnight. Death is as brief as restful sleep, from dusk to dawn, and when you awake: next to you in bed you see the young bride gleaming in renewed beauty.

So let us empty the golden cup to him, to powerful, beautifying death: for we go like a smile, dying away in the blessed kiss!

With its increasing ecstasy, this poem is cast somewhat in the mode of the Isolde's *Verklärung* in Wagner's *Tristan*. There is, however, nothing patently Wagnerian about Schoenberg's setting, which is one of the most magnificent among his early Lieder. As indicated by the letters to the right of the poem, the setting divides into two parts of unequal length, each of which, as Berg plausibly suggested, might be said to have a highly modified ternary form (Berg 1913, 46). (In the analysis above, the A segments of parts I and II are independent of each other.) These two sections of the song stand in relation to each other somewhat in the way that songs 5 and 6 do: the second functions as a fulfillment or completion of the first. In part I, the tonic G major is continually withheld or avoided in what Berg considers a prime example of Schoenberg's "schwebende Tonalität" (Berg 1913, 45). In part II, G is given broad thematic and harmonic confirmation.

EXAMPLE 6.4 *Gurrelieder*, "Du sendest mir einen Liebesblick," motives.

a.
656
y
z
Du sen - dest mir ei - nen Lie - bes - blick
b.
668
z
y′
3
Und du kannst noch seuf - zen um des Tod -

c.
675
z
y″
Die leuch - ten - den - Ster - ne am Him -

Schoenberg makes the division just before Tove's toast, "So laß uns," which represents the climax not only of this individual song, but also (as was suggested above) of the entire "dialogue" segment of part I of *Gurrelieder*.

The broader formal processes of Tove's song are linked up with, or generated by, motivic-thematic and harmonic procedures in ways that constitute a high point in Schoenberg's early tonal works. The song opens with the threefold statement, descending by octave, of an upward appoggiatura figure, D♯–E, in the orchestra (motive *x*; see Appendix ex. O). This motive becomes expanded and transformed in the vocal part into a melody comprising a neighbor-note figure (B–A♯–B, motive *y*; see ex. 6.4a) and one ascending chromatically by half-step (B–B♯–C♯–D, motive *z*).

In the second section of A, A2 (m. 668), these thematic elements are retained but in a sense reversed (ex. 6.4b): the rising scalar figure *z* appears first, the neighbor-note figure *y′* second. (Although the interval content of *z* has changed—it contains several whole steps—its association with the earlier figure seems indisputable.) The lyrical B-major melody that forms the B section of part I represents a further transformation of the theme as it was heard in A2 (ex. 6.4c). Although the neighbor-note configuration of the original *y* has been altered to

EXAMPLE 6.5 *Gurrelieder*, "Du sendest mir einen Liebesblick."

a. Final version

b. Version in piano-vocal draft

form a descending scale (hence *y″*), the motivic association with m. 668 is made clear by the similar rhythmic structure.

What I have called the transition back to A1′ is preceded on the final eighth note of m. 679 by a D or dominant chord (Appendix ex. P). (In the piano draft of this song, the dominant preparation is more extensive: there is actually an extra full measure of D^7 harmony between what are now the third and fourth beats of m. 679.) The transition, marked "Erstes Zeitmaß" (return to first tempo) by Schoenberg, begins with the disguised or ambiguous return to G in m. 680 and is based largely on motive *z*. At the actual return ("Bewegter, steigernd"), *x*, *y*, and *z* appear in their original sequence; but the thematic process is now speeded up—put into fast forward, so to speak—in order to prepare one of the most astonishing transformations in the song. In the accompaniment of mm. 686–88, the *z* motive evolves magically into the main theme of Tove's earlier song "Nun sag' ich dir zum erstenmal." The process, in which the earlier theme is "born again," as Berg puts it (1913, 49), is the splendid culmination of a motivic development reaching back to the beginning of the song.

The principal vocal melody of part II (m. 691) consists of essentially new material. Yet Schoenberg provides continuity with part I by introducing the rising semitones of *x* and *z* in the top line of the accompaniment: D–D♯–E (Appendix ex. N). The B section of part II is a clear transformation of the preceding A, and it, too, reveals close motivic links with part I in what is one of the most compelling transformations in the entire song. At the climax, "im seligen Kuß" (ex. 6.5a) the original complex is "born again" out of elements of part II, specifically out of the downward stepwise motive first heard at "Schale" in m. 692. In its initial appearance, as at subsequent ones, this figure (a half-step at mm. 692–93 and 702, a whole step at m. 700) is always followed by a descending leap. By analogy to the previous statements, we would expect F♯–E at "se-" to follow the same pattern, but rather than falling down by leap, the E rises in m. 704 back up to the F♯ and to G. Thus on "seligen" a broad augmentation of *y-z* is born out of a transformation of the "Schale" motive. The association with *y-z*, audible even in augmentation, would have been especially clear in Schoenberg's original draft, where "seligen" appears at twice the speed, in quarter notes (ex. 6.5b).

In part II of this song, the return to A′ takes place simultaneously with the vocal climax of B: the opening melody associated with "So laß uns die goldene" reappears in the orchestra underneath "Kuß." The recapitulatory procedure is thus different from that in any of the other ternary or return-oriented structures in part I of *Gurrelieder.*

The treatment of phrase structure in Tove's song is no less remarkable than the large formal-thematic design. As Berg suggested in one of the most perceptive analyses in his *Gurrelieder-Führer* (1913, 46–47), the opening section of the song (section A1 of part I) is based almost entirely on a repeated harmonic-bass pattern treated in the manner of a chaconne.[5] The pattern consists of the bass progression G–C♮–F♯–B–E–A–F♯, first set out in mm. 655–58. The bass line supports a chordal progression arranged entirely as a circle of fifths; except for the last chord, a first-inversion D-major triad, all are in root position.

The pattern begins on the tonic G, which is, however, attenuated by the D♯–E inner voice appoggiaturas (motive *x*) suggesting the relative minor, E. The D-major chord coming at the end of the pattern appears to function as the dominant of G, but the harmonic resolution coincides with the beginning of a new statement of the pattern in m. 659; G major is thus side-stepped once again.

The third statement of the pattern begins as if speeded up: each chord/bass note occupies a single beat in m. 663. As Berg points out, this acceleration brings about a harmonic displacement such that the E chord now falls on the strong beat of m. 664. Where, in the earlier presentations of the pattern, E major was just one stop on the circle, it now becomes the principal harmonic focus of the phrase: an E triad is articulated unequivocally in mm. 664 (here an augmented triad), 666, and 667. The veering from G major toward E implied at the beginning of the pattern is thus fully realized. Indeed, at the beginning of what would be the fourth statement of the pattern in m. 666, Schoenberg even substitutes G♯ for the expected G♮. This last statement of the pattern is in fact further truncated and compressed, extending only as far as the V–I resolution on E in m. 667.

5. It should be noted that Berg's measure numbering in his analysis, ex. 52 on p. 46, is off by one measure from that of the published vocal score; his starting measure, m. 650, is actually m. 651. In my analysis, I follow the vocal score.

~

Tove's song is at once one of the most ambitious and synoptic works of Schoenberg's early tonal period. If *Verklärte Nacht* can be said to have borrowed certain compositional strategies from the realm of the Lied—specifically from the Dehmel songs—for instrumental music, the song "Du sendest mir einen Liebesblick" repays the debt handsomely, and expansively. Tove's song is in fact the longest individual number in part I of *Gurrelieder*, lasting over five minutes. Schoenberg's ability to maintain structural and recapitulatory integrity over such a long span is a real triumph, of a kind that had in part eluded him in *Verklärte Nacht*.

CHAPTER SEVEN

Pelleas und Melisande, op. 5 (1902–1903)

With Schoenberg's move to Berlin in December 1901 and his assumption of a position at the Überbrettl cabaret, the relatively intense flow of composition represented by the Dehmel works of 1899 and the *Gurrelieder* of 1900–1 slowed up. Schoenberg's stay in the German capital, which lasted until the summer of 1903, is dominated by a single work, *Pelleas und Melisande*, which was probably begun in the summer of 1902 (one sketch leaf is dated 4 July 1902) and completed in February 1903 (the full score is dated 28 February 1903 at the end).

With the creation of a large instrumental work, Schoenberg returned to many of the structural issues he had faced in *Verklärte Nacht*. He now brought to bear the experience in counterpoint, harmony, and thematic structure—and, of course, orchestration—gained in the *Gurrelieder*.[1] *Pelleas* is almost twice the length of *Verklärte Nacht*. The nature of the programmatic source is very different: a large play, as compared with a short lyrical poem. What Schoenberg achieved in the sextet, capturing in relatively compact form the entire spiritual-dramatic content of a poem, was not possible—or was at any rate not his goal—in the case of *Pelleas*.

From Schoenberg's own remarks (all printed in Bailey 1984) and from Berg's well-known analysis of *Pelleas* (Berg 1920), it can be determined that Schoenberg actually selected about eight of the fifteen scenes in Maurice Maeterlinck's drama: Melisande wandering in the forest (Maeterlinck act I, scene 2); the episode at the fountain in the park (II, 1); the tower scene where Melisande combs her hair (III,

1. This chapter will not deal specifically with Schoenberg's orchestration, which is of course also an essential element of his early compositions. For an extended and sensitive treatment of this aspect of *Gurrelieder*, *Pelleas*, and the orchestral songs, op. 8, see Schubert 1975.

2); the vaults of the castle (III, 3); in the castle, when Golaud seizes Melisande by the hair (IV, 2); the love scene in the park (IV, 4); the entrance of the women servants in the castle (V, 1); the final scene of Melisande's death (V, 2). Schoenberg himself claimed that in *Pelleas* "I tried to mirror every detail of it [the play], with only a few omissions and slight changes in the order of the scenes" (cited in Bailey 1984, 61). As has long been realized, however, this process did not involve a mere translation of these scenes into music. Schoenberg used them to frame a genuinely symphonic work, based on a handful of themes that are continuously reshaped.

The large-scale form of *Pelleas*, like that of *Verklärte Nacht*, has stimulated different analytical interpretations. The one that has had the most authority is that of Berg, who proposes a four-part division according to the traditional symphonic model:

> In the four principal sections of this symphonic poem we can even identify clearly the four movements of a symphony. Specifically, a large opening movement in sonata form; a second movement consisting of three shorter episodes, thus a three-part form (of which at least one scene suggests a scherzo-like character); a broadly spun-out Adagio; and lastly a finale constructed as a reprise.
>
> BERG 1920, 3

Berg's detailed analysis also suggests how Schoenberg distributes elements of the first-movement form over the work as a whole. Although he is not always precise about the formal boundaries, Berg's scheme can be represented as in table 4 (a similar diagram is given in Bailey 1984, 70–71).

Schoenberg's strategy seems to be to introduce in part I a core of themes that are deployed almost continuously throughout the rest of the work. Like leitmotives, they are associated (as Schoenberg himself pointed out) with certain characters or more abstract concepts, and they undergo development that reflects the psychological or dramatic course of the play. For a work of such broad dimensions, there are actually relatively few recurring themes. These are shown in ex. 7.1, where the verbal labels, used mainly for ease of reference, correspond more or less to those provided in the commentaries of Berg and Schoenberg. In order to mark off the larger boundaries of the work—and to provide some needed contrast—Schoenberg presents new themes at or near the beginnings of parts II, III, and IV. Soon after, or even together with, their presentation, these themes are combined with the earlier themes of part I. As with *Verklärte Nacht*, a consideration of thematic relationships and thematic style is essential to an un-

TABLE 4 Formal Outline of *Pelleas und Melisande* (after Berg 1920)

Part I (first-movement sonata form)	Introduction (**0**): in the forest First theme group (**5**): Golaud marries Melisande Transition (6 after **8**) Second group (**9**): Pelleas Codetta (closing group) (7 after **11**): Awakening of love in Melisande Short recapitulation (**14**)
Part II (scherzo with episodes)	Scherzo: scene at the fountain in the park (**16**) Episode 1: scene at the tower (**25**) Episode 2: scene in the vaults (6 after **30**)
Part III (slow movement)	Introduction: fountain in the park (**33**) Love Scene (**36**) Coda: intervention of Golaud, death of Pelleas (**48**)
Part IV (recapitulatory finale)	Recapitulation of introduction to first movement (**50**) Recapitulation of principal theme of first movement (**55**) Recapitulation of love theme (**56**) Entrance of serving women and Melisande's death (**59**) Epilogue: further recapitulation of themes (**62**)

derstanding of *Pelleas*. It is to this aspect we should turn before considering further the matter of sonata form and the large-scale structure.

Thematic Relationships, Style, and Structure

The process of thematic transformation in *Pelleas und Melisande* is richer and more elaborate than in any of Schoenberg's earlier works. Some of the most obvious, audible relationships (many noted in Berg's thematic table of 1920) can be summarized as follows (see exx. 7.1 and 7.2):

1. The first theme of the work, MELISANDE 1, is based on a three-note motive, *x*, which is common to several important themes. The first three notes of MELISANDE 2 are clearly heard as an inversion of *x*, and the rising C–D♭–D♮ might be heard (although it is embedded in a longer rising line) as *x* in its original form. The motive appears prominently as the first chromatic element in the broadly diatonic F-major melody based on the GOLAUD motive (ex. 7.2a). It also forms a distinctive part of PELLEAS 1 and appears inverted across the first and second measures of PELLEAS

EXAMPLE 7.1 *Pelleas und Melisande*, principal themes.

2; in the latter spot, the inversion occupies the same metrical position with respect to the bar line as in MELISANDE 2. The programmatic import of these recurrences is clear: Melisande's chromatic motive *x* infiltrates the themes of the two men with whom she becomes involved, Golaud and Pelleas.

2. Another significant transformation on a larger scale involves the reworking of PELLEAS 2 into MELISANDE 4 (aligned in ex. 7.2b). Berg suggests further that MELISANDE 4 is a transformation of MELISANDE 2 (Berg 1920, "Thementafel," ex. 9).

3. Several elements of the themes of part I of *Pelleas* are reworked in the main LOVE theme of part III (ex 7.2c). Berg suggests that the first measure is a transformation of MELISANDE 1, although he is not specific

EXAMPLE 7.2 *Pelleas und Melisande*, transformations of themes.

about the transformation. His example (Berg 1920, "Thementafel," ex. 16) seems to imply that the rhythmic pattern of *x* and the rising stepwise contour are taken over as B–C♯–D♯ in LOVE. This derivation seems less persuasive than others pointed out by Berg. More convincing is his suggestion that mm. 6–7 of LOVE represent a further transformation of PELLEAS 2 via MELISANDE 4 (shown in ex. 7.2c). In addition, the figure of m. 7 of LOVE derives directly from the similar figure in MELISANDE 3.

EXAMPLE 7.3 *Pelleas und Melisande*, MELISANDE 2 theme.

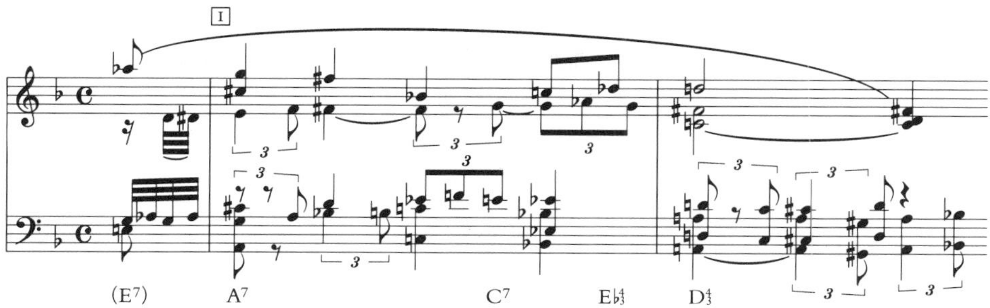

Though important, these (and similar) transformations form only a small part of what is most characteristic about the individual themes in *Pelleas*. A proper understanding of the *Pelleas* style must take account of the harmonic, formal, and rhythmic contexts. In his often-cited autobiographical essay, "My Evolution," Schoenberg suggested that in *Pelleas* "many of the melodies contain extratonal intervals that demand extravagant movement of the harmony" (Schoenberg 1975, 82). This statement (for "extratonal" we can probably read "non-diatonic") seems to imply that at least on the local level, harmonic motion is determined or motivated by thematic forces. In fact, the relationship between theme and harmony in *Pelleas* is really one of mutual interdependence. Not only do the chromatic melodies require unusual harmonic successions; the harmony and the very careful accompanimental voice-leading also tend to give definition to themes that taken by themselves would be almost unintelligible as tonal entities.[2] What is striking in *Pelleas* is how this interdependence of theme, harmony, and voice-leading generates thematic structures that are highly chromatic on the detailed level, but are governed by conventional progressions or cadential structures on the higher level. This process can be seen by examining three themes of increasing length and complexity.

The two-measure theme of MELISANDE 2 (ex. 7.3) is based on an open-ended progression of dominant-seventh chords, moving from the E^7 on the upbeat (spelled with A♭ instead of G♯ because of the downward resolution of the third), through the A^7 on the subsequent downbeat, to the D^7 (in second inversion) on the downbeat of m. 2. Although this kind of harmonic motion is not unusual in music after Wagner, or even by Wagner (for example, the chains of dominant sevenths at "O süsseste Wonne" in the Siegmund-Sieglinde duet in act I of *Die Walküre*), Schoenberg's voice-

2. A sensitive, if brief, discussion of the interaction between the vertical and horizontal dimensions of *Pelleas* is Harvey 1975, 375–79, who treats the "forest" music at rehearsal no. **2**.

leading and the intermediate harmonies it produces are distinctive. The vagrant sonorities actually sounded on the beats of the first full measure—an augmented B♭ triad, a half-diminished seventh chord on C, and a C minor-seventh chord in third inversion—make no sense as a "progression"; they are really produced by the motion of the individual parts. After the initial E–A resolution, the bass line progresses by step around A: A–B♭–C–B♭–A. This line makes extraordinary but logical counterpoint with the melody. The large downward melodic leap of an augmented fifth, F♯–B♭, which alone would sound highly dissonant, is in fact prepared or rationalized by the B♭ present in the bass underneath the F♯. Or it might be said that the melodic augmented fifth presents successively in the horizontal dimension what is also occurring simultaneously in the vertical dimension. This reciprocity between bass and melody continues in their exchange of C and B♭ on beats three and four.

The theme-complex PELLEAS (ex. 7.4) shows on a larger scale how an extremely chromatic melody and bass line can generate or fill out a harmonic skeleton and a phrase structure that are relatively conventional. The nine-measure theme consists of two phrases, divided 5+4. The first phrase moves from I (E major, in mm. 1 and 3) to V (m. 5); the second returns to the tonic (m. 9). The asymmetry, characteristic of Schoenberg (and of the Brahms themes he admired), is caused by the extension of the first phrase, and the concomitant delay of the arrival on the dominant, from m. 4, where we would normally expect it, to m. 5. The theme begins "on the run," with a remarkable superimposition of subdominant and tonic triads. The first three beats of m. 1 project a kind of rapid IV–V–I cadence; but, as in MELISANDE 2, the chords are produced or carried along by the interaction of a primarily stepwise bass line (and inner parts) with a highly mobile melody. In mm. 1–3 the bass traces a *descent* from A to the tonic E, then leaps down a major third to C, which moves down to the dominant, B. In the second half of the phrase there is a complementary stepwise *ascent* back to the tonic, whose final arrival is delayed by the upper chromatic neighbor, E♯. This unusual final approach to E in mm. 8–9, from a half-step above, creates an important (and undoubtedly intentional) parallel to mm. 4–5, where the dominant is likewise reached from a half-step above and from a note sustained for an entire measure. The E♯–E resolution of mm. 8–9 has also been directly anticipated in the bass motion across the bar line of mm. 2–3: indeed, in both cases the tonic triad is preceded by the identical half-diminished seventh (E♯–G♯–B–D♯).

Schoenberg fills out the initial I–V progression of mm. 1–5 by means of harmonic motion toward, respectively, chords a major third above and below the tonic. The first gesture is toward iii or G♯, suggested by the V^6 of iii in m. 2. Although the melodic D♯ "resolves" by fifth to the G♯ on the last beat of m. 2, the harmony and the bass line, which continues to descend, fail to support that resolution with a iii triad. Schoenberg returns instead to the tonic, on beat 2 of m. 3. The next move is to the lower major third, C major, on beats 3 and 4 of the measure. The A♭$^6_5$ harmony of m. 4 serves as mediator between C and the true dominant, B, reached in

EXAMPLE 7.4 *Pelleas und Melisande*, PELLEAS theme.

m. 5. The chord might initially be heard as a German sixth within C; but the outer voices resolve outward by step to the dominant seventh of E. A deceptive resolution of the dominant leads to an A-minor or iv triad on the downbeat of m. 6, then to a series of vagrant harmonies connected by stepwise voice-leading in the accompanimental parts, and finally back to the tonic in m. 9.

The filling out of diatonic *Stufen* and a normal phrase structure with chromatic harmonies and voice-leading is carried still further in the main LOVE theme (ex. 7.5). Although this theme is twice as long as the PELLEAS complex just examined, it is likewise clearly rooted in E major, and the principal secondary key is likewise the dominant, B, which is reached at about the halfway point, the end of m. 8, and at the conclusion, in mm. 16–17. On the way to the first dominant is a clear subdominant (m. 6), which is itself prepared by a dominant seventh in mm. 5–6. The mid-

EXAMPLE 7.5 *Pelleas und Melisande*, LOVE theme.

EXAMPLE 7.6 *Pelleas und Melisande,* rewriting of mm. 5–7 of LOVE theme.

a.

b.

point harmonic articulation is to some extent obscured by the thematic structure: four phrases, of which the third (mm. 9–11) is an almost exact sequence (up a whole step) of the second (mm. 5–8) and the fourth is an extended variation of the two preceding. The form might be schematized as:

A (mm. 1–4)
B (5–8)
B sequence (9–11)
B varied (12–17)

This is a theme that seems literally to get carried away with itself. Although the harmonic design is essentially symmetrical or balanced, the thematic content is progressive, abandoning A after four measures for sequential and variation treatment of B. The phrase structure, too, begins to unravel: after an initially well-balanced 4+4 measures, we get 3+6.

From the very opening, the theme also projects tension or asymmetry in an apparent conflict between the notated $\frac{3}{4}$ meter, supported by the bass and inner parts, and the tendency of the melody in mm. 1–3 toward $\frac{6}{8}$, or a duple division of the measure. The last measure of the first phrase, m. 4, seems to establish the $\frac{3}{4}$ more firmly, but the metrical grid begins to dissolve again at the beginning of the B phrase, where Schoenberg extends the initial E of the E–D♯–E neighbor motion. By analogy to the rhythm of mm. 1 and 2, we might expect this figure to be contained within m. 5, leading to the high C♯ on the downbeat of m. 6, as in ex. 7.6a. But the C♯ arrives only on the second beat of m. 6. Schoenberg has thus "stretched" the notated $\frac{3}{4}$ to an implied $\frac{4}{4}$, which is continued across mm. 6–7 (ex. 7.6b). This "melodic" meter by no means displaces the notated meter; it is in fact contradicted by the bass, which remains tied to the bar line and arrives on the dominant B on the downbeat of m. 8.

As suggested above, mm. 9–11 repeat the pattern of mm. 5–8 up a whole step, without the initial augmentation. The sequence seems about to continue with another leg in m. 12, but is broken by the appearance of the climactic half-diminished chord, B–D–F–A, which is sustained for two and a half beats, like the E of m. 5. This extension may be said to balance, or cancel out, the earlier one. It now brings the E♯ of m. 14 onto the notated downbeat (cf. the C♯ of m. 6 and D♯ of m. 9). Bass and melody are at last fully aligned and move together toward the half-cadence.

As in the PELLEAS theme-complex, Schoenberg expands or fills out the basic diatonic framework of the LOVE theme by means of harmonic substitutions and extensions. The first of these comes in m. 3, with the abrupt move to the C^7 chord. The relationship between this chord and the tonic, which, as we have seen, was central to *Verklärte Nacht*, is one Schoenberg exploits frequently in *Pelleas und Melisande*, where German sixths come to function almost as substitute dominants. Here, however, the chord moves neither to the real tonic nor to its own "tonic," F; it resolves to a half-diminished seventh on D, thence to a C-minor triad in first inversion. The result is that the first phrase, rather than concluding on the tonic, dominant, or another diatonic *Stufe*, ends on ♭vi.

The harmonic motion to this remote area has its corollary in the melodic avoidance of E in m. 3. Instead of ascending by step from C♯ to D♯ to E, the melody leaps up to G♯. This note then descends chromatically across mm. 3–4, through G♮ and F♮. The E that was avoided earlier appears at the start of the B phrase in m. 5, where the harmony also returns to the tonic region: the E is supported by an easily "readable" V^6_5 of IV.

In one sense, the phrase's ultimate goal in the bass, the dominant B, is reached in m. 8 and is then embellished and extended by what follows. The sequence of mm. 9–12, up a whole step from mm. 6–8, can be heard to move in the bass from the B up to C♮ to D♭, then back down stepwise (in m. 12) to the original point of departure, B. The B of m. 12 is harmonized not with a dominant seventh, but with the half-diminished seventh. The bass now continues to climb across mm. 13–14 up to the tonic E, which forms part of a final I–vi–V/V–V progression that concludes on the dominant seventh.

At a fundamental level, the three themes from *Pelleas* that we have examined in some detail all show traditional diatonic harmonies or progressions, as well as strong traces of conventional phrase structure. The basic skeleton supports a highly mobile melodic style and flexible, largely stepwise voice-leading. In Schoenberg's ability to expand or flesh out the skeleton by means of chromatic harmony and voice-leading, the thematic idiom or style of *Pelleas* goes far beyond that of *Verklärte Nacht*. The contrast can be seen most directly by comparing the LOVE theme of the symphonic poem with the somewhat similar theme 5 from the sextet (ex. 7.7). Both are slow, broad themes in E major that contrast with the more agitated passages preceding them. The *Verklärte Nacht* theme (incorporating 5a and 5b) is ten measures long, probably the longest individual theme in a work in which, as we have seen, themes tend to be quite brief. The first four measures of both themes show something of the "sentence" proportions and structure: 1 + 1 + 2. Both themes move, on the broadest span, between basic diatonic degrees, the tonic and dominant. But in the theme from *Pelleas und Melisande* the upper voice and the bass range much farther afield, and the span is filled in with denser chromatic harmonic motion and voice-leading.

Both themes show a certain metrical-rhythmic flexibility that overrides the notated bar lines. In *Verklärte Nacht* that flexibility is most apparent in 5b, where the basic unit is actually *two* beats long (a beat is a dotted quarter note) and begins not on the downbeat of m. 111, but on beat 2 (with a preceding upbeat). The metrical extension and displacement thus generated continue through m. 114 and are dispelled only with the return of 5a in m. 115. In the LOVE theme the metrical ambiguities begin right away and affect the entire theme up until the final cadence in mm. 16–17.

Tonality and Form

Having examined the thematic style of *Pelleas und Melisande* in some detail, we can now look again at the larger formal structure in which the themes are placed. Although there is some merit to Berg's analysis of the work as a sonata-symphony *Mischform* (see table 4), this approach becomes less persuasive the more specific it gets. Schoenberg himself, although he seemed on the whole to approve of Berg's analysis (Berg 1987, 293) and on two occasions referred to the first fountain scene as a "scherzo" (Bailey 1984, 61, 66), nowhere elaborated any sonata-like view of *Pelleas* (unlike in the case of the First Quartet, op. 7).

Berg's analysis is, as its title implies, almost purely thematic; he gives no tonal references for any of his sections. The sonata-form analogy becomes less plausible when the harmonic dimension is considered, as has been observed by both Philip Friedheim (1963, 207) and Walter Bailey (1984, 72). To be sure, *Pelleas* begins and ends in D minor, and the opening material is recapitulated in the final section (part IV). From the sonata-form point of view, however, the tonal relationships are odd: Berg's "introduction" is in D minor and the first theme (GOLAUD) in F major; in the "recapitulation" the introduction reappears (which makes one suspicious of calling it an introduction at all) and is not in the tonic, but in C♯ minor; the "first theme" is recapitulated in D minor. The sonata analogy is even hazy in Berg's analysis of part I. Although he locates the beginning of the "kurze

EXAMPLE 7.7 *Verklärte Nacht*, theme 5.

TABLE 5 Formal Plan of Parts I and II of *Pelleas und Melisande*

Formal unit	*Action/Theme*	*Key*	*Rehearsal no.*
A	MELISANDE wandering in forest, meets GOLAUD	D minor	**0**
	GOLAUD marries MELISANDE	F major	**5**
	GOLAUD—FATE—GOLAUD	A major	**6**
B	PELLEAS	E major	**9**
A′	MELISANDE—PELLEAS	[D minor: A^7]	4 after **12**
	GOLAUD; then MELISANDE and PELLEAS	F major	**14**
[C]	Scherzo	A major	**16**

Reprise" at the reappearance of GOLAUD in F major at rehearsal number **14**, he might more logically begin it seventeen measures earlier with what he calls the *Schlußsatz*, the return of the "forest" themes of Melisande (MELISANDE 1 and 2; at 4 after **12**), which leads into GOLAUD, as at the opening of the work.

If we avoid the urge to cast part I in sonata form and look instead at the tonal and thematic processes with a fresh eye—and an awareness of the programmatic source—a different kind of plan emerges (table 5). By stressing the status of F major, commentators on *Pelleas und Melisande* have ignored the large role played by A major in part I. The F major in which the GOLAUD theme appears at **5** is only a temporary stopping place on the way to A, whose key signature replaces that of D minor at **6**. The GOLAUD theme is presented as a point of tonal repose in A major at 4 after **7**, is interrupted by the FATE theme at **8**, and is then restored in A at 6 after **8**. Particularly in this latter passage, A has the feel of a fully established key area. Indeed, if there is a sonata-like "secondary key" in part I of *Pelleas und Melisande*, it would have to be A major, rather than F.

Up to the appearance of the PELLEAS theme at **9**, then, the tonal scheme of the work is based on a chain of ascending thirds, D–F–A, which outline the tonic triad. The close harmonic association of the keys D, F, and A is programmatically and psychologically appropriate: Golaud has found the wandering Melisande and has "captured" and married her. The appearance of PELLEAS in E major literally breaks apart this scheme; it is intended to be tonally distinct (but not remote: just one notch on the circle of the fifths past A). During the initial presentation of the PELLEAS complex, up to 7 after **11**, none of the previous themes is heard (I am ignoring in this context the *relationship* of the PELLEAS theme to the other themes).

At 4 after **12**, MELISANDE 1 and 2 from the opening reappear, followed by PELLEAS and MELISANDE 3 together. Despite the additions, we have a clear sense of some kind of return; and although D minor is even less in evidence than at the actual beginning of the piece, the distinct A^7 harmony at 4–5 after **12** could be said to stand in for the key. As before, this section is followed by GOLAUD in F major (at **14**), which is then followed by more MELISANDE and PELLEAS material, a climax, a ritardando, and the beginning of the "scherzo" at **16**. The scherzo begins in A major and thus replicates the ascent from F to A at **6**. Indeed, the A major of the scherzo could be said to fulfill or elaborate the earlier approach to that tonality.

The thematic-harmonic design outlined here suggests at the highest level an ABA′ form (as shown in table 5) whose basic tonal structure tends to override the actual formal boundaries of parts I and II. Even though many aspects of the scherzo—its mood, meter, and primary thematic material—are new, its key provides continuity with (or completes) what has preceded. It bears stressing, too, that the ABA′ structure is no conventional, tidy ternary form, but rather a skeleton, which Schoenberg fleshes out with an intricate layering of thematic and harmonic processes.

One of the harmonic relationships Schoenberg exploits most systematically throughout *Pelleas und Melisande* is that between the German sixth and the tonic. This tonal nexus, already prominent in *Verklärte Nacht* and *Gurrelieder*, can be said to govern many of the major articulation points of part I of the symphonic poem:

- **5**: F major is approached directly from $D\flat^7$, which (as noted by Friedheim 1963, 213) alternates with the true dominant, C^7.
- **6**: A major is reached from an F^9_7 chord, which has the seventh (D♯) in the bass just before the resolution.
- 4 after **7**: This is much like the preceding cadence, except that the F^7 is now sustained longer, for three measures. Again the bass note directly before the resolution is the seventh (here spelled E♭).
- 6 after **8**: A major is again approached directly from F, although not from an F^7. The bass F here is part of the first FATE harmony, a first-inversion D-minor triad with a G♯ in the melody.
- **14**: F major is approached from $D\flat^7$.
- **16**: The A major of the "scherzo" is reached from an F^7 chord.

These cadential patterns, in each case circumventing the traditional dominant-tonic resolution, create a distinctive harmonic syntax within part I of *Pelleas*. The question remains, however, just how these German sixths are actually *perceived* in context: do we come to hear the German sixth–tonic resolution as normative? Or, for instance at **7**, do we hear the F^7 clearly as pushing toward B♭, for which the A major acts as a deceptive resolution? Such questions are not easily answered. Indeed, Schoenberg seems consciously to be exploiting this very ambiguity of the German sixth, which is a dominant in its own right. It is clear too that Schoenberg is working with conventional dominant expectations. The F^7 that is (from one point of view) thwarted by the resolution to A at **6**, at 4 after **7**, and at **8** (here without the seventh), at last resolves normally at **15**, where MELISANDE 4 enters in the key of B♭. This resolution is short-lived, however, as the F^7 returns within a few measures and leads to the scherzo theme in A major (at **16**).

As was suggested by the scenario outlined in table 4, part II of *Pelleas* is more episodic, less formally and tonally focused than part I. Despite the *scherzoartig* opening, it certainly does not conform to a scherzo-trio-scherzo structure. Schoenberg may have intended the somewhat looser construction of part II to give freer rein to his powers of thematic transformation (and to his orchestral prowess). One is struck especially by the reworking of PELLEAS 2 and MELISANDE 4 into the theme that both Schoenberg and Berg refer to as "Golaud's jealousy" (first heard at **23**) and by the further transformation of MELISANDE 2 into the "flowing hair" figure in the tower scene at **25**.

We can pass on to part III, the love scene. The action of part III, in which the lovers meet, attempt to consummate their passion, and are interrupted by Golaud, is very close to that of act II of Wagner's *Tristan*, where the tryst is similarly broken off by King Mark. One commentator has suggested (but not demonstrated) that Schoenberg's movement is actually modeled on the love duet of *Tristan* (Nitsche 1974, 15). On the broadest level there may be some truth to this assertion. Schoenberg's love scene, like Wagner's, is based on increasing sexual passion, and the prominent half-diminished seventh chord in m. 12 of the theme (see ex. 7.5) seems an almost direct reference to the "Tristan" chord. But formally Schoenberg's scene has its own distinctive shape that is rondo-like and is also infused, like part I of *Pelleas*, with sonata-like elements (table 6).

The rondo aspect consists in the twofold return of the LOVE theme and its alternation with sections based on MELISANDE 1. The sonata-like features include the strong dominant reached and sustained before **43**, the development-like quality of what follows, and the return (not in E major, however) of LOVE at **44**. But both formal models, rondo and sonata, are overridden to a large extent by an ongoing developmental process that builds toward successive climaxes, the most powerful at **46–47**. These climaxes are based on three appearances of the thematic-harmonic component introduced in mm. 12–14 of LOVE (see ex. 7.5). The high A in m. 12, supported by the half-diminished chord B–D–F–A, serves to break the sequential pattern of mm. 6 and 9. Underneath the melody, the half-diminished chord now moves in m. 13 through stepwise voice-leading to a diminished seventh on B♯, which leads to a first inversion A-major triad.

The model of mm. 12–14 first recurs at **40**, where, through overlapping imitation, it now unfolds over five measures. The second recurrence is still more prolonged: at 7 after **46** Golaud appears, but Pelleas and Melisande continue their lovemaking a half-step higher (the half-diminished chord is now on C). The third and final pre-

TABLE 6 Formal Plan of Part III (Love Scene) of *Pelleas und Melisande*

Formal unit	*Theme*	*Principal key*	*Rehearsal no.*
A	LOVE	E major	**36**
B	MELISANDE 1, leading after 4 mm. into part of LOVE	E major	**37**
A′	LOVE, extended by sequences	begins in D♭ major	**38**
B′	MELISANDE 1	begins in D major; leads to sustained V of E	**41**
C	Episode/development based on a variety of earlier themes, including MELISANDE 2 and 3 and PELLEAS 1	begins in A♭	**43**
A″	LOVE, extended by sequences	begins in F major	**44**
D	Golaud interrupts; FATE	over F pedal	**48**
Coda	PELLEAS 1, MELISANDE 2	F pedal drops to E, then D	**49**

EXAMPLE 7.8 *Pelleas und Melisande*, climax of LOVE theme.

sentation, at 2 before **48**, deviates strikingly from the earlier ones. The initial harmony is no longer a half-diminished, but a dominant seventh (with ninth and thirteenth) of G♭ (ex. 7.8). Here we might expect a functional resolution. In fact, the bass D♭ does resolve by fifth to G♭ (in the low brasses), but instead of a triad, this pitch supports a diminished seventh, G♭–A♮–C♮–E♭. This is the same harmony (transposed) that occupies the second position in the original model in m. 13, and as in the model it leads stepwise to a triad in first inversion, here E♭. The modification, just before **48**, of the model of mm. 12–14 of LOVE is a signal that the scene is drawing to a close.

Berg suggests that part IV of *Pelleas und Melisande* serves the dual function of finale

EXAMPLE 7.9 *Pelleas und Melisande*, half-step approach to D.

to a four-movement work and "free reprise" of a single large sonata form (Berg 1920, 10). According to this scheme, the reprise begins with the "introduction" (comprising MELISANDE 1), followed by the full GOLAUD melody (Berg's *Hauptsatz*) and LOVE. The recapitulation is then interrupted at the death of Melisande, which leads to an "epilogue" in ABA′ form. A is the original *Hauptsatz*; B is based on earlier themes, including MELISANDE 1, 2, 3, PELLEAS 1, and LOVE.

As Bailey has rightly pointed out (1984, 73), the large-scale tonal scheme of this "finale" shows Schoenberg recreating almost exactly (although in reverse order) the procedures used in part II of *Verklärte Nacht*: the tonic D minor is approached first from a half-step below, C♯, then from a half-step above, E♭. The "introduction" or forest music is recapitulated in C♯ minor (beginning at **50**), a key that becomes explicit with a long sustained pedal at **53**. The pedal returns just before **55** and shortly thereafter moves to D (ex. 7.9). The thematic parallelism (bracketed in the example) makes this half-step juxtaposition as clear as possible: the C♯–E♯ motive (from GOLAUD) in the cellos and basses is imitated directly by the D–F♮ in the horn.

The scene of Melisande's death unfolds in E♭ minor, which is likewise sustained by a long pedal. Almost exactly as in *Verklärte Nacht*, the E♭ pedal moves, not directly to the D, but at the last moment to its own dominant, B♭, which resolves down by half-step to A, the dominant of D (ex. 7.10a and b). In both passages the resolution is marked "Breit."

Just as the basic tonal strategy in part IV of *Pelleas* is similar to that of the sextet, so too is Schoenberg's apparent desire to combine or associate the "twin" approaches to D with the phenomenon of recapitulation. And it is here that he still shows himself less than secure, even three and a half years after *Verklärte Nacht*. It will be recalled from chapter 5 that in *Verklärte Nacht*, the recapitulatory part II makes frequent approaches to D and actually culminates twice in the same passage of music. In part IV of *Pelleas*, where the harmonic language is more complex, the tonic is not implied as often or as directly, but it could be said that there is too much thematic recapitulation, that part IV is overlong.

In this respect it is significant that, just as Bruno Walter picked up on the potentially redundant climax of *Verklärte Nacht* and requested a cut, so did a conductor of *Pelleas*. In 1918 Zemlinsky, who was to conduct the work in Prague, apparently

EXAMPLE 7.10 *Verklärte Nacht* and *Pelleas und Melisande*, approaches to D from E♭.

a. *Verklärte Nacht*

b. *Pelleas und Melisande*

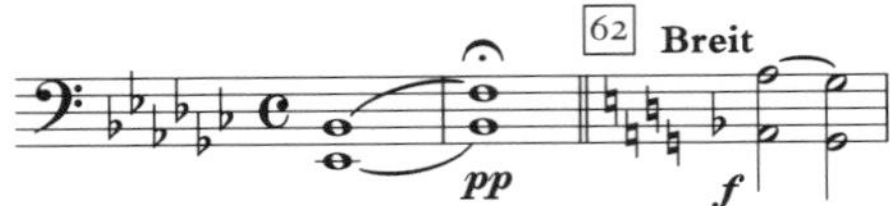

wrote to Schoenberg requesting permission to cut from **50** up to **59**—that is, from the beginning of the return of the introduction music in C♯ up to Melisande's death. As he was to do with Walter many years later, Schoenberg refused,[3] arguing that the passage in question is in fact "the best in the whole work" (Schoenberg 1964, 54), pointing out that a new theme is introduced at **50**, and attempting to demonstrate subtleties of phrase structure and motivic variation.

From the viewpoint of tonal balance or symmetry (something Schoenberg does not raise in his letter), the composer was right to veto the cut: it would mean the loss of the approach to D from the half-step below. But despite Schoenberg's clever analytical pleading, it must be admitted that—as in the case of *Verklärte Nacht*—the conductor was on to something. It does seem redundant to have the GOLAUD/*Hauptsatz* theme recapitulated four different times in the tonic: at **55**, and then three more times after Melisande's death, at **62**, at 4 before **67**, and at **69**. In the first two instances the theme leads similarly to the LOVE theme, at **56** and at 5 after **65**, respectively. (In the latter case, PELLEAS I intervenes.) The thematic recurrences are not, of course, identical: each time the *Hauptsatz* theme is given a new bass line/counterpoint, and the LOVE theme is presented differently. Yet in a work that despite its length has been, up to this point, as taut as *Pelleas*, the repetitions seem excessive. One could wish, with Zemlinsky, for a swifter denouement.

As in *Verklärte Nacht*, then, we see Schoenberg grappling with certain fundamental principles of large-scale form. Beneath all the brilliant thematic transformations and development in *Pelleas und Melisande* lies a basic uncertainty (not confessed by

3. See Schoenberg 1964, 54–56. Bailey 1984, 67–70, cites and discusses the letter, as well as including portions that were cut from Schoenberg 1964.

Schoenberg, of course) about how much tonic and how much thematic return are enough. It was an issue that had occupied Schoenberg as early as the songs of the mid 1890s and that continued to occupy him as he tried to reconcile the apparent demands of traditional tonal forms with newer impulses coming from within.

~

Although there are many wonderful moments in *Pelleas und Melisande*, it is probably the least successful of the large-scale instrumental works of Schoenberg's early period. That it falls chronologically between *Verklärte Nacht* and the First Quartet seems to have had technical and expressive ramifications. We sense Schoenberg struggling to reconcile programmatic and thematic-formal demands. In the relatively compact dimensions of *Verklärte Nacht*, problems of this kind tended to be swept away by the bold strokes of inspiration. Despite compositional awkwardnesses, the sextet easily convinces us of its status as a masterpiece. *Pelleas und Melisande* fails to do so; it seems bloated, its shortcomings (or longcomings) more exposed.

Pelleas und Melisande also shows obvious affinities with *Gurrelieder*, but here too it suffers by comparison. *Gurrelieder* represents the very best in Schoenberg's extravagant late romantic style; under its decorated, overripe surface lies a taut synthesis of harmonic, thematic, and formal processes. In *Pelleas und Melisande*, the lush orchestration and rich harmony, outwardly similar to those of *Gurrelieder*, are put to different use: they too often become a cloak for intricate contrapuntal experimentation, as in the whole-tone canon based on MELISANDE 2 that begins at 2 after **2**. Schoenberg soon came to realize that the cloak fitted such a technique poorly. In the songs of 1903–4, and then in the First Quartet, the contrapuntal preoccupations are laid bare in leaner textures that allowed (or inspired) Schoenberg to recapture something of the vitality of *Verklärte Nacht* and *Gurrelieder*.

PART III

"The Direction Much More My Own," 1904–1908

CHAPTER EIGHT

The First String Quartet, op. 7 (1904–1905)

Before the Quartet

After spending a year and a half in Berlin, Schoenberg returned to Vienna in the late summer of 1903 and began teaching classes in harmony and counterpoint at the school of Eugenie Schwarzwald and preparing piano arrangements for Universal Edition (Stuckenschmidt 1978, 78). Perhaps because of the move and these other activities, the early fall does not seem to have been a period of compositional productivity, but the late fall and early winter saw a flurry of songwriting and drafting (see table 7). It was at this time too that Schoenberg must have been revising *Warnung* for inclusion in his op. 3 (as discussed in chapter 4).

There is enormous technical and expressive diversity among the songs of 1903–4, greater than among the songs of the *Dehmeljahr*, 1899.[1] Perhaps the song that best adumbrates what Schoenberg was to achieve in the First Quartet is *Verlassen*, op. 6, no. 4, a powerful setting of a text by the naturalist poet Hermann Conradi.[2] The song is especially remarkable for its motivic concentration and for its contrapuntal, linear richness. On the largest scale the song is structured musically as an alternation between two thematic units—one cannot speak here of a single "theme"—which furnish virtually all the compositional material (ex. 8.1a and b). The piano part begins as a strict one-measure ostinato with two basic motivic

1. The songs *Traumleben*, op. 6, no. 1, and *Natur*, op. 8, no. 1, both from this period, will be treated briefly below in chapter 9 in the context of Neapolitan tonal relationships in the First Chamber Symphony, op. 9.

2. Conradi (1862–90) was one of the pioneers of naturalism in Berlin in the mid 1880s. He was a contributor to an important volume of poems, *Moderne Dichter-Charaktere*, ed. Wilhelm Arent and Karl Henckell (Berlin: The Editors, 1885), in which *Verlassen* first appeared. In an introduction to the collection, Conradi calls for German poetry to abandon the tradition of folklike, sentimental lyrics and to broach topics more relevant to modern sensibilities. His plea is much like that of Karl Bleibtreu, made in the same year (see above, p. 66).

TABLE 7 Schoenberg's Song Composition Preceding the First String Quartet, op. 7, Fall–Winter 1903–4

1903	
9 November	*Die Aufgeregten*, op. 3, no. 2 (Gottfried Keller)
10 November	*Geübtes Herz*, op. 3, no. 5 (Keller); song first drafted 2 September
26 November	*Das Wappenschild*, op. 8, no. 2 (*Des Knaben Wunderhorn*), incomplete piano draft; song completed 25 May 1904
18 December	*Traumleben*, op. 6, no. 1 (Julius Hart)
18 December	*Natur*, op. 8, no. 1 (Heinrich Hart), incomplete piano draft; song completed 7 March 1904
19 December	*Verlassen*, op. 6, no. 4 (Hermann Conradi)
1904	
23 January	*Ghasel*, op. 6, no. 5 (Keller)

components: rising chromatic steps unfolded in even quarter notes (*w*) and a figure containing a syncopated triplet (*x*). Above, the voice adds a third motivic idea (*y*), which shares or doubles the initial F♭–E♭ descent of *x*, but has a different rhythmic configuration and goes on to outline a D^7 chord. In the second thematic unit (ex. 8.1b), *w* is accelerated in diminution in eighth notes in the bass, while the voice has a figure clearly derived from an augmentation of *x*. In the right hand of the piano is a new sharply rhythmic motive, *z*. Later in the song (ex. 8.1c), motive *w* appears in the inner parts of the piano and in the voice itself; *y*, which was in the vocal part at the opening, is now in the piano, first in the right hand (m. 31), then in the bass (m. 32). Still later (ex. 8.1d), Schoenberg presents yet another inversion: *y* is back in the voice, but the lower two parts have exchanged positions so that *w* now lies above *x*.

The harmonic language is also, of course, affected by a texture so densely motivic that, as Webern said of op. 7, "everything is thematic" (Webern 1912; translated in Rauchhaupt 1971, 16). The opening is oriented around E♭ minor more because of the tonic pedal than because of any traditional harmonic progression (see also Morgan 1991, 64). In ex. 8.1c, the thematic complex, with its elements appearing at the *same* pitch level, is now governed by the D^7 harmony that was only suggested by the vocal part in ex. 8.1a. This chord functions not as a dominant of G (nor as a German sixth in F♯/G♭), but as a genuinely vagrant chord produced by the rearrangement or redisposition of the motivic voices. Motives *w* and *y* clearly function just as well (when enharmonically respelled) in the environment of D^7 as in that of E♭ minor.

EXAMPLE 8.1 *Verlassen*, op. 6, no. 4.

a.

b.

c.

EXAMPLE 8.1 *continued*

d.

The intensity of the motivic working, the emphasis on invertible counterpoint at thematic returns, and the large role played by vagrant chords all mark *Verlassen* as a significant precursor of the D-Minor Quartet. A still more immediate precedent is another string quartet in D minor, which was to remain incomplete. This prior D-minor quartet, perhaps begun as early as 1901, but worked on most intensively in 1903–4,[3] is first alluded to by Egon Wellesz, who notes that in the summer of 1903 Schoenberg was working on "a string quartet which may be regarded as the predecessor of the D minor, Op. 7" (Wellesz 1925, 18). This must be a reference to the movement in D minor and a scherzo in F major, which are sketched intensively alongside op. 7 in the early portions of the so-called Sketchbook I, first used in the spring of 1904.[4] In addition to these sketches, there survives a fully scored draft of eighty measures of the opening movement, evidently begun as a fair copy (printed in *SW* A20: 219–25).

This torso provides important evidence of Schoenberg's compositional devel-

3. Sketches for it appear in a pocket sketchbook used intermittently by Schoenberg between 1901 and 1908. See the discussion by Schmidt in *SW* B20: 279–84, who suggests (279) a starting date of 1901 for the fragmentary D-minor quartet because sketches for it are to be found among some for the *Brettl-Lieder*. Stylistically, however, the quartet fragment would seem to belong more to 1903.

4. Schoenberg's sketchbooks from the period 1904–16, now in the archives of the Arnold Schoenberg Institute in Los Angeles, were first mentioned by Wellesz (1925, 19–20). They were described in greater detail in 1959 by Josef Rufer (who called them Sketchbooks I, II, and III, a practice I shall follow in this study), and in 1972 by Jan Maegaard (Rufer 1962, 126; Maegaard 1972, 1: 20–21). The most definitive and complete account, including detailed bibliographic descriptions, is that prepared by Schmidt for *SW*. See *SW* B3: 21–23 (Sketchbook I); B11/II: 1–5 (Sketchbook II); and B11/II: 6–7, 82–90 (Sketchbook III).

EXAMPLE 8.2 Comparison of Fugue Subjects.

a. Schoenberg, String Quartet in D Minor (1901–4)

b. Beethoven, String Quartet in C♯ Minor, op. 131

opment in instrumental forms between *Pelleas und Melisande* and the quartet that became op. 7. It is a slow, highly chromatic double fugue in which two subjects are presented independently and then combined.[5] Although no material was taken over directly from the earlier D-minor effort into op. 7, Wellesz was right to consider one a "predecessor" of the other. Schoenberg did incorporate a slow, chromatic fugue into op. 7—not at the opening, but as the transition to the second group of the first movement. In fact, the initial fugue subject of op. 7 bears certain striking similarities to the subject of the earlier D-minor fugue (cf. ex. 8.2a and motive *b* of ex. 8.3). Both are in duple time and begin with a syncopated figure; both contain a pair of prominent downward leaps (minor sixths in the earlier fugue, diminished fifths in op. 7), followed by an upward semitone resolution.

The D-minor fugue subject not only anticipates the op. 7 transition; it also looks back to the most renowned nineteenth-century precedent for a fugal opening in a string quartet, Beethoven's Quartet in C♯ Minor, op. 131 (ex. 8.2b). Both the Beethoven and Schoenberg begin (like the op. 7 subject) with a strong syncopation, and both emphasize the leading tone, which is approached from the lower fifth degree. Both subjects also highlight the flatted sixth degree in its role as upper neighbor to the dominant: Schoenberg begins on the flatted sixth; Beethoven reaches it in the second measure. In both works, furthermore, the fugal answer begins on the subdominant, rather than the traditional dominant. Although Schoenberg never acknowledged this probable modeling, he did in fact point to the larger continuous structure of Beethoven's op. 131 as a precursor of

5. The fugue is analyzed in some detail, with transcriptions, by Schmidt in *SW* B20: 290–303. It is also discussed in Hattesen 1990, 167–90.

his op. 7.[6] The Beethoven quartet was obviously very much in his mind's ear as he worked toward, and on, op. 7 in the years 1903–4.

The first two bars of the earlier D-minor subject also hint at Schoenberg's characteristic interest in symmetrically arrayed tonal relationships. The dominant is decorated by the upper neighbor, B♭, the tonic by the lower neighbor, C♯. Schoenberg had explored these same relationships at the opening of another work in the same key, *Verklärte Nacht*, where B♭ and C♯, the first chromatic pitches to be heard, are introduced as upper and lower neighbors respectively. In op. 7 he was to make use of another, related phenomenon, what David Lewin has called "inversional balance" around a central pitch (Lewin 1968), where statements of the main theme in the tonic enclose statements in C♯ and E♭.

It is not clear either why Schoenberg abandoned work on the earlier D-minor quartet or what larger shape that work would ultimately have taken. Perhaps the massive double fugue came to seem too cerebral an opening for a quartet, even one by so committed a contrapuntalist as Schoenberg. In any case, in the spring of 1904, Schoenberg began work on the quartet that was to become op. 7 and was to occupy his energies on and off for a year and a half. In later years, Schoenberg would view this composition as representing a significant new direction in his musical development. He explained in 1949:

> Thereafter [after *Verklärte Nacht* and *Pelleas*] I abandoned program-music and turned in the direction that was much more my own than all the preceding. It was the First String Quartet, Op. 7, in which I combined all the achievements of my time (including my own) such as: the construction of extremely large forms; greatly expanded melodies based on a richly moving harmony and new chord progressions; and a contrapuntal technique that solved problems offered by superimposed, individual parts which moved freely in more remote regions of a tonality and met frequently in vagrant harmonies.
>
> RAUCHHAUPT 1971, 36

Although these remarks, as well as the D-Minor Quartet itself, would seem to signal a firm return to "absolute" instrumental music, Schoenberg would also allude frequently in later years to a "secret program" for op. 7 (see Bailey 1984, 130; Schmidt 1986, 230). When editing the quartet for *SW*, Schmidt discovered the outline of such a program on the inside cover of Sketchbook I; there can be

6. See Schoenberg's notes for the first recordings of his own string quartets, prepared in 1936 (Steiner 1978, 132–33). Schoenberg also mentions Beethoven's quartet in typed notes for a lecture given at the University of Southern California in the 1930s.

little doubt that it refers to op. 7.[7] This program constitutes neither a poem nor a story line, as in *Verklärte Nacht* and *Pelleas*, but rather a succession of feelings or moods, which, as both Schmidt and Mark Benson have suggested (Benson 1987), can be matched with some precision to portions of op. 7, especially in the scherzo, for which the first sketches in Sketchbook I are marked "Neues Leben fühlend," a phrase that also appears as part of the program outline.

Large-Scale Form and Thematic Process

Although the secret program is obviously not without significance for an understanding of op. 7, the real importance of the work lies in its relationship to, and transformation of, the absolute instrumental tradition of the eighteenth and nineteenth centuries. The D-Minor Quartet was unquestionably Schoenberg's most thoroughgoing attempt up to that date to compress and interweave into a continuous composition the standard three or four movements of an instrumental cycle, or, as he himself put it, "to include all the four characters of the sonata type in one single, uninterrupted movement" (Rauchhaupt 1971, 36). Schoenberg's quartet goes much further in this direction than Richard Strauss's tone poems or earlier nineteenth-century predecessors like Schubert's "Wanderer" Fantasy, Liszt's B-Minor Piano Sonata, and Schumann's Fourth Symphony. In each of the latter three works, the movements or sections succeed each other without pause (or with only a short pause); in each, there are clear thematic relationships between the movements; in each, the larger scheme is modified according to principles of sonata form, in that the first movement recapitulation is suppressed and its function largely taken over by the finale. Schoenberg does all this and more.[8]

The overall form of Schoenberg's D-Minor Quartet is outlined in table 8. The following description corresponds closely to Schoenberg's own prose analyses, which, significantly, invoke only the thematic dimension of "sonata form," not

7. The program is transcribed in *SW* B20: 109–10, and in Schmidt 1986. It also is included, in the original German and in English translation, in the booklet accompanying the 1987 reissue on compact discs of the La Salle Quartet's *Neue Wiener Schule: Schoenberg, Berg, Webern* (DG 419 994-2). This booklet is a reformatted and in some respects abridged version of Rauchhaupt 1971; the recently discovered program for op. 7 appears on pp. 18–19 (German) and 236–37 (English).

8. In his "Notes" of 1949, Schoenberg also suggests that the first movement of Beethoven's *Eroica* Symphony served as an important "model" for the "great expansion" of op. 7 (Rauchhaupt 1971, 36, 39). This tantalizing remark refers, I think, not to any large-scale formal principles, but to techniques of thematic and motivic development. Dika Newlin, taking Schoenberg at his word, has attempted to demonstrate specific similarities between some of the *Eroica* themes and those of op. 7 (Newlin 1978, 227–29); the analysis seems contrived and seems also to misintepret the broader kind of "modeling" to which Schoenberg was probably referring. Despite Schoenberg's mention of the *Eroica* as specific model, I feel that attempts to find any one-to-one relationship are misguided. (At least up to this point I have not seen or read any persuasive accounts.)

TABLE 8 Formal Overview of Schoenberg's First String Quartet, op. 7.

Four-movement form	*Sonata form*	*Starting measure*[a]
I. *Nicht zu rasch*	*Exposition*	
	first group	1
	transition	**A**1 (97)
	second group	**A**56 (152)
	Development 1	**B**1 (200)
	Recapitulation 1	
	first group	**C**1 (301)
	transition	**C**35 (335)
	second group	**C**49 (349)
II. *Kräftig*		
Scherzo		**E**1 (399)
Trio		**F**44 (575)
Scherzo reprise	*Development 2*	**G**34 (706)
	(first and second groups)	**H**1 (784)
	Recapitulation 2	
	first group	**I**38 (909)
III. *Mässig*		
A		**K**1 (952)
B		**K**52 (1003)
A′		**L**1 (1031)
	Recapitulation 3	
	second group	**L**52 (1082)
IV. *Mässig*		
A		**M**1 (1122)
B		**M**26 (1147)
A′		**M**48 (1169)
C		**N**1 (1181)
A″		**N**68 (1248)
	Coda	**O**1 (1270)

[a] Measure numbers (which begin again at 1 with each rehearsal letter) follow the original score (Berlin, 1907) and the widely available Kalmus reprint. The continuous measure numbers used in the new edition of the quartet, *SW* A20, are given in parentheses.

the harmonic one.[9] The first "movement" is comprised of a sonata-form exposition, development, and varied recapitulation. Then follows a full-fledged scherzo–trio–scherzo. The varied reprise of the scherzo functions as a continuation or resumption of the development, which begins with thematic material from the scherzo and then (at **H**) takes up material from the first group of the first movement. The development leads into a more literal recapitulation of the main theme on the tonic, then a dramatic "liquidation."

A long fermata marks the principal large division of the quartet. The tripartite slow movement opens with essentially new thematic material, which is gradually permeated by recollection of secondary themes from the first movement. This process is analogous to the infiltration of the scherzo reprise by first group themes in the first half of the quartet. Just as that process led up to recapitulation of the first group, so this one leads (at **L**52) to a recapitulation of the second group. The rondo finale theme is fashioned as a transformation of the slow movement theme; the contrasting episodes are all built from earlier themes. The coda, based on the opening and transition theme, functions as a conclusion to both the larger four-movement plan and the individual sonata-form plan.

Neither a diagram nor a verbal synopsis can do justice to the richness of op. 7, a work that, as Adorno claimed, "down to its last note . . . created an entirely new level of thematically coherent chamber-music composition" (Adorno 1981, 157). Something of the thematic-formal process that seems to generate the larger structure before our very ears can be sampled across the 300-measure segment comprising the transition, second group, first development and recapitulation, and scherzo. The transition is one of the least tonally oriented passages in the entire quartet (and in Schoenberg's music up to this point). A fugato based on a highly chromatic subject, it is almost pure counterpoint, pure "theme." First stated in full at the second entry, by the second violin, the subject has three related components or motives, labeled *a*, *b*, and *c* in ex. 8.3. (As will be shown below, in an examination of the sketches, these labels are in fact Schoenberg's own.) Subject *b* freely inverts the opening leap of *a*, then continues with a similar ascent

9. Schoenberg's principal analyses of op. 7 are those that appeared in *Die Musik* in 1907 (Schoenberg 1907), written in anticipation of the performance of the work at Dresden in June of that year; and in his "Notes on the Four String Quartets" of 1949. Both are reprinted (the former in translation) in Rauchhaupt 1971, 11–13 and 36–42. Other, briefer discussions are in *Style and Idea* (Schoenberg 1975, 42–46, 61–67) and in the album notes written for the private recordings made by the Kolisch Quartet in 1936 (Steiner 1978, 132–33) and now reissued on compact disc (Archiphon ARC-103/4). My analysis in table 8 is based upon Schoenberg's own, with one important modification: I hear the return of the main theme in C♯ minor at **C** as a first recapitulation, not as a continuing part of the first development. Although the thematic material is highly varied here, it does in fact return in its original order. I am indebted to Severine Neff (Neff 1984, 45) for suggesting this way of hearing the section from **C** through **D**. As Schmidt points out in his article on Schoenberg's commentaries (Schmidt 1984), the composer is not always precise about where the sonata-form sections begin and end; there is even some discrepancy between the analyses of 1907 and 1949.

EXAMPLE 8.3 First String Quartet, op. 7, transition.

through two half-steps. Subject *c*, rhythmically more animated, begins like a diminution of *b*, with the downward leap of a diminished fifth and ascent of a half-step. Its second measure contains what is to become an important syncopated figure oscillating within a half-step. The fugato opens with the *b* subject in the first violin; all subsequent entries employ *a*, *b*, and *c* in order.

The main theme of the second group of the exposition (ex. 8.4a) is derived directly from the transition material. The principal melodic line, in the first violin, is a rhythmically augmented version of the oscillating, syncopated seconds of motive *c*. The bottom part, at first played in parallel thirds by the viola and cello, takes over the first four notes and the rhythm of motive *b* (at a different transposition). In the continuation of the second group, Schoenberg fashions a magical transformation in E minor of the *c*-derived figure, which is now given a

EXAMPLE 8.4 First String Quartet, op. 7, second group and transformations.

a.

b.

c.

pulsating homophonic accompaniment (ex. 8.4b). In the first recapitulation, this theme appears in yet another homophonic transformation, now (in B♭ minor) with broken arpeggiated accompaniment (ex. 8.4c). These two modifications of the main theme of the second group constitute genuine thematic transformations in the tradition of Schubert, Schumann, Liszt, and Brahms. As in the passage from the middle section of the Dehmel song *Warnung* discussed in chapter 4, the

EXAMPLE 8.5 First String Quartet, op. 7, scherzo.

basic material is less "developed," less pulled apart, than it is placed, more or less intact, into a new rhythmic, textural, and harmonic context.[10] The transformations in op. 7 show clearly how Schoenberg seeks to link his work with nineteenth-century models, despite a style that is at other moments relentlessly developmental and modern.

The final part of the first recapitulation is occupied by energetic working of the transition theme and an extraordinary modulation from the dominant of F to that of G♭. From this, the scherzo theme emerges as a triumphant transformation of motives *a* and *b* (ex. 8.5). It is in a $\frac{3}{4}$ meter overlaid by a broad $\frac{3}{2}$—a hemiola characteristic of Brahms and early Schoenberg. The scherzo arrives as the goal of a long, virtually continuous, process extending back some eight minutes in real playing time, to the beginning of the transition. And it is primarily a thematic, not a harmonic process. The cadence to G♭ major is not prepared in any traditional sense. Indeed, it is intended to shock, and, by offsetting or contradicting the smooth thematic evolution, to help mark off the beginning of an important new formal segment of the quartet. In this regard, it seems significant that (as will be shown below) the scherzo theme was originally drafted in B♭, a key area much closer to the tonic D minor; only later did Schoenberg create a harmonic disjunction to demarcate the formal boundary.

The First Group: Thematic Aspects

In the discussion up to this point, I have concentrated on what might be called the higher-level thematic process, which shapes the broader segments of the form. The quartet is as intensely "thematic" on the more local level, as can be seen in the first group (mm. 1–96; first portion reproduced in Appendix ex. Q). The later Schoenberg, even the composer of the First Chamber Symphony of

10. On the basic distinctions between thematic transformation and development, see Frisch 1984, ch. 2, and Friedheim 1963, 13–14.

1906, would undoubtedly have deemed excessive the first group's duration of two and a half minutes and the numerous varied repetitions of the main theme; but for the Schoenberg of 1904, such breadth was necessary to assure the comprehensibility and memorability of the basic thematic material of the quartet.

The structure of the first group is a fascinating hybrid or interweaving of what might be called strophic form, in which the main theme is subjected to successive variation, and ternary form, which has a contrasting middle section. (We have seen how Schoenberg used ternary form for the first group of the first movement of his D-Major Quartet [chapter 2] and how he modified it for many of the thematic statements of *Verklärte Nacht* [chapter 5].) Emphatic statements of the main, or A, theme are placed like pillars at roughly thirty-measure (or, in real time, fifty-second) intervals: A (m. 1), A′ (m. 30), A″ (m. 65). This structure comprises the strophic aspect of the first group. But A′ also serves to some extent as a contrasting middle section in that A and A″ begin firmly in the tonic, D minor, while A′ contains statements of the theme outside (literally, around) the tonic, in E♭ minor (m. 30) and C♯ minor (m. 54), as well as an extensive developmental segment (from about m. 37 on).

Another ternary aspect of the structure of the first group is suggested by the contrasting (but related) material beginning at m. 14, in the key of B♭ minor. When this section is followed by the return of the A theme (as A′) in m. 30, we are inclined to hear a conventional ABA′ form: A (m. 1), B (m. 14), A′ (m. 30). But as the first theme group continues to unfold, this smaller ternary form becomes nested, or subsumed, into the larger strophic structure.[11]

As was pointed out long ago by Berg in his renowned essay on Schoenberg's quartet, the opening "theme" of op. 7 actually consists (as in the song *Verlassen*) of three separate lines, which come to be treated independently (Reich 1965, 199).[12] This opening thematic complex (Appendix ex. Q) extends thirteen measures and consists of two related segments, which we can call x (m. 1 through beat 3 of m. 8) and y (beat 4 of m. 8 through 13). (Measures 7–8 are really transitional, serving both to continue elements of x and to introduce the sixteenth-note motion that is characteristic of y.) In the areas of phrase structure and metric-rhythmic manipulation, this thematic complex goes well beyond opp. 4 and 5.

Berg analyzed what I call x^1 as comprising two phrases of two and a half mea-

11. This embedding of formal structures within one another is discussed by Michael Cherlin in a stimulating unpublished study, "Formal Problems in Schoenberg's First String Quartet," prepared as a seminar paper at Yale University in 1980. I am grateful to Professor Cherlin for sharing his essay with me.

12. Berg's essay, "Warum ist Schönbergs Musik so schwer verständlich," first appeared in 1924 in a special issue (*Sonderheft*) of the Viennese journal *Musikblätter des Anbruch*, devoted to Schoenberg (*Arnold Schönberg zum fünfzigsten Geburtstage*). It has been translated three times: in *Music Review* 13 (1952): 187–96; in Reich 1965, 189–204 (from which my citations are taken); and in Rauchhaupt 1971, 20–30.

EXAMPLE 8.6 Berg's analysis of the main theme from Schoenberg's First String Quartet, op. 7 (from Reich 1965, 191).

sures each (ex. 8.6); he pointed with admiration (as his teacher Schoenberg would do to themes in Brahms) to Schoenberg's avoidance of the conventional two- or four-measure unit. In fact, the structure is more intricate than Berg suggests. The basic phrase cannot be said to end in midair on the D of m. 3, as Berg's parsing suggests, but on the low E that follows. Such an interpretation—of the E as the conclusion of the phrase—is borne out by the slur linking the D and E (in the real score) and by the diminuendo across beats 2–4 of m. 3.[13]

And yet there is an important element of accuracy in Berg's analysis. Classical-romantic practice would lead us to expect a second phrase beginning on the low E, the note that corresponds in duration and in register to the D of m. 1. A second or consequent phrase built as a sequence of the first and beginning on the supertonic degree is a time-honored device for opening themes (for example, the first Allegro theme of Beethoven's First Symphony, or of Brahms's Second). In his cheeky rewrite of Schoenberg's theme, intended to smooth out the irregularities, Berg puts it in exactly such a form: two two-measure phrases, the second beginning on the second degree (Reich 1965, 193). (Even here, however, there is overlap, since the E is still heard as conclusion to the first phrase.) Schoenberg is clearly playing upon such an expectation here: the note E remains tantalizingly ambiguous, both an ending and a beginning. In this sense it functions like section A′ of the first group, looking both backward and forward.

Each of the two lower elements of the theme falls into a phrase structure (and relationship to the notated bar line) different from x^1. The viola part, x^2, unfolds in regular one-measure units. The bass, x^3, consists, like x^1, of two essentially sequential phrases, but the second phrase (up a minor third from the opening pitch D) begins in beat 2 of m. 4, well after the beginning of the second phrase of x^1. Thus, the second phrases of x^1 and x^3 lie differently with respect to each other than did the first phrases.

By m. 6 the original metrical alignment of x^1 is restored: the dotted figure D–E is now in its original position on the fourth beat (like the C♯–D in m. 1). In m.

13. For further discussion of the structure of this theme and of its genesis as reflected in the sketches for op. 7, see Frisch 1984, 165–69.

7 all parts begin clearly and emphatically on the notated downbeat with what is the first real development of *x* material. As Berg plausibly suggested, the top line here is like a compressed version of x^1 (Reich 1965, 192). Now the elusive pitch E is fully integrated into the theme. The bottom line is clearly a variant, in dotted rhythm, of the portion of x^3 that descends from the B♭ on beat 3 of m. 2.

After this measure, Schoenberg builds to the climax of the A theme by introducing essentially new material (hence *y*). Each of the three elements is distinct from what has preceded it: the top line (y^1), in which an essentially stepwise descent (F–E♭–D–D♭–C–B♮–B♭–A♮–G♯) is decorated by leaps; the middle part with parallel quintuplets (y^2); and the starkly rising arpeggiation of the bass line (y^3). The accented fourth beats of mm. 8 and 10 serve to upset the metrical grid that had begun to be restored in mm. 7–8. The *y* theme is repeated sequentially up a major third (beat 4 of m. 10), then extended (mm. 12–13) and broken off.

Unlike a conventional contrasting B section in a ternary group, B begins in m. 14 almost as if resuming the development of *x*, which has been interrupted by *y*. The top part seems to pick up rhythmically in the second measure of x^1, as does the bass in the second measure of x^3. The viola line has the rhythm and the tremolo of x^2, but the pitch structure of x^3. Just as the first half of B is a recollection or development of *x*, so too its continuation in mm. 19–24 is clearly based on *y*. The chromatically descending line y^1 is now augmented to quarter-note triplets; the sixteenth-note quintuplets of y^2 have become eighth-note ones. Only at the very end of B, with the "etwas langsamer" theme of m. 24, does Schoenberg introduce genuinely contrasting material (*z*); this, however, gives way almost immediately to A′.

In A′ the original *x* returns, but with its outer parts inverted: x^1 is now the bass, x^3 the melody. In its eighth measure, the restatement of *x* veers away from its initial form into an extended contrapuntal development of material from A (*x*, *y*, and *z*) and B. The arrival of the A theme in D minor at m. 65, with its components in their original position (x^1 on the top, x^3 on the bottom) signals the real return within the first group; because of the extensive development that has preceded in A′, the return is especially forceful. It leads to a full liquidation of A material.

The First Group: Harmonic Aspects

The thematic process of the first group rides on the surface of, and of course helps to generate, a chromatic harmony that is no less volatile. In his 1924 essay Berg presents a harmonic skeleton of the first ten measures of op. 7 in what he calls "chorale style" (ex. 8.7). He attempts to show that despite the profusion of chords that occurs within a short space, all represented in half notes in his example, "there is no single sonority, not even on the unaccented semiquavers

EXAMPLE 8.7 Berg's "chorale" or harmonic reduction of the first theme of Schoenberg's First String Quartet, op. 7 (from Reich 1965, 197).

[eighth-notes] of these ten quartet bars, that cannot be immediately clear to any ear educated in the harmony of the last century" (Reich 1965, 198). As Christopher Wintle has shown, many of the verticalities in Berg's chorale can be explained along the lines of Schoenberg's own *Theory of Harmony*, as chromatic alterations of certain basic chords (Wintle 1980, 52–55). And although, as Wintle also suggests, Berg's harmonies are sometimes dubious representations of what seems actually to be happening in the music, the chorale nevertheless offers a good starting point for an assessment of the local-level harmonic component of op. 7.

One of the striking things about the quartet—and this is readily apparent at the opening—is the avoidance of functional dominants on the small scale and the concomitant pervasiveness of vagrant harmonies. Berg's chorale displays a dominant-seventh harmony across (his) mm. 5–7; although the harmony is somewhat obscured by the motion of the voices, it is explicit in the first half of

m. 6 and throughout m. 7. In the actual piece, this dominant is even less apparent, and less structural. Although the A in the bass on the last eighth note of Schoenberg's m. 2 supports a C♯ and G in the viola, the first violin sustains F. When this F resolves to E, the viola part moves on to D and B♭, and thus away from the dominant.

The harmonic goal of the first phrase is not the elusive dominant, but the ii^6_5 half-diminished chord supporting the first violin's E of m. 3, the note that, as has been suggested above, represents both the melodic end point of the first phrase (x^1) and the beginning of the second. The ii^6_5 chord is, as we have seen, one of Schoenberg's favorite and most versatile vagrant chords. As early as the song *Mädchenfrühling* of 1897 (see chapter 3), he exploited its potential for ambiguity by thwarting its tendency to move to the dominant. In the opening measures of op. 7, the ambivalence of this chord becomes a direct counterpart or corollary to the fluid phrase structure: the ii^6_5 is a kind of free agent, as "vagrant" in its function as is the melodic E that it underpins.

Across the A portion of the first group, Schoenberg's strategy seems to be to increase the level of dissonance and chromaticism progressively. The B♭-A seventh, which is sustained between the outer parts for two full beats in m. 5 and supports a VI^7 harmony, is the most powerful or prominent dissonance up to this point. From here the next two measures sound a range of vagrant harmonies, including diminished chords on the downbeats of mm. 6 and 7. The half-diminished ii^7, now in root position, reappears on the downbeat of m. 8; on the fourth beat, the root E♮ drops suddenly to E♭, against which sounds a ninth, F, high in the first violin. From the registral and harmonic standpoints, this is the most intense sonority yet to appear: all six notes of the whole-tone scale are sounded on this beat. Through m. 9, whole-tone chords alternate with dominant sevenths and a diminished seventh, as shown in ex. 8.8; the *y* theme cuts off abruptly on another whole-tone sonority on the downbeat of m. 10. The bass that underpins this extraordinary progression (y^3) moves by fifth and third in alternation: E♭–A♭ / C–F / A–D–F♯. Despite the cadential, dominant-sounding fifth resolutions, this progression cannot be explained in traditional terms. The bass can be said to outline interlocking triads of, respectively, A♭ major, F minor, F major, D minor, and D major. The roots of these triads spell out a diminished triad, A♭–F–D, and thus project horizontally the principal vagrant harmony of the first group.

The two-beat silence of m. 10 is shattering in effect: the musical discourse seems paralyzed or frozen by the disorienting harmonic-thematic spiral of theme *y*. The shock is then intensified, rather than dissipated, by the sequential repetition of *y* up a major third (and now *fortissimo*). The use of exact sequence (it is exact up to m. 12) is rare in Schoenberg's works after 1900, and is especially strik-

EXAMPLE 8.8 First String Quartet, op. 7, alternation of whole-tone and seventh chords in mm. 8–10.

EXAMPLE 8.9 Derivation and resolution of six-note whole-tone chord, from Schoenberg 1978, p. 392 (ex. 323).

ing in view of the negative opinion he often takes of it in his writings (see, for example, Schoenberg 1975, 129–31). Here the sequence seems specifically intended to exaggerate or prolong the disruption represented by *y*.

The combination of vagrant harmonies with fifth motion in the bass is reminiscent of certain works of 1899 and 1900, especially the song *Jesus bettelt* from op. 2 (see chapter 4) and Tove's "Du sendest mir einen Liebesblick" from *Gurre-lieder* (see chapter 6). However, the whole-tone complex now plays a greater role, and does so in a way that has important implications for Schoenberg's compositional language in 1904–5. In op. 7, Schoenberg does not treat the whole-tone scale/chord as a purely symmetrical, rootless phenomenon. It is used less to weaken or loosen tonal implications than to intensify chromatic and vagrant harmonies. By resolving the whole-tone harmonies of mm. 8–9 emphatically up by fourth, as if they *were* dominant chords, Schoenberg seems to stress their functional aspect.

It is essential in this context to consider Schoenberg's discussion of whole tones in *Theory of Harmony*, where a chord containing all six notes of the whole-tone scale is derived from a dominant ninth, by "simultaneously raising and lowering the fifth" (Schoenberg 1978, 392). This ninth chord is then resolved by fifth, like a normal dominant, as in ex. 8.9. This resolution can be compared with those in theme *y* of op. 7, as shown in the first four chords of ex. 8.8. (In ex. 8.8 the

EXAMPLE 8.10 First String Quartet, op. 7, transition to return of main theme (A″).

whole-tone chords are represented with four, not six, notes; but, as suggested earlier, all six notes of the scale are in fact sounded in the music, where the effect and function are similar to Schoenberg's *Theory of Harmony* example.) This root-oriented view of even the most vagrant chords is fully characteristic of Schoenberg. As with any chord discussed in *Theory of Harmony*, he stresses the way in which the whole-tone sonorities are to be resolved and linked with other harmonies. In this respect he contrasts his own early compositions with those of his contemporaries:

> Debussy uses this chord and scale more in the sense of impressionistic expressive devices, somewhat as a tone color (so does Strauss in *Salome*); but they entered my work more for the sake of their harmonic and melodic possibilities: the chords for the sake of their connection with other chords, the scale for the sake of its peculiar influence on the melody.
>
> SCHOENBERG 1978, 393

The role of the whole-tone complex in op. 7 as intensification, rather than dissolution, of diatonic-chromatic relations is reinforced at the transition to A″ in the first group (ex. 8.10). After the imitative statement of the main theme beginning on C♯ minor (m. 54, not shown in the example), the harmony arrives at a chord like a German sixth on A♯/B♭ (mm. 59–60). This chord resolves more or less normally, as an augmented sixth, to a V^7 of D (mm. 60–61); but the dominant does not resolve directly to the tonic. Instead the bass A is pushed back up to B♭ on the downbeat of m. 62. On the second beat, above the B♭, the upper parts form a four-part whole-tone chord (B♭–D–F♯–G♯), which then breaks off into a run containing all notes of the whole-tone scale. The scale here is literally generated from the kind of whole-tone chord that in his *Theory of Harmony* Schoenberg calls a dominant seventh with augmented fifth (Schoenberg 1978, 391). In his ex. 319a and b, Schoenberg derives the whole-tone scale by stepping between the tones of precisely this chord. Like the whole-tone harmonies of mm. 8–9, the whole-tone scale of mm. 62–63 is made to grow out of, and thus to heighten, the preceding chromaticism.

The whole-tone scale breaks off abruptly in m. 63; the reappearance of the main theme in D minor is preceded in m. 64 by a transitional measure identical with the first measure of x^2 (see ex. 8.10). Schoenberg's use of this thematic fragment as a transition is a masterstroke, for it serves genuinely to mediate between the preceding whole-tone scale and the subsequent D-minor return. Whole-tone elements are still present in the C–B♭–G♯ scalar descent of x^2, but Schoenberg introduces two notes that significantly form part, *not* of the whole-tone scale, but of the tonic triad: A (also the dominant) and F♮. When the main theme resumes in m. 65, x^2 retreats to its original position in an inner part (it is varied in sixteenth notes in the second violin). But now we hear x^2—and, consequently, the whole of the main theme—differently, since in the preceding measure it has evolved directly from the whole-tone scale. In this regard the "reborn" x^2 now fulfills a role barely suggested at the opening of the quartet.

Here we might do well to glance back at Berg's chorale (ex. 8.7), where the harmonic reduction of the second half of Schoenberg's m. 1 (the first half of m. 2 in the chorale) reveals a whole-tone chord of the French sixth type, with E in the bass. Berg's harmonic entity may not at first seem an accurate rendering of Schoenberg's music, since it freezes into a fictional simultaneity two pitches, B♭ and G♯ of x^2, that are presented successively as chromatic neighbors to the A. And yet it is precisely this simultaneity displayed by Berg that is incorporated into the whole-tone chord on the second beat of m. 9 of the quartet (the downbeat of m. 23 in Berg's chorale) and that is contained as well in the whole-tone scale of mm. 62–63.[14] By reiterating x^2 alone as a transitional gesture in m. 64, Schoenberg in effect realizes its original whole-tone implications.

The whole process is a splendid example of the intimate, reciprocal relationship between the vertical and horizontal dimensions—betweeen "harmony" and

14. The relation of the whole-tone chord of m. 2 of Berg's chorale to that of m. 23 has been pointed out by Wintle (1980, 54).

"theme"—in the quartet. What begins as an apparently linear, thematic detail in the viola part of m. 1 becomes a harmonic element in the whole-tone sonorities of mm. 8–9, then evolves back into the former role with the whole-tone scale of mm. 62–63.

Sketches: The Genesis of Op. 7

Schoenberg was occupied with the D-Minor Quartet intermittently for over a year and a half, from the spring of 1904 to the fall of 1905. More sketches survive for this than for any other early work, and they bear separate consideration here for the richly detailed and suggestive—if not always easily decipherable—picture offered of how Schoenberg planned his most ambitious large-scale instrumental work to date. Perhaps the strongest impression gained from such a study is how intensively Schoenberg labored to create the dense web of thematic interconnections—what I have above called the large-scale thematic process.

With the exception of a handful of loose leaves, all the extant preliminary graphic activity for op. 7 is contained on almost 100 pages in the two sketchbooks (I and II) that Schoenberg used consecutively in the years 1904–6. In the critical report for the D-Minor Quartet in *SW* (B20: 1–13), Schmidt divides the material in the sketchbooks into two categories, a "first fair copy" *(erste Niederschrift)* and "sketches" *(Skizzen)*. The former constitutes a nearly complete full-score draft of the work, although not a continuous one, since the music is distributed widely over the sketchbooks and sections are connected by Schoenberg with numerous "VI-DE" cross-references. (The final fair copy of the score, which served as *Stichvorlage*, is a separate autograph at the Library of Congress, dated 29 September 1905 at the end.) The latter category includes every other kind of musical jotting not part of the first fair copy.

On the whole, the sketchbooks bear out Schoenberg's own testimony about the composition of the quartet. In the essay "Heart and Brain in Music" (1947), he noted, "I personally belong to those who generally write very fast, whether it is 'cerebral' counterpoint or 'spontaneous' melody" (Schoenberg 1975, 55). He implies that this was the case with the composition of the D-Minor Quartet: "Some forty years ago I was composing my First String Quartet, Op. 7. Usually taking morning walks, I composed in my mind 40 to 80 measures complete in almost every detail. I needed only two or three hours to copy down these larger sections from memory" (ibid., 61).

These "larger sections" would correspond to what Schmidt has called the first fair copy (although neither he nor Schoenberg accounts for why these sections appear so scattered, and their sequence so jumbled, in the sketchbooks). But in addition to these segments, the sketchbooks contain several smaller fragments, usually of only a few bars, in which Schoenberg is clearly engaging less in active

TABLE 9 Overview of Sketches for Schoenberg's First String Quartet, op. 7

Sketch pages	*Portion of work sketched*
Sketchbook I	
4–17	first group
18–30	other compositions
31	scherzo
32	second group
33	transition
34–60	first group—transition—second group—dev. 1—recap. 1
Sketchbook II	
1–16	scherzo—trio
17–18	scherzo reprise / dev. 2
19–20	slow movement—finale
21–27	slow movement
29–39	trio—scherzo repr. / dev. 2—recap. 2
39–60	slow movement—recap. 3—finale—coda

Italicized numbers indicate most significant concept sketches. Sketchbook I was begun in March 1904 and completed on 20 April 1905; sketchbook II was begun in April 1905, and the quartet completed on 29 September 1905.

"composition" than in reflective or exploratory work. Following Alan Tyson's term for certain of Beethoven's similar jottings, we may call these "concept" sketches (Tyson 1970, 68–69), although it is important to note (and will be shown) that Schoenberg's concept sketches tend to appear in coherent groups, while Beethoven's are usually more isolated. If we assume that the order of the material as set down in the sketchbooks for the most part represents the order in which Schoenberg conceived or drafted it—and I think it is reasonable to do so, since the books were bound before any entries were made—then a fascinating sequence of creation emerges. Table 9 shows the position of these concept sketches within the sketchbooks and their relation to the formal scheme outlined in table 8.[15] Pages with the most significant concept sketches are indicated in italics. These represent what I believe to be the "crisis" points in Schoenberg's draft-

15. The dates given in table 9 are taken from Schoenberg's own annotations in the sketchbooks. When referring to a particular sketch, I shall for the convenience of the reader provide a reference to the transcription in *SW*, including (in brackets) the "S" number assigned by the editor, Schmidt, to each sketch. My own readings occasionally differ in details from Schmidt's.

EXAMPLE 8.11 First String Quartet, op. 7, sketch for scherzo theme, in Sketchbook I, p. 31.

ing of the quartet, moments at which the generally smooth flow of composition was interrupted.

After working out much of the first group on I/4–17 (Sketchbook I, pp. 4–17), Schoenberg set aside the quartet to work on other projects, principally the songs that were to become op. 8.[16] Some fourteen pages later, he returned to op. 7, but did not, as we might expect, pick up where he left off, in the first group. He began instead to sketch the scherzo theme, well in advance of its eventual appearance. The theme appears in short score in the key of B♭ (as transcribed in ex. 8.11; *SW* B20: 67 [S12]). Despite its tonality (briefly discussed above) and certain striking differences of harmony and voice-leading, the theme is quite close to its final form. After six measures the sketch trails off to only the top part, and it ends altogether after sixteen measures. The rest of the page is occupied by brief sketches of possible developments or continuations of the scherzo.

Schoenberg attempted no larger draft of the scherzo at this point, but began instead to work immediately on the second group, another step backward to his previous stopping point. The first concept sketches appear in short score on the following page, I/32;[17] the sketches for the second theme are partially transcribed in ex. 8.12 (*SW* B20: 52–53 [S22–23]). In its initial form, ex. 8.12a, the theme makes no apparent reference to motives *b* and *c*; the principal melody and the bass part lack the syncopation characteristic of these motives. Schoenberg thus seems to work more from a harmonic skeleton than from a fully thematic conception. Directly beneath this sketch, however, Schoenberg in effect "thematicizes" the same passage (ex. 8.12b). The top line is now much closer to *c*; the bass syncopation, which derives from motive *a*, is added in the margin of the sketch leaf and thus appears to be an afterthought. It was most likely tacked on some-

16. This would have been in mid July 1904. In a letter to Oskar Posa written on 13 July, Schoenberg notes that he has begun a new orchestral song and has set aside the quartet for the time being: "Mein Quartett ruht. Vielleicht komme ich aber doch noch dazu" (cited in Szmolyan 1974, 193.)

17. A facsimile reproduction of this sketch page appears in Frisch 1988a, 300.

EXAMPLE 8.12 First String Quartet, op. 7, sketches for second group, in Sketchbook I, p. 32.

a.

b.

what later, after Schoenberg had continued his conceptual path back through the exposition of the first movement.[18]

Schoenberg now abandoned the second group to work on the transition. First he jotted down in a very light pencil the scherzo theme itself, in triple meter and still (by implication) in the key of B♭ (*SW* B20: 44 [S17]). He probably did this as a reminder, to keep the theme visually before him.[19] Beneath it appears the first concept sketch for the transition (ex. 8.13; *SW* B20: 44 [S19]), in which Schoenberg recast the scherzo theme, with both its *a* and *b* motives, in quadruple meter

18. Schmidt has suggested that a sketch with the G-major key signature on staves 2–3 of p. 32 (*SW* B20: 52 [S16]) is a *Vorentwurf* for the second group. I am not persuaded by this argument, since this sketch bears no resemblance to the final form of the theme and has no significant trace of motives *b* or *c*. It might be entirely unrelated to op. 7. Schmidt's conjecture, however, would support my broader thesis that the idea of thematicizing the second group—and making it relate to the scherzo and transition—did not occur to Schoenberg immediately. Schmidt has also proposed that the sketch on staves 6–7 (*SW* B20: 71 [S20]) is related to the trio of the scherzo. This seems even less likely than the previously mentioned hypothesis, since the trio is (like most pieces of the genre) in triple meter and is a transformation of the scherzo. The sketch is clearly in 4/4 and manifests no obvious derivation from the scherzo; it is probably unrelated to op. 7.

19. A similar phenomenon is to be found in the sketches for the First Chamber Symphony, op. 9, in Sketchbook II. In the midst of sketches for the development section, Schoenberg wrote out the first two measures of the secondary theme of the exposition (mm. 84–85). Schmidt suggests plausibly that this jotting represents an aide-mémoire (*Gedächtnisstütze*), since the head motive of this theme plays an important role in this particular passage of the development (*SW* B11/II: 65).

EXAMPLE 8.13 First String Quartet, op. 7, sketch for transition theme, in Sketchbook I, p. 32.

EXAMPLE 8.14 First String Quartet, op. 7, sketch for motive *b*, in Sketchbook I, p. 33.

and in something like the chromatic form it would assume in the transition. Motive *b*, however, still ascends by whole step, C♯–E♭–F♮ (in mm. 3–4), rather than by semitone.[20]

On the next page of the sketchbook, I/33, Schoenberg began to sketch the transition in earnest by separating and actually labeling the component parts of the transformed scherzo theme, *a*, *b*, and *c*.[21] At the upper left of the page, we find motive *b* isolated (ex. 8.14; *SW* B20: 44 [S24]). This is very much like the *b* subject of the actual transition, beginning with the syncopation and the downward leap of a diminished fifth. But the disjunct leaps of the continuation (F–D♭–G♭–C♭) still show the immediate derivation from the second half of the scherzo theme and from the transformation of that theme sketched on the preceding page. Beside this fragment, in short score, is a first, six-measure mini-draft of the transition itself (ex. 8.15; *SW* B20: 46 [S25]), in which the imitative texture and all the thematic material are present, including a new motive, *c*, which Schoenberg has derived from the syncopations in the second theme on the previous page (see above, ex. 8.12). Schoenberg has himself now labeled the motives *a*, *b*, and *c*. Motive *b* still has a prominent whole step (G♭–A♭, in m. 2); its ascent does not yet consist only of half-steps.

On the remainder of this page, we see the "cerebral" Schoenberg trying out various three-part combinations of the motives in four more short sketches.[22] At

20. In S19, Schmidt mistakenly interprets the E in m. 4 of the sketch as a natural; the accidental preceding it is clearly a flat.

21. A facsimile reproduction of this page appears in Frisch 1988a, 301.

22. For transcriptions of these sketches, see *SW* B20: 45–48. Related sketching activity for the transition—in which Schoenberg tries out various combinations of the motives labeled *a*, *b*, and *c*—is found on two loose leaves and in a pocket sketchbook, which must have been used concurrently with Sketchbook I. These sketches are transcribed in *SW* B20: 44–51. In one sketch (S134), Schoenberg wrote out the scherzo theme in its original form, apparently again as an aide-mémoire.

EXAMPLE 8.15 First String Quartet, op. 7, sketch for transition, in Sketchbook I, p. 33.

some point during, or soon after, his work on this page—that is, after isolating motive *b*—Schoenberg turned back to I/32 and added the syncopated measure in the margin for the bass part of the second theme (above, ex. 8.12). He thus tightened the net of thematic associations between this theme, the transition, and the scherzo still further. He also confirmed the final form of motive *b*, with ascending semitones (here C♯–D–E♭, in the viola).

In his critical and theoretical writings Schoenberg often stresses that a motivic or thematic idea must have generative power—that all the events of a piece must be implicit in, or foreseen in, the basic shape, or *Grundgestalt*, presented at the opening.[23] In some of the exercises in his textbook *Fundamentals of Musical Composition*, he shows student composers how to elaborate an initial motive into an entire small work (Schoenberg 1967, 64–67). The transition, second group, development, and scherzo of the D-Minor Quartet can be heard as an extremely sophisticated example of this process on a massive scale. But the series of sketch pages (I/31–33) we have just examined suggests that the hearing and the making were hardly as congruent as Schoenberg's textbook (or his own statements on the creative process) might suggest. The "basic shape" from which Schoenberg forged this particular complex of thematic material was the scherzo theme. The

23. See, for example, his remarks in the essay "Linear Counterpoint," where he postulates: "'Whatever happens in a piece of music is nothing but the endless reshaping of a basic shape.' Or, in other words, there is nothing in a piece of music but what comes from the theme, springs from it and can be traced back to it; to put it still more severely, nothing but the theme itself. Or, all the shapes appearing in a piece of music are *foreseen* in the 'theme'" (Schoenberg 1975, 290).

EXAMPLE 8.16 First String Quartet, op. 7.

a. Slow movement

b. Finale

compositional process appears to have involved a gradual chromaticization of a diatonic scherzo theme into the transition theme—a process that is then reversed in the actual quartet, where the scherzo is made to serve as the culmination, rather than the germination.

With these three pages of concept sketches, Schoenberg resolved many of the problems of creating a thematically integrated and continuous form. He now returned to the first group and, on I/34–II/16, wrote out an extensive and more or less continuous draft of the entire first half of the quartet, through the trio. The matter of thematic and formal logic arose again, however, as Schoenberg planned the second half of the quartet. As table 9 suggests, the steady flow of composition came to a halt on II/16, at the beginning of the passage that was to serve as both scherzo recapitulation and second development. Schoenberg had here to reconcile two demands: that of the larger sonata-form design, which necessitated the further development of earlier material, and that of the individual movement, which required a symmetrical restatement of the scherzo theme.

He also began to think—or at least set down the first evidence of that thinking—about the shape that the latter part of the quartet would take. Here as well there were potentially conflicting demands. A slow movement and finale had to have sufficient independence as movements; yet to fulfill their role in the larger sonata-form design, they had also to recapitulate earlier material. Schoenberg's ultimate answer was to fashion the main theme of the slow movement of op. 7 (ex. 8.16a) as essentially new material. Unlike the scherzo, it does not grow out of or emerge from any obvious thematic process. Indeed, the slow movement comes as a distinct contrast or relaxation after the recapitulation and intense liquidation of the first theme. The main theme of the finale is virtually a Lisztian transformation of the slow movement, whose first six measures are taken over note for note (ex. 8.16b).

This ingenious formal and thematic design was anything but obvious to Schoenberg when he was at II/18 of the sketches, as he broke off a tentative attempt at the scherzo recapitulation to draft a slow movement (see ex. 8.17; the sketch is fully transcribed in *SW* B20: 78–79 [S75]). This fragment, in the key of B♭ minor, extends thirty-nine measures in full score. Unlike the eventual theme of the slow movement, this one is based entirely on material from the second group of the exposition and from development 1. It begins with eight measures of syncopated chordal accompaniment (ex. 8.17a), whose characteristic "sighing" appoggiatura figure derives from development 1 [**B**14]. In m. 9 the first violin enters with a melody derived quite clearly from the oscillating syncopated half-steps of motive *c*, as heard in the principal theme of the second group (cf. ex. 8.12b). After a cadence to B♭ minor (ex. 8.17b), the violin sustains D♭ while the lower parts introduce the other main theme of the second group (from m. 61), in its original $\frac{6}{4}$ meter. As the first violin resumes its melodic status, the lower parts continue in $\frac{6}{4}$, with the sighing figure. After another cadence to B♭ minor in m. 33, and two bars of transition, the second violin begins the original theme (ex. 8.17c), accompanied by a new decorative figure in the first violin. Although the sketch trails off here, there is enough to suggest that, like the scherzo recapitulation sketched on the previous pages, this passage was to serve a dual function, as both slow movement and recapitulation of the second group.

Schoenberg's mind turned now to the last movement. Directly beneath this slow movement fragment, we find the first sketches for the finale theme. There are three, one above the other (excerpted in 8.18a, b, c; *SW* B20: 87–88 [S77–79]). The first, in A major, has lithe, energetic eighth notes. The second, still in A, slows down the motion and eliminates the melodic diminution; the theme now has also the beginnings of an accompaniment. The third sketch transposes the second to D major, the tonic of the work as a whole. In ex. 8.18b and c, the theme is quite close to its final form, except for the contour of the opening three-note figure, which here is a transformation of motive *b*, a descending leap followed by a chromatic ascent. As in the preceding draft of the slow movement, then, Schoenberg was deriving his thematic material exclusively (and audibly) from the first movement of the quartet. But this logical chain of thematic associations did not satisfy him. Indeed, he may have felt that he had linked that chain too tightly, that his quartet lacked enough genuine contrast.

He broke off these concept sketches for the finale and, on the next page, II/21, began a draft in full score of the slow movement as we now know it. Its theme is clearly related to the finale theme just sketched, but any direct association with motive *b* has been eliminated. The opening three-note figure now repeats the first note and leaps down a fifth. It is thus essentially new thematic material. When

EXAMPLE 8.17 First String Quartet, op. 7, draft for slow movement, in Sketchbook II, pp. 19–20 (reduction).

a.

b.

c.

EXAMPLE 8.18 First String Quartet, op. 7, sketches for finale theme, in Sketchbook II, p. 20.

a.

b.

c.

Schoenberg came to write out the draft for the finale, beginning on II/42, he began to write the theme out as in ex. 8.18c, but then crossed out that version and rewrote the theme to bring it into conformity with the slow movement (see *SW* B20: 89–90 [S94]). As already demonstrated, the finale became an almost literal transformation of the slow movement.

Establishing this relationship between the slow movement and finale was, I believe, the last major conceptual problem Schoenberg encountered in planning the D-Minor Quartet.[24] He had found a way to give the second half of the quartet

24. The autograph score of the quartet, however, is far from a clean copy. It contains numerous revisions, most notably large cuts in development 1 and recapitulation 1 (see *SW* B20: 101–9).

(the portion after the fermata) its own thematic integrity or identity without abandoning its purely recapitulatory function in the larger sonata design.

That Schoenberg decided to cast the finale theme in A major, and not in D, as in the third of the concept sketches (ex. 8.18c), is highly suggestive from the viewpoint of large-scale tonal planning. Very much as in *Verklärte Nacht* and *Pelleas*, he was faced in the latter part of the quartet with the challenge of reestablishing the tonic by means of the kind of dominant relationships that had been largely absent up to this point. One way of generating dominant tension was to place the rondo theme in the key of A.

In fact, however, in none of its three main appearances (indicated by A, A′, and A″ in movement IV of table 8) does the rondo theme resolve directly to the tonic. The magisterial coda of the quartet may be said to assert, rather than achieve, D major. The coda is certainly successful on its own terms, but its effect is different from a conclusion that grows out of extensive dominant preparation. One suspects that for Schoenberg, placing the rondo theme of op. 7 in the key of the dominant was something of a gesture toward a compositional procedure he no longer could or would easily follow. In the next chapter, we shall consider a very similar gesture, one that also seems to have generated uncertainty on the composer's part, in the B-major slow segment near the end of the First Chamber Symphony.

Schoenberg and Reger: A Brief Comparison

In chapter 1 it was suggested that among the younger Brahmsians of the 1890s, Max Reger came the closest to Schoenberg in his assimilation of and response to the compositional techniques of Brahms. By 1904 both composers had moved well beyond overt imitation or emulation; basic Brahmsian precepts, such as dense thematic-motivic development and flexible phrase structure, were now put in the service of highly individual chromatic languages. Yet there remain strong and instructive points of contact between the styles of Reger and Schoenberg. These are perhaps especially apparent in the string quartets in the same key, D minor, written by both composers at this time.

Reger's D-Minor Quartet, op. 74, completed and published in 1904, just as Schoenberg was working on his own op. 7, is one of his most imposing and ambitious pieces of chamber music, lasting almost an hour in performance.[25] It would be impossible to prove any direct impact of the Reger work upon Schoenberg, who at any rate began work on op. 7 before he could have encountered

25. The timings given in Stein 1953, 139, total 58′: I, 24′; II, 4′30″; III, 19′30″; IV, 10′.

Reger's work (which appeared in the summer of 1904). Yet during the protracted composition of his own op. 7, Schoenberg may well have become familiar with, and interested in, Reger's op. 74.

The circumstances are as follows. Reger's quartet was to have been premiered at the annual Tonkünstlerfest of the Allgemeiner Deutscher Musikverein in Frankfurt in May 1904, but because of the illness of one of the players, the performance was postponed until December in Frankfurt (Stein 1953, 608).[26] That same summer, Schoenberg and several Viennese colleagues formed the Vereinigung schaffender Tonkünstler (Society of Creative Composers) and were on the lookout for works to program in their first (and in the event, only) season. Reger himself joined the Vereinigung in July and agreed to participate as pianist (playing Bach transcriptions) in a concert on 20 February 1905.[27] As is apparent from the Vereinigung's concert program of 20 January 1905 (a copy is held at the Arnold Schoenberg Institute), plans were changed somewhat for the February concert, which was now announced to include the Reger D-Minor Quartet, op. 74. At the actual concert, however, the quartet was not performed; the Violin Sonata in C Major, op. 72, was substituted, played by Arnold Rosé and Bruno Walter. Reger himself was almost certainly present, as he was in Vienna on 19–20 February to participate in an all-Reger concert of the Ansorge-Verein (Schreiber 1981, 283).

It is well known that Schoenberg found much to admire in Reger's music. In 1918–21 he programmed numerous Reger works—indeed, more than by any other composer—in the concerts of the Society for Private Musical Performances (see Szmolyan 1981, 84–96); in his writings he would refer to Reger sympathetically (see, e.g., Schoenberg 1975, 129–30, 427). It is certainly possible that as Schoenberg resumed work on his quartet after a pause during the summer of 1904, and as he continued to labor over problems of large-scale structure in ways that we have examined above, Reger's op. 74, especially its first movement, provided a powerful model for the integration of sonata style and large-scale form.

Reger's movement, cast in sonata form without repeated exposition, and lasting nonetheless over twenty minutes, is surely one of the most massive composed at the turn of the century. Carl Dahlhaus has rightly characterized it as having "truly symphonic proportions" (Dahlhaus 1989, 339). Although it forms part of a piece of chamber music, the movement is really comparable in scope and duration to the sonata-form first movements of Mahler's Second, Sixth, and Sev-

26. In the Schoenberg Collection at the Library of Congress there is an issue of the *Mittheilungen* of the Allegemeiner Deutscher Musikverein from May 1903, which announces Schoenberg as a new member of the society. There are also issues for August 1903 and for April and May 1904; the latter two announce the impending performance of the Reger quartet.

27. Letters from Oskar Posa to Schoenberg, 12 July and 26 August 1904, Schoenberg Collection, Library of Congress.

enth Symphonies. In a contemporary assessment of Reger, the critic Max Hehemann suggested that the first movement of op. 74 stood as one of the composer's masterpieces because of its "exceedingly fecund invention both in the chiseled thematic working and the splendid architectonic structure" (Hehemann 1905, 416).

Like Schoenberg, Reger relies strongly on large and distinct thematic pillars to give definition to the sonata structure.[28] The design of Reger's expansive exposition can be represented as:

First group, D minor, mm. 1–68
- theme 1a, m. 1
- theme 1b, m. 6
- 1a, m. 10
- 1b, m. 15
- 1a, m. 29
- transition, m. 34
- 1b, m. 49
- 1a, m. 55

Transition, mm. 69–90
Second theme, F major, mm. 91–116
Transition, mm. 117–38
Closing group, G♯ minor (ending in F major) mm. 139–77

Like many composers in the sonata tradition, Reger builds his large first group from two alternating and contrasting themes, but he greatly extends the process (to almost eight and a half minutes) and builds a considerable amount of variation and development into the thematic statements.

Reger's deployment and treatment of the 1a theme is similar to Schoenberg's in that the theme comes to represent a point of focus or orientation within the unfolding sonata form. Yet his developmental style is much less densely and continuously motivic than Schoenberg's. There is also much greater contrast between Reger's 1a and 1b than between Schoenberg's themes, which, as we have

28. An extended analysis of the first movement of Reger's op. 74 is contained in Mattner 1985, 28–49. See also the motivic analysis in Wilke 1980, 170–76. Reger himself provided a brief commentary/analysis in the journal *Die Musik* (Reger 1904), intended to introduce the work before its projected premiere in Frankfurt.

seen, tend continuously to rework the opening material. Moreover, despite the rampant chromaticism, Reger's overall plan is more conservative than Schoenberg's. Schoenberg tends to avoid certain traditional harmonic relationships: in the first group of op. 7, D minor does not lead to, and is not often supported by, the dominant A major or the relative major F. Schoenberg prefers the more unusual ♭VI and key areas that circumscribe the tonic by half-step. Reger by contrast employs both the dominant and its own dominant, as well as the relative major F, the key of the second group and of the ending of the exposition as a whole.

What Reger shares with Schoenberg—and what is, I think, rare among composers working in an advanced chromatic language and with larger instrumental forms at this time—is the ability to control broad spans with a fusion of harmonic tension, subtle phrase structure, and thematic construction. We have seen this on a small scale with Schoenberg's main theme; it is also readily apparent in the masterful second theme of Reger's movement (ex. 8.19). Reger's theme is wonderfully mobile in a way that seems quite close to the more homophonic segments of Schoenberg's quartet. The principal statement begins on F and moves at the halfway point to A minor (mm. 93–94). The second phrase concludes (or elides) in m. 99 on an E♭^{7} chord with an augmented fifth; this is the kind of dominant that, as we have seen, Schoenberg also tends to employ (in mm. 62–63), although he goes farther than Reger in the direction of exploiting its whole-tone possibilities. The repetition of the theme begins in m. 99 up a minor third, in A♭. It proceeds as a sequence of the original up to m. 103, where instead of a melodic E♭, supported by a C-minor chord, we get E♮ and an A$^{6}_{4}$ harmony. In this way Reger pulls or reins in the centripetal harmonic tendency and gradually moves back toward the original starting point, F major, which is reached, via a cadence from its own dominant, in m. 106.

The two phrases of Reger's theme overlap in a fashion not unlike those of the main theme of Schoenberg's quartet. Phrase 1 concludes with a half-cadence to A minor (locally iii). This harmony is reached on the last half of m. 94, but the melody note at this point, D, is dissonant with the chord. In fact, the C♮ of m. 95, part of the A-minor harmony, really serves as the end point of the descending line; it also serves (somewhat like the ambiguous E in Schoenberg's m. 3) as the beginning of the second phrase.

The junction between the second phrase of the theme and the counterstatement of the first is treated in a similar fashion. The high B♮ near the end of the phrase in m. 99 is dissonant with the E♭^{7} chord underneath. When this chord resolves to A♭ on the second half of the measure, the B moves up to the chord tone C. The C serves as both end point to the preceding phrase and as the beginning of the counterstatement. These techniques of phrase elision, and their coordination with harmonic processes, owe much to the fluid practices of Brahms. Both Reger

EXAMPLE 8.19 Max Reger, String Quartet in D Minor, op. 74, I, second theme.

and Schoenberg display here, as in their youthful works, a profound affinity with these principles and an ability to transmute them into personal styles of great integrity.

After the D-Minor Quartet

The completion of the D-Minor Quartet was followed by a period of Lieder composition almost as intense as that of 1903–4. If the compositional energies of songs like *Verlassen* can be said to have been channeled into op. 7, those of the quartet itself seem to have flowed out into the group of songs from the fall of 1905, including *Alles*, op. 6, no. 2 (6 September 1905); *Der Wanderer*, op. 6, no. 8 (15 October); *Am Wegrand*, op. 6, no. 6 (18 October); *Lockung*, op. 6, no. 7 (26 October); and *Mädchenlied*, op. 6, no. 3 (28 October). Also drafted at this time was the fragmentary programmatic piano quintet, *Ein Stelldichein*, based on a Dehmel poem (published as Schoenberg 1980).[29]

Schoenberg claimed to have composed the Dehmel song *Alles* "very fast," while waiting for music paper with which to finish copying the D-Minor Quartet.[30] It is remarkable for its use of invertible counterpoint in the manner of op. 7 and for the extremely ambiguous tonal language, which settles into the tonic A♭ only at the very end of the song. The first vocal phrase consists of three independent parts, of which the top two (voice and right hand of the piano) are related initially by free inversion. In the second phrase of the song, the lines are redistributed, as they are yet again at the return of the opening. Despite the elegant compositional technique, however, *Alles* is a curiously detached song, especially compared with the white-hot Dehmel settings of 1899.

Similar contrapuntal preoccupations are joined to a much more expressive language in *Am Wegrand*. The poem, by John Henry Mackay, which communicates alienation and despair in a manner not unlike Conradi's *Verlassen*, called forth an equally powerful response from Schoenberg. *Am Wegrand* shares the key of the quartet, D minor, and the wide-ranging, athletic opening melody of the voice seems cut from the same cloth as the main theme of op. 7. As in *Verlassen*, *Alles*, and the D-Minor Quartet, this melody forms part of a contapuntal complex that

29. It has been claimed by Allen Forte (1978, 138) that "set consciousness"—that is, an intentional use of unordered pitch-class sets—begins for Schoenberg with the op. 6 songs composed in the fall of 1905. Forte bases his suggestion principally on what he analyzes as a frequent recurrence in the songs of Schoenberg's "musical signature," a six-note set made up of the pitch equivalents of letters from the composer's last name. Forte's analyses seem to me farfetched, in that to find the signature, he must often acknowledge complementation, transposition, and inversion of the set, atonal operations with which Schoenberg is not likely to have been acquainted at this time.

30. See Newlin 1980, 63. Schoenberg does not mention *Alles* by name here, but it seems clear from the context of his remarks that he is referring to this song; there is no other song that corresponds in time to the final stages of the completion of the quartet in fall 1905.

EXAMPLE 8.20 *Am Wegrand*, op. 6, no. 6.

EXAMPLE 8.20 *continued*

c.

is subjected to inversion. From the three-note descending chromatic motive in the piano left hand (E♭–D–C♯; ex. 8.20a), *x*, Schoenberg derives a more extended melodic idea, *x′*, which at the first return of the opening (ex. 8.20b) is now placed in the voice, while the original vocal line, *y*, is in the bass.

Other similarities to the quartet are evident in Schoenberg's treatment of the main key. The opening bass motive, *x*, circumscribes the tonic D by semitone, a feature elaborated in the vocal version of the motive, *x′*. The upper half-step, E♭, plays a large role in the song, as it does in the first group of op. 7. It is to the key area of E♭ major that Schoenberg shifts suddenly in m. 15 for the setting of "Hier bin ich," the imagined answer to the poet's urgent search. Once introduced, the E♭ continues to permeate the D-minor tonality, especially at the first return in m. 22.

The introduction of the whole-tone complex in *Am Wegrand* is also related to procedures in op. 7. E♭ major collapses into a whole-tone environment in mm. 16–18. Here, unlike in op. 7, the whole-tone complex has the effect of dissolving or evaporating the tonality, rather than intensifying it. A bit later, however, at the approach to G minor in mm. 26–27, the whole-tone scale is used to enrich the dominant (ex. 8.20c), much as in the first group of op. 7. As in the example from *Theory of Harmony* cited above (ex. 8.9), the dominant appears in m. 26 with its fifth simultaneously raised and lowered (B♭–A♭). (Unlike in the *Theory of Harmony* example, the chord has no ninth.)

Schoenberg's creative rhythm in the period 1903–6 seems to have dictated an alternation between Lieder and instrumental works. The achievements of the songs of late 1905—the integration of whole-tone with diatonic-chromatic procedures in *Am Wegrand*; the contrapuntal intricacy of *Alles*; the "fluctuating" tonality, as Schoenberg called it, of *Lockung*, a song that "expresses an E♭-major tonality without once in the course of the piece giving an E♭-major triad in such a way that one could regard it as a pure tonic" (Schoenberg 1978, 383)—all these techniques were adumbrated to some degree in the D-Minor Quartet. They were to be carried over, in imaginative ways that Schoenberg himself could not have envisioned in 1905, into his next large-scale project, the First Chamber Symphony.

CHAPTER NINE

The First Chamber Symphony, op. 9 (1906)

Judging from the disposition of materials in Sketchbooks II and III, Schoenberg began work on the First Chamber Symphony sometime between the end of 1905—after the spate of post-quartet song composition—and April 1906. The piece was completed by midsummer: the date at the end of the sketches and drafts for op. 9 in Sketchbook III is 17 July 1906; that at the end of the autograph score, 25 July. The First Chamber Symphony thus seems to have had a relatively swift and unproblematic genesis in comparison with the First Quartet, to which it is in many respects the direct heir.[1] The larger formal design of op. 7 is here condensed into a structure about half as long. The basic plan is shown in table 10. The streamlining results largely from the presence of a single development and from the drastic compression of the individual "movements." Unlike in op. 7, the finale introduces no new themes, but is purely recapitulatory.

Timings from two of the best recent recordings of the Chamber Symphony are included in table 10 to indicate not only how compact the work is in relation to op. 7, but also how well-balanced the various segments are from the viewpoint of duration.[2] The two outer movements, which are of approximately equal du-

1. The publication history of op. 9, extending from 1912 to 1924, is slightly more complicated than its *Entstehungsgeschichte*. For full details, with a collation of the different printed sources, see *SW* B11/II: 14–28; see also Brinkmann 1977, 134–36.

2. It should be noted that neither recording comes anywhere near the fast tempi suggested by Schoenberg's metronome markings for the first movement in 1922 edition of the Chamber Symphony. At the "sehr rasch" of m. 5, Schoenberg indicates that a half note should equal about 104. Reinbert de Leeuw, whose tempi seem very fast indeed here, takes the half note somewhere between 80 and 84. Although de Leeuw's tempi in the fast parts of the piece are noticeably quicker than Giuseppe Sinopoli's, his slow movement takes almost half a minute longer.

My own final tallies for timings in table 10 differ slightly from the totals given on the record liners; the difference can be accounted for by the fact that I have added the individual sections or movements individually, not always taking the same measure as the recording engineers of the silences or pauses in between.

TABLE 10 Overall Formal Plan of Schoenberg's First Chamber Symphony, op. 9.

Section	Starting measure	Timings: Sinopoli[a]		de Leeuw[b]
First movement/exposition	1	4′54″	ca. 7/8′	4′17″
Transition	133	1′00″		57″
Scherzo	160	2′11″		1′49″
Development	280	3′30″		2′59″
Transition	368	1′10″		1′09″
Slow movement	378	2′45″	ca. 9′	3′14″
Episode/transition	415	1′00″		1′13″
Finale/recap.	435	5′03″		4′28″
TOTAL:		21′33″		20′06″

[a] Giuseppe Sinopoli and members of the Berlin Philharmonic (Deutsche Grammophon DB 4233072).
[b] Reinbert de Leeuw and the Schönberg-Ensemble (Koch-Schwann CD 311009 H1).

ration (4–5 minutes), are the lengthiest. As is suggested by the curved braces in the table, there is also greater balance, on either side of the central development and transition, between the first movement-transition-scherzo complex and the slow movement-transition-finale complex. (This balance is clearer in the timings of the recording by Sinopoli cited in table 10.)

Thematic and Formal Structure

The themes of op. 9 tend to be briefer, tauter, more compact than those of op. 7 (as has been observed by Brinkmann 1977, 138), but there are more of them. In the first movement, this profusion of material is accommodated within an ingenious design, which has not, to my knowledge, been previously clarified in print. Alban Berg (1921),[3] and most analysts following him (for example, Brink-

3. Following the printed catalog of Berg's manuscripts prepared by Rosemary Hilmar (Grasberger and Stefan 1980, 99–100), I give the publication date of Berg's *Thematische Analyse* as 1921. The pamphlet itself bears no imprint date. It may in fact have appeared well before 1921, since Berg's contract for it, still in the archives of Universal Edition, bears the date 4 May 1918. (I am grateful to Sabine Franz of Universal for providing me with a copy of this document.) According to Willi Reich, the *Analyse* was completed and published in 1918 to coincide with a series of ten open rehearsals of the Chamber Symphony led by Schoenberg in June of that year (Reich 1965, 45). The one letter in the Berg-Schoenberg correspondence that mentions the analysis (Berg 1987, 268) gives no information about publication.

TABLE 11 Plan of Exposition/First Movement of Schoenberg's First Chamber Symphony, op. 9.

Formal/thematic function	*Starting measure*	*Initial or primary key area*
Cadence 1 (=slow intro.)	1	F major
Horn motto	5	Fourths
Cadence 2	8	E major
Exposition I		
Theme 1a	10	E major
Theme I/1b	16	E major
Theme I/2	32	F minor
Transition+cad. 2	50	cad. to E major
Exposition II		
Theme 1a (=I/1a)	58	E major
Theme II/1b	68	E major
Theme II/1c	75	F major
Theme II/2	84	A major
Transition	106	F major
Codetta (based on II/2)	113	A major
Cadence 3	127	A major

mann 1977, 144), have discerned a single exposition with a slow introductory portion (mm. 1–4), a large and multifarious first group (mm. 5–67), a transition (mm. 68–82), a lyrical second subject (mm. 82–113), and a fast closing group (mm. 113–32). But the first movement of op. 9 is best heard as comprising a *double* exposition, or pair of expositions (see table 11). We have seen in chapter 5 that such a design is proposed by Richard Swift for *Verklärte Nacht* (Swift 1977), but that this parsing is not supported by the thematic and harmonic disposition of the sextet. A much more persuasive case for this kind of plan can be made in op. 9. The principle of a double exposition is not, of course, without precedent. An obvious forebear is the classical-romantic first-movement concerto form. Richard Strauss's *Don Juan*, a piece Schoenberg surely knew well (it has the same tonic as op. 9, and its athletic thematic style may also have been influential) can also be heard as employing two expositions (a perspective discussed in Hepokoski 1992, 147). Although the conception of op. 9 may owe something to both models, Schoenberg's double exposition is sui generis; with it, he created a new formal synthesis of procedures with which he had been grappling imaginatively for over a decade.

The first exposition is preceded by two passages, which I shall call "cadences" because they serve to map out, or introduce emphatically, the two key areas, F

EXAMPLE 9.1 First Chamber Symphony, op. 9.

a. Cadence 1

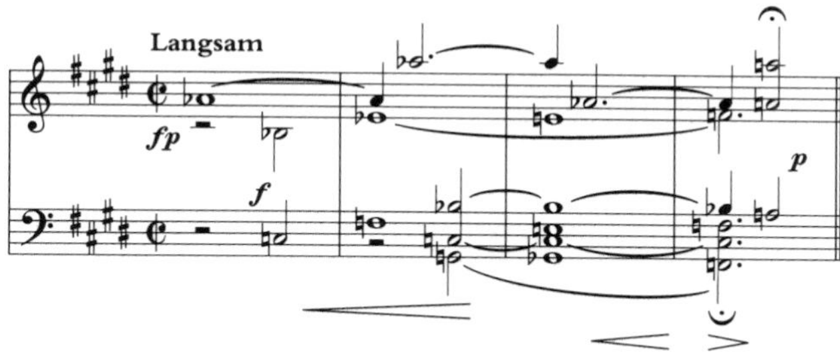

b. Cadence 2

and E, that are to dominate the succeeding expositions, especially the first (ex. 9.1).[4] Cadence 1 also behaves like a brief slow introduction. (I shall return below to the more specifically harmonic aspects of the expositions.) The two cadences also enclose the first statement of the horn "motto" of rising fourths that is to assume importance at larger formal articulation points in the piece. (In table 11 and in the discussion that follows, themes are distinguished by the exposition in which they originate; thus I/2 refers to theme 2 in exposition I. Since 1a is the same in both expositions, it will be referred to without a roman numeral.)

Each of the two expositions begins with the same theme (1a), which in both cases cadences on the tonic, E major. As has been suggested by Philip Friedheim (who, however, follows the tradition of perceiving a single exposition), this theme and subsequent ones tend to preserve the "thematic character" of the traditional sonata form, where "principal melodies remain strong and aggres-

4. Berg 1921, 5, also refers to mm. 8–10 as the "cadencing theme," which, he suggests, appears throughout the piece when there is a strong cadence in E major.

sive, secondary melodies expansive and lyric" (Friedheim 1963, 337). Theme 1a is indeed aggressive; it is also somewhat asymmetrical and open-ended. It is succeeded by theme I/1b, which definitely has the character of a modulatory transition, especially by virtue of its prominent use of sequence (in overlapping four-measure units).

In both expositions, the "second" themes provide genuine contrast—in mood, in key, and in thematic material. The first of these (I/2, m. 32) differs from what has come before in extending a full (and regular) eight measures and in being accorded an actual counterstatement or repetition (beginning at m. 39), which, however, soon begins to deviate from the original. Similarly, the A-major theme (II/2) is an expansive one, lasting nine measures (clearly heard as an extension of eight by the varied repetition of m. 88 as m. 89). After a transitional addition of five measures, this theme too has a counterstatement, beginning (in the horn) at m. 97. Like the counterstatement of I/2, this one soon deviates from the original model.

After the cadences at the close of exposition II, cadence 2 and theme 1a make yet another return (mm. 133–36)—one that might suggest either another exposition or the beginning of a development section. In fact, however, the primary thematic material takes a different direction at m. 142 and leads toward the introduction of scherzo material at m. 148.

From the formal/thematic viewpoint, the scherzo of op. 9 is no less remarkable than the first movement. Schoenberg here moves away from the clear scherzo–trio–scherzo plan of op. 7, but retains the essential thematic dualism of that design. The two principal themes are closely related. The nervous accompanimental figure to theme 1 (ex. 9.2b) is modified to become theme 2 (ex. 9.2c). The principal voice of theme 1 can also be heard to derive from the prominent ascending semitones in the second violin at cadence 1 (ex. 9.2a).

The way in which the two themes are introduced and developed gives the scherzo a shape closer to sonata form than to the tripartite scherzo plan:

Theme 1 [scherzo], m. 160
transition, m. 184
Theme 2 [trio], m. 200
Development, m. 215
Recapitulation [scherzo], m. 249

The passage in mm. 215–18, with the final appearance (for the moment) of theme 2, followed by the sustained horn pedal, clearly indicates the end of an important

EXAMPLE 9.2 First Chamber Symphony, op. 9, derivation of scherzo themes.

segment. It is followed by the reappearance of a portion of theme 1, precisely in the way we might expect at the beginning of a development section. The "recapitulation" is remarkable for its extreme compression, which in a sense fulfills the latent identity between themes 1 and 2: they are now recapitulated simultaneously in mm. 253–58.

The reader will recall that in op. 7 the reprise of the scherzo leads directly into a large development section, in which scherzo material gradually gives way to that from the first movement. Schoenberg's strategy in op. 9 is somewhat different. The end of the scherzo is clearly demarcated by the sustained *fortissimo* Es of mm. 274–79, and by the reappearance of the horn motto, now descending in fourths (mm. 279–80). The development section begins with a distinct contrast of key, tempo, and thematic material. The initial motive of theme I/2 reappears in its original key, F minor. It is followed—interrupted, one might almost say—by cadence 1, then by theme II/2, which dominates the first part of the development.

Berg rightly observes that the development section of the Chamber Symphony divides into three segments: part I, mm. 280–312; part II, mm. 312–35; and part III, mm. 335–67 (Berg 1921, 9–11). The segments are distinguished primarily by means of thematic material, which is arranged in order of progressively greater

EXAMPLE 9.3 First Chamber Symphony, op. 9, derivation of slow movement theme.

rhythmic activity, so that a listener might perceive an increase in tempo, although there is none. Throughout this process, Schoenberg preserves the essential character of the themes as they were introduced in the expositions and the scherzo. Thus part I of the development begins with the slower "second" themes from the first movement expositions and is dominated especially by II/2, whose lyricism makes an appropriate contrast with the headlong pace of the scherzo. At the beginning of part II, the tempo quickens to the *Anfangszeitmaß*, the "sehr rasch" of the opening of the piece. It remains essentially at this tempo for the rest of the development; the impression of increasing speed is created by Schoenberg's choice of themes.

Part II is governed by theme II/1b, which in its original appearance (m. 68) *preceded* II/2 and formed a kind of transition from the assertive II/1a. Here it has the opposite function, representing an increase in rhythmic activity from II/2. Part III begins with part of theme 1 of the scherzo, which represents a still greater increase of rhythmic activity. The scherzo theme is combined with II/1b; gradually the other "fast" theme, 1a, emerges (beginning at m. 341).

The development culminates with the triple *forte* chords in fourths of mm. 363–68. This sonority represents a compression into a simultaneity of the horn motto powerfully presented in mm. 358–62. (I return to the significance of this moment below.) This passage at 363–68, standing essentially at the midpoint of the work, is the formal analogue of the massive liquidation of the first theme before **K** in the D-Minor Quartet. In the quartet, the liquidation was followed directly by the slow movement; in the Chamber Symphony, this moment is followed by a kind of regeneration of the motto and of cadence 1 in mm. 368–77.

The main theme of the slow movement derives audibly from the twofold dotted figure of cadence 2 (ex. 9.3a, b). The relationship is especially appropriate here since the theme comes after the horn motto and cadence 1 and thus occupies a formal position analogous to that originally occupied by cadence 2 (in mm. 8–10). By making this analogy to the opening of the piece, Schoenberg signals the beginning of a large new segment of the Chamber Symphony.

The slow movement proper has a lucid design, in which material of great variety is fitted into a compact structure:

Introduction/cadence (mm. 378–81)
Main theme (mm. 382–85)
Contrasting theme (mm. 385–90)
Main theme repeated and varied (mm. 391–94)
Contrasting theme repeated and varied (mm. 395–97)
Introduction/cadence repeated and extended (mm. 398–404)
Main theme (mm. 405–7)
Coda (mm. 407–10)

One distinctive aspect of this design is the reappearance of the introduction/cadence at m. 398 to form the real climax of the section.

The slow movement is followed by the return of the fourths motto and by cadence 1; this leads into a lengthy passage, mm. 415–34, that in the overall analysis of op. 9 (table 10) has been called episode/transition. This segment seems to have two functions. First, it is a continuation and thematic variation of the slow movement. The last segment of the theme of this section, consisting of two descending semitones and rising major third (diminished fourth), is derived clearly from the slow movement theme, a derivation made more obvious in the horn melody that emerges at m. 430 (ex. 9.4a, b). Second, the segment of mm. 415–34, which has a B-major key signature, appears intended to function as a transition to the recapitulation, which may be said actually to begin with the E-major key signature at m. 435. Despite its apparent functions, however, the passage from mm. 415–34 is one of the most puzzling in the Chamber Symphony, as will be discussed below in conjunction with the recapitulation.

The recapitulation/finale of the Chamber Symphony posed the kind of challenge Schoenberg had faced several times before in his large-scale instrumental compositions. In op. 9 the solution proves as ingenious as the exposition. Schoenberg creates a double recapitulation that is analogous but in no way identical to the double exposition in terms of harmonic areas and thematic disposition (see table 12). The thematic components of the two expositions are now intermingled

EXAMPLE 9.4 First Chamber Symphony, op. 9, relation of slow movement theme to episode/transition.

in a logical yet flexible way. The double recapitulation is followed by a two-part coda.

The analysis suggested in table 12 differs not only in detail but overall from that of Berg, who places the start of the recapitulation at m. 410, with the horn call, and the "coda" at m. 497, at the beginning of what I have called recapitulation II. Berg calls my coda II an *Endkoda.* Berg's coda seems unusually and disproportionately long and does not take sufficient account of the treatment of the slow movement theme, which is actually taken up at *greater* length than its original presentation. In the slow movement proper, the theme unfolds for only twenty-seven measures before giving way (at m. 410) to a new transitional theme in B major. The fuller treatment of the theme at mm. 508–41 would seem more appropriately considered part of a recapitulation than a coda. Placing the beginning of the coda at m. 555, as I have suggested, creates an analogy with the codetta in exposition II: in both, a transformed, fast version of II/2 leads into cadence 3 (ex. 9.5a, b).

Wherever one chooses to place the traditional formal boundaries, it is important to remember that these are only labels of convenience that fix—and thus to some extent falsify—what is in the Chamber Symphony an extremely fluid process. This fluidity makes it particularly difficult to pinpoint the actual beginning of the recapitulation. Schoenberg's principal compositional goal is to prepare the return of the tonic, E major. The portion of the slow movement that comes after the horn motto and fourth chords of mm. 410–14 is given a B-major key signature. The tonic key signature returns at m. 435, with the appearance of theme II/1b, which, however, really continues in the previous B major. The tonic itself begins

TABLE 12 Plan of Recapitulation/Finale of Schoenberg's First Chamber Symphony, op. 9.

Formal/thematic function	*Starting measure*	*Initial or primary key area*
Recapitulation I		
II/1b + slow mvt. theme	435	B major
II/2	448	E major
II/transition	463	A♭ major
Horn motto	473	Fourths
1a + cad. 2 in augm.	476	E major
I/1b	488	C major
Cad. based on II/1a	491 (cf. 65)	B major as V
Recapitulation II		
1a	497	E major
I/1b	498	E major
Slow mvt. theme	508	E major
I/2	541	C minor
I/transition	552	(ambiguous)
Coda I		
II/Codetta	555	B♭ major
Cad. 3	562	C major / E major, to B as V
Horn motto	574	Fourths
Coda II		
1a + horn motto + motive of cad. 2	576	E major
Cad. 2 augmented	589	E major

to emerge only at m. 448 with theme II/2, then more definitively with the simultaneous presentation of 1a and cadence 2 at m. 476. Following convention, I give the moment at which the key signature changes as the beginning of the recapitulation, but one might with equal justification point to the *fortissimo* statement of the horn motto at m. 473.

Dominant Relationships

The matter of recapitulation—and, indeed, of formal structure in general—is intimately bound up with the harmonic dimension of op. 9, especially with the structural role of the dominant. The principal rationale for arguing for a double

EXAMPLE 9.5 First Chamber Symphony, op. 9, relation between codetta (a) and final coda (b).

EXAMPLE 9.6 Schoenberg's analysis in *Structural Functions of Harmony* of cadence 2 in First Chamber Symphony, op. 9.

recapitulation is that as in the exposition there is a double approach to the tonic: first at m. 448, then again more explicitly at m. 497. This procedure is roughly, but surely intentionally, parallel to the double approaches at mm. 8–10 (with cadence 2) and mm. 56–58. What is significantly different from the exposition is the role played by the dominant, B major, in these later passages and in coda II at mm. 573–76.

In the expositions, Schoenberg tends to avoid any sustained or explicit dominant of E major. Thus in cadence 2, as the composer himself demonstrated in *Structural Functions*, there is no B in the bass of the dominant chord; it must be inferred through "multiple root reference of a diminished 7th chord" (Schoenberg 1969, 110–11; see my ex. 9.6). (In fact, a B root is heard fleetingly in the horns on the last beat of m. 8.) But at the recapitulation, as in the recapitulatory portions of opp. 4, 5, and 7, Schoenberg clearly felt the need for a stronger V–I

EXAMPLE 9.7 First Chamber Symphony, op. 9, cadences to E from the dominant.

a.

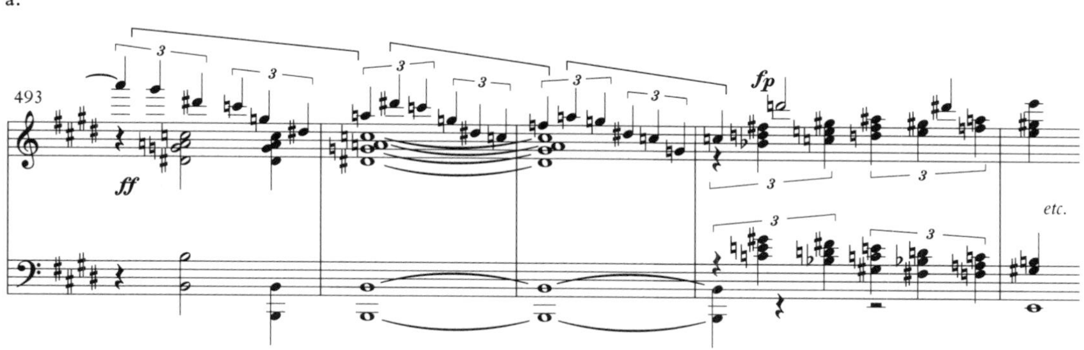

b.

resolution. The most forceful such cadences, with a clear B in the bass, come at mm. 493–97 and at 572–76 (ex. 9.7a and b).

During the compositional process of the Chamber Symphony, as in that of *Verklärte Nacht* and the First Quartet, Schoenberg was clearly concerned with, and somewhat uncertain about, how much dominant preparation would be necessary or appropriate toward the end of the work. The one major compositional change indicated—but then revoked—in the autograph score of op. 9 was made, I believe, precisely because of this concern. In the autograph (at the Pierpont Morgan Library), all of mm. 415–34, the passage with the B-major key signature that has been referred to above as an episode/transition, is indicated for deletion with a red pencil; Schoenberg used a "VI-DE" to cut directly from m. 414 to the present m. 435—that is, from just after the horn motto and cadence 1 to the recapitulation of theme II/1b in B major. Then he changed his mind and wrote "bleibt" above the passage, thus restoring it in full. It is not clear exactly when he would have made these markings, but it was certainly after the autograph was written out.[5]

Schoenberg's vacillation about the episode/transition is suggestive. As a listener to the Chamber Symphony and student of the score—well before I had ever consulted the autograph—I had found the passage at mm. 415–34 oddly stagnant for so relentlessly logical a composition. Are we to take it as a resumption of the slow movement after the interpolation of the horn motto and cadence 1? As such, it would break the precedent of using the motto as a marker of important formal junctions in the large-scale form. Or is it a transitional episode meant to lead into the recapitulation? In this latter role, it seems unusually, uncomfortably long for this work, where transitions tend to be relatively brief and focused.

That Schoenberg considered cutting mm. 415–34 can be taken as an indication that he too was somewhat puzzled about the function of the episode/transition. As he realized, the horn motto and cadence of mm. 411–14 could lead quite smoothly and logically, as indicated by the provisional cut, to the reprise of theme II/1b in m. 435. And Schoenberg may have felt that since the slow movement theme already receives such an extensive recapitulation—expansion, really—at mm. 508–41, an extensive episode derived from the slow movement theme at mm. 414–34 would come to seem redundant.

In the end, however, Schoenberg's instincts told him to leave the passage intact. He did so, I believe, not because of its contribution to the development of the slow movement theme, but because of its harmonic implications: these measures provide necessary time spent in or about the *dominant.* The appearance of II/1b in the dominant at m. 435 (it is heard in B despite the change of key signature to E) would not alone be sufficient; the passage at mm. 414–35 gives additional weight to the dominant. Even so, very little of the episode/transition actually sustains a dominant of E, since harmonic stability is constantly threatened by the pervasive chromatic counterpoint. One suspects that the key signature of B retains an almost purely symbolic value for Schoenberg. Somewhat like the A major of the rondo theme of op. 7 examined in chapter 8, it represents the dominant that Schoenberg was finding increasingly harder to sustain as a functional element in his music.

Whole-Tone and Quartal Elements

The role of dominants in op. 9 is intimately bound up with Schoenberg's extensive use of whole-tone and quartal elements. At the opening of the work,

5. Similar cuts are indicated in the autograph score of Schoenberg's own four-hand arrangement of op. 9 (at the Schoenberg Institute). For a description of both cuts, see *SW* B11/II: 13; and B5: 85.

EXAMPLE 9.8 First Chamber Symphony, op. 9, whole-tone chord as dominant seventh of F.

Schoenberg explicitly—almost didactically—demonstrates how whole tones and fourths can (and will) penetrate both the vertical and horizontal dimensions of the music. First, with cadence 1, comes an essentially chordal or vertical presentation, a fourths–whole-tone–triad progression resolving to F major. The horn motto then horizontalizes the fourths, and the transition to cadence 2 does the same for whole tones by successively unfolding the augmented triads F–A–C♯ and E♭–G–B♮ (mm. 6–8), thus exhausting one entire six-note whole-tone complex. The E triad of m. 10 is also laid out in a mainly successive way. In both the vertical and horizontal presentations—that is, in both cadences 1 and 2—the fourths–whole-tone–triad succession involves altered but functional dominant sonorities, the dominant of F in mm. 2–4, and that of E in m. 9.

I have already reviewed Schoenberg's own theoretical derivations of the whole-tone complex and demonstrated something of its realization in op. 7 (chapter 8). We recall that in both theory and practice Schoenberg treats whole-tone scales or chords not as purely symmetrical, rootless phenomena, but as harmonically functional ones; he often derives whole-tone structures from, or relates them to, conventional dominants. In this respect, as in so many others, the First Chamber Symphony is a worthy successor to the First Quartet, making good on the inheritance. The second chordal component of cadence 1 contains five notes of the whole-tone scale (ex. 9.8). If inverted so as to put the C in the bass, the chord can be heard to function as a dominant of F major, with the fifth simultaneously raised and lowered, in the way suggested by Schoenberg in *Theory of Harmony* (1978, 392) and discussed above in connection with the D-Minor Quartet. (See the similar analyses of the opening of op. 9 in Morgan 1991, 66, Rexroth 1971, 356–59, and Brinkmann 1969, 6–8.) The dominant function might be said to be reinforced by the doubling of the leading tone, E♮, in chord 2 of cadence 1.

This aspect of the whole-tone complex becomes still more explicit at the cadence to theme I/2 in F minor at mm. 30–32 (ex. 9.9). In m. 30, all six notes of the whole-tone scale are present; although not sounded as a chord, they are clearly oriented around or toward the C root. In the next measure, the C fully

EXAMPLE 9.9 First Chamber Symphony, op. 9, cadence to theme I/2.

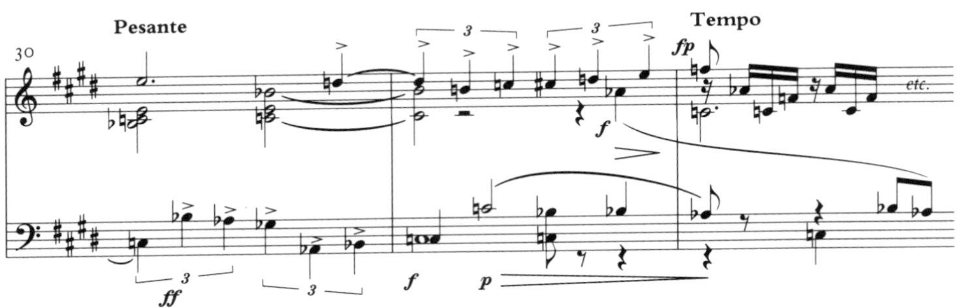

establishes itself as a dominant, and the whole-tone scale gives way to a more conventional half-step approach to F in the violins.

Schoenberg's theoretical and compositional treatment of chords built of fourths is similar to his approach to the whole-tone complex. In *Theory of Harmony,* he observes that fourth (quartal) chords "are chords like all others" (1978, 404) and can be produced by—and thus can function as—alterations within the triadic system (see also Rexroth 1971, 318–25). He also stresses their possible dominant function: both four-part and five-part quartal harmonies "can be substitutes for a dominant, from which they are derived by lowering the root (if one wishes to admit such), the seventh, and the fifth for the four-part quartal chord" (Schoenberg 1978, 405). It is striking that Schoenberg should suggest—even if diffidently and parenthetically—the lowering of the root, the one chord component that he elsewhere claims not to be subject to alteration: "The roots are, in our conception, fixed points from which relationships are measured. The unity of all the measurements we have found is guaranteed by the immobility of these points. But then one may not move them!!" (Schoenberg 1978, 234). Schoenberg's willingness to condone the possibility of root alteration in quartal harmonies shows how strong is his impulse to relate even the most exotic constructions to diatonic roots.

The resolutions of the quartal harmonies demonstrated in *Theory of Harmony* are especially relevant to an understanding of compositional practice in the Chamber Symphony. Schoenberg observes that in a six-part quartal chord, the top voice forms a minor ninth with the bass. Because this ninth represents "the first 'rather sharp' dissonance among the fourth chords," he suggests that the resolution of the ninth be a priority (Schoenberg 1978, 405–6). One of his solutions in *Theory of Harmony*, as reproduced in ex. 9.10a, is quite close to cadence 1 in op. 9 (ex. 9.10b, which is a reduction of ex. 9.1a). Both begin with a six-

EXAMPLE 9.10 Resolution of six-part fourth chord.

a. After Schoenberg 1978, 406, ex. 337b

b. First Chamber Symphony, op. 9, mm. 2–3

part quartal chord; in both, three notes, including the ninth above the bass, are held over into the next chord, which is in both cases a whole-tone sonority.

In the *Theory of Harmony* example, Schoenberg claims to demonstrate "a connection that also appears in my *Kammersymphonie*" (406). In fact, however, the six-note quartal harmony in mm. 2–3 of op. 9 does not resolve precisely as indicated in Schoenberg's textbook example, because as can be seen in ex. 9.10b, the whole-tone chord of resolution in cadence 1 has *five*, not six, pitch classes. Instead of moving down by half-step, as in the model (ex. 9.10a), the second voice from the top resolves up, from E♭ to E♮, which thus doubles the E♮ in the third voice from the bottom. The deviation in cadence 1 from the model given in *Theory of Harmony* is revealing because the doubled pitch E♮ is (as was observed above) the leading tone of F. The doubling of the leading tone thus serves to strengthen our hearing the progression of cadence 1 as a V–I in F.

In all, cadence 1 appears five different times in the Chamber Symphony: once at the opening, twice in succession just before the slow movement at mm. 374–77, and twice again at the end of the slow movement, mm. 411–14. In none of these places does the pattern correspond to Schoenberg's model in *Theory of Harmony*. In the passages at mm. 374–77 and 411–15, the cadence first behaves as at the opening, leading to F major (ex. 9.11a and d), and is then refashioned to lead toward the key of the succeeding passage. The reworking at mm. 376–77 (ex. 9.11b) corresponds to a different model proposed in *Theory of Harmony* (ex. 9.11c; Schoenberg 1978, ex. 336, m. 3), where the six-part quartal chord leads to

EXAMPLE 9.11 First Chamber Symphony, op. 9, appearances of cadence 1 (a, b, d, e); resolution of six-part fourth chord after Schoenberg 1978, 406, ex. 337, m. 3 (c).

a first-inversion dominant seventh. In op. 9, the dominant seventh is V of G, the key of the slow movement. It could be said that this passage makes explicit or overt the dominant function that was implied in the original form of cadence 1, which has just been heard once again before the reworking. At the final occurrences of cadence 1, in mm. 411–15, Schoenberg repeats the original form once again (ex. 9.11d), then modifies it still further to resolve eventually to the dominant of E major (minus the fifth; ex. 9.11e).

Neapolitan Relationships

In *Theory of Harmony*, Schoenberg notes that quartal sonorities "place their stamp on everything that happens" in the Chamber Symphony (Schoenberg 1978, 404). While it is true that both cadence 1 and the horn motto blaze a trail through the work, they constitute only one aspect of its richly complex tonal world. Indeed, one harmonic relationship that seems to lie at the core of much of op. 9 derives directly from neither whole tones nor fourths (although an affinity to the latter will be suggested): it is generated by the half-step E–F. The Chamber Symphony, especially its first movement and finale, constitutes Schoenberg's most profound exploration to date of the relationship between a tonic and its Neapolitan upper neighbor.

The key areas of F major and E major are emphatically juxtaposed at the very opening, where cadence 1 is in the former, cadence 2 in the latter (see above, ex. 9.1). This juxtaposition, so portentous for the work as whole, was apparently not

EXAMPLE 9.12 First Chamber Symphony, op. 9, sketch for cadence 1, in Sketchbook II, p. 92.

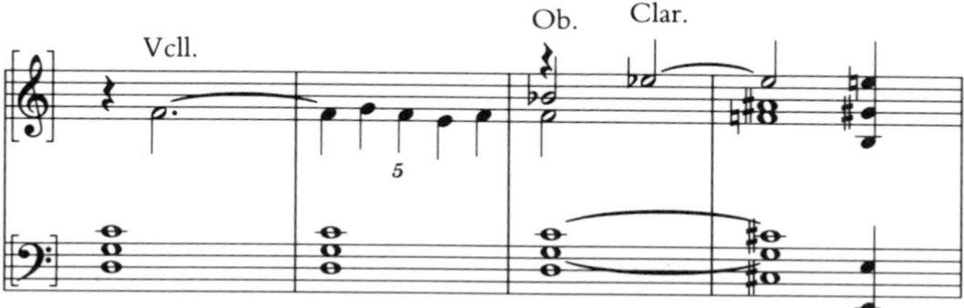

part of Schoenberg's earliest notated conception. In the first surviving sketch for cadence 1 (ex. 9.12; see also *SW* B11/II: 42 [S3]) the opening chord is built from a different set of fourths, D–G–C–F–B♭, and the cadence is made to E major. (At this point in the compositional process—at least in its graphic representation—there is as yet no whole-tone chord in cadence 1. This appears in the next sketch, S6.)

Cadence 2 is more conventional than cadence 1 and is accompanied by (or accompanies) a dynamic melodic gesture. This can be taken as a sign that E major, and not the F major of the introduction, is the real tonal center of the work. Another sign is the prominent motivic gesture within cadence 2, C♮–B (or ♭$\hat{6}$–$\hat{5}$ in E major), which clearly subordinates the C♮, the upper fifth of the Neapolitan, as an upper neighbor to B.

The cello theme, 1a, also embodies within itself the crucial F–E harmonic-thematic relationship. In m. 12, the theme swerves sharply from its E-major orbit with the ascending figure, D♮–E♮–F♮. The arrival on the important F♮ is reinforced by the entrance of the horn, which then joins the cello for (and only for) the resolution down to E. The F–E half-step is heard prominently again in the bass at the next cadence to E in mm. 15–16, and is made still more prominent at the beginning of the overlapping statement of theme I/1b in m. 19, where in the winds and horns an F-major triad moves directly to E major.[6]

It is instructive to consider the pervasiveness and the boldness with which Schoenberg exploits the Neapolitan in op. 9 (and there is more to say about this below) in light of his own theoretical statements. Like other nineteenth-century

6. Friedheim (1963, 343) suggests that this theme (I/1b) is actually in A minor, in other words that the E major is heard here as a dominant and that F♮ is functioning as ♭VI. This seems to me a mishearing. Although it is true that the ♭VI–V was prominent in cadence 2 (as C♮–B), the F–E does not function in an analogous way here. For one thing, the F–E appears not as a motive in its own right, but as an answer to the motive D♮–C♮, which consists of a whole step. Friedheim is correct to imply that the E is somewhat unstable, but it is not a dominant.

theorists, Schoenberg sees the tonic and its Neapolitan as related through the mediation of the subdominant minor (A minor in the case of op. 9), in which region the Neapolitan triad forms a diatonic chord (VI, F major). But Schoenberg also decides that "in spite of the mediation of the minor subdominant relation: these two chords [a tonic and its Neapolitan] are about as remotely related as chords can be. And if we connect them so directly we are right on that boundary where we can say: all chords can be connected with one another" (Schoenberg 1978, 235). Even in Schoenberg's more systematic treatment of harmonic relationships in *Structural Functions of Harmony*, the Neapolitan is still a remote, slippery phenomenon; in the schematic chart of the regions, in which keys are visually arranged around a central axis according to nearness or remoteness to the tonic, the **Np** hovers ambiguously outside the main grid (Schoenberg 1969, 20).

Despite the remoteness of the Neapolitan in theory, this scale degree is explored in practice in Schoenberg's earlier tonal works with great imagination. We have already examined some of these procedures in *Verklärte Nacht* (chapter 5) and *Gurrelieder* (chapter 6). More direct precedents for op. 9 are to be found in three works in which this tonal relationship occurs at the same pitch level, that is, E–F. Two of these are the songs *Traumleben*, op. 6, no. 1, and *Natur*, op. 8, no. 1, which were drafted on the same day, 18 December 1903. (*Natur* was completed and orchestrated in March 1904.) In both songs, the tonic E major is frequently enriched by, and inflected toward, the Neapolitan F. In *Traumleben*, the opening melodic phrase contains all the notes of the F-major triad, spelled enharmonically as A, E♯, and B♯. The phrase is at first harmonized in E, then at its reappearance in m. 22 at the same pitch level is magically reharmonized in F.[7] In *Natur*, the recapitulation or return of the opening theme occurs in m. 46 in F major, a half-step higher than its original key; the theme returns to the tonic in m. 52. In both songs, Schoenberg resolves the dominant seventh of F (C^7) directly to E (*Traumleben*, mm. 24–25; *Natur*, mm. 21–23), an expansion of the cadence from German sixth to tonic that we observed in *Verklärte Nacht* and *Pelleas*, and that is also a frequent device in *Gurrelieder*.

A still more direct way of shuttling between the key areas of F and E—and one highly relevant to Schoenberg's method in op. 9—appears in the slow movement of the D-Minor Quartet, op. 7. Although this movement, which has an ABA′ form, begins in A minor, the principal key area of the A section is F minor/major. Toward the end of this section (one measure before **K**45 in ex. 9.13), Schoenberg confirms F major with its own dominant. At the cadence in **K**45, Schoenberg introduces in the second violin (imitated in the cello) a phrase from the second group of the first movement. In its final statement, in the viola in

7. For further discussion of *Traumleben* and these particular Neapolitan relationships, see Cone 1974, 30–32; Wintle 1980, 57–64; and Lewis 1987, 32–37.

EXAMPLE 9.13 First String Quartet in D Minor, op. 7, slow movement.

K47–48, this phrase emphasizes the neighbor-note motives G♯–A and F–E. The G♯ clearly functions as lower neighbor to the A, and the E as leading tone to F. F major is therefore still the prevailing key.

On the final beat of **K**48 (just before the double bar and change of meter), the lower voices sustain the dyad E–G♯, which seems all at once to lose (or at least waver in) its dissonant status. High above, the first violin sounds on F♮ the characteristic sixteenth-note upbeat of the slow movement theme. This note is now dissonant to the chord below, and on the downbeat of the next measure, with the change of time signature to $\frac{12}{8}$, the E–G♯ dyad metamorphoses as if by magic into E major. In a shift of aural perspective, the high F♮ in the first violin, previously the tonic, now becomes the Neapolitan to the more stable E. As the key signature changes to E major and the B theme of the movement enters in **K**52, the F♮, and indeed the whole Neapolitan triad, continue to play a prominent role in both the accompaniment and the melody (note especially the F♮–G♮–A figure in the melody in **K**53). The tonal shift from F to E in the slow movement of op. 7 is achieved without the mediation of any dominant or German sixth. It is accomplished essentially by stepwise voice-leading and by the assertion of E–G♯ as tonic in **K**49. Stepwise voice-leading of this kind also plays a crucial role in the Chamber Symphony, as can be seen if we return to theme I/2, cast in F minor.

In an abstract theoretical sense, the relationship between E major and F minor, between a tonic and its Neapolitan *minor*, is still more remote than the conventional one, since it involves a further transformation or substitution, that of F minor for F major. This particular relationship is so remote that Schoenberg addresses it specifically nowhere in either *Theory of Harmony* or *Structural Functions*.[8] And yet in the tonal world of the First Chamber Symphony, F minor is really *closer* to the tonic than is F major. The key area of theme I/2 represents an attempt to reconcile or bring together the two key areas, F and E, which have been juxtaposed in the first theme group. The F-minor triad shares one note, A♭/G♯, with that of E major. F minor can be reached from E major in two steps with semitone voice-leading, as shown in ex. 9.14, by a successive raising of the tonic and fifth degrees. Raising the fifth, B, yields an augmented triad, which can be understood to have a C root, and thus to be a dominant of F. A resolution of the leading tone, E♮, to F yields the F-minor triad.

Schoenberg himself may well have been thinking along these lines when composing op. 9. Such at least is one possible interpretation of some of the fascinating sketches for the F-minor theme, I/2. The position of these sketches within

8. In the chart of the regions in *Structural Functions* (Schoenberg 1969, 20), Schoenberg acknowledges no Neapolitan minor triad; a minor triad built on the flatted second degree appears only as the mediant minor of the minor five of the flat mediant, or ♭**mvm**. (Thus in C, D♭ minor is the mediant minor of B♭ minor, which is the minor five of the flatted mediant, E♭ minor.)

EXAMPLE 9.14 Connection of E major to F minor through stepwise voice-leading.

the sketchbook suggests that this theme may originally have been intended as the main theme (a hypothesis advanced by Schmidt in *SW* B11/II: 43). These sketches directly follow those for the opening cadence 1 and precede those for the theme that eventually became 1a. Schoenberg himself transcribes five of the twelve sketches for the F-minor theme in his essay "Heart and Brain in Music" (Schoenberg 1975, 59–60).[9] He makes no comment on the harmonic, or enharmonic, implications of the theme's evolution; his goal is only to give an idea of how much labor and revision was involved in forging the theme. But nothing speaks more tellingly of the relationship Schoenberg attempts to establish between E and F than the successive drafts of I/2, in which the theme, always at the *same* pitch level, is first cast in the key of E major, then gradually shifted toward F minor.

It is not necessary here to trace the entire evolution of the theme across the surviving sketches (the reader can consult the transcriptions and commentary in *SW* B11/II: 45–49 [S8–9, 11–20, 33, 39, 40]); but some idea of this process can be given. In the first surviving sketch (S8, excerpted in my ex. 9.15a), the theme appears underneath a sustained dyad E–G♯ in the treble. The first four notes are G♯–B♯–A♯–G♯, an exact enharmonic equivalent of the eventual A♭–C–B♭–A♭. Although no further harmonic support is indicated, the continuation of the theme clearly implies an E-major center. E-major is outlined by the arpeggios of m. 3, and the final motion of the bass can only indicate a V–I cadence in E. In the fourth sketch (S12; my ex. 9.15b), the end point of the initial melodic descent has become E♯, the enharmonic equivalent of the eventual F♮.

The new harmonic context of F minor is made explicit in S16 (ex. 9.15c), where, in the upper staff, Schoenberg moves by semitone voice-leading from E major to F minor (and then beyond, to A major) in exactly the fashion suggested above in my ex. 9.14: the fifth of the E triad is raised to C, which is then interpreted as a dominant of F minor, so that the E resolves up by half-step to F. The sequence by which F minor is reached is now repeated, so that we end up at F♯ minor. In one of the final sketches for the passage (S33; reduced in ex. 9.15d), as in the published version, there is no longer any trace either of the initial E-major

9. Schoenberg's examples correspond to those transcribed in *SW* B11/II: 46–48, as follows: Schoenberg's ex. E=S11; ex. F=S12; ex. G=S13; ex. H=S16; ex. I=S17.

EXAMPLE 9.15 First Chamber Symphony, op. 9, sketches for theme I/2, in Sketchbook II, pp. 92–94, 102.

EXAMPLE 9.16 First Chamber Symphony, op. 9, Schoenberg's derivation of theme I/2 from 1a (from Schoenberg 1975, 85).

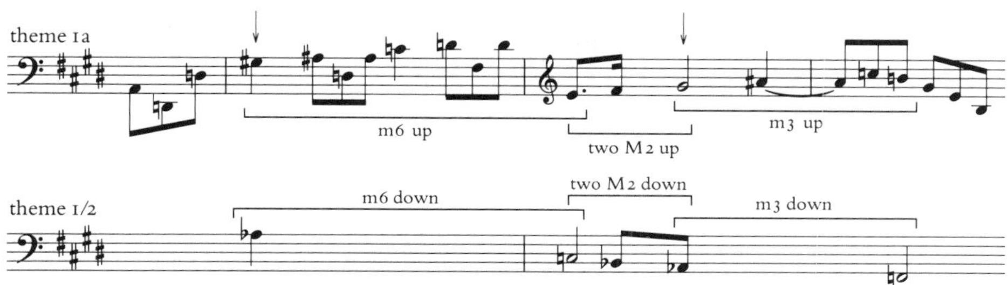

triad or of the following augmented triad; the progression now begins in F minor. The earlier sketches thus spell out explicitly (almost as if in a theory book) the voice-leading relationship between E major and F minor, a relationship that can only be inferred in the final version.

In one of his best-known musical analyses, presented in two different essays, "My Evolution" and "Composition with Twelve Tones," Schoenberg showed how his "subconscious" (as dictated by the "Supreme Commander") had created a deep structural relationship between the two apparently contrasting principal themes (my 1a and I/2) in the first group of the Chamber Symphony (Schoenberg 1975, 85, 222–23). He isolates certain pitches of 1a and demonstrates how by inversion they form the notes of I/2 (ex. 9.16). The derivation may seem a little farfetched, calling to mind the more fanciful thematic analyses of Rudolf Réti (Réti 1951), but from the viewpoint of the E–F relationship investigated here, Schoenberg's analysis is suggestive indeed; it establishes an identity between the G♯ of 1a and the A♭ of theme I/2 (indicated by the arrows I have added in the example). Schoenberg can thus be said to suggest the latent unity, or at least the great intimacy, created between E major and F minor in op. 9. The closeness of the relationship is also suggested by the possibility (mentioned above) that theme I/2 was originally intended, even in its evolved F-minor form (ex. 9.15d), to be the first allegro theme of the work. It is intriguing to speculate that it was only after Schoenberg had cast theme I/2 in F minor and decided to precede it with theme 1a in E major that he went back and modified his original conception of cadence 1 (transcribed in my ex. 9.12) to move toward F major, rather than E major. In other words, he now surrounded two E-major themes (cadence 2 and theme 1a) with two F-oriented ones (cadence 1 in F major and theme I/2 in F minor).

To continue with the Neapolitan story of the Chamber Symphony: the relationships between E and F set out in exposition I come into play again at the end

EXAMPLE 9.17 First Chamber Symphony, op. 9, climax of F–E juxtaposition.

of the development section, at mm. 355–68, where the two pitches are forcefully juxtaposed in one of the most compelling passages of the work (ex. 9.17). Here the fourths motto reappears, triple *forte*, in a form that at first descends and ascends between the outer extremes of G♭ and F♮. When the motto begins a second descent from G♭ on the last beat of m. 356, the intervals are adjusted to alternate between tritones and major thirds, such that the end point now becomes E♮ (downbeat of m. 358). In the ascent that follows (horns, last beat of m. 357), which we would expect to mirror the preceding descent, Schoenberg normalizes the interval sequence to produce a set of pure fourths bounded by E and F. This version of the motto is now given out repeatedly in ascending and descending form and in diminution over the next five measures, where the two pitches F and E are thus thrown together as forcefully as possible. The end result is fusion: on the downbeat of m. 364 (see ex. 9.17) the motto congeals or freezes into a six-note fourth chord, which is reiterated and sustained over four measures.

This remarkable passage, which Adorno (citing an anonymous conductor) aptly characterizes as resembling a "glacier landscape" (Adorno 1981, 158), lies virtually at the midpoint of the Chamber Symphony and can be said to represent its most powerful and dissonant climax. Here the F and E have been brought together in (or around) a six-note quartal harmony of the type that, as discussed above, Schoenberg characterized as "rather sharp," with the minor ninth between the outer parts. It is here, at the climax, that we are made aware of the relationship between fourths and Neapolitan half-steps, phenomena that have up to this point been manipulated more or less separately. Both are embodied in the chord of m. 364, with F at the top and E at the bottom.

The F–E relationship is fully resolved only near the very end of the Chamber Symphony, at mm. 582–84 (ex. 9.18). Here a sustained F-major triad moves, via an intervening whole-tone run, to E major for the last time. This cadence follows, and is meant to be heard in apposition to, the more conventional dominant cadence of mm. 573–76 (see above, ex. 9.7b). Indeed, it seems to replace or su-

EXAMPLE 9.18 First Chamber Symphony, op. 9, resolution of F–E relationship.

persede that earlier cadence, as if Schoenberg is saying that in the Chamber Symphony, Neapolitan relationships have greater force than dominant ones. In these final pages, which seem to tie together all the harmonic and thematic threads of the work, the F–E nexus is further enriched by the strong presence of C major, which is both the dominant of F and Neapolitan to B. It is in the latter role that C functions principally here, although at first it moves directly to E major without any intermediate resolution to the dominant.

At m. 562, cadence 3 appears for the first time since the first movement. It is reiterated forcefully over the next nine measures. The first two times it resolves to C (ex. 9.19a); then it moves twice to E major (ex. 9.19b). On the downbeat of m. 567 the cadence resolves again to C; this resolution is now prolonged or expanded over four measures as the bass descends through the complete whole-tone scale from C to C. In mm. 572–73, the C at last resolves downward to B♮ and to the dominant harmony (see above, ex. 9.7b) and is thus reintegrated into the world of E major. In the final segment of the coda, Schoenberg drives home the basic Neapolitan relationships of the Chamber Symphony with a series of exhilarating cadences to E (m. 576), C (m. 578), E (m. 580), F (m. 582), and E again (m. 584). The very last cadences to E, in mm. 585, 587, and 593, are made, not from the dominant, but from the triads of F and B♭, underpinned the final time by A (as shown in ex. 9.18). This is surely one of the most extraordinary plagal cadences in all of music. Neapolitan-plagal, we might call it, since the A

EXAMPLE 9.19 First Chamber Symphony, op. 9, final appearances of cadence 3.

a.

b.

in the bass derives not from a traditional A major but from the Neapolitan realm of F (and its related keys, C and B♭), which has played such a critical role in the harmonic-thematic world of the Chamber Symphony.

More than any other instrumental work of Schoenberg's early period, the Chamber Symphony is characterized virtually throughout by an urgent, occasionally frantic, quality. One has the feeling that (to adopt an Adornian mode of expression) the musical material itself is pressing up against its own technical and expressive limits. With its fifteen individual voices competing for attention, the Chamber Symphony represents, as Reinhold Brinkmann has suggested, an extreme of polyphonic subjectivity (Brinkmann 1977, 148). Schoenberg's suggested metronome markings (virtually impossible to execute) make the faster themes of op. 9 seem especially breathless. The themes of op. 9 also generally have an expansive range, both tonally and registrally. Cadences or cadential figures are often repeated, as if insisting on closure in the face of skeptical disbelief. Indeed, as I have suggested, the piece begins with two cadences that take on important structural and thematic functions. In this way Schoenberg seems to be exploring the possibility, or the adequacy, of closure in a complex, tonally advanced composition.

Schoenberg considered op. 9 to represent the "climax" of his "first" (or tonal) period:

> Here is established a very intimate reciprocation between melody and harmony, in that both connect remote relations of the tonality into a perfect unity, draw logical consequences from the problems they attempt to solve, and simultaneously make great progress in the direction of the emancipation of the dissonance. This progress is brought about here by the postponement of the resolution of "passing" dissonances to a remote point where, finally, the preceding harshness becomes justified.
>
> SCHOENBERG 1975, 84

Our investigation of the E–F relationship in the sketches and the finished work has, I hope, revealed a profound example precisely of Schoenberg's ability to bring "remote relations" into a "perfect unity" in a logical fashion. We have not looked closely here at the opposite tendency mentioned by Schoenberg, at the incipient emancipation of dissonance. The emphasis has been primarily on forces of resolution and coherence, for I believe that the First Chamber Symphony is ultimately a work that confirms or affirms the power of tonality to articulate large-scale form. Within the frantic voice of op. 9, there is also a tone of joy, a sense of exuberance ("stormy jubilation," as Schoenberg described the horn motto in his *Theory of Harmony* [1978, 403]). The First Chamber Symphony is the last big composition of Schoenberg's early period to embody this attitude. As we shall see in the next chapter, the Second Chamber Symphony and Second Quartet take a more somber, sober approach to the problems of tonal composition.

CHAPTER TEN

The Second Chamber Symphony, op. 38, and the Second String Quartet, op. 10 (1906–1908)

After completing the First Chamber Symphony in July 1906, Schoenberg immediately set to work on another one; the first sketches for the Second Chamber Symphony were made in August. Yet he was to complete neither this nor any other large-scale work for two years. From the winter of 1906–7 on, Schoenberg's writing of op. 38 (I shall refer to the Second Chamber Symphony by the opus number it eventually bore) was essentially overtaken by the composition of other works, including the songs opp. 12 and 14; the chorus *Friede auf Erden*, op. 13; the Second Quartet, op. 10, begun on 9 March 1907; and some of the songs of the *Hanging Gardens* cycle, begun in March 1908. (In Sketchbook III, which contains material for most of these works, there are also sketches from this period for songs based on the poetry of Dehmel, Goethe, Gottfried Keller, C. F. Meyer, and Hermann Löns, as well as for an opera based on Gerhard Hauptmann's *Und Pippa tanzt.*) Schoenberg returned intermittently to the Second Chamber Symphony, most notably during 1911 and 1916, but was not to complete the work until 1939.

It is not possible to give consideration here to all the significant works composed—let alone those sketched—during the extraordinarily creative two-year period between mid 1906 and mid 1908. This was a critical time in Schoenberg's early career, during which he began to make the break with triadic, functional tonality as an organizing principle, completed with the Piano Pieces, op. 11, of 1909. A detailed investigation of the technical means by which Schoenberg's music evolved into atonality (a word he himself disliked) is beyond the scope of this study.[1] Here I shall attempt to convey something of this development through an

1. Although there are studies of individual pieces from the period 1906–9 (a notable one is Brinkmann 1969, on op. 11), there has been no study of this period as a whole in Schoenberg's output. Two articles that deal, in very different ways, with the transition to atonality across a broad range of works are Cone 1974 and Forte 1978.

analysis of the two instrumental works that span this period, the Second Chamber Symphony and the Second String Quartet (the latter also, of course, a vocal work). The first movement of op. 38 can be seen as perhaps Schoenberg's last fully tonal masterpiece of the early period. The quartet begins to call into question the kind of procedures handled with such assurance in op. 38; indeed, the quartet is, in a sense, "about" the conflict or differences between tonal and atonal procedures.

An essential kinship between these two pieces has gone largely unnoticed in the Schoenberg literature, perhaps because the Chamber Symphony was completed only in 1939 and is thus taken to be one of Schoenberg's later works. But as Sketchbook III reveals, the two pieces were to a large extent composed in tandem during 1907–8 (see table 13). By the fall of 1907, simultaneously with the completion of the first movement of op. 10, Schoenberg had completed in the sketchbook a continuous draft, in short score, of almost all of the first movement of the Second Chamber Symphony (through m. 143) and 85 full measures of the second. He also began to copy a full score, which was then broken off in August 1908, shortly after the completion of op. 10. As far as it extends, this full-score fragment, printed in *SW* B11/I: 147–97, is in all important respects identical to the final version published as op. 38, apart from some aspects of instrumentation and orchestration. Thus we can legitimately assess the first movement up to the coda (m. 143) as a work of 1906–8.

It is not only the chronological proximity and the intertwined sketching that suggest that opp. 10 and 38 be considered together. They are also both *Gegenstücke* to their immediate predecessors in their respective genres: that is, the Second Chamber Symphony is to the First somewhat as the Second Quartet is to the First Quartet. This relationship is most obvious in the larger formal design. Both the Second Chamber Symphony and Second Quartet appear to have been conceived at the outset as (or, at any rate, soon evolved into) works in separate movements. In this sense they both depart from the larger four-in-one-movement design of opp. 7 and 9. The similarity extends further into the very stuff of musical style and compositional technique. Both op. 10 and op. 38 tend to move away from the dense, almost self-consciously dissonant and gritty contrapuntal style so characteristic of opp. 7 and 9. This is not to say that there is any shortage of counterpoint, but the overall impression, especially in the first movements, is of a more lyrical idiom and a less cluttered texture.

The sketches bear out this assertion to a large extent, especially if one compares the first notated thoughts for the respective opening themes of opp. 7 and 10. The sketch for op. 7 (*SW* B20: 36) shows initially only the bass and theme (some inner parts are filled in at mm. 6 and 9); it is essentially a two-part contrapuntal framework. The first sketch for op. 10 (*SW* B20: 174) is more clearly homophonic: a melody line supported by harmony (with some contrapuntal move-

TABLE 13 Sketching and Drafting of Schoenberg's Second String Quartet, op. 10, and Second Chamber Symphony, op. 38, in Sketchbook III, 1906–8 (other compositions not included)

Pages	*Work/movement sketched/drafted*	*Dates in sketchbook*[a]
32–35	op. 38/I, sketches	1, 14 August 1906
38–39	op. 38/I, draft of mm. 1–57	
56	op. 10/II, sketches	
57	op. 10/I, sketches	9 March 1907
74–75	op. 10/I, draft of mm. 17–84	
76	op. 38/I, sketches	8 July 1907
77–79	op. 38/I, draft of mm. 57–143	
80–85	op. 38/II, drafts of mm. 3–41, 43–55, 53–158, 86–105	
86	op. 10/II, sketches	
87–88	op. 38/II, sketches	
90–92	op. 10/I, drafts of mm. 143–45, 159–end	1 September 1907
93	op. 10/II, sketches	
94–95	op. 10/II, drafts of mm. 53–62, 65–94	
96	op. 10/II, sketches; op. 10/III (?), partial draft of mvt. in E♭ min.	
97	op. 10/II, sketches	
99–101	op. 10/II, drafts of mm. 1–52, 98–132, 160–76	
105	op. 10/IV, sketches	
106	op. 10/III (?), partial draft of mvt. with B♭ key sig.	
108, 108^{1-8}	op. 10/III, sketches	
109	op. 10/III, draft of mm. 1–25	
110–11	op. 10/III, sketches; op. 10/II, drafts of mm. 132–60, 177–99	
113–15	op. 10/II, draft of mm. 200–end	27 July 1908
(116	op. 38/II, work resumed	23 November 1911)

[a] Incomplete fair copy of full score (*SW* B11/I: 146–97) has two dates on p. 1: *(29/8 1908) / 14/I. 1907.*

ment indicated in the implied second violin line). (A similar harmonic conception dominates the sketches for the themes from mm. 16 and 43; see S4 and S5.)

The effect of this more homophonic texture in both op. 10 and op. 38 is to place more emphasis—at least in the opening themes—on fluent motivic development in the primary voice. Both themes unfold by a process in which a very brief initial motivic gesture is presented, then immediately modified. In op. 38 (Appendix ex. R), the motive becomes displaced rhythmically by an eighth beat and takes on an additional eighth note; the melodic pattern is modified to move upward past the initial F♭ to A♭. In op. 10 (Appendix ex. S), the one-measure motive becomes compressed rather than expanded, so that the high C♯ in the varied repetition in m. 2 is now reached on beat 3 rather than beat 4. The rhythmic diminution allows for the addition to the melody of the B.

The Second Chamber Symphony, op. 38

Christian M. Schmidt has suggested that op. 38 represents a "regression" in Schoenberg's development during the years 1906–8:

> Op. 9 opened up new paths: its harmony, with its extremely tight-knit relation to the motivic-thematic occurrences, thrusts out to the very limits of the tonal system. In this respect the Second Chamber Symphony represents a regression: neither can its harmony be regarded as a further step towards the dissolution of tonality, nor are its harmonic formations so organically rooted in the structure of the musical substance as is the case in Op. 9.
>
> PREFACE TO PHILHARMONIA EDITION NO. 461

The practice of evaluating a work primarily on the basis of its progressiveness, although widespread in critical literature about the arts (and evident in portions of this study as well), seems especially wrongheaded here. The harmonic-motivic language of the work is certainly different from that of op. 9, but it is no less progressive. Indeed, op. 38 can be seen to represent an elegant refinement of some of the compositional techniques of op. 9.

The formal plan of the first movement is, to be sure, outwardly less adventurous than that of the double exposition of the first part of op. 9. Schoenberg turns to a large ternary design:

A (mm. 1–52)
B (mm. 53–94)
A′ (mm. 95–140)
Coda (mm. 141–65)

The conservative aspect of this plan, however, disguises a musical structure and language of great fluency. By comparison with the first movements of opp. 7 and 9, the A and B sections of op. 38 are tonally more closed, in E♭ minor and A♭ minor respectively. The A′ reprise is greatly transformed; segments of A are not only varied, but some are also transposed in a way that suggests that Schoenberg was still thinking, however subliminally, of sonata form. Although the A section certainly does not have the tonal thrust of a sonata-form exposition, its thematic process imparts an exposition-like feel. The design of the A section can be represented as:

A1 (mm. 1–11), tonally ambiguous, moves to V of E♭ minor
A2 (mm. 11–22), begins in E♭ minor, moves to V
A3 (mm. 23–31), begins in E♭ minor
A1′ (mm. 32–35), begins in E♭ minor
A2′ (mm. 36–47), begins in E♭ minor
Codetta, based on A1 (mm. 48–53)

Although it provides the principal motivic-thematic material for the movement, A1 almost has the feel of a slow introduction. It entirely avoids presenting the tonic E♭ minor until m. 11, as Schoenberg himself proudly pointed out in an annotation on the full-score draft (*SW* B11/II: 92). And it unfolds almost tentatively, questioningly. Steady rhythmic motion comes only with the cadence to E♭ minor in m. 11. In a sonata-form sense, then, A2 might be said to represent the "first theme"; it is followed by the imitative A3, which might be said to serve as a "second theme." This in turn is followed by a substantial developmental passage of sixteen measures (A1′-A2′), of the kind that often follows a second group in a sonata form.

Sonata-like procedures tend to be vestigial in the face of the wonderfully fluid thematic process that unfolds across the entire A section (Appendix ex. R). Indeed, Schoenberg may have consciously renounced overt sonata-like processes in order to focus on less "formal" thematic ones. It has been shown by Klaus Velten that the first movement of op. 38 is a supreme example of the simultaneous use of the Schoenbergian concepts of developing variation, in which thematic materials are generated from the continuous modification of a very few motivic ideas, and fluctuating (*schwebende*) tonality, in which many key areas are touched upon (Velten 1976, 91–98). Velten suggests that the themes tend to develop successively from the intervals of the fifth and half-step presented in the initial motive. "While the fifth leap stresses the tonic and thereby suggests the tonality, the chromatic step oversteps the tonal boundaries," he notes (ibid., 91).

Although he tends to remain only on the level of the individual theme and does not in fact take much account of harmony in his analyses, Velten is certainly right. Throughout themes A1 and A2, one can hear Schoenberg quite consciously (even self-consciously) reworking, reshaping, and recombining the basic intervals of the fifth and the half-step (which we may call *x* and *y*). A1 consists of six phrases or units leading toward a cadence in E♭ minor in m. 11. These units cannot be said to shape themselves into any traditional antecedent-consequent or period structure. Rather they seem to unfold by a successive reinterpretation of the basic harmonic-motivic material. The first four units form complementary pairs (*a, a′, b, b′*) in which the first element of the pair presents a motive and the second modifies it in some way such as to lead toward a new harmonic area. The fifth and six (*c, c′*) serve to "liquidate" the material and move toward the cadence. But even the use of the different letters *a, b,* and *c* tends to conceal the genuine continuity of the process.

We can hear quite clearly how *b* modifies the basic elements of *a*. Across mm. 3–4, *x* is contracted to a fourth, A♭–E♭, then followed by *y*. The process of contraction can be perceived as occurring through an inversion of *y* as the descending half-step B♭♭–A♭. Indeed, the figure B♭♭–A♭–E♭, in which the inversion of *y* is attached to the beginning of a contracted (or inverted) *x*, becomes a significant enough motivic element that it can be given its own designation, *z*. At the end of *b′*, the second interval of *z* is now expanded to a minor sixth. Phrase *c* consists solely of a presentation of *z*, in which the original descending fifth of *x* is restored. The original *x* is then repeated at the beginning of *c′*.

The harmonic component of the first movement of op. 38 is just as remarkable as the thematic-motivic one. The four phrases of theme A1 move through a wide range of root relationships before reaching the tonic E♭ minor. Some of these relationships seem to share in or reflect in particular the motivic identity of *y*, the half-step. Indeed, across the phrases *a, a′, b,* and *b′*, the roots rise by half-step from A♭ to B♮. Phrase *a* moves from A♭ minor up a half-step to A minor; phrase *a′* carries the same succession up a further half-step to a half-diminished seventh chord on B♭. Phrase *b* moves back to A minor; *b′* then pushes still further up to B minor. Phrase *c* and the first three notes of *c′* remain in the orbit of B, with moves to F♯ minor and D major.

D major represents one of the remotest possible keys from the tonic: it is the key of the leading tone. The way in which Schoenberg moves from here to the tonic is fully characteristic of the range of his powers at this time. In m. 9, the F♯ of the D-major chord is respelled as G♭. Underneath the sustained G♭ comes the same B♭ half-diminished seventh chord heard in phrase *a′* (m. 3), together with the original descending sixth motive B♭–D♭ in the cellos and double bass. The melodic F♯/G♭ is thereby redefined as a suspension within that chord. In another harmonic surprise, the G♭ of m. 10 resolves not to the expected F♭, but to

F♮; and with the concomitant change of D♭ to D♮, the half-diminished chord has reshaped itself as a dominant seventh of E♭ minor. This change is indeed remarkable—almost magical—for half-diminished chords and dominant sevenths normally have very different tonal functions. That through voice-leading Schoenberg can transform one into the other shows both how flexible and at the same time how root-oriented his harmonic language is: the common root B♭ is enough to give identity and logic to the chord during its evolution from half-diminished to dominant seventh.

The whole eleven-measure process of A1 thus integrates extremely remote harmonies into what comes to seem a coherent, purposeful succession from the initial subdominant heard in mm. 1–4 to the dominant reached in m. 10. The harmonic process of theme A3 is also worthy of analysis. The first entry of the theme, beginning on the note B♭, functions essentially as a V–i cadence in E♭ minor, sustaining the dominant adumbrated in m. 22. The tonic is reached on the second beat of m. 25. The second entry, beginning a half-step higher on B♮ (here is another half-step relationship), fulfills an entirely different tonal function. Although the theme itself is transposed up a half-step through the F♯ on the downbeat of m. 27, the second entry does not function as a dominant; instead it remains in B minor. By analogy to the first entry, the chord on the final eighth note of m. 26 should be a dominant of E minor. Instead, we get the dominant of B minor, which resolves onto B minor on the downbeat of m. 27. Schoenberg has thus radically reharmonized the three-measure theme while keeping its melodic component essentially intact. The third entry, beginning on G, is quickly followed by a stretto (new entries in mm. 28 and 29) and leads into the "developmental" return of A1 in m. 32.

The manipulation of phrase structure and the harmonic vocabulary of op. 38 are different in significant respects from opp. 7 and 9, the two preceding instrumental works of the 1904–6 period. Perhaps the style of the first movement of op. 38 comes closest to that of the slower, more lyrical portions of these earlier works, especially the A-major theme of op. 9 (theme II/2, m. 84) and the slow movement theme of op. 7 (**K**). But there is a distinct difference. The theme in op. 9 remains clearly rooted in the key of A major, which is articulated in mm. 86 and 91–92. The rate of harmonic change is slower; there are fewer different chords and the melody is thus more consistently and pungently dissonant with the underlying harmony. This intense kind of dissonant writing is part of the distinctive style of op. 9 (and op. 7). In op. 38, the simultaneous motion of the voices makes for more frequent local shifts of harmony; there are thus fewer dissonant melodic appoggiaturas.[2] Another difference from op. 9 is in the nature of the harmonies. Theme II/2 of op. 9 makes considerable use of dominant-seventh

2. This point has been made by Neighbour 1980, 718.

EXAMPLE 10.1 Second Chamber Symphony, op. 38, I, fourth chords at climax of A2.

chords not directly related to the local tonic A: specifically the D^7 and $B\flat^7$ chords in mm. 85, 87, and 90. These kinds of chords, which help give the theme its peculiar flavor, are not present in op. 38.

A revealing point of comparison between the First and Second Chamber Symphonies is their respective treatment of quartal elements. As we recall, fourths play a prominent role in op. 9, especially at important formal junctures. We may recall too that the quartal harmonies of op. 9 tend to arise through stepwise voice-leading and that Schoenberg often seems to conceive these outwardly symmetrical formations in terms of root functions. There are no six-part quartal chords in op. 38 of the kind found in op. 9; from this point of view, the work is indeed less radical—more "regressive," in Schmidt's terms. But there are distinctly quartal elements, and the way in which they are integrated into the overall harmonic language is just as persuasive as in op. 9.

The first quartal sonority comes in m. 9, in phrase *c'* at the approach to the first cadence in E♭ minor (Appendix ex. R). Underneath the sustained G♭ of the flute, the violas play D♭ and A♭. But any true quartal property of the chord is undermined by the root, B♭ in the bass, which clarifies the chord (at least by the end of the following measure) as a dominant. Fourth chords appear more prominently at the climax of the A2' theme, at m. 43 (ex. 10.1). In m. 43, the fourths are projected horizontally, in the melody. Genuine four-part fourth chords appear on the strong beats, alternating with normal triads (B♭ and C respectively). The harmonic-melodic progression is carried along by strong stepwise voice-leading in the bass. This passage forms, on a smaller scale, a kind of structural analogy to that at mm. 355–67 in the development section of the First Chamber Symphony. There the treatment of the quartal sonorities reaches its climax in both the vertical and horizontal dimensions: both harmony and melody consist only of simultaneous and/or successive fourths. In mm. 43–44 of the first movement of the Second Chamber Symphony, Schoenberg achieves something similar. Yet, befitting the whole tone and style of op. 38, the climax is much more understated than in op. 9, although no less subtle.

EXAMPLE 10.2 Second Chamber Symphony, op. 38, I, fourth chords.

a. End of A

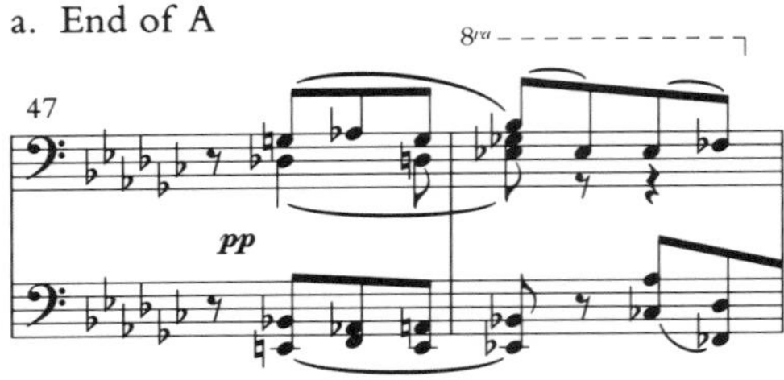

b. Coda

Purer fourth chords are encountered at the important cadential points at the end of A and the coda, in particular at mm. 47–48 and 159–63. In the former (ex. 10.2a), the tonic is approached directly from a four-part fourth chord, which stands in for the conventional dominant. As in the climax four measures earlier, the radical nature of the cadence is muted, understated by the smooth voice-leading. The cadential passage at the end of the coda (ex. 10.2b), although apparently not composed or drafted in 1906–8, merits consideration here. The melodic figures of descending fourths are harmonized first by A minor, then by a four-part fourth chord built up from B♭, then a five-part fourth chord on B♮. Schoenberg moves back down through B♭ with an exact transposition of the preceding five-part chord down a half-step, to A minor and back up to B♮. All these

EXAMPLE 10.3 Second Chamber Symphony, op. 38, I, recapitulation of A3.

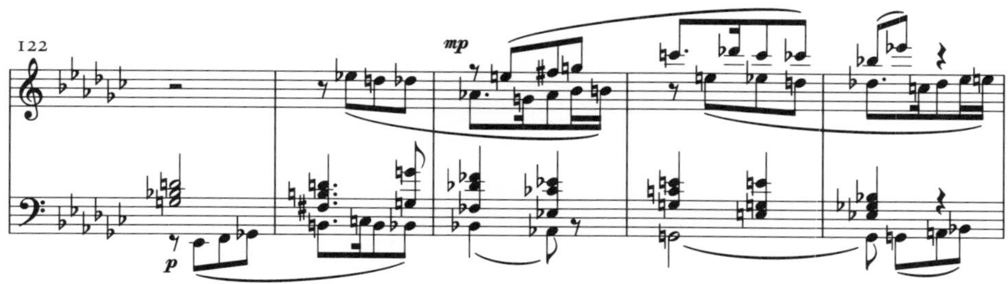

chords are connected clearly and conspicuously by stepwise voice-leading. Schoenberg thereby manages to achieve logical yet untraditional continuity between sonorities and also manages, as in mm. 47–48, to avoid utterly any conventional V–i approach to the tonic.

This process of voice-leading is so smooth and so idiomatic that it forces us to redefine our own normal perceptions of tonal functions. Thus, it is hard to say whether the chord in m. 163 is to be taken as a substitute dominant, because of the B♭ in the bass, or as a genuine tonic with the fifth in the bass (the tonic E♭ is provided in the bass only at the very last moment, in m. 165). The simultaneous arrival of phrase *a* of the A1 theme with the chord on the downbeat of m. 163 might argue for a "real" tonic. In any case, the very ambiguity shows how fluent Schoenberg's utilization of the quartal chords is—and how closely it is tied in with the half-step motivic figure *y*. The final cadence across mm. 164–65 contains, and in an important sense resolves, the E♭–F♭ semitone relationship.

Before leaving the Second Chamber Symphony, we should devote some attention to the transformations of the A section in the reprise A′. It is here that we see in especially vivid form the synthesis of sonata and ternary procedures. The moment of return in m. 95 arrives quietly, unobtrusively. The original theme, accompanied by chords at its first appearance, is now surrounded by, or enmeshed in, a contrapuntal web comprised of three other voices: a syncopated theme in the first flute; a line descending in semitones, played by the bass clarinet and the first cello; and a theme played by the viola. The viola line is based rhythmically on the second, third, and fourth measures of theme A2 (cf. mm. 12–14).

Real transposition occurs with the approach to theme A3 (ex. 10.3). In true sonata-like fashion, the theme begins (in m. 122) on E♭, down a fifth from its original appearance (m. 23). This brings the first entry to cadence on A♭ minor, rather than the original E♭ minor of m. 25. The second entry begins on E♮, also down a fifth from the original B, but Schoenberg modifies this entry so that its final notes lead back to E♭ minor. In its original appearance (Appendix ex. R, mm. 25–27), the second entry of the theme remained in B minor (unlike the first entry, which cadenced from V to i in E♭ minor). Were the reprise exact, the theme would now sustain E minor: the last two notes (on the downbeat of m. 124) would be C♭–F♭ (or B♮–E♮). Instead, Schoenberg changes these to B♭–E♭, down a half-step from the expected location. This change, together with the accompanying harmonies, serves to steer the theme back toward the tonic E♭ minor. Such far-reaching transformations of A material in the reprise of op. 38 show Schoenberg manipulating sonata-like principles with extraordinary fluency.

The Second String Quartet, op. 10

As is suggested by Sketchbook III (table 13), Schoenberg began work on the Second Quartet in March 1907, about seven months after making the first sketches for op. 38. Over the next year and a half, the quartet was to supplant the Chamber Symphony as the focus of his creative activities. Although the genesis of the work as a whole was protracted, Schoenberg appears to have composed the individual movements at lightning speed; such, at least, is suggested by his claim to have written "three-fourths of both the second and fourth movements of my Second String Quartet in one-and-a-half days each" (Schoenberg 1975, 55).

Schoenberg himself saw the Second Quartet as marking "the transition to my second period" (Schoenberg 1975, 86) in two particular ways. First, large, continuous structures were replaced by separate movements (something also true, as I have suggested, of op. 38): "By abandoning the one-movement form and returning . . . to the organization of four movements, I became the first composer of the period to write short compositions. Soon thereafter I wrote in the extreme short forms" (ibid., 78). Second, the quartet intimated the renunciation of tonal centers that was to characterize the works of 1909: "In the first and second movements there are many sections in which the individual parts proceed regardless of whether or not their meeting results in codified harmonies. Still, here, and also in the third and fourth movements, the key is presented distinctly at all the main dividing-points of the formal organization" (ibid., 86). As has been suggested above (and will be elaborated below), Schoenberg's second point, about the juxtaposition of key-centered and non-tonal passages, forms the basic compositional premise of the quartet as a whole. In this important sense, the Second Quartet is different from either op. 7 or op. 9, pieces for which Schoenberg had made similar claims about the individual parts moving independently of harmonic implications.

As to the first point: although the division into distinct movements is, to be sure, significant, one of the great achievements of op. 10 is precisely Schoenberg's adaptation of the long-range cyclic or recapitulatory techniques of opp. 4,

5, 7, and 9 to the separate-movement format. One of the main themes of the first-movement exposition (1b, m. 12; Appendix ex. S) is recalled near the end of the trio in the scherzo movement (m. 180), just after the renowned "O du lieber Augustin" citation. The thematic material of the third movement, a setting of Stefan George's "Litanei" in variation form, comes almost exclusively from the preceding two movements; in this sense, the movement functions as a cyclic return. The coda of the finale is clearly intended to round off the quartet as a whole. The syncopated triplet figures (cello, m. 134) recall the opening theme of the first movement. The tonal return to the key of the first movement, F♯ minor, followed by a resolution to F♯ major, is also in this context, as Schoenberg himself acknowledged, a genuinely cyclic gesture.

The first movement of op. 10 is in outward respects a more conservative sonata form than the analogous movements of op. 7 or op. 9 (or op. 38). The exposition (mm. 1–89), development (90–145), recapitulation (146–201), and coda (202–33) are not hard to locate. (For Schoenberg's own analysis, which employs sonata form, see Rauchhaupt 1971, 43–44; see also the analysis in Whittall 1972, 20–21.) The exposition of op. 10 has the following design:

1a, m. 1
1b, m. 12
1a′/transition, m. 33
2a, m. 43
2b, m. 59
2c, m. 70

What is distinctive is the way Schoenberg manipulates the sonata structure into a technical and expressive conflict between tonal and atonal gestures, a conflict that prefigures that of the quartet as a whole. The contrast between themes, especially between 1a and 1b (and 1a and 2a, which is closely related to 1b, as will be shown below), is distinctly sharper than that between the analogous themes in op. 38 and is, indeed, perhaps more extreme than in any previous sonata form by Schoenberg.

Theme 1a (see Appendix ex. S) begins in F♯ minor, passes through the chords of A♭ major and A minor, and breaks off in m. 11 on a *fortissimo* F major. Even though the syntax or succession of chords is surprising and unconventional, the theme is clearly based on triadic structures; as such it seems almost to embody tonality or tonal processes. In theme 1b, no triad is evident; tonal associations are stretched to the limit through the primacy of counterpoint, dissonant appoggiaturas, and stepwise voice-leading. For the first five-measure phrase of 1b, the melodic line alone could be heard as a conventional unit in F♯, descending from scale degree 5 to a half-cadence on 7, a half-step below 1. A "normal" harmonization might move from I or i to V, perhaps with a strong G-major Neapolitan in m. 15. But the context into which Schoenberg places the phrase is far from harmonically normal. The melody is underpinned by two lines, one in the second violin, the other in the cello. The bass line descends in appoggiaturas by half-step from B to G♮. Except for the A♯ of m. 13, this descent fails utterly to support a progression from I to V. In this sense, then, we may speak of "atonality," fully realizing that the theme is not as resolutely atonal as the music written by Schoenberg after this quartet.

Schoenberg's bold stroke here—one that has implications not only for sonata form but for his entire musical style—is to reverse the expected associations of tonality/consonance with stability, and of atonality/dissonance with instability. Despite its triadic orientation, theme 1a is highly unstable. It refuses to hold to its F♯-minor point of origin, but begins right away to wander tonally and in m. 11 literally falls apart on F major (one can certainly not speak of any cadence or close on F). The theme is also temporally unstable: it begins slowly, then speeds up dramatically, impulsively, across its eleven measures, as if propelling itself headlong toward its own demise.

From the viewpoint of phrase structure as well, 1a seems unstable. Outwardly, it has a two-part, antecedent-consequent structure of the kind Schoenberg himself might have analyzed as a "period" (mm. 1–7, 8–11). But the proportions and the general *Stimmung* are awry. The first phrase or antecedent begins with a proper two-measure unit, which is followed by a three-measure one. But the succeeding measures undermine any incipient regularity. The consequent is too short, and it is violent: instead of "completing" or complementing the antecedent, it grabs the theme and in m. 11 brings it abruptly to a halt.

The contrasting theme of the first group, 1b, presents a very different picture. It unfolds at a relatively constant tempo, which Schoenberg marks significantly as the *Hauptzeitmaß*, or principal tempo, almost as if what preceded is to be taken as *Vorspiel*. The smooth linearity of its bass line and the regularity of the melodic structure (5 + 5, mm. 12–16 and 17–21) give the theme a stability or solidity. Unlike theme 1a, 1b is accorded a full counterstatement beginning in m. 24. With its regular *Hauptzeitmaß*, its smooth voice-leading, and its substantial length, theme 1b, then, takes on the character of a principal or primary theme in a sonata form. In that a relatively unstable opening theme leads to a more stable second one, Schoenberg's procedure in op. 10 is analogous to that in the first movement of op. 38. But the tonal implications are now reversed. In op. 38, the reader will recall, the opening theme gives way to a firm (if temporary) E♭ minor at m. 11. In the quartet, the triadic sonorities of 1a are made to sound less stable than the tonally more ambiguous 1b.

EXAMPLE 10.4 Second String Quartet, op. 10, I, comparison of themes 1b and 2a.

The approach to the second group replicates (and thus reinforces) to some extent the process of the first twelve measures of the movement. The return of 1a as a transitional element (1a′/transition) brings with it the unsteady tempo of the opening measures. In a sense this passage shows 1a in its "true" light; it is more suited to be an unstable transition than an opening theme. The transition gives way in m. 43 to *Zeitmaß* (presumably the same as the *Hauptzeitmaß* of m. 12) and to theme 2a, which is derived directly and unmistakably from 1b.

This derivation or relationship becomes clear when the two themes are superimposed as in ex. 10.4. Both consist of two phrases (5 + 5 measures in 1b, 4 + 5 in 2a). Both begin with a C♯–D neighbor motion and proceed with similar contours. It is perhaps not surprising to find that the two themes were actually sketched by Schoenberg very close together on the same page of Sketchbook III (see *SW* B20: 174–75). But more significant than their common or simultaneous genesis is their disposition in the sonata form. By using similar (indeed, aurally almost identical) themes in the middle of the first group and then at the beginning of the second group, Schoenberg is calling into question some of the perceptual foundations of sonata form. To be sure, Haydn had long before written so-called monothematic expositions, in which there is no distinct second subject to coincide with the arrival of the dominant. But in the later nineteenth century, when tonality (or at any rate, tonic-dominant polarity) no longer played such an important role in the articulation of sonata forms, composers tended to rely strongly on thematic dualism or contrast. As we have seen, Schoenberg certainly does so in earlier works, even where the second theme can be motivically derived from the primary one. In the first movement of op. 10, however, we seem to have a deliberate attempt to overturn the normal associations or conventions of thematic dualism.

Schoenberg also plays with the formal implications of thematic groupings. In one sense, the first 43 measures present an ABA′ form, a conventional arrangement within sonata traditions from Schubert onward (see, for example, the first movement of Brahms's Violin Sonata in G Major, op. 78, or of Schoenberg's own D-Major Quartet of 1897). But the ternary design, in which the longer, more stable theme normally encloses the shorter, unstable one, does not fit or suit the thematic material in op. 10. We are thus forced, or invited, to hear beyond the 43 measures to a larger two-part design, AB A′B′, in which each part begins unstably and moves to a more stable theme (Appendix ex. S). The essential identity that Schoenberg creates between the B and B′ themes (respectively 1b and 2a in my sonata-form analysis) overrides the conventional sonata plan, in which we expect a distinct contrast between first group and second group. In op. 10 Schoenberg has built that contrast right into the first group.

The continuation of the second group at m. 58 (not shown in ex. S) further complicates and extends the AB A′B′ design by adding a suggestion of A″: the theme that begins at m. 58 ("belebend"), which can be labeled functionally as 2b, or the second idea within the second group, is in fact derived rhythmically from the second measure of theme 1a (m. 2 of the movement).[3] The derivation becomes explicit at the recapitulation, where 2b (m. 150) follows immediately upon 1a (m. 146) as part of the first group. The presence of 2b in the exposition as a developmental variant of 1a serves as a kind of complement to the relationship of 2a and 1b. In both cases, first-group material (1a and 1b) comes back more or less overtly in the second group (as 2b and 2a, respectively).

In the recapitulation, Schoenberg continues to explore the dualistic relationship between themes. At the opening of the recapitulation in m. 146, he strikingly reverses the process from the analogous part of the exposition. Theme 1a now begins in F major, the key or triad on which it fell apart upon its first appearance (m. 11); it then moves smoothly, through stepwise voice-leading to the tonic F♯ minor in m. 159. Instead of the agitated, ever-accelerating tempo of the opening, the theme now begins slowly, broadly, and gets still slower across fourteen measures, so that the *Zeitmaß* of m. 159 really comes to seem quicker than the initial tempo. Schoenberg gives 1a still greater weight or status in the recapitulation by presenting the theme in augmentation in the cello (mm. 146–49). In these ways, then, the recapitulation of 1a effects a genuine reversal and accords theme 1a a stability it was denied in the exposition.

In his own analysis of op. 10, Schoenberg suggests that theme 2a is omitted from the recapitulation (Rauchhaupt 1971, 44). But it seems clear that the passage beginning at m. 196 serves precisely a recapitulatory function and leads to the coda at the resolution to F♯ minor in m. 202. Furthermore, in following 1b (m. 159) and 1a′/transition (m. 186), 2a occupies the same position as in the exposition. At m. 196, theme 2a is actually divided into its two basic thematic units, which are presented simultaneously rather than successively. This is a typically

3. I am grateful to Julian Treves for suggesting this relationship to me.

economical recapitulatory strategy for Schoenberg, one that is also present in the finale of op. 10. The half-step figure (from mm. 43–44, but without the whole-step descent of m. 44) appears in the upper voices; the descending figure (from mm. 45–46) is in the cello. The isolation of the half-step neighbor figure helps reinforce the close identity between themes 1b and 2a.

The first movement of op. 10 calls many sonata-like precepts into question, while nevertheless adhering with relative strictness to the formal prototype. The impetuous scherzo seems to throw any such caution to the wind. It is one of the most extraordinary and unorthodox instrumental movements among Schoenberg's early works, and certainly far more radical than the scherzos in opp. 7 and 9. Elaborating the *Formübersicht* prepared by Erwin Stein for the Philharmonia pocket score of op. 10 (no. 229), Schmidt has divided the scherzo proper into a brief, nineteen-measure "exposition" and a "development" lasting from m. 20 to m. 97 (*SW* B20: 178–79). Here the use of sonata-form terminology seems to me (even with my own strong propensity to read "sonata" into instrumental movements) misleading and inappropriate. To be sure, the absence of an immediate "recapitulation," or its displacement to the return of the scherzo after the trio, would perhaps not be surprising from the composer of the First Quartet and First Chamber Symphony. But in the Stein-Schmidt scheme, the proportion of "exposition" to "development" is out of balance. Moreover, that the three basic thematic ideas in the scherzo are separated by a fermata but no "transition" suggests a formal dynamic very different from sonata form. Indeed, the process seems almost to dismiss or turn its back on the rather orthodox sonata form of the preceding movement.

The body of the scherzo consists essentially of an alternation and cumulative development of three basic thematic units, A (mm. 1–13), B (14–17), and C (17–19), which seem constantly to react to each other (see Appendix ex. T). Unit A begins with only a rhythmic figure (*x*) in the cello (perhaps an echo of Beethoven's equally unusual scherzo in op. 59, no. 1?). In m. 4, this figure is overlaid with two other ideas (*y* and *z*). Beginning in m. 7, the upper two parts are inverted so that the staccato *z* appears below the legato *y* (whose rhythmic profile is now varied). In unit B, the rhythmic motive *x*, which was deprived of any melodic shape, is now accorded one; but after three and a half measures, C seems to dismiss the preceding lyricism with a chuckle of sixteenth notes. Later in the scherzo (m. 65), C is itself transformed from its original skittish shape into a lyrical melody "mit sehr zartem Ausdruck."

In the critical report to *SW* (B20: 178–89), Schmidt has described in illuminating detail Schoenberg's extensive sketches and drafts for the "development" section of the scherzo (mm. 20–97). His essential point is that the various thematic units that I have called A, B, and C (and that are called *Gedanken* 1, 2, and 3 by Schmidt), were continuously reshuffled and recombined, almost like pieces of a

EXAMPLE 10.5 Second String Quartet, op. 10, II, first sketch for scherzo theme, from Sketchbook III, p. 56.

puzzle, until the final form was reached (and indicated by Schoenberg in the sketchbook by a characteristic profusion of cross-reference symbols). The sketching process shows Schoenberg working in this movement toward a new kind, or a new degree, of developmental form.

It is worthy of notice too that according to the sequence of Sketchbook III, the scherzo was both the first movement of op. 10 to be sketched and the last to be completed (see table 13); it can thus be said to have preoccupied Schoenberg on some level throughout the eighteen-month genesis of the work (although he claims to have composed most of it in a day and a half). The first notated ideas for the quartet in Sketchbook III are contained in two sketches on p. 56 (see table 13; *SW* B20: 177). The first contains a single-line draft for the eighth-note motive *z* of theme A (ex. 10.5); it is identical to its final form except that it contains an immediate repetition of the first measure (and thus is three measures long in the sketch, rather than two as in the final version). The second appears to be a sketch for the trio and is, as Schmidt suggests, "very close to the 'O du lieber Augustin passage' in gesture and rhythmic shape" (*SW* B20: 177).

The first sketch is of relevance to the present study because it shows that Schoenberg's first notated idea for the Second Quartet was in the key of his previous quartet (and several other early works), D minor, and that, somewhat like the opening theme of op. 7, it seems intent on exploring the chromatic range around a D center. Indeed, this little theme can almost be taken as representative or symbolic of Schoenberg's tonal language at this time (probably early 1907). The tonic is obviously D, and it is complemented or supported by a clear dominant tone, A, as well as by two tonic-defining neighbor notes (part of the dominant chord), C♯ and E. But the tonal field of D is, as it were, so sprinkled with chromatic "weeds" that the tonic becomes obscured. This overgrowth becomes especially evident when the theme is heard in its real context (as *z*), near the beginning of the scherzo. The D pedal sounding insistently in the cello throughout the first ten measures (*x*) is really tonic by assertion, above which *y* and *z* range widely over the chromatic space. In these ways, the scherzo of op. 10 can be considered the last great D-minor exploration of Schoenberg's early tonal period.

The disintegration of D becomes still more extreme in the trio, which is given a key signature of D major. Here the main theme, a combination of a rapid descending figure in the violin and a lyrical rising melody in the cello (ex. 10.6), is

EXAMPLE 10.6 Second String Quartet, op. 10, II, main theme of trio.

to my ear the least tonally centered of any so far in the quartet: that is, it has less audible relationship to D major than do the themes of the scherzo proper to D minor. Schoenberg refers to the violin figure of m. 98 as having "seven notes . . . because this was the form in which this theme came to mind" (Rauchhaupt 1971, 45). Indeed, in the sketches for the trio, the figure consists entirely of eighth notes, divided between two measures, $\frac{2}{4}+\frac{3}{8}$ (*SW* B20: 189). Schoenberg then changed it to a single measure of 4 + 3 "because I feared to be called a revolutionary." Not only the rhythmic profile, but also the tonal outline of this figure (which remained unchanged) might perplex a listener. The downward sequence through m. 101 descends by major third: the starting notes are respectively F♯, D, A♯, F♯. Although this kind of symmetrical division of the octave was hardly new in 1907 (it already appears in Schubert almost a century earlier), its combination with a figure that is already highly chromatic and unstable makes for virtual atonality. In this sense, the sequence is not unlike the more famous and vivid one at the opening of the fourth movement.

The cello theme that is placed underneath the sequence beginning in m. 100 is also extremely dissonant. Its nine notes expose eight different chromatic tones (only the F♯ appoggiatura in m. 103 is a repetition) and fail in any sense to project D major (or any other key). The pure A-major "dominant" triads that follow in mm. 104–5, 107, and 108 seem intended as a witty—but ineffective—corrective to the wanderings of the first theme.

The essential dramatic scenario of the scherzo and trio of op. 10 appears, then,

EXAMPLE 10.7 Second String Quartet, op. 10, II, transformation of "Augustin" theme.

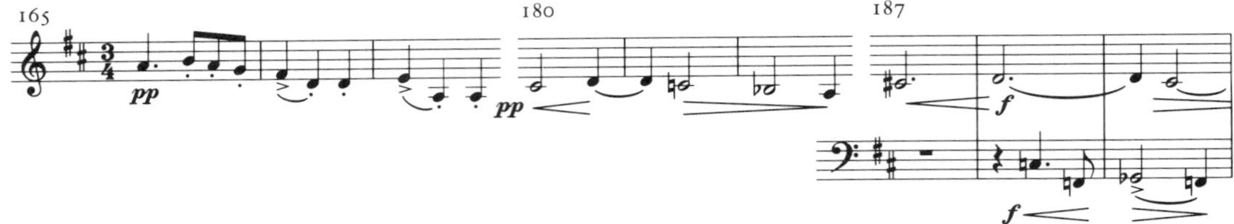

to be the dissolution or evaporation of conventional tonality. This tale reaches its overtly programmatic climax at the end of the trio, in m. 160, where the musical development of the trio themes screeches to a halt and yields to the renowned quotation of "O du lieber Augustin." The intrusion of this popular song, especially of its last phrase, "Alles ist hin," serves, as is often remarked, as a kind of self-referential commentary on the distintegration of the musical language. What is perhaps not so often articulated is what Schoenberg himself points out (Rauchhaupt 1971, 45): that the liquidation or taking-apart of the "Augustin" theme in mm. 171–92 yields the principal motives of themes 1b and 2a of the first movement. Specifically (ex. 10.7), the opening neighbor-note figure, A–B–A (or $\hat{5}$–$\hat{6}$–$\hat{5}$), of the song (m. 165) becomes transmuted first (m. 180) into the head motive of 2a (C♯–D–C♮), then into the C♯–D–C♯ figure of 1b (at m. 187). Underneath this latter transformation, Schoenberg turns the other part of the "Augustin" melody, the descending fifth (E–A, m. 167) and the rhythmic figure it embodies (three quarter notes with an accent on the first), into the third and fourth measures of theme 1b.

Here we have an extraordinary example of the kind of thematic transformation that we have been tracing throughout Schoenberg's early works and that is now put into the service of a programmatic statement. With the transformation of the banal, tonal street song back into the intense, dissonant thematic material of the quartet, Schoenberg seems to be saying that the step between tonality and atonality (or between consonance and dissonance), which was presented in exaggerated form in the opening segment of the first movement and then further exposed in the scherzo and trio, is in fact not so great. It is not an unbridgeable, absolute gap. This is, of course, the viewpoint repeatedly propounded by Schoenberg in his *Theory of Harmony*, where he argues that "dissonances are the more remote consonances of the overtone series" (Schoenberg 1978, 329).[4] Here, in the trio of

4. This quotation comes from the crucial chapter on "non-harmonic" tones (chapter 17). See also chapter 3, "Consonance and Dissonance."

op. 10, he makes the point musically by referring back to precisely that spot in the first movement where the tonal-atonal or consonant-dissonant juxtaposition was made, in the first theme group. It is to create this association for the listener, rather than to fufill any purely "cyclic" impulse, that Schoenberg here makes reference to a theme from the first movement. Thus in this way, as in so many others, the Second Quartet makes over traditional techniques.

The apparent genesis of the last two movements of op. 10 sheds further light on the important issue of cyclicism or return in the work. According to the sequence of sketches, as well as certain notations, in Sketchbook III, the present fourth movement, "Entrückung," was originally projected to be in third position. The sketches for it are headed "III Satz Streichquartett"; they follow sketches for movements 1 and 2, and precede those for "Litanei" (see table 13). "Litanei" was thus not only the last movement conceived (although the scherzo was the last actually to be completed), but appears to have been intended as the finale, even though no sketches are marked specifically as such. Such is the reasonable speculation of Schmidt, who notes that an ordering "Entrückung"–"Litanei" would have placed the most obviously recapitulatory movement last, according to nineteenth-century tradition (*SW* B20: 193).

I would concur with Schmidt's interpretation of the evidence, in part because, judging by the example of Schoenberg's earlier instrumental works that have been examined in this study, we would expect him instinctively to place some kind of important large-scale return near the end of a piece. The key of "Litanei," however, which is E♭ minor even in the earliest sketches, presents something of a challenge to the theory that the movement might have been intended for last place. As we have seen, Schoenberg (unlike Mahler in this period) tends to end his large-scale instrumental compositions in the key in which they began. It is certainly possible that for op. 10, which departs from the earlier works in many respects, Schoenberg would have opted for a tonal conclusion away from F♯ minor. But in a sketch for stanza 4 of "Litanei" there is strong evidence that he did indeed plan a return to F♯ minor, one that would moreover coincide with a direct recall of theme 1a from the first movement, in its original triple meter ("Litanei" as we know it remains in $\frac{4}{4}$ throughout). In this sketch (ex. 10.8; see *SW* B20: 194), in which a tonic and dominant of F♯ minor are clearly articulated, the bass is ingeniously fashioned from what I called theme 2b of the first movement (m. 58), a theme that also plays a large role in "Litanei" (first appearing in augmentation in mm. 4–9). As was pointed out above in the discussion of the first movement, theme 2b was itself derived from 1a, and the two themes were juxtaposed in the recapitulation; their actual contrapuntal combination in the "Litanei" sketch thus seems especially appropriate. This sketch was rejected when "Litanei" assumed its third-movement position in the completed work.

When he reversed the order of "Entrückung" and "Litanei," thus displacing

EXAMPLE 10.8 Second String Quartet, op. 10, III, sketch for fourth stanza of "Litanei," from Sketchbook III, p. 108.

the most substantial cyclic return from its customary end position, Schoenberg effected a profound change not only in the shape of the quartet but in his whole conception of large-scale form. From the viewpoint of the texts alone, the decision was both significant and logical. In the final version of the quartet, the questioning, anguished persona of "Litanei" is liberated and released in "Entrückung," literally set afloat in the atmosphere. Here the "qual" (torture, anguish) of "Litanei" is completely "erloschen" (extinguished). George uses the word *qual* in both poems, and Schoenberg clearly picks up on the verbal association. An ordering of movements "Entrückung"–"Litanei," as intially planned, would have given a completely contrary motion, from liberation toward pain and suffering (albeit with the hope of redemption).

As is well known, Schoenberg dedicated the Second Quartet to his wife, Mathilde. The composition of the work coincided with a particularly painful point in their marriage, just after the end of Mathilde's affair with the painter Richard Gerstl (who committed suicide). Schoenberg's apparent vacillation over the ordering of the last two movements may well reflect his own emotional conflict over the Gerstl affair. From an initial pessimistic despair, from an "Entrückung"–"Litanei" ordering, he moved toward a more optimistic, life-affirming (really art-affirming) position, signified in part by the ordering "Litanei"–"Entrückung."

Although many commentators, including Schoenberg, have a tendency to speak of "shorter" forms in op. 10, the finale is, in fact, an expansive structure. Lasting almost eleven minutes, it is twice as long as any of the preceding three movements and half as long as the entire First Chamber Symphony. In its fusion of song and instrumental form, "Entrückung" is one of the masterpieces of Schoenberg's early period. As in the first movement, and as in so many other structures we have examined in this study, Schoenberg relies on sonata-like processes to give the finale its shape. In his *Formübersicht* in the Philharmonic pocket score, Erwin Stein gives the large outlines of the sonata structure, which may be expanded or filled out as follows:

INSTRUMENTAL INTRODUCTION

Part I, mm. 1–9

Part II, mm. 10–15

Part III, mm. 16–21 (=transition to exposition)

EXPOSITION

Theme 1, mm. 21–26

Transition/development, mm. 27–51

Theme 2, mm. 51–66

DEVELOPMENT

Part I, mm. 67–82

Part II, mm. 83–99

REPRISE

Themes 1 and 2 combined, mm. 100–19

CODA, mm. 120–56

The renowned introduction to this movement is a masterpiece of tone painting that both illustrates the "transport" of the poem and epitomizes or captures the essential tonal-atonal conflict that lies at the basis of the quartet. The opening of the introduction is built from essentially two different melodic figures or types. The first, introduced by the instruments in rising imitation in the first measure, can be called the "floating" figure. Although the entries come at the interval of a fifth (G♯–D♯–B♭–F), thus paying lip service to contrapuntal tonal tradition, the "subject" itself has no tonal base; it consists of eight different notes (categorized as pitch-class set 8–12 in Forte 1978, 165). The floating figure and its close relatives dominate in the upper strings in mm. 2–5. Underneath, in the viola and cello in m. 3, Schoenberg introduces the second basic motive, the descending fifth. With its downward, cadence-like gesture, this fifth works as a kind of counterforce to the floating figure and thus might be said to embody "gravity."

The descending fifth and the open-fifth interval itself play an important role in this movement. In the introduction, they serve not only as a melodic figure, but also as closing gesture for parts I and II. Part I ends with an emphatic pizzicato G–C (m. 9); this same fifth is reiterated as a simultaneity at the end of part II (m.

15). It is then raised a half-step to C♯–G♯ to begin part III, which serves as the transition to the entry of the voice. In the primarily atonal context of this introduction, the prominent fifths cannot be said to be harmonically functional: that is, parts I and II cannot be said to end or cadence in C major. Nor can the successive entries of fifths in mm. 3 or 6 be said to establish any key (although as Forte rightly points out, the succession in the first violin in m. 6 produces the G♭-major scale, enharmonically F♯, the tonic of the movement [Forte 1978, 170]). Rather, to my ear, the fifths seem somehow to symbolize the tonal processes Schoenberg is about to abandon.[5]

The tonic of this movement makes its first real appareance, over a dominant pedal, at the cadence in theme 1, "ich fühle luft." This theme, as suggested above, functions much like the first theme in a sonata form, essentially stable and tonally focused. It is followed by a developmental transition based entirely on motives derived from the introduction and from theme 1. In the tonal world of this movement, as in the first movement, we cannot expect the traditional harmonic markers of sonata form—that is, a clear modulation to a second key area within the exposition. Nevertheless, the entry of "ich löse mich in tönen" functions much like a second theme, except that it is still more strongly oriented around the tonic than theme 1. F♯ now appears in root position, and the theme moves harmonically from I to V in mm. 54–55 (the dominant seventh chord has the fifth in the bass).

The development divides into essentially two sections, of which the second, beginning at m. 83, is remarkable for having the feel of a lilting scherzo or waltz. Here Schoenberg transforms the previously angular, staccato triplets into lyrical melodic lines. The floating of the introduction has turned into a more rhythmically defined dance on the "sea of crystalline radiance."

We have looked frequently in this study at the phenomenon of recapitulation in Schoenberg's early works and have investigated some of the ways in which he manages to effect a reprise of material without any exact repetition. In the first movement of op. 10, the reader will recall, Schoenberg compressed the reprise greatly, in part by presenting the two halves of theme 2a in counterpoint with each other. This kind of compression is carried even further in the finale. Here Schoenberg brings themes 1 and 2 together contrapuntally. The voice part at "ich

5. Forte's analysis of the opening of this movement (1978, 164–71) contains many persuasive observations on atonal procedures, but tends to disregard the tonal implications and gestures that are so clearly part of Schoenberg's compositional strategy. In his zeal to attribute "set consciousness" to Schoenberg, Forte downplays the role of conventional tonal structures by referring to them in quotation marks ("descending fifths," "augmented triads," and the like), as if such gestures were unwelcome foreign objects within the world of pitch-class sets, rather than an integral part of Schoenberg's musical language. Forte also analyzes the pitch content of theme 1, "ich fühle luft" (set 4–23), with no reference to the harmonic underpinning that is an essential element (1978, 165). A more sensitive, tonally oriented analysis of this movement is Ballan 1986, 190–205. See also Whittall 1972, 23–24.

bin ein funke" is a reprise of theme 1, first heard at "ich fühle luft." Surrounding this theme above (first violin) and below, or roughly in the same register (second violin), is theme 2 in octaves. Also brought in from theme 2 here is the bass line ascending stepwise from the tonic F♯. Originally this bass had ascended only as far as E♮ (m. 59). Now it continues up to the A a tenth above its starting point. Here the line breaks off and the bass drops down to a low D (m. 110).

Now begins perhaps the most astonishing aspect of the reprise: theme 1, at its original pitch level (D–G–A–C), appears in augmentation in the bass underneath the climactic final words "heilige stimme." A sequential repetition begins in m. 114 on E♭, but is broken off on the third note, B♭, with the end of the vocal line (m. 116). This reprise of theme 1 as bass is logical because at its first appearance in m. 21, the theme *was* the bass—that is, the lowest voice in the texture. When it appears at the beginning of the recapitulation, "ich bin ein funke," the theme is, as noted, accompanied by the stepwise bass brought in with theme 2, and it is accordingly transposed to begin in the key area of F♯. Thus Schoenberg felt it appropriate to bring theme 1 back once again at its original pitch level and in its original function, as bass. The vocal part at "heilige stimme" can also be heard as part of this recapitulatory process, since it begins like the viola counterpoint in the original "ich fühle luft" presentation: A–B♭–G (mm. 21–22). The condensed recapitulation of the finale of op. 10, lasting only nineteen measures, is surely one of the finest of Schoenberg's early period. It also serves as a harbinger of the kind of polyphonic compression, or simultaneous presentation of themes, that was to characterize his later music.

The moving instrumental coda to the movement serves to balance the introduction and, as has been suggested, to round off the entire quartet. If the introduction can be said to have stressed "floating" and atonality, the coda moves in the other direction, toward tonal resolution. Here we get the longest sustained tonic and dominant phrases in the movement. The final cadence of the work is, however, made not from the dominant, but from the trichord D–A–G♯ that has appeared frequently throughout the movement: as the first chord accompanying theme 1 (m. 21); at the original-pitch reprise of theme 1 in m. 110; and again in the coda (m. 140, now as a D-minorish tetrachord with F♮).

The cadential resolution is combined with or accompanied by a reference to the initial "floating" motive of the introduction, and as such it seems to epitomize the remarkable blend of traditional tonal procedures and newer atonal ones in this quartet. From the high G♯, the first violin makes a fifth descent to C♯. The stark D–A fifth in the cello, the relative of the open fifths we have heard since the introduction, proceeds by parallel motion to the tonic fifth F♯–C♯. The A, already present in the trichord, remains as part of the tonic minor articulated in the penultimate measure, then moves stepwise to the major third A♯. It is hard to envision a more satisfying cadence; it is still harder to articulate why the conclusion is so right. At this point, critical analysis must leave off and mute admiration take over.

In his writings Schoenberg attributes to his subconscious, the "Supreme Commander," many aspects of the composition of his works, such as elegant motivic and thematic relations. In the final stanza of "Entrückung," we encounter an artist who has in effect placed himself in the hands of, or made himself the vehicle of, a "heilige stimme" beyond his own direct, conscious control. It is clear from the music he wrote for this movement that the "stimme" was now leading Schoenberg away from many of the compositional preoccupations traced in this study. Consideration of op. 10, then, serves as an appropriate end point.

Appendix of Longer Musical Examples

EXAMPLE A Piano Piece in C♯ Minor (1894), mm. 1–23. Reproduced by permission of Universal Edition A. G., Vienna, from *SW* A4: 75.

EXAMPLE B Scherzo for Piano in F♯ Minor (ca. 1894), mm. 1–44. Reproduced by permission of Universal Edition A. G., Vienna, from *SW* B4: 101–2.

EXAMPLE B *continued*

EXAMPLE C Scherzo for String Quartet in F Major (1897), mm. 80–128. Reproduced by permission of Universal Edition A. G., Vienna, from *SW* A20: 171–72.

EXAMPLE C continued

102
103
104
105
106
107
arco

108
109
110
111
112
113
ff

114
115
116
117
118
119
120
121

122
123
124
125
126
127
128
ff

EXAMPLE D *Schilflied* ("Drüben geht die Sonne scheiden"), mm. 1–13. Reproduced by permission of Universal Edition A. G., Vienna, from *SW* A2: 4.

EXAMPLE E *Ecloge*, mm. 1–51. Reproduced by permission of Universal Edition A. G., Vienna, from *SW* A2: 67–69.

17
18
19
20
hör' ich's wie von Pfei - fen schal - len, und vom Ha - ge-dorn
B
lebhafter
21
22
23
24
25
fällt hel - ler Blü - ten - gruß.
p
pp
26
27
28
29
Und das Aug' von Freu - de naß, fragst du: Ja, was
p
A″
30
31
32
33
p
soll all das? „Was?" ruft der Vo - gel und die Blu - me
p

EXAMPLE E *continued*

spricht: „Anders kommen doch des Lenzes holde Wunder
nicht, anders kommen doch des Lenzes holde
rit.
Wunder, des Lenzes Wunder nicht!“
rit.
dim.
Tempo I

EXAMPLE F *Mädchenlied*, mm. 1–13. Reproduced by permission of Universal Edition A. G., Vienna, from *SW* A2: 79.

EXAMPLE G *Waldesnacht*, mm. 1–24. Reproduced by permission of Universal Edition A. G., Vienna, from *SW* A2: 81–82.

Sehr ruhig

pp

Wal - des-nacht, du wun - - der - küh - le, die ich tau - send Ma - le grüß', nach dem lau - ten Welt - ge - wüh - le

rit.
o wie ist dein Rau - schen süß!
pp
Träu - me-risch die mü - den Glie - der berg' ich weich ins
f
Moos, — und mir ist, als würd' ich — wie - der all der ir - ren
f
Qua - len los.
Fer-nes

EXAMPLE H *Mädchenfrühling*. Reproduced by permission of Universal Edition A. G., Vienna, from *SW* A2: 86–88.

es sprießt der Grund,
und sein Mund bleibt so ver - schlos - sen?
rit.
f
Ruhiger
pp
Mai - - son - nen - re - gen; al - le
pp

EXAMPLE H *continued*

EXAMPLE I *Nicht doch!* mm. 1–12. Reproduced by permission of Universal Edition A. G., Vienna, from *SW* A2: 89.

EXAMPLE J *Nicht doch!* mm. 73–84. Reproduced by permission of Universal Edition A. G., Vienna, from *SW* A2: 94–95.

EXAMPLE K *Mannesbangen.* Reproduced by permission of Universal Edition A. G., Vienna, from *SW* A2: 99–101.

11
12
sol - chen zu - cken - den Hän - den wie mit Dol - - - -

13
14
- chen durch die Haa - - - re fährst, und mein

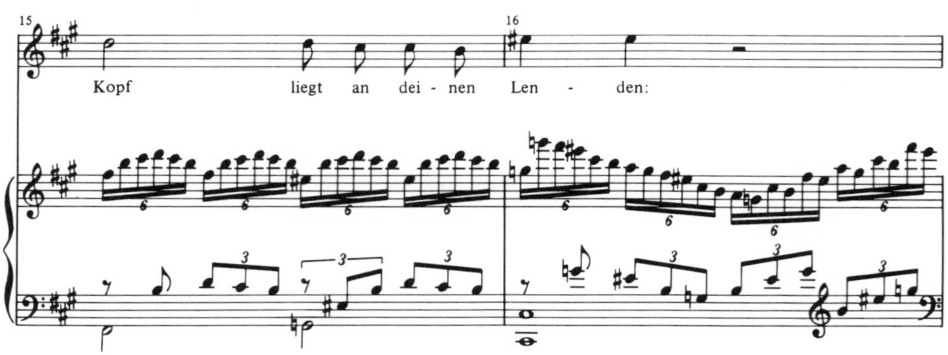
15
16
Kopf liegt an dei - nen Len - den:

17
18
dann,
du
Sün
-
drin,

rit.
19
20
beb'
ich
vor
dir—
p

21
22
23
24
25
pp
pp

EXAMPLE L *Warnung* (1899 version), mm. 1–15. Reproduced by permission of Universal Edition A. G., Vienna, from *SW* B1/2/II: 18–19.

EXAMPLE M *Im Reich der Liebe*, mm. 1–8. Reproduced by permission of Universal Edition A. G., Vienna, from *SW* B1/2/II: 149.

EXAMPLE N "So tanzen die Engel," from *Gurrelieder* (1900–1), piano-vocal score, mm. 443–88. Reproduced by permission of Belmont Music Publishers, Pacific Palisades, CA 90272.

Wal.
rit.
har - ten Er - lö - sungs - strei - te, als Wal - de - mar stolz nun und
p
rit.
Wal.
kö - nig - lich ist an To - ve - lil - les Sei - te. Nicht
(rit.)
Wal.
sehn - li - cher möch - ten die See - len ge - win - nen den Weg zu der Se - li - gen
p
47
Wal.
Bund, als ich deinen Kuß, da ich Gur - res
p
p

EXAMPLE N *continued*

EXAMPLE O "Du sendest mir einen Liebesblick," from *Gurrelieder*, mm. 653–67. Reproduced by permission of Belmont Music Publishers, Pacific Palisades, CA 90272.

EXAMPLE P "Du sendest mir einen Liebesblick," mm. 676–97. Reproduced by permission of Belmont Music Publishers, Pacific Palisades, CA 90272.

To.
Schön - ——z——→ "Nun sag' ich dir" - - len die
jun - - - - ge Braut.
rit.
69
fff
rit.
ppp
Sehr breit. (♩.) 3/2 = 6/4.
So laß uns die gol - de - ne Scha - le lee - ren ihm, dem
x/z
pp
mäch - tig ver - schö - nen - den Tod:
pp
p

EXAMPLE Q First String Quartet, op. 7, mm. 1–35. Reproduced by permission of Universal Edition A. G., Vienna, from *SW* A20: 3–5.

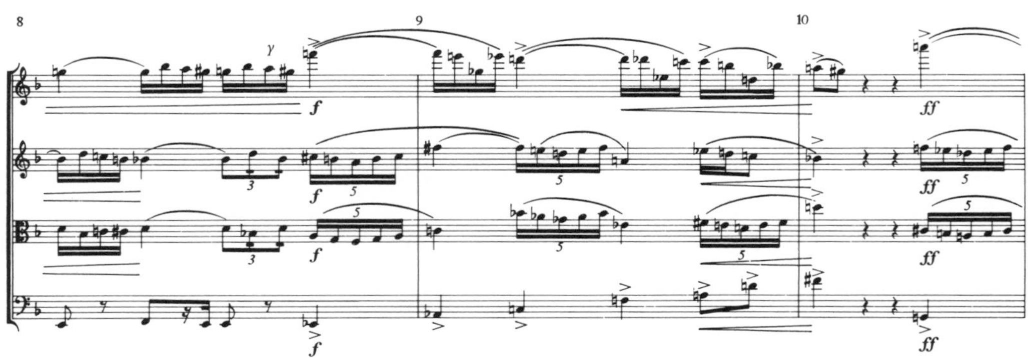

B
p
mf
f

EXAMPLE Q *continued*

EXAMPLE R Second Chamber Symphony, op. 38, I, two-piano arrangement, mm. 1–28. Reproduced by permission of Universal Edition A. G., Vienna, from *SW* A5: 31–32.

EXAMPLE R *continued*

EXAMPLE 5 Second String Quartet, op. 10, I, mm. 1–55. Reproduced by permission of Universal Edition A. G., Vienna, from *SW* A20: 83–85.

1a

Mäßig (moderato) (♩ = ca 100)

etwas langsamer anfangen

1. Geige

2. Geige

Bratsche

Violoncello

1b

Hauptzeitmaß (𝅗𝅥. = ca 52- 56)

EXAMPLE S *continued*

rit.
breit
rit.
f
sf
2a (≈ 1b′)
Zeitmaß
sehr ausdrucksvoll
p
pp
espr.
hervortreten

EXAMPLE T Second String Quartet, op. 10, II, mm. 1–18. Reproduced by permission of Universal Edition A. G., Vienna, from *SW* A: 95–96.

BIBLIOGRAPHY OF WORKS CITED

Adler, Guido. 1911. *Der Stil in der Musik.* Leipzig: Breitkopf & Härtel.

Adorno, Theodor W. 1978. "Zemlinsky." In *Gesammelte Schriften,* vol. 16, edited by Rolf Tiedemann, 351–67. Frankfurt: Suhrkamp. Originally published in 1959.

———. 1981. *Prisms.* Translated by Samuel and Shierry Weber. Cambridge, Mass.: MIT Press. Originally published in 1951.

Alpers, Svetlana. 1987. "Style Is What You Make It: The Visual Arts Once Again." In *The Concept of Style,* rev. ed., edited by Berel Lang, 137–62. Ithaca, N.Y.: Cornell University Press.

Arnold Schönberg zum fünfzigsten Geburtstage, 13. September 1924. 1924. Special number of *Musikblätter des Anbruch.* Vienna: Universal.

Arnold Schönberg zum 60. Geburtstag, 13. September 1934. 1934. Vienna: Universal.

Bab, Julius. 1926. *Richard Dehmel: Die Geschichte eines Lebens-Werkes.* Leipzig: Haessel.

Bach, David Josef. 1924. "Aus der Jugendzeit." In *Arnold Schönberg zum fünfzigsten Geburtstage, 13. September 1924,* 317–20. Vienna: Universal.

Bailey, Walter B. 1979. "The Unpublished Songs of Arnold Schoenberg, c. 1893–c. 1900." Master's thesis, University of Southern California.

———. 1984. *Programmatic Elements in the Works of Schoenberg.* Ann Arbor: UMI Research Press.

Ballan, Harry. 1986. "Schoenberg's Expansion of Tonality, 1899–1908." Ph.D. diss., Yale University.

Benson, Mark. 1987. "Schoenberg's Private Program for the String Quartet in D Minor, Opus 7." Paper read at the national meeting of the American Musicological Society, New Orleans.

Berg, Alban. 1913. *Arnold Schönberg. Gurrelieder Führer.* Leipzig and Vienna: Universal.

———. 1920. *Pelleas und Melisande . . . von Arnold Schönberg Op. 5. Kurze thematische Analyse.* Vienna: Universal.

———. 1921. *Arnold Schönberg. Kammersymphonie Op. 9: Thematische Analyse.* Leipzig and Vienna: Universal.

———. 1987. *The Berg-Schoenberg Correspondence: Selected Letters.* Edited by Juliane Brand, Christopher Hailey, and Donald Harris. New York: Norton.

Birke, Joachim. 1958. "Richard Dehmel und Arnold Schönberg: Ein Briefwechsel." *Die Musikforschung* 11: 279–85.

———. 1964. "Nachträge zum Briefwechsel zwischen Dehmel und Schönberg." *Die Musikforschung* 17: 60–62.

Brahms, Johannes. 1908–22. *Johannes Brahms Briefwechsel.* Rev. ed. 16 vols. Berlin: Deutsche Brahms-Gesellschaft.

Brinkmann, Reinhold. 1969. *Arnold Schönberg: Drei Klavierstücke Op. 11: Studien zur frühen Atonalität bei Schönberg.* Wiesbaden: Steiner.

———. 1977. "Die gepreßte Sinfonie: Zum geschichtlichen Gehalt von Schönbergs Opus 9." In *Gustav Mahler: Sinfonie und Wirklichkeit,* edited by Otto Kolleritsch, 133–56. Graz: Universal.

———. 1984. "On the Problem of Establishing 'Jugendstil' as a Category within the History of Music—With a Negative Plea." In *Art Nouveau and Jugendstil and the Music of the Early 20th Century.* Adelaide Studies in Musicology, 13: 19–47.

Challier, Ernst, ed. 1885. *Grosser Lieder Katalog.* Berlin: Ernst Challier. Supplements (*Nachträge*) published every two years: *Nachträge* I–V (1886–94).

———. 1906. *Grosser Lieder Katalog. Nachtrag XI.* Giessen: Ernst Challier.

Cone, Edward T. 1974. "Sound and Syntax: An Introduction to Schoenberg's Harmony." *Perspectives of New Music* 13: 21–40. Reprinted in Cone, *Music: A View from Delft,* 249–66. Chicago: University of Chicago Press, 1989.

———. 1990. "Harmonic Congruence in Brahms." In *Brahms Studies: Analytical and Historical Perspectives,* edited by George S. Bozarth, 165–88. Oxford: Clarendon Press.

Cross, Charlotte. 1980. "Three Levels of 'Idea' in Schoenberg's Thought and Writings." *Current Musicology* 30: 24–36.

Dahlhaus, Carl. 1987. "Schoenberg and Programme Music." In *Schoenberg and the New Music,* translated by Derrick Puffett and Alfred Clayton, 94–104. Cambridge: Cambridge University Press.

———. 1989. *Nineteenth-Century Music.* Translated by J. Bradford Robinson. Berkeley and Los Angeles: University of California Press.

Deggeller-Engelke, Eleonore. 1949. *Richard Barth (1850–1923): Leben, Wirken und Werke. Ein Beitrag zur Brahmsfolge.* Marburg: Elwert Gräfe & Unzer.

Dehmel, Richard. 1923. *Ausgewählte Briefe aus den Jahren 1883 bis 1902.* Berlin: Fischer.

———. 1926. *Bekenntnisse.* Berlin: Fischer.

———. 1963. *Dichtungen, Briefe, Dokumente.* Edited by Paul J. Schindler. Hamburg: Hoffmann & Campe.

Dümling, Albrecht. 1981. *Die fremden Klänge des Hängenden Gärten: Die öffentliche Einsamkeit der Neuen Musik am Beispiel von Arnold Schönberg und Stefan George.* Munich: Kindler.

Fellinger, Imogen. 1983. "Zum Stand der Brahms-Forschung." *Acta Musicologica* 55: 131–201.

———. 1984. "Das Brahms-Jahr 1983: Forschungsbericht." *Acta Musicologica* 56: 145–210.

Forte, Allen. 1972. "Sets and Non-Sets in Schoenberg's Atonal Music." *Perspectives of New Music* 12: 43–64.

———. 1978. "Schoenberg's Creative Evolution: The Path to Atonality." *Musical Quarterly* 64: 133–76.

Friedheim, Philip. 1963. "Tonality and Structure in the Early Works of Schoenberg." Ph.D. diss., New York University.

Frisch, Walter. 1984. *Brahms and the Principle of Developing Variation.* Berkeley and Los Angeles: University of California Press.

———. 1986. "Schoenberg and the Poetry of Richard Dehmel." *Journal of the Arnold Schoenberg Institute* 9: 137–79.

———. 1988a. "Thematic Form and the Genesis of Schoenberg's D-Minor Quartet, Opus 7." *Journal of the American Musicological Society* 41: 289–314.

———. 1988b. Review of Arnold Schönberg. *Streichquartette I. Sämtliche Werke,* vol. 20, series A and B (Mainz and Vienna: Schott and Universal, 1987). *Journal of the Arnold Schoenberg Institute* 11: 181–88.

———. 1990a. "The 'Brahms Fog': On Analyzing Brahmsian Influences at the Fin de Siècle." In *Brahms and His World,* edited by Walter Frisch, 81–99. Princeton: Princeton University Press.

———. 1990b. "Music and Jugendstil." *Critical Inquiry* 17: 138–61.

Fritz, Horst. 1969. *Literarischer Jugendstil und Expressionismus: Zur Kunsttheorie, Dichtung und Wirkung Richard Dehmels.* Stuttgart: Metzler.

Garland, Henry, and Mary Garland. 1976. *The Oxford Companion to German Literature.* Oxford: Clarendon Press.

Gerlach, Reinhard. 1972. "War Schönberg von Dvořák beeinflußt?" *Neue Zeitschrift für Musik* 133: 122–27.

———. 1985. *Musik und Jugendstil der Wiener Schule, 1900–1908.* Laaber: Laaber Verlag.

Glienke, Bernhard. 1975. *Jens Peter Jacobsens lyrische Dichtung: Ein Beitrag zur Geschichte der modernen Poesie.* Neumünster: Wachholtz.

Goehr, Alexander. 1977. "Schoenberg's *Gedanke* Manuscript." *Journal of the Arnold Schoenberg Institute* 2: 4–25.

Grasberger, Franz, and Rudolf Stefan, eds. 1980. *Katalog der Musikhandschriften und Studien Alban Bergs im Fond Alban Berg und der Weiteren Handschriftlichen Quellen im Besitz der Österreichischen Nationalbibliothek* [prepared by Rosemary Hilmar]. Alban Berg Studien, vol. 1. Vienna: Universal.

Hamann, Richard, and Jost Hermand. 1973. *Stilkunst um 1900.* Munich: Nymphenburger.

Harvey, Jonathan. 1975. "Schönberg: Man or Woman?" *Music and Letters* 56: 371–85.

Hattesen, Heinrich Helge. 1990. *Emanzipation durch Aneignung: Untersuchungen zu den Frühen Streichquartetten Arnold Schönbergs.* Kassel: Bärenreiter.

Hehemann, Max. 1905. "Max Reger." *Die Musik* 4/4: 410–24.

Hepokoski, James. 1992. "Fiery-Pulsed Libertine or Domestic Hero? Strauss's *Don Juan* Reinvestigated." In *Richard Strauss: New Perspectives on the Composer and His Work*, edited by Bryan Gilliam, 135–75. Durham: Duke University Press.

Hermand, Jost, ed. 1971. *Jugendstil.* Wege der Forschung, vol. 110. Darmstadt: Wissenschaftliche Buchgesellschaft.

Hilmar, Ernst, ed. 1974. *Arnold Schönberg: Gedenkausstellung 1974.* Vienna: Universal.

———. 1976. "Zemlinsky und Schönberg." In *Alexander Zemlinsky: Tradition im Umkreis der Wiener Schule*, edited by Otto Kolleritsch, 55–79. Graz: Universal.

Holl, Karl. 1928. *Friedrich Gernsheim: Leben, Erscheinung und Werk.* Leipzig: Breitkopf & Härtel.

Just, Martin. 1980. "Schönbergs 'Erwartung' op. 2, nr. 1." In *Bericht über den internationalen musikwissenschaftlichen Kongreß Berlin 1974*, edited by Hellmut Kühn and Peter Nitsche, 425–27. Kassel: Bärenreiter.

Kalbeck, Max. 1904–14. *Johannes Brahms.* Rev. ed. 4 vols. Berlin: Deutsche Brahms-Gesellschaft.

Kandinsky, Wassily. 1977. *Concerning the Spiritual in Art.* Translated and with an introduction by M.T. H. Sadler. Reprint. New York: Dover.

Kimmey, John A., Jr., ed. 1979. *The Arnold Schoenberg–Hans Nachod Collection.* Detroit: Information Coordinators.

Kohleick, Werner. 1943. *Gustav Jenner, 1865–1920: Ein Beitrag zur Brahmsfolge.* Wurzburg: Triltsch.

Kropfinger, Klaus. 1984. "The Shape of Line." In *Art Nouveau and Jugendstil and the Music of the Early 20th Century.* Adelaide Studies in Musicology, 13: 131–67.

Leichtentritt, Hugo. 1963. "German and Austrian Chamber Music." In *Cobbett's Cyclopedic Survey of Chamber Music,* edited by Walter W. Cobbett, 2d ed. (1st ed. 1929), 2:444–51. London: Oxford University Press.

Lewin, David. 1968. "Inversional Balance as an Organizing Force in Schoenberg's Music and Thought." *Perspectives of New Music* 6: 1–21.

———. 1982. "Vocal Meter in Schoenberg's Atonal Music, with a Note on a Serial Hauptstimme." *In Theory Only* 6: 12–36.

———. 1987. "On the Ninth-Chord in Fourth Inversion from *Verklärte Nacht.*" *Journal of the Arnold Schoenberg Institute* 10: 45–64.

Lewis, Christopher. 1987. "Mirrors and Metaphors: Reflections on Schoenberg and Nineteeth-Century Tonality." *19th-Century Music* 11: 26–42.

Lindner, Adalbert. 1938. *Max Reger: Ein Bild seines Jugendlebens und künstlerischen Werdens.* 3d ed. Regensburg: Bosse.

Loll, Werner. 1990. *Zwischen Tradition und Avantgarde: Die Kammermusik Alexander Zemlinskys.* Kassel: Bärenreiter.

McGeary, Thomas. 1986. "The Publishing History of *Style and Idea.*" *Journal of the Arnold Schoenberg Institute* 9: 181–209.

Maegaard, Jan. 1972. *Studien zur Entwicklung des dodekaphonen Satzes bei Arnold Schönberg.* 3 vols. Copenhagen: Hansen.

———. 1983. "Arnold Schönbergs Scherzo in F-Dur für Streichquartett." *Dansk Arbog for Musikforskning* 14: 133–40.

Mattner, Lothar. 1985. *Substanz und Akzidens: Analytische Studien an Streichquartettsätzen Max Regers.* Wiesbaden: Breitkopf & Härtel.

Morgan, Robert. 1991. *Twentieth-Century Music.* New York: Norton.

Musgrave, Michael. 1980. "Schoenberg and Brahms: A Study of Schoenberg's Response to Brahms's Music as Revealed in His Didactic Writings and Selected Early Compositions." Ph.D. diss., King's College, University of London.

Neff, Severine. 1984. "Aspects of *Grundgestalt* in Schoenberg's First String Quartet, op. 7." *Theory and Practice* 9: 7–56.

Neighbour, Oliver. 1980. "Schoenberg, Arnold." *New Grove Dictionary of Music and Musicians,* ed. Stanley Sadie, 16: 701–24. London: Macmillan.

Newlin, Dika. 1978. *Bruckner, Mahler, Schoenberg.* Rev. ed. New York: Norton.

———. 1980. *Schoenberg Remembered: Diaries and Recollections, 1938–1976*. New York: Pendragon Press.

Niemann, Walter. 1912. "Johannes Brahms und die neuere Klaviermusik." *Die Musik* 12/2: 38–45.

Nitsche, Peter. 1974. "Schönbergs Orchesterwerke." In *Arnold Schönberg. Publikationen des Archivs der Akademie der Künste zu Arnold Schönberg-Veranstaltungen innerhalb der Berliner Festwochen*, 15–20. Berlin: Berliner Festspiele GmbH.

Oncley, Lawrence A. 1975. "The Published Works of Alexander Zemlinsky." Ph.D. diss., Indiana University.

———. 1977. "The Works of Alexander Zemlinsky: A Chronological List." *Music Library Association Notes* 34: 291–302.

Osborne, Harold, ed. 1970. *The Oxford Companion to Art*. Oxford: Clarendon Press, 1970.

Pfannkuch, Wilhelm. 1963. "Zu Thematik und Form in Schönbergs Streichsextett." In *Festschrift Friedrich Blume: Zum 70. Geburtstag*, edited by Anna Amalie Abert and Wilhelm Pfannkuch, 258–71. Kassel: Bärenreiter.

Rauchhaupt, Ursula von, ed. 1971. *Schoenberg, Berg, Webern: The String Quartets*. Hamburg: Deutsche Grammophon. Reissued in abridged format in 1987 with compact disc set.

Reger, Max. 1904. "Streichquartett op. 74 in d-moll." *Die Musik* 3/3: 244–47.

———. 1928. *Briefe eines deutschen Meisters*. Edited by Else von Hase Koehler. Leipzig: Koehler & Amelang.

———. [1957]. *Sämtliche Werke*, vol. 10. Edited by Helmut Wirth. Wiesbaden: Breitkopf & Härtel.

Reich, Willi. 1965. *The Life and Work of Alban Berg*. Translated by Cornelius Cardew. London: Thames & Hudson. Reprint, New York: Da Capo Press, 1982.

———. 1971. *Schoenberg: A Critical Biography*. Translated by Leo Black. New York: Praeger.

Reilly, Edward. 1982. *Gustav Mahler and Guido Adler: Records of a Friendship*. Cambridge: Cambridge University Press.

Réti, Rudolf. 1951. *The Thematic Process in Music*. New York: Macmillan.

Rexroth, Dieter. 1971. *Arnold Schönberg als Theoretiker der tonalen Harmonik*. Bonn: Friedrich-Wilhelms-Universität.

Rosen, Charles. 1980. "Influence: Plagiarism and Inspiration." *19th-Century Music* 4: 87–100.

Rufer, Josef. 1962. *The Works of Arnold Schoenberg*. Translated by Dika Newlin. New York: Free Press. Original German edition, Kassel, 1959.

Ruprecht, Erich, ed. 1962. *Literarische Manifeste des Naturalismus, 1880–1892.* Stuttgart: Metzler.

Ruprecht, Erich, and Dieter Bänsch, eds. 1970. *Literarische Manifeste der Jahrhundertwende, 1890–1910.* Stuttgart: Metzler.

Schapiro, Meyer. 1953. "Style." In *Anthropology Today*, edited by A. L. Kroeber, 287–312. Chicago: University of Chicago Press.

Schmidt, Christian M. 1978. "Formprobleme in Schönbergs frühen Instrumentalwerken." In *Bericht über den 1. Kongreß der Internationalen Schönberg-Gesellschaft*, edited by Rudolf Stephan, 180–86. Vienna: Elisabeth Lafite.

———. 1983. *Johannes Brahms und seine Zeit.* Laaber: Laaber Verlag.

———. 1984. "Schönbergs analytische Bemerkungen zum Streichquartett op. 7." *Österreichische Musikzeitschrift* 39: 296–300.

———. 1986. "Schönbergs 'Very Definite—But Private' Programm zum Streichquartett Opus 7." In *Bericht über den 2. Kongreß der Internationalen Schönberg-Gesellschaft*, edited by Rudolf Stephan and Sigrid Wiesmann, 230–34. Vienna: Elisabeth Lafite.

Schmidt, Leopold. 1922. *Aus dem Musikleben der Gegenwart.* Berlin: Max Hesses Verlag.

Schmutzler, Robert. 1962. *Art Nouveau.* New York: Abrams.

Schoenberg, Arnold. 1907. "Streichquartett Op. 7 von Arnold Schönberg. Analyse anläßlich einer Aufführung zum 43. Tonkünstler-Fest des Allgemeinen Deutschen Musikvereins in Dresden." *Die Musik* 6/3: 332–34.

———. 1950. *Style and Idea.* New York: Philosophical Library.

———. 1964. *Letters.* Selected and edited by Erwin Stein. Translated by Eithne Wilkins and Ernst Kaiser. London: Faber & Faber. Paperback reprints, 1974, 1987.

———. 1966. *String Quartet in D Major (1897).* Edited by Oliver W. Neighbour. London: Faber & Faber.

———. 1967. *Fundamentals of Musical Composition.* Edited by Gerald Strang and Leonard Stein. New York: St. Martin's Press.

———. 1969. *Structural Functions of Harmony.* Rev. ed. Edited by Leonard Stein. New York: Norton.

———. 1975. *Style and Idea: Selected Writings of Arnold Schoenberg.* Edited by Leonard Stein. New York: St. Martin's Press. Paperback reprint, Berkeley and Los Angeles: University of California Press, 1984.

———. 1978. *Theory of Harmony.* Translated by Roy E. Carter. Berkeley and Los Angeles: University of California Press.

———. 1980. *Ein Stelldichein.* Edited by Rudolf Stephan. Vienna: Universal.

———. 1984. *Scherzo for String Quartet, F Major (1897).* Revised and edited by Jan Maegaard. Los Angeles: Belmont.

———. 1987. *7 Early Songs.* Edited by Leonard Stein. London: Faber & Faber.

———. 1994. *The Musical Idea and the Logic, Technique, and Art of Its Presentation.* Edited, translated, and with a commentary by Patricia Carpenter and Severine Neff. New York: Columbia University Press.

Schreiber, Ingeborg, ed. 1981. *Max Reger in seinen Konzerten, Teil 2: Programme der Konzerte Regers.* Bonn: Dummler.

Schubert, Giselher. 1975. *Schönbergs frühe Instrumentation: Untersuchungen zu den Gurreliedern, zu op. 5 und op. 8.* Baden-Baden: Koerner.

Schuh, Willi. 1982. *Richard Strauss: A Chronicle of the Early Years, 1864–1898.* Translated by Mary Whittall. Cambridge: Cambridge University Press.

Sichardt, Martina. 1990. "Zur Bedeutung der Dichtung Richard Dehmels für die Liedkomposition um 1900." In *Neue Musik und Tradition: Festschrift Rudolf Stefan zum 65. Geburtstag,* edited by Josef Kuckertz et al., 365–88. Laaber: Laaber Verlag.

Smith, Charles. 1986. "The Functional Extravagance of Chromatic Chords." *Music Theory Spectrum* 8: 94–139.

Smolian, Artur. 1894. "Max Reger und seine Erstlingswerke." *Musikalisches Wochenblatt* 25: 518–19, 546–49.

Stein, Fritz, ed. 1953. *Thematisches Verzeichnis der im Druck erschienen Werke von Max Reger.* Leipzig: Breitkopf & Härtel.

Stein, Leonard. 1977. "Toward a Chronology of Schoenberg's Early Unpublished Songs." *Journal of the Arnold Schoenberg Institute* 2: 72–80.

Steiner, Fred. 1978. "A History of the First Complete Recording of the Schoenberg String Quartets." *Journal of the Arnold Schoenberg Institute* 2: 122–37.

Stephan, Rudolf. 1974. "Schönberg als Symphoniker." *Österreichische Musikzeitschrift* 29: 267–78.

———. 1976. "Über Zemlinskys Streichquartette." In *Alexander Zemlinsky: Tradition im Umkreis der Wiener Schule,* edited by Otto Kolleritsch, 120–36. Graz: Universal.

Steuermann, Clara. 1979. "From the Archives: Schoenberg's Library Catalogue." *Journal of the Arnold Schoenberg Institute* 3: 203–18.

Stuckenschmidt, H. H. 1978. *Arnold Schoenberg: His Life, World and Work.* Translated by Humphrey Searle. New York: Schirmer.

Swift, Richard. 1977. "1/XII/99: Tonal Relations in Schoenberg's *Verklärte Nacht.*" *19th-Century Music* 1: 3–14.

Szmolyan, Walter. 1974. "Schönberg in Mödling." *Österreichische Musikzeitschrift* 29: 189–202.

———. 1981. "Die Konzerte des Wiener Schönberg-Vereins." *Österreichische Musikzeitschrift* 36: 82–104. Partially reprinted in *Musik-Konzepte* 36 (1984), edited by Heinz-Klaus Metzger and Rainer Riehn, 101–14.

Thieme, Ulrich. 1979. *Studien zum Jugendwerk Arnold Schönbergs: Einflüsse und Wandlungen*. Regensburg: Bosse.

Trezise, Simon. 1987. "Schoenberg's *Gurrelieder*." Ph.D. diss., Oxford University.

Tyson, Alan. 1970. "The 1803 Version of Beethoven's *Christus am Oelberge*." In *The Creative World of Beethoven*, edited by Paul Henry Lang, 49–82. New York: Norton.

Velten, Klaus. 1976. *Schönbergs Instrumentation Bachscher und Brahmsscher Werke als Dokumente seines Traditionsverständnisses*. Regensburg: Bosse.

Weber, Horst. 1977. *Alexander Zemlinsky*. Vienna: Elisabeth Lafite.

Webern, Anton. 1912. "Schönbergs Musik." In *Arnold Schönberg*, 22–48. Munich: Piper.

Wellesz, Egon. 1925. *Arnold Schoenberg*. Translated by W. H. Kerridge. London: Dent. Reprints, New York: Da Capo Press, 1969; London: Galliard, 1971. Original German edition, Leipzig, 1921.

———. 1985. *Arnold Schöenberg*. Reprint of the original German edition (1921), with an afterword by Carl Dahlhaus. Wilhelmshaven: Heinrichshofen.

Whittall, Arnold. 1972. *Schoenberg Chamber Music*. Seattle: University of Washington Press.

Wilke, Rainer. 1980. *Brahms, Reger, Schönberg Streichquartette: Motivisch-thematische Prozesse und formale Gestalt*. Hamburg: Wagner.

Wintle, Christopher. 1980. "Schoenberg's Harmony: Theory and Practice." *Journal of the Arnold Schoenberg Institute* 4: 50–67.

Wirth, Helmut. 1974. "Johannes Brahms und Max Reger." *Brahms-Studien* 1: 91–112.

Zemlinsky, Alexander. 1922. "Brahms und die neuere Generation: Persönliche Erinnerungen." *Musikblätter des Anbruch* 4: 69–70. Translated as "Brahms and the Newer Generation: Personal Reminiscences," in *Brahms and His World*, edited by Walter Frisch, 205–7. Princeton: Princeton University Press, 1990.

———. 1934. "Jugenderinnerungen." In *Arnold Schönberg zum 60. Geburtstag, 13. September 1934*, 33–35. Vienna: Universal.

INDEX OF SCHOENBERG'S COMPOSITIONS AND WRITINGS

Boldface page numbers indicate a more extended analysis. Italic page numbers indicate a musical example.

Compositions

Alles, op. 6, no. 2, 83n, 216, 219

Am Wegrand, op. 6, no. 7, **216–18**, *217–18*, 219

Andantino in C♯ Minor. *See* Three Piano Pieces (1894)

Die Beiden, 80

Besuch, 80n

Book of the Hanging Gardens, op. 15, 51n, 248

Chamber Symphony No. 1, op. 9, 113, 181n, 192–93, 204n, 211, 219, **220–47**, *223*, *225*, *226*, *228*, *230*, *231*, *233*, *234*, *235*, *236*, *237*, *242*, *243*, *244*, *245*, *246*, 248, 251, 254–55, 258, 263, 268

Chamber Symphony No. 2, op. 38, xv, 247, 248–49, **251–58**, *255*, *256*, *257*, 260, *305–6*

Dank, op. 1, no. 1, 79n

Drei Klavierstücke (1894). *See* Three Piano Pieces (1894)

Ecloge, 50, **54–61**, 57–59, 62, 65, *280–82*

Entrückung. *See* String Quartet No. 2, op. 10

Erhebung, op. 2, no. 3, 82, 83, **105–8**, *106*, *107*

Erwartung, op. 2, no. 1, 82, 83, **92–98**, *95*, *96*, 100, 105, 107–8

Friede auf Erden, op. 13, 248

Frühlings Tod, 79, 109

Gethsemane, 83, 98

Gurrelieder, 65, 105, **140–45**, *144*, 158, 172, 177, 238; "Du sendest mir einen Liebesblick" (song 8), 105, **152–57**, *154*, *155*, 198, *299–301*; "Nun sag' ich dir zum erstenmal" (song 6), **151–52**, *151*; "O, wenn des Mondes Strahlen" (song 2), **146–47**; "So tanzen die Engel" (song 5), **148–51**, *150*, *296–98*; "Sterne jubeln" (song 4), **147–48**

Hans im Glück, 109

Im Reich der Liebe, 83, **98–99**, *295*

In hellen Träumen, 51

Jesus bettelt ("Schenk mir deinen goldenen Kamm"), op. 2, no. 2, 82, 86, **99–104**, *101*, *103*, *104*, 105, 106, 107–8, 128, 129, 198

Klavierstücke. *See* Three Piano Pieces (1894)

Lieder, op. 1, 48, 79

Lieder, op. 2, 48, 82, 92. *See also Erwartung*, *Erhebung*, *Jesus bettelt*

Lieder, op. 3, 48, 82. *See also Warnung*

Litanei. *See* String Quartet No. 2, op. 10

Lockung, op. 6, no. 7, 216, 219

Mädchenfrühling, 25, 50, 67, **68–72**, 73–74, 75, 85, 86, 89, 96, 127, 197, *286–88*

Mädchenlied (1897), 50, 60, **61–62**, 67, 72, *283*

Mädchenlied, op. 6, no. 3, 216
Mailied, 80
Mannesbangen, 69n, 82n, **84–87**, *85*, *86*, 88, 89, 94, 97, 98, 99, 100, 103, 104, 107–8, *291–93*
Natur, op. 8, no. 1, 238
Nicht doch! 50, 67, **72–75**, *74*, *289*, *290*
Orchestral Songs, op. 8, 203, 238
Pelleas und Melisande, op. 5, 109, 113, 115n, 133, **158–77**, *161*, *162*, *163*, *165*, *166*, *167*, *174*, *175*, *176*, 185, 186–87, 211, 238
Piano Pieces (1894). *See* Three Piano Pieces (1894)
Piano Pieces, op. 11, 248
Presto in A Minor. *See* Three Piano Pieces (1894)
Scherzo for Piano (1894), 21, **27–28**, *275–76*
Scherzo for String Quartet, F Major (1897), 20, 32, 33, **39–43**, *40*, 52, *277–78*
Schilflied, **50–54**, *53*, 55, 60, *279*
Serenade for Small Orchestra, D Major (1897), 20, **28–32**, *30–31*, 34, 35, 37
Songs. *See* Lieder
Ein Stelldichein, 216
String Quartet, D Major (1897), 20, **32–39**, *35–36*, *38*, 40, *42*, **43–47**, *45–46*, 50, 52, 66, 74, 109, 110, 113, 139, 193, 262
String Quartet, D Minor (fragment, 1903–4), **184–86**
String Quartet No. 1, op. 7, 91, 113, 169, 177, 181, 184, 185, *185*, 186, **187–211**, *190*, *191*, *192*, *194*, *196*, *198*, *199*, *203*, *204*, *205*, *206*, *207*, *209*, *210*, 212–19, 220, 226, 231, 232, 233, 238–40, *239*, 249, 254, 258, 263, *302–4*
String Quartet No. 2, op. 10, xv, 247, 248–49, **258–72**, *261*, *264*, *265*, *266*, *268*, *307–9*, *310*
Three Piano Pieces (1894), 20; Andantino in C♯ Minor, **21–24**, *23*, *274;* Presto in A Minor, **24–28**, *25–26*, 29
Three Piano Pieces, op. 11, 248
Toter Winkel, 109
Traumleben, op. 6, no. 1, 181n, 238
Verklärte Nacht, op. 4, 79, 83, 98, 105, **109–39**, *117*, *128*, *130*, *131–32*, *133*, *137*, 140, 141, 146, 151–52, 157, 158–59, 169, *170*, 172, 175–76, *176*, 177, 186–87, 193, 211, 222, 231, 238
Verlassen, op. 6, no. 4, **181–84**, *183–84*, 193, 216
Vorfrühling, 33n
Waldesnacht, 50, 56n, 60, **62–66**, *65*, 67, 72, 103, *284–85*
Waldsonne, op. 2, no. 4, 82
Der Wanderer, op. 6, no. 8, 216
Warnung, op. 3, no. 3, 82, 83, **87–92**, *89*, 97, 100, 102, 105, 118, 191, *294*

Writings

"Brahms the Progressive," 5n, 9n
"Composition with Twelve Tones," 243
Fundamentals of Musical Composition, 22, 87n, 206
"Heart and Brain in Music," 201, 241
"Konstruktives in der Verklärten Nacht," 123–26
"Linear Counterpoint," 206n
Der Musikalische Gedanke und die Logik, Technik und Kunst seiner Darstellung, 6
"My Evolution," 20n, 243
"Notes on the Four String Quartets," 20n, 189n
"*Pelleas and Melisande*, Notes by Arnold Schoenberg," 158–59
"Streichquartett Op. 7 . . . Analyse," 189n
Structural Functions of Harmony, *230*, 230, 238, 240
Style and Idea, 6, 189n, *243*
Theory of Harmony, xv, 69n, 85, 91n, 135, 196, *198*, 198–200, 218, 233–36, *235*, *236*, 240, 247, 266
"*Verklärte Nacht*, Notes by Arnold Schoenberg," 112–13

GENERAL INDEX

AA′ form, 119, 262
ABA′ form. *See* Ternary form
Absolute music, 186, 187
Absorption, 15, 19, 32, 75
Adler, Guido, 6n
Adorno, Theodor W., 10, 189, 244, 246
Allgemeine Musik-Zeitung, 3
Allgemeiner Deutscher Musikverein, 212
Allusion, 15, 32
Ansorge-Verein, 212
Antecedent-consequent structure. *See* Period structure; Phrase structure
Arnold, Robert Franz, 142, 146, 148
Arnold Schoenberg Institute, 20n, 29, 56, 69n, 140, 212
Asymmetry, 10, 28, 63, 143, 164, 167, 224
Atonality, 248; conflict with tonal procedures, 249, 258–60, 265–67, 270, 271; and "set consciousness," 216n, 270n
Auerbach, Ida, 81, 112
Augmented chord, 10, 53, 84, 99, 104, 127, 128, 164, 243; as dominant, 152, 240; as source for whole-tone scale, 91n. *See also* Vagrant chord; Whole-tone formations
Augmented sixth chord. *See* French sixth chord; German sixth chord; Vagrant chord
Austrian National Library, 82n
Autographs. *See* Manuscripts; Revisions; Sketches

Bach, David Josef, 24, 26, 50
Bach, J. S., 212
Bailey, Walter, 48, 50, 115n, 169, 175
Barcelona, 123
Basic shape, 206
Beethoven, Ludwig van, 201; WORKS: Piano Sonata, op. 2, no. 1, 22; String Quartet, op. 59, no. 1, 263; String Quartet, op. 131, 185–86; Symphony No. 1, op. 21, 194; Symphony No. 3 (*Eroica*), op. 55, 43, 187n
Benson, Mark, 187
Berg, Alban, xiii; analysis of Chamber Symphony No. 1, op. 9, 221–22, 223n, 225, 228; analysis of *Gurrelieder* (*Gurrelieder-Führer*), 140, 148, 151, 153, 155, 156; analysis of *Pelleas und Melisande*, op. 5, 158, 159, 161–62, 169–71, 174–75; analysis of String Quartet No. 1, op. 7, 193–96, 200; *Nachlaß*, 82n; "Warum ist Schönbergs Musik so schwer verständlich?" 193–96, 200
Berlin, 158, 181
Binary form, 119, 262
Bleibtreu, Karl, 66, 181n
Brahms, Johannes: asymmetry of phrases in, 9, 10, 164, 194; "Brahms fog," 3–4, 5, 7; Brahms tradition, 109; compositional techniques of, 37, 98, 211, 214; influence on Reger, 3–5, 14–19, 214; influence on Schoenberg's instrumental works, 5, 20, 21, 23, 24, 29, 31, 32, 37, 38–39, 40, 41–42, 43, 47, 192; influence on Schoenberg's songs, 5, 50, 52, 66, 71–72, 82; influence on Zemlinsky, 6–14; metrical techniques in, 11, 17, 21–22, 24; piano style of, 16; thematic transformation in, 191; WORKS: Academic Festival Overture, op. 80, 7n;

Brahms (*continued*)
An die Nachtigall, op. 46, no. 4, 9; *An ein Veilchen*, op. 49, no. 2, 9; Capriccio, op. 76, no. 1, 24n; Cello Sonata No. 2, op. 99, 4n; *Dein blaues Auge*, op. 59, no. 6, 9; *Es liebt sich so lieblich im Lenze*, op. 71, no. 1, 38–39; *Feldeinsamkeit*, op. 86, no. 2, 10n, 62; Intermezzi, *see* Piano Pieces; *Klavierstücke*, *see* Piano Pieces; *Die Kränze*, op. 46, no. 1, 71n; *Maienkätzchen*, op. 107, no. 4, 9; *Die Mainacht*, op. 43, no. 2, 9; *Mein wundes Herz*, op. 59, no. 7, 9, 26n; Piano Pieces, opp. 116–19, 17, 21, 23, 24; Piano Quintet, op. 34, 22n; Rhapsodies, op. 79, 15n; *Sehnsucht*, op. 49, no. 3, 9; Serenades, opp. 11 and 16, 29; *Ständchen*, op. 106, no. 1, 61; String Quartet No. 3, op. 67, 11, 24, 40, 41–42; Symphony No. 2, op. 73, 11–12, 22n, 26n, 29, 30, 194; Symphony No. 3, op. 90, 19n, 22n, 31n; Symphony No. 4, op. 98, 15, 17; Tragic Overture, op. 81, 21; Violin Sonata No. 1, op. 78, 262; "Von waldbekränzter Höhe," op. 57, no. 1, 9; *Waldesnacht*, op. 62, no. 3, 63–64; "Wie bist du, meine Königin," op. 32, no. 9, 9; *Wie Melodien zieht es mir*, op. 105, no. 1, 9. *See also* Hemiola; Meter; Motivic development
Brinkmann, Reinhold, 246

Canon, 23, 43, 44
Chaconne, 156
Challier, Ernst, 51
Cherlin, Michael, 193n
Chromatic harmony. *See* Diminished-seventh chord; French sixth chord; German sixth chord; Half-diminished seventh chord; Vagrant chord
Chromatic voice-leading. *See* Stepwise voice-leading
Coda, 26, 32, 133, 150, 228, 245, 249, 255, 259, 262, 269, 271
"Color" chord, 94–97
Color complementarity, 94
Concept sketch. *See* Sketches
Concerning the Spiritual in Art (Kandinsky), 94
Cone, Edward T., 96, 97
Conradi, Hermann, 181, 216
Counterpoint, 23, 43, 177, 181, 184, 189, 201, 232, 249, 257, 259, 269, 270. *See also* Canon; Fugato; Fugue; Invertible counterpoint
Cyclic form, 258, 259, 267, 268. *See also* Recapitulation

Dahlhaus, Carl, xiii, 33n, 113, 114, 212
Debussy, Claude, 199
Dehmel, Richard, 50, 248; influence on Schoenberg, 67, 110; Schoenberg's settings of, *see* Index of Schoenberg's Compositions under individual song titles; POEMS AND COLLECTIONS: *Aber die Liebe*, 66n, 67, 72; "Alles," 216; "Entbietung," 82n; "Erhebung," 82, 83, 105; *Erlösungen*, 66n; "Erwartung," 82, 83, 92–98, 108, 110; "Gethsemane," 83; "Jesus bettelt," 99–104; "Mädchenfrühling," 68–72; "Nicht doch!" 72–75; "Im Reich der Liebe," 98–99; "Ein Stelldichein," 216; "Verklärte Nacht," 83, 110–13; *Weib und Welt*, 67, 79–82, 83, 93, 100, 110; *Zwei Menschen*, 112
Developing variation, 70–71, 86, 87n, 105, 252. *See also* Motivic development; Thematic transformation
Development (section), 115, 116; in Chamber Symphony No. 1, op. 9, 220, 224, 225–26, 244, 255; in *Schilflied*, 53; in Serenade for Small Orchestra, 29–31; in String Quartet in D Major, 37; in String Quartet No. 1, op. 7, 189, 206, 208; in String Quartet No. 2, op. 10, 259, 262, 263, 269, 270; in *Verklärte Nacht*, 114, 116, 121. *See also* Motivic development; Recapitulation; Retransition; Sonata form
Diminished-seventh chord: in Chamber Symphony No. 1, 230; in early piano works, 24; in early songs, 84, 85, 102; in *Gurrelieder*, 147, 148, 150–51; in *Pelleas und Melisande*, 173; in Serenade for Small Orchestra, 31, 32, 37; in String Quartet in D Major, 46; in String Quartet No. 1, 197; in *Verklärte Nacht*, 128, 129, 134, 136. *See also* Vagrant chord
Dominant preparation, 29, 41, 75, 107–8, 116, 129–30, 135, 155, 173, 211, 231
Dominant seventh chord, 31, 74, 96, 103–4, 134, 163–64, 196–97, 200, 236, 254–55, 270; with added tones, 96, 174; as alteration of half-diminished seventh, 254; altered to French sixth, 91; relation to German sixth chord, 135, 165, 172–73, 238; as vagrant chord, 182.

See also Dominant preparation; German sixth chord
Door, Anton, 7
Double exposition. *See* Exposition; Sonata form
Double recapitulation, 227–28, 229–30. *See also* Recapitulation; Sonata form
Dvořák, Antonín, 29, 37, 38–39, 61

Emulation, 14, 16, 32, 62, 211
Exposition, 11–12, 115, 213–14, 261; in Chamber Symphony No. 1, op. 9, 222–24, 227, 230, 251; in Chamber Symphony No. 2, op. 38, 252; in *Schilflied*, 53; in Serenade for Small Orchestra, 29; in String Quartet in D Major, 33–37; in String Quartet No. 1, op. 7, 189, 208; in String Quartet No. 2, op. 10, 259, 262, 263, 269, 270; in *Verklärte Nacht*, 116. *See also* Sonata form

Falke, Gustav, 109
Film technique, 143
Fitzner Quartet, 33
Fluctuating tonality, 153, 252
Folk style, 50, 61, 67, 79
Form. *See* Binary form; Rondo form; Sonata form; Ternary form
Forte, Allen, xiv, 216n, 270
Fourths, 232–36, 244, 255–57
Frankfurt, 212
French sixth chord, 84, 86n, 91, 103, 104, 200. *See also* Augmented chord; Vagrant chord; Whole-tone formations
Friedheim, Philip, 169, 223–24, 237n
Fuchs, Robert, 7, 29
Fugato, 189–90
Fugue, 185, 186, 189

George, Stefan, 66, 259, 267–68, 272
Gerlach, Reinhard, 37–38
German sixth chord, 32, 37, 47, 53, 65, 99, 130, 135, 136, 147, 165, 168, 172, 182, 200, 238, 240; derivation of, 135. *See also* Dominant seventh chord; Vagrant chord
Gerstl, Richard, 268
Gesellschaft der Musikfreunde, 7n, 33
Glienke, Bernhard, 143, 144, 145, 146
Goethe, Johann Wolfgang von, 66, 80, 248
Gold, Alfred, 51
Grundgestalt, 206

Half-diminished seventh chord: in Chamber Symphony No. 2, op. 38, 253–54; in *Gethsemane*, 83; in *Im Reich der Liebe*, 99; in *Jesus bettelt*, 102, 103, 104; in *Mädchenfrühling*, 69, 70; in *Mannesbangen*, 84, 85, 87; in *Pelleas und Melisande*, 164, 168, 173, 174; in Presto in A Minor, 24, 26, 27; in *Schilflied*, 52; in String Quartet No. 1, op. 7, 197; in *Verklärte Nacht*, 127–28, 129. *See also* Pre-dominant chord; Vagrant chord
Harmonic congruence, 9, 39
Harmony. *See* Diminished-seventh chord; Dominant seventh chord; French sixth chord; German sixth chord; Half-diminished seventh chord; Vagrant chord
Hart, Julius, 66
Hauptmann, Gerhard, 248
Haydn, Franz Joseph, 261
Hehemann, Max, 213
Hemiola, 11, 17, 39–40, 70, 91, 192. *See also* Brahms, Johannes; Meter
Heyse, Paul, 20, 50, 61, 62, 63, 66, 75, 79
Hofmannsthal, Hugo von, 80

Iambic pentameter, 146
Inversional balance, 186
Invertible counterpoint, 11, 195, 216–18. *See also* Counterpoint

Jacobsen, Jens Peter, 141, 142
Jugendstil, 94

Kandinsky, Wassily, 94
Keller, Gottfried, 248
Klangfarbe, 42
Knittelvers, 143n, 146
Knüpftechnik, 99. *See also* Phrase structure
Kropfinger, Klaus, 114

Leeuw, Reinbert de, 220n
Leichtentritt, Hugo, 4
Leitmotiv, 149, 159
Lenau, Nikolaus, 51, 109
Lessmann, Otto, 3
Levetzow, Karl von, 79
Lewin, David, 22, 186
Library of Congress (Schoenberg Collection), 33, 115n, 120, 201
Lindner, Adalbert, 3, 4
Linkage technique, 99. *See also* Phrase structure
Liquidation, 23, 31, 35, 118, 119, 189, 195, 207, 226, 253, 266
Liszt, Franz, 52, 109, 187, 191
Löns, Hermann, 248

Mackay, John Henry, 216
Maeterlinck, Maurice, 158
Mahler, Gustav, 7, 212–13, 267
Manuscripts, xvi; of Chamber Symphony No. 1, op. 9,

Manuscripts (*continued*) 220, 231–32; of Chamber Symphony No. 2, op. 38, 249–50, 252; of Dehmel songs of 1899, 80, 82, 84; of early instrumental works, 20, 28; of early songs, 48, 54, 56, 68, 72; of *Gurrelieder*, 140–41, 145, 155, 158; of "Konstruktives in der Verklärten Nacht," 123–26; of String Quartet fragment in D Minor (1903–4), 184; of String Quartet in D Major, 33, 39, 44; of String Quartet No. 1, op. 7, 201, 210n; of *Verklärte Nacht*, 109, 110, 120, 129–30, 136–38. *See also* Revisions; Sketches
Marschalk, Max, 115
Mary Magdalene, 100
Meter: development of, 39–40, 72, 86, 97–98, 106, 138, 193; displacement of, 17, 21, 23, 26, 167–68, 169; stresses within, 89, 90. *See also* Brahms, Johannes; Hemiola
Metronome markings, 220n, 246
Meyer, C. F., 248
Model-and-sequence constructions, 83. *See also* Sequence
Modernism, 66
Motivic development: in Brahms, 11–14, 41–42; in Reger, 213–14; in Zemlinsky, 11–14; in *Am Wegrand*, 218; in Chamber Symphony No. 2, op. 38, 251, 252–53; in early songs, 52, 55, 62, 70–71, 83, 86–87, 100–102, 105, 107; in *Gurrelieder*, 154–56; in Piano Pieces of 1894, 23, 26, 28; in Scherzo in F Major, 39–42; in Serenade for Small Orchestra, 29, 31; in String Quartet in D Major, 34–35, 43, 44–45; in String Quartet No. 1, op. 7, 189–92, 193–95, 200, 203–7, 208; in String Quartet No. 2, op. 10, 251, 261–62; in *Verklärte Nacht*, 116–22; in *Verlassen*, 181–82. *See also* Developing variation; Meter; Thematic transformation
Motivic process. *See* Developing variation; Motivic development
Musikalisches Wochenblatt, 3

Nachod Collection (North Texas State University), 20n, 56
Naturalism, 66, 181
Neapolitan relationships, 38, 41, 43, 70, 149, 150–51, 218, 236, 260
Neff, Severine, 189n
Neighbour, Oliver, 33n, 254n
Newlin, Dika, 123n, 126, 142, 187n
Niemann, Walter, 4, 16
Nietzsche, Friedrich, 66

"O du lieber Augustin," 259, 266
Oppenheimer, Paula, 81
Österreichische Nationalbibliothek, 82n
Ostinato, 181–82

Pentatonic scale, 38, 61
Period structure, 24, 34, 39–40, 43, 194, 253, 260. *See also* Phrase structure
Pfannkuch, Wilhelm, 113–14, 116
Pfau, Ludwig, 50, 61
Phrase structure, xv, 27, 47, 88, 108, 156, 164, 165, 167, 168, 176, 193–94, 211, 214, 254, 260. *See also* Asymmetry; Period structure; Sentence structure
Phrygian mode, 17
Pierpont Morgan Library, 56, 231
Pitch-class sets, 216n. *See also* Atonality
Plagal cadence, 9, 136, 152, 245–46
Pocket sketchbook. *See* Sketches
Polyhymnia Orchestra, 28, 29, 51
Pre-dominant chord, 9, 17, 69, 70, 85, 129. *See also* Dominant preparation; Half-diminished seventh chord
Program music, 158, 171, 177, 186–87, 216, 266
Progressive form, 146, 167. *See also* Recapitulation; Sonata form

Quartal formations. *See* Fourths
Quotation, 15

Recapitulation, 187; in Chamber Symphony No. 1, op. 9, 220, 225, 227–29, 232, *see also* Double recapitulation; in Chamber Symphony No. 2, op. 38, 252, 257–58; in *Ecloge*, 60; in *Erwartung*, 97, 98; in *Gurrelieder*, 146, 148, 149–51, 156, 157, 169; in *Mädchenfrühling*, 71–72; in *Pelleas und Melisande*, 169, 171, 175–77, 230; in Scherzo in F Major, 41; in *Schilflied*, 53; in Serenade for Small Orchestra, 29; in String Quartet in D Major, 37; in String Quartet No. 1, op. 7, 189, 191, 192, 207, 208, 211, 230; in String

Quartet No. 2, op. 10, 258–59, 262–63, 267–68, 270–71; in *Verklärte Nacht*, 98, 114, 116, 121, 122, 129, 130, 136, 138, 139, 175, 230; in *Warnung*, 89, 92. *See also* Retransition; Sonata form
Reger, Max: admiration for Brahms, 3–5; contact with Schoenberg, 212; influence of Brahms upon, 4n, 14–19, 211, 214; settings of Dehmel, 67; WORKS: *Resignation*, op. 26, no. 5, 14–19, 23; *Rhapsodie (Den Manen Brahms)*, op. 24, no. 6, 15n; String Quartet, op. 74, 211–16; Violin Sonata No. 2, op. 3, 3
Reich, Willi, 221n
Reprise. *See* Recapitulation; Sonata form
Réti, Rudolph, 243
Retransition, 115; in Scherzo in F Major, 41; in *Schilflied*, 53; in Serenade for Small Orchestra, 29–31; in *Verklärte Nacht*, 139. *See also* Development; Recapitulation; Sonata form
Retrograde, 34, 39, 40, 105
Return. *See* Recapitulation; Retransition; Sonata form
Revisions: of Chamber Symphony No. 1, op. 9, 231–32; of *Ecloge*, 56–60; of *Gurrelieder*, 140–42, 144, 145, 155, 156; of *Mannesbangen*, 84; of *Pelleas und Melisande*, 133–34, 175–76; of String Quartet in D Major, 33, 41, 42, 44; of String Quartet No. 1, op. 7, 210n; of *Verklärte Nacht*, 110, 120–21, 129–34, 136–39; of *Waldesnacht*, 65n; of *Warnung*, 82, 90–92. *See also* Manuscripts; Sketches
Riegl, Alois, 6n
Riemann, Hugo, 4
Rilke, Rainer Maria, 81
Romanticism, 51
Rondo form, 27, 113, 173, 211
Rosé, Arnold, 212
Rosen, Charles, 19
Rosé Quartet, 110

Schenker, Heinrich, 99
Schlaf, Johannes, 82
Schmidt, Christian M., xiii, 48, 186, 187, 189n, 201, 202n, 204n, 205n, 251, 263, 264, 267
Schmidt, Leopold, 4
Schoenberg, Mathilde, 82, 268
Schoenberg Collection (Library of Congress), 33, 115n, 120, 201
Schoenberg Institute. *See* Arnold Schoenberg Institute
Schubert, Franz, 187, 191, 261, 265
Schumann, Robert, 50, 187
Schwarzwald, Eugenie, 181
Schwebende Tonalität, 153, 252
Sentence structure, 22–23, 24, 118, 169. *See also* Phrase structure
Sequence, 41, 55, 83, 90, 100, 102, 116, 138, 147, 167, 173, 194, 195, 197–98, 214, 224, 265. *See also* Model-and-sequence constructions
Simrock, Fritz, 7, 10
Sinopoli, Giuseppe, 220n
Sketchbooks. *See* Revisions; Sketches
Sketches: for Chamber Symphony No. 1, op. 9, 220, 237, 240–43; for Chamber Symphony No. 2, op. 38, 248, 258; concept sketches, 202, 207, 208, 211; for *Pelleas und Melisande*, 158; pocket sketchbook, 184n; sketchbooks, 184, 186–87, 201–2, 220, 248, 249, 258, 261, 264, 267; for String Quartet fragment in D Minor (1903–4), 184; for String Quartet No. 1, op. 7, 201–10, 249–51; for String Quartet No. 2, op. 10, 249–51, 258, 261, 263–64, 265, 267–68; for *Verklärte Nacht*, op. 4, 110, 136n, 138n. *See also* Manuscripts; Revisions
Society for Private Musical Performances, 212
Society of Creative Composers, 212
Sonata form: 29, 33, 53–54, 113–16, 118, 121, 171, 173, 212, 213, 223–24, 251, 257, 259, 260, 261, 262, 263, 268–69, 270; combination of sonata form and four-movement form, 113, 159–60, 169–71, 175, 187–89, 207, 220–21, 249; combination of sonata and ternary form, 252, 257–58. *See also* Development; Exposition; Recapitulation; Ternary form
Song cycle, 141–42, 144–45
Stein, Erwin, 263, 269
Stephan, Rudolf, 11
Stepwise voice-leading, 52, 102, 103, 163–64, 165, 168, 173, 240, 241, 243, 254, 255, 256, 257, 259
Stilkunst, 6n
Strauss, Richard, 3, 66, 67n, 82, 109, 115–16, 187, 199, 222
Strophic form, 55, 61, 63, 71, 100, 105, 146, 147–48, 193. *See also* Sonata form
Stuckenschmidt, H. H., 82
Style, xiv, 5, 66; vs. idea, 5–6
Subconscious, 126, 272

Subdominant. *See* Half-diminished chord; Predominant chord
Subjectivity, 66, 68, 246
Suk, Josef, 29
Swift, Richard, 113, 114, 116, 122, 129, 222
Symmetry, 46–47, 84, 110–11, 123, 126, 127, 176, 186, 198, 207, 233, 255; symmetrical division of octave, 42, 135, 265. *See also* Augmented chord; Fourths; Whole-tone formations
Symphonic poem, 109

Tappert, Wilhelm, 3
Ternary form, 11, 17, 23, 34, 71, 84, 88, 98, 100, 119, 121, 153, 156, 172, 175, 189, 193, 238, 251, 257–58, 261–62
Thematic development. *See* Motivic development; Thematic transformation
Thematic dualism, 261, 262
Thematic process. *See* Motivic development; Thematic transformation
Thematic structure. *See* Motivic development; Period structure; Phrase structure; Sentence structure
Thematic transformation, 83, 88–89, 100, 102, 116, 154–55, 160–63, 173, 176, 189, 190–92, 205, 207–8, 210, 266. *See also* Motivic development
Thieme, Ulrich, 48, 50, 84–85, 86
Tone color, 42
Transformational beat, 22, 23, 26
Trezise, Simon, 141, 142, 146
"Tristan" chord. *See* Half-diminished seventh chord; Vagrant chord
Tyson, Alan, 202

Überbrettl cabaret, 158
Universal Edition, 181

Vagrant chord, 52–53, 69, 84, 86, 91, 98, 102, 103, 104, 106, 108, 128, 129, 164, 165, 182, 184, 196, 197, 198, 199; defined, 24, 85. *See also* Augmented chord; Diminished-seventh chord; French sixth chord; German sixth chord; Half-diminished seventh chord; Whole-tone formations
Variant, 87n. *See also* Motivic development; Thematic transformation
Variation form, 43–47, 259
Velten, Klaus, 252–53
Vereinigung schaffender Tonkünstler, 212
Verlag Dreililien, 82n, 110, 115n
Vienna Conservatory, 7
Vienna Society of Composers, 7, 33, 110, 141
Voice-leading. *See* Stepwise voice-leading
Volkmann, Robert, 29
Vrchlický, Jaroslav (pseud. for Emil Frida), 54
Wagner, Richard, 3, 4, 52, 82, 163; Wagnerian techniques, xiv–xv, 48, 98–99, 109; WORKS: *Tristan und Isolde*, 83, 153, 173; *Die Walküre*, 163
Walter, Bruno, 130–31, 133, 134, 139, 175, 176, 212
Webern, Anton, 6n, 67, 112, 182
Wellesz, Egon, xiii, 6n, 32–33, 110, 113, 114, 184, 185
Whole-tone formations, 65, 91, 103–4, 108, 177, 197–201, 214, 218, 219, 232–34, 237, 244. *See also* Augmented chord; French sixth chord
Wiener Tonkünstlerverein, 7, 33, 110, 141
Wilde, Oscar, 100
Wintle, Christopher, 196
Wolf, Hugo, 52, 82

Zemlinsky, Alexander von, 19, 66, 94n, 110, 133, 141, 142, 175–76; admiration for Brahms, 7; early training, 6–7; involvement with Schoenberg's D-Major Quartet, 32–33, 41, 42, 43; as teacher of Schoenberg, 7, 8; WORKS: Clarinet Trio, op. 3, 7, 41, 60; *Entbietung*, op. 7, no. 2, 82n; *Heilige Nacht*, op. 2, no. 1, 7–10, 60; Lieder, opp. 7, 8, and 10, 82n, 141n; String Quartet No. 1, op. 4, 10–14, 41. *See also* Brahms, Johannes
Zemlinsky, Mathilde, 82, 268

Designer: Nola Burger
Compositor: Wilsted & Taylor
Text: 10/13 Bembo
Display: Bembo
Printer: Malloy Lithographing, Inc.
Binder: John H. Dekker & Sons